Victorian Literature and Culture Series

Jerome J. McGann and Herbert Tucker, Editors

VERNON LEE

A LITERARY BIOGRAPHY

Vineta Colby

UNIVERSITY OF VIRGINIA PRESS
CHARLOTTESVILLE AND LONDON

University of Virginia Press
© 2003 by the Rector and Visitors of the University of Virginia
All rights reserved
Printed in the United States of America on acid-free paper

First published 2003

9 8 7 6 5 4 3 2 1

LIBRARY OF CONGRESS CATALOGING-IN-PUBLICATION DATA
Colby, Vineta.
    Vernon Lee : a literary biography / Vineta Colby.
        p.   cm. — (Victorian literature and culture series)
    Includes bibliographical references and index.
        ISBN 0-8139-2158-9
    1. Lee, Vernon, 1856–1935.   2. Authors, English—19th century—
Biography.   3. Lesbians—Great Britain—Biography.   I. Title.   II. Series.
    PR5115.P2 Z63 2003
    824'.8—dc21   2002013489

FRONTISPIECE: Portrait of Vernon Lee by John Singer Sargent, 1881.
(© Tate, London 2002)

To the Italy of Vernon Lee's memory and my imagination

CONTENTS

Illustrations follow page 94

PREFACE

IT IS A SMALL COMPANY WHO READ VERNON LEE TODAY. IT IS AN even smaller one who read her with delight for her quirky prose, her flashes of brilliance, her bold and stubborn spirit, and her grasp of the culture of a Europe that no longer exists. Reading Vernon Lee is also a process of discovery, layer by layer, of the complex intellect that informed her work—as protean as the mythical god for whom she named one of her last books. She quoted Whitman—"And if I contradict myself, why, I contradict myself" —with no apologies, and she challenged her readers to accept her terms or reject her altogether.

Yet it is the thesis of this book that over the course of her long and turbulent intellectual life, she remained much as she had always been: an idealist clinging to the values she had absorbed in her childhood. The masculine pen name she assumed at the beginning of her publishing career was appropriate because it identified her as a strong, independent woman of letters. But she never abandoned her birth name of Violet Paget, using it in personal correspondence interchangeably with Vernon Lee; some of her friends addressed her as Violet or Miss Paget until her last days. I plead guilty, though not so brazenly as Whitman, to inconsistency in referring to her as Violet Paget when discussing her personal relationships and Vernon Lee as an author, but often slipping from one to another as seemed in the context appropriate.

This is a literary biography, reading her life in terms of the large body of writing she produced. Because it is her mind that first attracted my interest, I have read Vernon Lee to discover what she read and what influences, personal and intellectual, shaped that mind. Although she never published an autobiography, she left a wealth of material in her published work and in the unpublished letters, journals, and essays that survive (the bulk of them in the Miller Library at Colby College in Waterville, Maine). There is one brief but solid biography by Peter Gunn, published by Oxford University Press in 1964, that surveys her life admirably but gives little attention to the literary and intellectual content of her work. In recent years there has been a flurry of interest in her stories of the supernatural and these mainly as expressions of her lesbianism. My book is an attempt to read her entire work in its fullest context—biographical, literary, and intellectual. In the end Vernon Lee fits into no single category. She was too late to be a Victorian, too early to be a Modernist. She was a nonmilitant feminist, a sexually repressed lesbian, an aesthete, a cautious socialist, a secular humanist. In short, she was protean.

ACKNOWLEDGMENTS

No scholar seriously interested in the life and writings of Vernon Lee can long ignore her archive in the Special Collections of the Miller Library at Colby College in Waterville, Maine. Thanks to the generous cooperation of Suanne Muehlner, Director of Colby Libraries; Special Collections Librarian Patricia Burdick; Nancy Reinhardt, her predecessor in that office; Margaret Libby, of the Colby Slide Library and Special Collections; and Eileen M. Curran, Professor Emerita of English at Colby College, I have been able to assemble much of the material for this book. I am also grateful to Pauline Adams, Librarian of Somerville College, Oxford, for sending me copies of Edith Wharton's letters to Vernon Lee, and to David Elliott for copies of Mary Berenson's letters to Vernon Lee in the Somerville collection. Aspects of Vernon Lee's busy life are documented in many other research libraries, gratefully acknowledged here: the Beinecke Rare Book and Manuscript Library of Yale University, the Berg Collection of the New York Public Library, the Rare Book and Manuscript Library of Columbia University, the Fales Library of New York University, the Houghton Library of Harvard University, and the Huntington Library in San Marino, California.

Most valuable of all research libraries is the New York Public Library, where I have worked happily and, I would like to think, productively over virtually a lifetime. What little that library could not supply, the staff has obligingly sought out and furnished me through interlibrary loan. I am also indebted to the Accademia Letteraria Italiana in Rome, which allowed me to visit the small but exquisite site of the Arcadian Academy, and to the Harold Acton Library of the British Institute of Florence, which has a small collection of books from Vernon Lee's library, richly embellished with her marginalia. I have benefited also from the interest in my work demonstrated by Robert Bledsoe, Robin Brancato, Donald Stone, Martha and Albert Vogeler, Sally Mitchell, my editors at the University of Virginia Press—

Cathie Brettschneider, Ellen Satrom, and David Sewell—and manuscript editor Ruth Melville.

Beyond my powers of expression is my gratitude to Robert A. Colby for his knowledge and his generosity in sharing it with me, his patience with my impatience, and his enduring love.

 VERNON LEE

1 THE INFANT PRODIGY

ENGLISH BY NATIONALITY, FRENCH BY ACCIDENT OF BIRTH, Vernon Lee was Italian by choice. Italy was the subject of her best writing and the object of her quest as a scholar and traveler. There are in fact two Italys in Vernon Lee's life: the country in which she lived for more than half a century and the country she created in her imagination and re-created in her work. For her, Italy was a refuge, an escape from what she perceived as the encroaching evils of modern society and, in a way that she did not perhaps recognize herself, an escape from her bondage as a woman. In transforming herself into an authority on Italian culture of the distant past and on the Italian rural landscape so little changed from the past, she created a new identity for herself as a woman and as a writer who could retreat at will from the present into a timeless past of which she was the interpreter and guardian. She was thus able to liberate herself from her socially engineered roles of baby sister, submissive daughter, and genteel unmarried female. Her unchallenged authority as a writer on Italian culture allowed her to travel freely and unchaperoned, to mingle with artists and intellectuals, to assert herself (not always to her social advantage), and to demand recognition, not for the beauty and charm she conspicuously lacked, but for the intelligence and erudition she had in abundance.

"Had I ever really cared for any country except Italy?" Vernon Lee asked sometime around 1912 (*Tower of the Mirrors* 153). Though she was to live for nearly another quarter century, she had already lived long enough to know that while she cared for other countries, she loved only Italy. It was a poor substitute perhaps for the human love that persistently eluded her, for although Italy gave her in generous measure what no other country could offer, it could not satisfy her emotional needs. It did, however, provide her with a vocation that filled her life with productive work and brought her recognition as a woman of letters. She was a prodigious worker. Much as Italy possessed her, she was never touched by the *dolce far niente*. At a moment of personal crisis when her companion Kit Anstruther-Thomson left her, she adopted as her motto: "Labora et noli contristari." Work she did all her life, whether as a balm to unhappiness, an outlet for her not inconsiderable ego, or an act of obedience to her Anglo-Puritan heritage, which made a virtue of industry and a vice of idleness.

"Vernon Lee" was born when Violet Paget assumed the name for a series of articles that she published in the Italian journal *La rivista europea* in 1875. The use of a masculine pseudonym was hardly unusual in the nineteenth century, although by the last quarter of the century many women were publishing under their own names. But it was a necessity for an unknown young woman who chose to write on weighty subjects: "I am sure that no one reads a woman's writing on art, history or aesthetics with anything but unmitigated contempt," she wrote her mentor Henrietta Jenkin with characteristic conviction (18 December 1878). But more than expedience was involved in becoming Vernon Lee. Although she used both names interchangeably in her personal life, her use of the pseudonym thereafter in all her published work suggests that she preferred the strong masculine ring of Vernon to the flowery feminine of Violet. In July 1871 Mrs. Jenkin, herself a novelist, cautioned the very young and precocious Violet: "Violets never were nor can be vain—but I see that there is some record of a Violet ambitious to be an oak." Ambitious she certainly was. By 1875 she had firmly decided to be Vernon Lee. As she wrote another of her mentors, Cornelia Turner, on 6 April: "The name I have chosen as containing part of my brother's [Eugene Lee-Hamilton] and my father's [Henry Paget] and my own initials is H. P. Vernon Lee. It has the advantage of leaving undecided whether the writer be a man or a woman." The initials were soon dropped, but the androgynous identity was preserved.

Years later, in a moment of self-analysis following a nervous breakdown, Vernon Lee wrote to an Italian friend, Carlo Placci: "I recognise now that my family is, on one side, acutely neuropathic and hysterical; and that my earlier years were admirably calculated, by an alternation of indiscipline and terrorism, by excessive overwork and absolute solitude, to develop these characteristics. Had I known this at 22 or 23, instead of learning nearer forty, I should now be a good deal sounder and happier" (9 August 1894). Allowing for the inevitable depression and self-pity of a midlife crisis, her observation is nevertheless sound. Hers was a childhood and youth programmed by heredity and environment for lifelong emotional instability. That it left her in the end, and in spite of repeated mental crises, an intellectually active and productive woman is a tribute to her dedication to her craft. Though filled with bitter disappointment and frustration, constantly struggling but failing to come to terms with her lesbianism, she led a life rich in achievement. The obvious explanation for that achievement is sublimation, but this ignores the complexity and contradictions of Vernon Lee's character which she was quick enough to acknowledge herself. Her persona and spokesman in a series of dialogues collected under the eponymous title *Baldwin* is "a negative being, in many respects . . . perhaps all the more that, as you see, there is much that is positive in his nature. An illusive [*sic*], shimmering personality, seemingly full of contradictions, yet at the same time almost repulsively cut and dried. Negative, self-contradictory, abstract, as becomes an inhabitant of the country which lies, as I have observed, upon the boundaries of fact and fiction" (13).

The mother who ruled Violet Paget's life absolutely until her death in 1896 was born Matilda Adams in 1815 in Carmarthenshire, Wales, to Edward Hamlin Adams (1777–1842), son of a colonial family in Barbados, and his wife Sarah, who had lived for some period of her early life in Philadelphia. Having made his fortune in Jamaica in banking and trading during the Napoleonic Wars, Edward Adams retired to England with his wife and bought a country estate, Middleton Hall, in Carmarthenshire, but he never enjoyed the tranquil life of an English country gentleman. Testy and litigious, he was, his granddaughter wrote, "extremely doctrinaire and moral, an ardent Voltairian who spent most of his time disputing with the local persons and refusing to pay tithes" (Gunn 14). Although he represented his county in the Reform Parliament of 1832, Edward Adams was too much involved in disputes with his neighbors for a successful political career. He instilled in his two sons and two daughters the same defiance of convention that ruled his life. They also inherited his passion for litigation, with damaging results to family harmony and finances. On his death in 1842, his elder son Edward prefixed the Welsh patronymic *Ab* to the family name and challenged the claims of his younger brother William's children by declaring them illegitimate.[1] The long lingering case of Abadam vs. Abadam, with its painful echo of Jarndyce vs. Jarndyce, consumed most of Edward's fortune and left the other heirs embittered and in financial difficulties of their own.

Matilda Adams appears to have been very much her father's daughter. Her education was even more irregular than her daughter's was to be, consisting mainly of French grammar, classic English rhetoric, music, some mathematics, and considerable independent reading in eighteenth-century radical philosophy. We learn this from Vernon Lee's loving memoir of her in an essay in *The Handling of Words*. Of Matilda's girlhood and early years, little is known. There was apparently a period of more conventional education at a school for young ladies in London and presumably a debut in society. An early portrait suggests that she was pretty, with delicate features and silky curls, a model young Victorian. But whether impelled by her family's stormy relationships to escape from home or genuinely in love, Matilda made an imprudent marriage to a Captain James Lee-Hamilton, of whom there appear to be no surviving records. Her daughter described the marriage as "deplorable." Its only happy result was the birth of a son, James Eugene, in 1845. Captain Lee-Hamilton died in 1852, and his widow and son moved to France. Matilda explained later, in typically perverse fashion, that her motive was to escape the English Sundays. More realistically, since the family estate was still in litigation, with fees eating up most of the principal, and she had only a small inheritance of her own, she found it cheaper to live abroad. She joined her brother William and his family in France, thereby antagonizing her brother Edward even more. Nor could her second marriage have pleased him. Requiring a tutor for her seven-year-old son, she hired a man of French and English parentage with a mysterious European background and no money, Henry Ferguson Paget, who became her second husband and the father of her daughter Violet.

With the years Matilda grew increasingly eccentric, but in ways that her patient second husband endured and her adoring children accepted without protest. As Vernon Lee acknowledged, her mother was "a mass of contradictions, but these were all grown into each other, made organic and inevitable by her passionate and unmistakable individuality, which recognized no law but its own, and while unceasingly influenced by others, was never once checked or interfered with" (*Handling of Words* 299). She scorned religious orthodoxy (her views were "Voltairian, or derived from Rousseau and Tom Paine"), but for all her free thinking she held and instilled in her daughter a rigorous personal morality that permitted no deviations or compromise. "Her two husbands bored her and she gave them their liberty after having a child by each." So Vernon Lee summed up her mother's marital life. Like her daughter, Matilda seemed to have had little taste for sex. Whatever cravings for love and affection she had were amply satisfied by her son Eugene.

What had attracted her to Henry Paget, other than the convenience of having a tutor at hand for her son, is a mystery. Possibly, for all her indifference to convention, she felt the need for the social status of marriage. Moreover, Henry had an unusual family heritage that would have appealed to her eighteenth-century fascination with the ancien régime. His connections to aristocracy were remote (Vernon Lee dismissed them as pure romance): he was the son of an émigré from France who claimed the noble name of De Fragnier. When De Fragnier settled in England, he became a naturalized citizen and anglicized his name to Ferguson. He married a Miss Paget, and for reasons unclear, his son Henry was christened Henry Ferguson Paget.[2] The family moved to Warsaw, where they lived during Henry's boyhood. His father, however, spent much of his time in St. Petersburg running a school for young aristocrats that he had established at the personal request of the czar. This at least was the account that Mrs. Paget gave in a memoir of her husband. Henry studied engineering in Warsaw and became involved in the struggle for Polish independence in 1846. Forced to flee to England, he supported himself by teaching and no doubt welcomed the opportunity to tutor the young son of a widow who had expectations of a family inheritance and was not without personal charm and good looks.

They were married in Paris in the summer of 1855, and their daughter Violet was born on 14 October 1856 in the chateau of St. Léonard, just outside Boulogne-sur-Mer, a town much favored by improvident English families. The attending physician, one Dr. Perrichod, congratulated his patient: "'Madame, je n'ai rien à vous reprochera' [*sic*]—words repeated to me many times during my childhood as a reason for filial gratitude and soundness of reproach" ("Vernon Lee Notebook," 20 June 1930).[3] Living on Matilda's modest income, the Pagets followed the custom of many such families drifting about France, Switzerland, Germany, and Italy, living in country inns or in rented rooms in town wherever they could afford to maintain a marginally genteel lifestyle: "[W]e had a pensive preference to watering-places, out of date or out of season" (*Sentimental Traveller* 16–17). They were not tourists. Indeed, Violet recalled her family's wanderings as the antithesis of tourism. "We shifted our quarters invariably every six months and by dint of shifting, crossed Europe's length and breadth in several directions. But this was *moving*, not *travelling*, and we contemned all travellers." The "we" was Matilda, her husband ever a silent partner. She despised sight-seeing, had not the slightest enthusiasm for monuments, grand vistas, and holy shrines or for the quaintness of local color, but was apparently content to read her favorite eighteenth-century authors, lecture her children on the irrationality and corruption of organized religion, and play the piano, which she did exceptionally well:

> *We* never saw any sights. We moved ourselves and our luggage regularly . . . and, obeying some mysterious financial or educational ebb and flow, backwards and forwards between the same two places, and every now and then between a new couple of places in a different part of the globe. But we were careful to see nothing on the way, save the inns where we slept, the refreshment rooms where we ate, and the Custom-houses where we opened our boxes whose contents must have been familiar to the officials.

Henry Paget was no more enthusiastic about travel than his wife. "The members of my family ate, drank, slept, made music, constructed machines, fished, shot, read, and walked, particularly walked, in one place and one quarter of Europe exactly as in the other" (*Sentimental Traveller* 6–8).

Although the Pagets stubbornly resisted roots, they managed to make themselves at home wherever they were: bourgeois gypsies—the term is patently contradictory, but so was the Paget character. However irregular it was, their way of life offered rich intellectual nourishment for their young daughter. Eugene had good enough tutoring to prepare him for Oxford; he entered Oriel College in 1864 with a scholarship in modern languages. For his sister, who was "Baby" or "Bags" to the family for far too many years, there were no such ambitious plans. She received a haphazard early education at the hands of Swiss and German governesses and fitful instruction from her mother out of Blair's *Rhetoric* and Cobbett's *Grammar,* textbooks from Matilda Paget's own girlhood. From her current reading she lectured Violet on the phrenologist George Combe's moral philosophy and the free-thinking Henry Thomas Buckle's *History of Civilization.* She corrected her daughter's compositions "from the point of view of good sense and good manners" and instructed her in Euclid "without allowing me to glance at a diagram or even to draw one furtively in the road's dust" (*Handling of Words* 298). Violet's early musical education was even more haphazard, confined largely to listening to her mother performing on the piano or playing duets with some of the governesses. Casual as all this was, it must soon have become apparent to Mrs. Paget and to Eugene, who took a keen interest in his young sister's development, that Violet was no ordinary child. She had inherited none of her mother's delicacy of features and silky curls. Instead she had her father's heavy jaw (which he concealed with a fashionable thick beard) and stubbornly straight hair. As if in compensation, she early showed signs of intellectual precocity, a passion for reading, a lively imagination, and a gift for languages. If Matilda could not produce a beautiful daughter, she could produce a learned one. "While my father thought poorly of writing, described it (I now think not quite unjustly) as a 'gift of gab,' my mother had made up her mind that I was to become, at the very least, another de Staël" (*Handling of Words* 301).

A stern, intimidating master, Matilda Paget demanded and received not only obedience but undivided loyalty and love. In return she offered her daughter respect and approval; but it was Eugene, and he alone, who had Matilda's love and devotion. Her bright and beloved firstborn went off to Oxford full of promise. His adoring young sister followed her mother's example and looked up to "Bruder," as she called him, with pride. She sent him a childish watercolor inscribed "Hail E. Hamilton—The Pride of Oxford and Oriel," and wrote him letters in execrable spelling, an academic discipline that Matilda and the governesses evidently ignored. She faithfully observed his admonitions to study and improve herself. Young and inexperienced as he was, Eugene was happy to play the role of father in the absence of any substantial interest from Mr. Paget in his child's education. He addressed her in his letters as "Dear Baby," followed the progress of her studies, and advised her mother on her instruction. "At Rome she should be working at Italian by which I mean not only the language but the literature. She should be talking the language daily with persons of cultured taste. The great advantage of lessons is that they introduce regularity and method into one's work" (Gunn 47).

Violet's education and well-being were of far less concern to Matilda than the health and well-being of her son at Oxford. The letters they exchanged are an extraordinary record of an obsessively loving mother and a passive, yielding son who became increasingly attached to her, ironically, during his absences abroad. She reserved an intimate form of address for Eugene, using the "thee" and "thou" she may have learned from her mother's Philadelphia background. She wrote him daily with salutations like "My darling," "My beloved," "Life of My Soul," "Beloved of My Heart," followed by anxious inquiries about his health, his diet, his activities. True to her antisocial disposition, she advised him to keep to himself, "Be firm in refusing to become a member of the club," and the only time she referred to her husband it was to report his suggestion to be "cautious" with Polish students: "They are charming but they want morality." The letters always end with expressions of her longing for him: "How I miss thee!," "I kiss thee a thousand times dearest child." Eugene's letters are also full of loving salutations—"My little darling," "Dearest little Mama"—and complaints of loneliness and homesickness.

Clearly Henry Paget and his daughter were excluded from this intimate relationship. Indeed, his wife complained to her absent son that her husband "with all his virtues . . . is a dreadful bore and torment very often," out of spirits when he could not find good fishing or hunting. Violet, however, appreciated his presence in the household and had affectionate regard for him. When she was with her mother in Paris in 1870, she wrote him lively, chatty letters, and years later she fondly recalled a Christmas in Germany when he decorated a tree for her. One snowy afternoon, returning from a walk with her governess, she caught a glimpse of him through the window. "I could see, drawn in black upon the white window blind, the outline of a fir-tree, the sharp apex, the majestic triangular sweep of the branches; and along with this the outline of my father's face—the nose, the lock of hair which bobbed when he stooped, the points of his moustaches, the fingers twisting something . . . " (*Juvenilia* 2:186–87). But the child's hunger for affection had to be filled elsewhere, and early on she adopted a series of surrogate mothers, initiating what were to become her many attachments to women in later life.

In the early years that need was easily satisfied. There were the governesses, "our spiritual foster mothers who put a few drops of the milk of German kindness, of German simplicity and quaintness and romance, between our lips when we were children," she remembered in an essay, "In Praise of Governesses." Her favorite was a young Fräulein Marie Schülpach, with whom she shared an easy intimacy that she never had with her mother. They read Goethe and Schiller and the Grimms' fairy tales and played Bach and Mozart on the piano. She recalled sitting with her "in the little room above the rushing Alpine river, eating apples and drinking *café au lait,* hours in which the whole world of legend and poetry, and scientific fact and theory more wonderful still, passed from your ardent young mind into the little eager puzzled one of your loving pupil" (*Hortus Vitae* 15–22).

Later there were kindly matrons, British and American expatriates in Nice or Rome for the winter or in the Swiss alpine town of Thun for the summer, who took an interest in the precocious child and encouraged her to write. Mrs. Paget rarely mingled with others, but she had no objection to Violet's friendships, especially her attachment to one American family, the Fitzwilliam Sargents of Philadelphia, whom the Paget family met in Nice in 1866. The Sargents had come to Europe in pursuit of health for the presumably ailing Mrs. Sargent. In fact, no one seems to have been in better health than this ebullient matron, whom Vernon Lee remembered years later in her memoir of John Singer Sargent for her "unquestionable youthfulness" and "jocund personality." The Pagets and the Sargents maintained a polite distance from each other, but the children—ten-year-old Violet, John Singer, also ten, and his younger sister Emily—became immediate and, as it proved, lifelong friends.

Mrs. Sargent was an enthusiastic tourist. While her husband patiently endured his homesickness for America, she led the family a nomadic life: "[T]he Spring comes and we strike our tents and migrate for the Summer; the Autumn returns, and we must pack our duds and be off to some milder region," Dr. Sargent wrote wearily to his mother from Florence in 1870. "I wish there were some prospect of our going home and settling down among our own people and taking permanent root" (Mount 26). Mrs. Sargent had no such complaints. She took the children, Violet included, on exhausting expeditions in search of the *genius loci.* "The high priestess . . . the most favoured and inspired votary of the Spirit of Localities . . . this most wisely fantastic of Wandering Ladies," Vernon Lee wrote of her in *The Sentimental Traveller* (20). The children discovered worlds of the imagination totally alien to the Pagets' narrow vision. Mrs. Sargent guided, but she also allowed the children freedom to explore on their own. She took them to museums and to the opera, encouraged them to read and play music and draw together.

Under her leadership her son discovered the artistic talent that was to make him the foremost painter of his day in England and America, and Violet discovered her vocation as a writer.

In the winter of 1868 both families were in Rome, the Sargents in a house at the top of the Spanish Steps on Trinità dei Monti and the Pagets a short distance away in rooms on the Piazza Mignanelli. Violet's days were crowded. On afternoon walks with her mother on the Pincio or in the Borghese gardens she continued to absorb miscellaneous instruction in mathematics, philosophy, and rhetoric, always filtered through Mrs. Paget's eclecticism and idiosyncrasies. Vastly different were her outings with the Sargents. They explored a Rome only beginning to emerge from its monumental ruins into a modern, cosmopolitan city. Thanks to Mrs. Sargent, Violet's social horizon widened. The Pagets rarely entertained, nor did they visit with Anglo-Roman society. But Mrs. Sargent knew everyone and went everywhere, the children tagging along. She was a frequent guest of her fellow New Englander William Wetmore Story, who since 1856 had lived in a spacious apartment in the Palazzo Barbarini. There, as his friend and biographer Henry James recalled, he had "an overflowing personal and social life . . . in which curiosity, hospitality and variety never ceased to renew themselves" (*W. W. Story* 1:337). At the Storys', Violet could have seen with proper awe some of the bold American women who might have served as role models—the roving journalist who wrote under the name "Grace Greenwood"; the sculptor Harriet Hosmer, who dazzled Hawthorne, James, and all Rome with her self-assurance and her practice of riding horseback through the streets ("Hatty takes a high hand here with Rome and would have the Romans know that a Yankee girl can do anything she pleases," Story wrote James Russell Lowell); and the Shakespearean actress Charlotte Cushman, who, in addition to her Lady Macbeth, played Romeo, Hamlet, and Cardinal Wolsey ("the Cushman sings savage ballads in a hoarse, manny voice, and requests people recitatively to forget her not") (*W. W. Story* 1:255). In Florence some years later Violet would open the Paget household to distinguished visitors, but at this early stage she absorbed society vicariously. She was seeing people who had actually known Thackeray, George Eliot, and the Brownings, and she was discovering the lively transplanted Anglo-American society that defied the conventions of their homelands yet remained essentially and eminently respectable.

Now twelve years old, moving rapidly from childhood into that condition of adolescent self-discovery that constantly surprises, Violet followed Mrs. Sargent around Rome with at first little appreciation of the city: "the dreary, horrible Rome of the popes: this warm, wet place with its sordid houses, its ruins embedded in filth and nettles . . . its whole atmosphere of decay and sloth . . . " (*Belcaro* 25). She missed the colorful, fragrant landscapes of Switzerland and southern France and especially "the homely and sentimental . . . Germany of the humbler and greater days, when no one talked of Teutonic superiority or of purely Teutonic idiom" (*Hortus Vitae* 19).

Her discovery of Rome at this early age was not the gradual awakening that comes with education and maturity; rather it was in the nature of an epiphany. In "The Child in the Vatican," an essay that openly imitates Walter Pater's "The Child in the House" in more than its title, she sees this huge and formidable palace-museum as "the most desolate, the most unintelligible of places . . . a dreary labyrinth of bricks and mortar." The sculpture galleries through which she is led are chilly, their contents lifeless and unfamiliar. She longs to be outside playing in the courtyard: "For there, outside, is life, movement, green; little hedged beds to run around, fountains to be made to spirt [*sic*] aside by sticking fingers into their pipes; walls on which to walk balanced, and benches to jump over; there is field and food for the child's fancy, and here within, among all these cut stones there is none" (*Belcaro* 20–21). Then one evening in spring, returning from a ramble and waiting for supper at the Sargents', she looked out of the window from the height of Trinità dei Monti at sunset and discovered Rome:

> This child would watch the bank of melting colours, crimson and smoke purple and gold, left by the sun behind the black dome of St. Peter's; and as the white vapours rose from the town below, and gathered on the roofs like a veil, would feel a vague, acheless pain within it; and at any stray, trifling words or bar of dance music, its eye and its whole little soul would fill with a mist of tears. The spell cast by the statues was not idle, the mysterious philter which they had poured into it was working through that childish soul; the child was in love: in love with what it hated; in love, intensely, passionately, with Rome. And as a part of love it loved blindly, for no other reason, that desolate Vatican. (*Belcaro* 26)

Along with Rome, Violet was discovering her vocation. "From that moment, I devoted myself to reading books on art; I began to have theories on the subject, and the idea of occupying myself with aesthetics confusingly entered my literary ambitions."[4] She honed her imagination with the reading she shared with John Sargent—gory episodes from English history like the executions of Mary of Scotland and the Earl of Essex, which they delighted in acting out; the opera libretti of Verdi and Donizetti, some of whose works Mrs. Sargent had taken them to see performed; Hawthorne's *The Marble Faun;* the publisher John Murray's travel guides; Sir William Smith's *Smaller Dictionary of Greek and Roman Antiquities;* and all the novels they could find in the circulating library. In Rome as nowhere else, the past came alive, not only in the relics of antiquity but, equally fascinating to her, in the rococo charm of the Piazza San Ignazio, "where the semi-circle of houses, each with its plaster laurel-branch and shell, its little balconies of twisted iron, seems arranged as a background for a comedy by Goldoni" (*Juvenilia* 1:138). Her childish imagination was stimulated by the shabby vestiges of great eighteenth-century palaces, which she recalled years later as part "Piranesi grandeur" and part "Callot picturesqueness."

The Rome of her childhood was also full of tangible realities; on her walks she absorbed not only sights but sounds and smells. Everyday occurrences like papal processions and church rituals appealed immediately to her sense of mystery and drama. There was even a glimpse of Pio Nono (Pius IX) himself, "a white sash around his portly white middle, distributing benedictions with two extended fingers among the bay hedges and mossy fountains of the Villa Borghese." With no religious training herself, she responded to Rome as pageant and playground. "I took part in 'bombarding' the pigs, then kept outside Porta del Popolo, with acorns and pebbles from the Pincian Terrace; and in burning holes in bay-leaves with a burning glass, until we were expelled as 'enfants mal élevés' by the ferocious French porter of the Medici Gardens" (Charteris 242).

In the dusty streets the children collected shards and scraps of what they liked to believe were antique Roman coins and artifacts. Already fired with the instinct of a scholar, Violet polished her coins in the hope of finding an effigy of Nero or Marcus Aurelius and fulfilled her family's expectations of a prodigy by producing her first publication at the age of fourteen. Written in French, a language she had already mastered, this was a story told as the biography of an ancient coin, *Les aventures d'une pièce de monnaie,* published serially in the Lausanne journal *La famille* in May, June, and July 1870. The narrator is a coin bearing the effigy of the emperor Hadrian that passes through history from the golden age of the Roman Empire, when it belongs variously to a gladiator, a Roman sculptor, and a Christian; it survives into the Renaissance, when it comes into the possession of the artist Guido Reni; in the eighteenth century it passes through the hands of the boy wonder Mozart when he performs in Rome; and it ends finally in the collection of a modern numismatist. Altogether *Les aventures* is a creditable and, for the author's age, remarkable little story, a work of diligent scholarship supported with footnotes on Roman history and customs and relieved with lively imaginative detail.

At an early age Violet tasted both the delights and the frustrations of authorship—praise and approval from her friends and family, anger at the Swiss editor for cutting and making changes in her manuscript. And once published she knew no limits to her ambitions. Her failure to find a publisher for a short story, "Capo Serpente: A Legend of the Roman Campagna," did not discourage her. Folklore and history alike attracted her and set the pattern for her later work, and she planned ambitious writing ventures, encouraged by her mother and by Eugene, who had his own literary ambitions. Unhappily, and to his mother's dismay, Eugene had dropped out of university in 1866. He traveled about Europe, wrote some poetry, and fell in love with his cousin Pauline, the daughter of Matilda's brother William. His mother encouraged the romance, but Pauline was not interested and later married a Frenchman, M. de Cargouet. Eugene consoled himself with poetry, his mother's sympathy, and his little sister's education. Convinced of her genius, he suggested programs of study, books to read, and topics for essays. Referring to the latter, he wrote his mother in January 1871: "Bags' two last are magnificent productions. Her comparison between the 16th and 18th centuries is first rate, eloquent, and (I doubt not) perfectly correct. I will enter further into the subject with her. I suggest for her consideration the Political Decline of the Dutch Republic. It is a subject belonging chiefly to her favorite century." A few weeks later he wrote: "Few indeed are the beings who can unite in themselves such double superiority, nor should I dream of such a result if I had not reason to believe Bags to be one of those very few." His ambitions for her soared. "She has an admirable ear for music," he continued, "and the interest she takes in the productions of the brush and chisel afford a fair presumption that her mind is equally adapted to success in painting and sculpture."

   Eugene's attention to Violet's education was not, however, an occupation, and he was keenly aware of his lack of a suitable vocation. Without a university degree but widely traveled in Europe and fluent in French, German, and Italian, he chose a career in diplomacy, passed the examinations for the civil service, and was posted to the British Embassy in Paris in February 1870. The following summer his mother and Violet visited him. It was a treat for the young girl, because in spite of the nomadic nature of their lives, the Pagets never "traveled," and Violet had been away from home, wherever home was, only once before, in 1862 when the family summered on the Isle of Wight. In spite of the impending Franco-Prussian War and Mrs. Paget's distaste for travel, young Violet was an enthusiastic, though critical, tourist. To her father, settled in Thun, where the fishing was good, she wrote long letters, her spelling now improved and her powers of observation sharpened by her burgeoning self-confidence. She shared her family's iconoclasm. "Oh my dearest Papa you cannot conceive what bad taste is shown in the new public buildings here!" The Paris Opera is "a monstrosity . . . a shapeless mass . . . of useless masonry. The whole is surmounted by a hideous bronze statue of Apollo in a nightgown, holding up with both arms a gilded lyre." The churches are "so hideously ugly that one would fain hide one's eyes." She deplores the mixture of architectural styles and the vulgarity of the gilded dome of Les Invalides and describes with wit the bust of Napoleon III: "his thin modern face and thinner moustache (like a paint-brush held between his teeth)" (23 June 1870). Some of this cynicism may have been calculated to console her father for staying in Thun, but more likely it was intended for the approval of her mother and Eugene, for it ex-actly expressed her practice of negative reporting in her letters to them, al-ways conscious of her family as her readers, always seeking their approval.

The stay in Paris was shortened by the outbreak of war in August. Vio-let's letters to her father vividly describe the street fighting, some of it di-rectly in front of the rooms they had taken in the rue de Luxembourg. She relished the tension of the soon-to-be-besieged city:

> Everyone here, the Paget-Hamilton family entre autres . . . is in the most melodramatic state of excitement, the slightest thing "sets them off." If a fiacre is heard to pass, heads appear at every window, the barking of dogs is like cannon, the crying of potatoes is like an émeute [riot]. The most beau-tiful thing of all was this. We were sitting quietly in the drawing room when Mamma and Bruder exclaim that they hear a noise like the discharging of riffles [*sic*]—it must be riffles—so they rush to the window. It turns out to be—what do you think! a cart with baskets full of empty Eau de Seltz si-phons, the jogging of which appeared to their excited brains like the noise of a shot! (9 August 1870)

By this time the Pagets, like most foreign visitors, were ready to leave the city. They rejoined Mr. Paget in Thun, then went on to Rome for the winter.

For Violet the Paris visit had been a rewarding excursion. First, it con-firmed her resolve to become a writer, not simply to record her impressions but to communicate to readers the learning she was only just beginning to acquire herself. Second, she was discovering that others outside the Paget family nest had much to offer her—professionally by encouraging her writ-ing and emotionally by taking a personal interest in her. In childhood her warmest relationships had been with the governesses who gave her an educa-tion far better suited to her early needs than her mother's lectures. Mrs. Pa-get's idea of motherhood was to shape her bright but homely daughter into an eighteenth-century bluestocking, a role she might have fancied for her-self had time and fate permitted it. But the governesses were content with more-modest goals like regular schoolroom lessons, country walks, piano practice, and long hours of storytelling. A few, the beloved Marie Schülpach especially, were genuinely fond of the affection-starved child, and to them Violet responded with almost pathetic gratitude: "We are loved, when we

are, not as a matter of course and habit, not with any claim; but for ourselves and with the delicate warmth of a feeling necessarily one-sided" (*Hortus Vitae* 21–22).

As she grew older, Violet adopted other surrogate mothers, mature,
worldly women who recognized her precocity and responded to her need
for attention. Mrs. Sargent was the first, but she was too preoccupied with
her own still growing family to be much concerned with Violet's intellectual promise. But at the very moment that she was developing her literary
ambitions, Violet was fortunate in meeting two older women who took a
lively interest in her. One was Henrietta Camilla Jackson Jenkin (ca. 1807–
85), whom the Pagets had known in Rome and in Thun. A published novelist herself, she encouraged Violet's writing ambitions and introduced her
to people who could help her find publishers. The other was Cornelia Boin-
ville de Chastel Turner (1793–1874), a longtime friend of Mrs. Jenkin whom
Violet met during her 1870 Paris visit. Both were women of uncommon intelligence and independence of spirit whose lives touched many literary
bases. Both recognized Violet's potential and understood her in ways that
quite eluded her mother.

Of Scottish heritage, Henrietta Jenkin was born in Kingston, Jamaica,
to a customs official. She married a young midshipman, Charles Jenkin,
who rose to the rank of captain in the Royal Navy. Gifted not with beauty but
with energy and personality, she tried to make the best of a less than happy
marriage. Captain Jenkin was good-natured, but as Robert Louis Stevenson
described him in a memoir of their son Fleeming Jenkin (who became a distinguished electrical engineer and professor at the University of Edinburgh),
"[H]is mind was largely blank. He had indeed a simplicity that came near
to vacancy." Stevenson summed up their marriage briskly: "His wife, impatient of his capacity and surrounded by brilliant friends, used him with a
certain contempt. She was the managing partner; the life was hers, not his."
After her husband retired from the navy, Mrs. Jenkin assumed most of the
financial obligations of the family, including the education of their son. Finding it cheaper to live abroad, they were in Paris in 1847, where they mingled
with writers, artists, and political exiles from the revolutions in Italy and
central Europe. Mrs. Jenkin delighted in this bohemian society and drew
on it for the plots of some of her novels. Stevenson wrote that her novels,
"though they attained and merited a certain popularity both in France and
England, are a measure only of her courage. They were a task, not a beloved
task; and they were written for money in days of poverty and they served
their end."[5] In 1848 the Jenkins were in Genoa, a center of Risorgimento activity, and in 1851 they returned to Scotland for their son's education. They

resumed their travels on the Continent as soon as they could and met the Pagets in Thun in 1868.

Henrietta Jenkin and Cornelia Turner shared curiously linked romantic pasts. Years earlier, living in Edinburgh, Mrs. Jenkin had met a young Italian, Agostino Ruffini, exiled from his homeland for his activities in Giovane Italia (Young Italy), a revolutionary group led by Giuseppe Mazzini that fought for a republican monarchy and freedom from Austrian domination. Agostino was one of three brothers, natives of Genoa who had dedicated their lives to the cause. The oldest, Jacopo, was arrested and committed suicide in prison. Agostino and a younger brother, Giovanni, found refuge in England. The story was that Mrs. Jenkin, then close to forty, left her husband for a passionate fling with Agostino. The relationship ended unhappily in Paris under obscure circumstances. Mrs. Jenkin suffered a collapse and was nursed back to health by her lover's brother Giovanni, who was living at the time with an Englishwoman some fifteen years his senior, Cornelia Turner.

Mrs. Turner's past was even more romantic than Mrs. Jenkin's, who eventually returned to her husband. Cornelia Turner had been born to an English mother and a French father who had served under Lafayette and died in Napoleon's Russian campaign. Her widowed mother lived on a fine country estate, Bracknell, in Berkshire, where she maintained a salon, entertaining writers and political radicals of William Godwin's circle. At eighteen, already married to Thomas Turner, a lawyer, Cornelia enchanted one of their guests, Percy Shelley, himself unhappily married and eager for consolation. Intelligent, well-educated, and pretty, Cornelia gave him lessons in Italian and listened raptly to his poetry and conversation. She was said to have inspired his "transient passion" expressed in "Alastor" and "Epipsychidion." Although there is no evidence of anything more than an idealized relationship between them, in a letter to Mrs. Godwin Shelley's wife Harriet reported that her erring husband had "paid her [Cornelia] such marked attention [that] Mr. Turner, the husband, had carried off his wife to Devonshire" (Cameron 4).[6]

To have "seen Shelley plain" was enough to give Mrs. Turner some modest fame for the rest of her life. But there was more romance in store for her. After giving birth to three children, only one of whom survived her, Mrs. Turner left her husband and went to live in Paris with her mother. They shared an apartment on the rue de Clichy and continued to entertain a variety of colorful figures—artists, writers, political exiles. In 1844 she met Giovanni Ruffini, who was struggling to support himself by writing opera libretti, one of them for Rossini's *Don Pasquale.* Mrs. Turner and her mother offered him housing in their building, and it was presumably during this period that they came to the assistance of the ailing Mrs. Jenkin. In 1849, after the death of her mother, Mrs. Turner and Ruffini set up housekeeping together and lived in harmonious bliss until her death in 1874. Irregular as the relationship might have appeared in Victorian society, it did not shock the English colony in Paris. Margaret Oliphant, the eminently respectable Scottish novelist, visited them in the winter of 1864–65 and recalled fondly in her *Autobiography* that they lived together "as if there had not been such a thing as an evil tongue in the world . . . an elderly romance, in old fidelity and friendship, made innocent, almost infantile, as of old babies, independent of sex and superior to it, amid all the obliterations of old age" (103).

By this time Giovanni, who mastered English during his long exile in England in the 1830s and published there as John Ruffini, had won some prestige as a novelist. His most popular, and to this day still an engaging, novel was *Dr. Antonio* (1855), allegedly inspired by Mrs. Jenkin's unhappy affair with his brother. It is the story of a gentle Italian country doctor who treats a young English girl after a carriage accident. They fall in love, but the story ends with his heroic death in the struggle for Italian independence. Eugene Lee-Hamilton met Ruffini in Thun, where he and Mrs. Turner were summering in 1868. An admirer of Ruffini's novel, Eugene showed him his yet unpublished poems, and they became good friends. When Eugene was sent to Paris in 1870, they resumed their friendship.

For Violet the visit was especially exciting. These were people with solid literary connections. Mrs. Turner had published two novels anonymously (*Angelo Sammartino, a Tale of Lombardy* [1859] and *Charity, a Tale* [1862]); Ruffini not only knew several English publishers but also wrote for Italian periodicals. Eugene and Violet, young as she was, were eager to make as many publishing contacts as possible. Ruffini and his companion went out of their way to encourage them. "They have the funniest little drawing room conceivable," Violet wrote enthusiastically to her father, "full of sketches, sepias, photos, daguerrotyphs [*sic*] and etchings of the different people they know. . . . We talked about Rome, Paris, Mrs. Jenkin, books, statues and Mr. Story the sculptor and his well known book Roba di Roma." But it was Mrs. Turner who won Violet's heart. She was "oh so kind! She made me promise to send her my *Biographie d'une Monnaie* to Thun and to write to her" (16 June 1870). Mrs. Turner promptly read and praised Violet's book and wrote to console her for the cuts the editor had made: "'Never mind,'" as poor Shelley the poet used to say when he was vexed, there is enough there to do you great credit, and the subject as well as its treatment suffices to place you at once out of the category of what my friend Shelley used to name with horror 'young ladies.' You have taken on superior standing to this offending class" (Corrigan, "Ruffini's Letters" 185).

From this time until her death four years later, Mrs. Turner corresponded regularly with Violet, encouraging her interests both in writing and in music, sprinkling her letters with references to Shelley, whom she cited as an example of another writer who was unappreciated in his time. She also used her good offices on behalf of Eugene, who was seeking English publishers for his poems and essays. Only a few hours before she died, on 25 October 1874, she wrote to Violet expressing her and Ruffini's interest in an article Violet wanted to write on Bologna. The most touching and tangible evidence of her affection for the girl was the gift to her of a watch that had once belonged to the musicologist Charles Burney and had been given to Mrs. Turner's mother by his daughter Fanny. Ruffini responded to Violet's thanks, 28 June 1875: "A vous, enfant précoce, revenant de droit le souvenir de cette autre enfant précoce, qui fut Mme D'Arblay" (Corrigan, "Ruffini's Letters" 187).

The Paris visit gave the "enfant précoce" renewed confidence in her talent and strengthened her determination to publish as soon and as widely as possible, a resolution fully supported by her mother and brother. As a family they recognized that her unusual background could be capitalized on for at least two audiences—English readers whose appetites for all things foreign, and especially Italian, were insatiable, and a smaller Italian public eager to learn about English writers and their own contemporary culture. While Eugene was unsuccessfully sounding out editors of English journals, his young sister had plans of her own—a long historical novel along the lines of George Sand's *Consuelo,* the romantically charged story of a brilliant singer in eighteenth-century Venice. Like Sand's, hers was to be "a grand historical musical novel," but it was to have an Italian tenor for hero rather than a soprano heroine like Consuelo. Violet's ambition was to create "a perfect eighteenth-century ideal of the Télémaque, Sir Charles Grandison, and Re Pastore sort" (*Juvenilia* 1:143–44).

The Paget family was musical: even Henry played the concertina. Violet never demonstrated a talent for performing and stopped formal piano lessons in 1870, but she managed to pick up an excellent musical education. At fifteen she discovered early Italian music, which was still being performed in churches and academies though it had no appeal for the general public. She was enchanted by the classical purity of Pergolesi, Paisiello, Scarlatti, Galuppi, and a host of others respected but largely forgotten in the nineteenth-century rage for romantic music. On one of her visits to the Ruffini-Turner apartment in Paris in 1870, Ruffini suggested that she read the poet-dramatist-librettist Pietro Metastasio, now unappreciated, "a bit flaccid ["un peu slombato"], but full of grace and high quality," he wrote her in September 1871 (Corrigan, "Ruffini's Letters" 184). It was an irresistible challenge. Violet promptly resolved to follow in the footsteps of Dr. Charles Burney and write a biography of Metastasio. Only Mrs. Jenkin had the foresight to warn her to go slowly. "I believe that you are a born writer," she wrote her in 1871. "Your letters are very graphic—lively in your descriptions—and you have a poetic tendency. . . . At the same time, my dear little friend, don't forget that you are a complex machine—body, soul, mind, and heart—and that all your component parts must have a due share of attention" (Gunn 57).

At fifteen Violet was indeed "a complex machine." If no more complex than other bright and ambitious teenagers, she was certainly more focused. From that age, and even earlier, she had a passion for the past. It had been acquired in part from her mother, who lived in her own self-created version of the eighteenth century, in part from the *Arabian Nights,* fairy tales, legends, and folklore she had read with such intense pleasure that they remained alive to her throughout her life. But in even greater measure it came from her itinerant childhood in premodern Europe—provincial German and Swiss towns and cities like Rome and Bologna that for her and her companion John Sargent were vast and exciting playgrounds where all these impressions of the past came together:

> Those genuine feelings of those youthful days of mine I can sometimes almost recapture, catch the swish of them vanishing in the distance of years, I mean the ineffable sense of the picturesqueness and wonderfulness of everything one came across: the market-place with the stage coach of the dentist, the puppet show against the Gothic palace, the white owl whom my friend John and I wanted to buy and take home to the hotel, the ices we eat [*sic*] in the medieval piazza, the skewered caramelles and the gardenias and musky, canary gaggias hawked about for buttonholes; the vines festooned over corn and hemp, the crumbling villas among them, the peasants talking like W. W. Story's *Roba di Roma,* "Kennst du das Land?" . . . a land where the Past haunted on, with its wizzards, sphinxes, strange, weird, *curious.* (*For Maurice* xlii–xliii)

When her conversations with Giovanni Ruffini in Paris began to focus on Metastasio, Violet found a center for her future work. She bought a copy of Burney's biography and read as much as she could find on eighteenth-century Italian music. Once again Mrs. Jenkin was a steadying influence. "Why should you not first try your hand at Essays about Metastasio and his times—Essays of about 40–50 pages or shorter, and so allow your subject to grow with a natural growth. . . . I think you might write something extremely interesting and amusing and less fatiguing than a History." Mrs. Turner also took a sympathetic interest in the young girl's work. Now well launched on her project, Violet wrote her in February 1873 that she was finally beginning to recognize her limitations:

> When last I wrote to you I was full of an idea of a work on Metastasio, and of beginning it immediately but on attempting to do so I found that I had scarcely anything to say on the subject. . . . I saw that for any such work to be really interesting, its writer must not only have an unusual degree of knowledge on the precise subject on which he is treating, but also a large general view of all the subjects at all connected with it; for to hope to get at the real rules of any particular branch of art seems to me preposterous without out a more or less thorough acquaintance with aesthetics in general. . . . I have also been studying counterpoint, but I find it horribly difficult to understand. Having so many subjects at the same time I can of course give but a short time to each, but the variety is pleasant, and I find that I can do even a *little,* only when I propose to myself to do a great deal.

To this Mrs. Turner replied, recalling her own youthful ambition to master classical studies and her advice to a despairing Shelley in the throes of writer's block that "a poet's mind is like a China rose. It is covered with a first crop of roses. Then the blossoms fall and the mere green leaves all forlorn remain, but after a while a fresh set of buds come forth and blossom, and thus crop succeeds crop of beautiful flowers through the years" (Gunn 60).

After Cornelia Turner's death, the bereaved Ruffini retired to the small town of Taggia on the Italian Riviera, where he spent his last years. He found consolation in corresponding, in French, with the young girl his companion had so admired. "C'est pour moi un besoign de coeur, c'est aussi un devoir en quelque sorte religieux envers la mémoire de celle qui vous a tant aimés" (Corrigan, "Ruffini's Letters" 189). Eugene had first come to their attention, but it was Violet, Ruffini recognized, who had a genuine literary vocation. By this time, too, Eugene was showing signs of the mysterious paralysis that was to keep him an invalid for some twenty years. As a result of his infirmity, the Pagets finally settled down in what was their first family home, in Florence, in 1873. Violet wrote faithfully to her elderly friend, reporting on her brother's health, on Florentine politics and society, and on her mother's and her own never ending battle against vivisection and for humane treatment of animals, a cause that he and Mrs. Turner had supported. But most important, she kept him informed of her studies and her writing plans. Living as he did in a remote seaside village, he had no opportunity to hear great music or see classic drama, and still a committed Italian nationalist, he did not share her passion for the past. He was, however, moved and impressed by her knowledge of Italian culture, and he actively helped her to break into print.

Her early efforts to find an outlet for her articles in English journals had failed, as had Eugene's, but knowing that she was fluent in Italian, Ruffini suggested that she apply to the editor-publisher of *La rivista europea,* Angelo de Gubernatis, with an offer to write a series of articles on contemporary English women novelists. De Gubernatis was happy to have the work of a writer whom he identified in a footnote to the first article he published, "I romanzieri inglesi di Afra [*sic*] Behn a Dickens e a Thackeray" in September 1875, as "H. Vernon Lee . . . who lives in Italy and writes with much ease in our language." Thus while still spending most of her time preparing for her book, which by 1875 she no longer saw as a biography of Metastasio but as a collection of essays on eighteenth-century Italian music and drama, she dashed off a series of articles on English novelists for *La rivista.* The assignment was not altogether to her taste; she complained to Ruffini of having to write on "cette odieuse Ouida." Nevertheless she was now becoming a professional writer with a voice and an outlet in which she could express her strongly held critical opinions.

Her first article opens with some breathtaking generalizations about the origins of not just the English novel but the German novel as well. She sees them linked in a common Teutonic heritage, sharing a common limitation as "a genre of middle character, capable of rising to beauty, but incapable of achieving the sublime, as in epic and tragedy." Her critical judgments on individual novelists are conservative and for the most part conventional. Like all her later critical writing on the novel, they are heavily weighted on the side of morality, with condemnation of the licentiousness of Restoration literature (from which charge she exempts Aphra Behn) and the bawdiness of Smollett and Fielding but with praise of Richardson. Even this early, she is more the moral relativist than puritan judge. *Tristram Shandy,* though she finds it scarcely less gross than some of Fielding's work, is—once purged by careful editing—"full of enchanting naturalness," and *A Sentimental Journey* is "immortal." A few of her judgments are strictly personal and stated as such. She concedes that Jane Austen's work is of "outstanding merit," but confesses that Maria Edgeworth gives her greater pleasure and that she prefers Charlotte Brontë's *Villette* for its spirited and strong-minded heroine to the more popular and romantic *Jane Eyre.* The article concludes with a comparison of Dickens and Thackeray in a series of glib antitheses: "Dickens laughs to divert, Thackeray laughs to correct; Dickens is more universally known, Thackeray is more widely respected." More important than the critical content of this survey is the particular attention she gives to lesser known women novelists. Although Violet had already assumed her masculine pseudonym, she makes no effort to conceal her pride in the achievements not only of major figures like Fanny Burney, Edgeworth, Austen, and Charlotte Brontë (she makes no mention of Emily Brontë) but also of the almost forgotten Aphra Behn, Amelia Opie, Elizabeth Inchbald, and Anne Radcliffe, who inspired hosts of imitators with her "blood-chilling and hair-raising" novels.

The omission of Trollope and George Eliot is not an oversight because her article covers only authors no longer living. She does, however, give Eliot honorable mention in her second article (October 1875), "I romanzi inglesi viventi: *Once and Again* [*Di bel nuova*] della Signora Jenkin." She refers to her as "la signora Lewis [*sic*], nata Evans, famosa sotto il pseudonim di George Eliot," the leading practitioner of the realistic novel. This, she writes, is the genre distinguished not for plot or character but for its depiction of real life; its chief merit is truth. The article itself is shameless puffery of Mrs. Jenkin, seventeen pages devoted to a dreary piece of hackwork. Violet was repaying a debt of gratitude to the friend who had given her so much encouragement. In the same spirit she proposed to Ruffini that he contribute to the series an article on Mrs. Turner, who had published two quite forgotten novels some years earlier; he wisely refused, saying that the subject would be too painful for him. Violet had no such delicacy with Mrs. Jenkin, whom she unblushingly ranked above George Eliot as the chief of the school of realistic novelists. Like Eliot, she wrote, Mrs. Jenkin drew on her own experiences—in this novel her life in France—with more skill than Ouida or M. E. Braddon ever manifested. Beyond this, however, H. Vernon Lee is hard-pressed to find anything to praise. Instead she offers a detailed synopsis and long passages of direct quotation, turning fourteen pages of her article into a capsule condensation of the novel.

The third article in this series (January 1876) discusses a better but still hardly memorable novel and novelist—*Daisy Burns* by Julia Kavanagh. The series ended here, suggesting that Violet's interests were moving in other directions. She had meanwhile learned that de Gubernatis had no intention of paying her for her work. Ruffini had initially advised her to submit articles without mentioning payment; if he asked for additional work, Ruffini advised that she "take the bull by the horns" and request compensation. But as he had foreseen, de Gubernatis not only expressed surprise that she expected to be paid but asked her to pay for galley corrections.

H. Vernon Lee's most interesting contribution to *La rivista* was an essay of sociocultural criticism, "Sulla necessità della coltura estetica in Italia" (November 1875), written in the form of a seven-page letter to the editor by "un cosmopolitana." Readers could not have known that the author of this fiery attack on the Italian public for its indifference to its cultural heritage

was a nineteen-year-old English girl. The editor, relying on the favorable reception of her articles on English novelists, printed a discreet footnote saying that the criticism was made in good faith and that there were currently
in Italy signs of a movement toward a cultural revival ("un risorgimento estetico"). Elsewhere in the article he added footnotes citing positive developments, but overall he did not challenge her charges because they were not
confined to Italy. Italy, she argues, was simply another victim of the materialism and utilitarianism that had produced sterile cultures everywhere in Europe—bland domestic painting in England, coarse social realism in France,
cold classicism in Germany. Italians cannot discriminate between a lightweight operetta like Offenbach's *Grand Duchess of Geroldstein* and Pergolesi's *Stabat Mater.* They chatter during operas and ignore and neglect the
great art that tourists come from all over the world to admire. The article is
a powerful though shrilly stated indictment, but it ends on a more hopeful
note, urging programs of education for women as well as for men, reading
the best writers on aesthetics from Taine and Burckhart, and the study of
early Italian music: "I wonder why in the country of Pergolesi and Marcello
there should be such ignorance, such frivolous heedlessness of that art that
is the wonder of other nations." And in a final appeal to the rising nationalism of Italy, she reminds her readers that although the great ages of creativity have passed, they still have a vast and rich heritage that it is in their
power to restore.

Violet had anticipated that her article would be controversial. Before
submitting it to de Gubernatis she sent a copy to her mentor Ruffini. He
suggested a few changes in wording, observing that her tone was "too im-
moderate not to give offense." But he acknowledged the justice of her arguments: "You do not spare my compatriots hard truths. . . . the evil is profound enough to demand frank speech." On 25 November 1875 he reported
that the article had indeed raised a tempest, but he added reassuringly in
English, "a tempest in a teapot." The fact that she published only one more
article in *La rivista europea* is not evidence of de Gubernatis's dissatisfaction
with her work. More likely it was because she was beginning to break into
English journals, which not only paid her (she received 31 guineas for an article entitled "Contemporary Italian Poets" in the *Quarterly Review,* October 1877) but offered her the audience she was seeking. Making her English
debut with "Tuscan Peasant Plays" in *Fraser's Magazine* in February 1877,
an article signed with a demure "V. Paget," she launched a career that saw
almost no year between 1877 and 1933 without some representation of her
work in English, American, or European periodicals.

The apprentice years were over, but the big book was still in the making. Throughout the 1870s, from the first suggestion by Ruffini in 1870, she

was preparing for and writing that book. The most remarkable feature of the work she produced in this period is the emergence even so early of certain implicit assumptions that were to dominate all her later work: the enduring values of the past, the intellectual equality of men and women, the natural superiority of an intellectual elite, the moral obligation of the artist to produce beauty in defiance of social ideologies and material advantage. In her survey "Contemporary Italian Poets" she praises Aleardi, Carducci, Bernardo Arnaboldi, but ranks them inferior to their predecessors because they are distracted from their art by the politics of the age: "The poet or the artist who prefers an ulterior object to his poem or his picture will necessarily sacrifice the latter to the former." Contemporary Italian poetry suffers too from the absence of women poets: "Italy has now no great female poet as she had in former days, and it would be as discreditable to a young unmarried lady to be a writer nowadays as to be so was creditable to her in the sixteenth and eighteenth centuries" (237).

Almost obsessively during this decade Violet was drawn back to the eighteenth century. Her prescription for a "risorgimento estetico" in aesthetically barren nineteenth-century Italy was a revival of its eighteenth-century musical heritage. Her first published travel essay, "Tuscan Peasant Plays," traces a link between a simple rural custom and the urbane neoclassicism of Metastasio's opera libretti. Fascinated by a song she hears the peasants sing as they work in the fields near Lucca, she visits a remote Tuscan village to attend a *maggio,* an annual celebration in song and recitation of ancient stories. To her surprise she recognizes one of them as derived from Metastasio. The local carpenter had prepared the script from a rough copy of the poet's *Ciro Riconosciuto:* "Someone went to Lucca and saw an opera," a villager explains to her; "he returned to the country and imitated it." The music that accompanied the spoken words had no relation to what was played in the opera house and was a simple traditional chant. But the lingering presence of Metastasio in remote Tuscan villages testified to the vitality of eighteenth-century Italian music.

Even when she surveyed the writings on aesthetics of the French critic Hippolyte Taine for the *British Quarterly Review* of July 1878, she turned the article ("Taine's Philosophy of Art") into a celebration of Italian music, a subject that Taine had failed to appreciate: "The eighteenth century in Italy is not what M. Taine represents it, misled, doubtless, by the account of a few superficial travellers and disreputable memoir-writers. It is almost a kind of minor Renaissance, a very jog-trot one certainly, but none the less distinctly one." She reminds her readers that the Italians were the masters and the rivals of Gluck and Mozart, and that "the eighteenth-century was to music what antiquity was to sculpture and the Renaissance to painting."

Italy's greatest glory then was its "deification of the human voice," and the ideal medium for that voice was "the old heroic opera, as perfected by Metastasio" (13).

In essays written decades later, Vernon Lee described the excitement of these early years when she was absorbed in discovering the past. Modest as her achievements may have been—the groundwork had already been done by Dr. Charles Burney and a handful of Italian scholars—they were for her, a precocious child at last confronting the challenges of adult criticism and scholarship, an initiation into a vocation that was to define her life.

2 THE EIGHTEENTH CENTURY AND AFTER

As a guide to myself, I am quite satisfied I have endowed my eighteenth-century people with virtues and graces of my own making; it was more satisfactory and perhaps more just than insisting on them from poor living creatures. Be this as it may, it was a case of Browning's "Was a lady such a lady?" the people, the places, and things becoming exquisite and wonderful by dint of brooding over them. It is utterly impossible for instance, that any real singer of any age should ever have stirred an audience as those dead singers I had never heard moved my childish heart. Indeed, I suspect that some of the extraordinary poignancy which eighteenth-century music still possesses for me may be due to the imaginative fervour with which I spelt out those songs or sonatas, to the inner dramas by which their hearing were accompanied. I have heard a good deal of music since, but none has ever had the quality of that.

　　　　　"Retrospective Chapter," *Studies of the Eighteenth Century in Italy*

🐚 LAUNCHING HER AMBITIOUS PROJECT TO WRITE A HISTORY of eighteenth-century Italian opera, Violet Paget became Vernon Lee. She was no longer the precocious child seeking to impress her family but, as she saw herself many years later, "a half-baked polyglot scribbler of sixteen." Thirty-five years later, when she added a "Retrospective Chapter" to the 1907 second edition of *Studies of the Eighteenth Century in Italy,* she looked back with an air of diffidence, almost apologetically, to her youthful naïveté. Yet for all her later protests that "my *Eighteenth Century* must be brimful of presumptuousness and folly," there was a distinct pride in what she had accomplished:

> My eighteenth-century lore was acquired at an age (more precisely between fifteen and twenty) when some of us are still the creatures of an unconscious play instinct. And the Italy of the eighteenth century, accidentally opened to me, became, so to speak, the hay-loft, the tool-house, the remote lumber-room full of discarded mysteries and of lurking ghosts, where a half-grown

young prig might satisfy, in unsuspicious gravity, mere childlike instincts of make-believe and romance. . . . These essays are the log-book of my explorations through that wonder-world of things moth-eaten and dust-engrained, but sometimes beautiful and pathetic in themselves, and always transfigured by my youthful fancy; they are the inventory of my enchanted garret. (xvi) [1]

In those exciting early years, liberated at last from governesses and her mother's erratic tuition, spared the discipline and arid curriculum of a proper girls' school, Violet flourished in the joys of independent scholarship. An older Vernon Lee looked back at that industrious prodigy with a mocking echo of Browning's grammarian: "At eighteen I had written an essay demonstrating why Cimarosa's recitative was less good than, say, Leo's, and wherein consisted the subtle superiority of Pergolesi's setting of *Se cerca, se dice* over Galuppi's. There were six weeks of struggles to settle Mozart's position towards Sarti and Paisiello, which have made me appreciate the wrestlings of divines with Predestination and the Procession of the Holy Ghost" (xxiii–xxiv). [2] Fortunately, her youthful imagination triumphed over her pedantry. Scholarly essays on Cimarosa and Pergolesi were valuable educational preparation, but they were merely schoolroom exercises. Even the teenaged Violet Paget knew that she must move from these into the profession for which her mother had destined her, and which she was eager to embrace herself.

Wherever the Pagets settled for a short stay—Florence, Padua, Bologna, Rome—she scoured the bookstalls and the archives of libraries for eighteenth-century materials: books, musical scores, libretti. The dust and neglect these had suffered had romantic appeal:

> An old book of cantatas of Porpora, an old volume of plays by Carlo Gozzi, does not affect us in the same manner as a darkened canvas by Titian, or a yellowed folio of Shakespeare; these latter have passed through too many hands, been looked at by too many eyes: they retain the personality of none of their owners. But the volume of Gozzi's plays was probably touched last by hands which had clapped applause to Trufaldino-Sacchi or Pantalone-Darbes; the notes in the book of cantatas may last have been glanced over by singers who learned to sing them from Porpora himself; with this dust, which we shake reluctantly out of the old volumes, vanishes we know not what subtle remains of personality. (*Studies* 293)

When the family wintered in Rome in 1873, she took lessons in counterpoint and singing, not that she should sing but that she should appreciate vocal technique. Her teacher was Gaetano Capocci, chapel master of

St. John Lateran. In 1875, in Florence, she studied with an unnamed ancient music master, "who had sung with boyish voice to Cimarosa and Paisiello those airs which he hummed over for us in faint and husky tones" (*Studies* 294).[3] Her research became a family enterprise, engaging even her father at one point to work with her on an essay on Clementi (apparently never completed).[4] Eugene's health was by now failing, but he followed her progress with keen interest. Mrs. Paget, far more expert in music than her daughter, played out on the piano the old scores she had bought or copied in libraries, and Violet recalled in her "Retrospective Chapter" that on one occasion she was so emotionally stirred that she could not remain in the room but had to go out into the garden to listen:

> And the first piece she played was *Pallido il Sole,* one of the three legendary airs . . . with which the madness of Saul-Philip of Spain had been soothed by virtuous David-Farinelli . . . I can still feel the sickening fear, mingled with shame, lest the piece should turn out hideous. . . . It is impossible to put into reasonable words the overwhelming sense that on that piece hung the fate of a world, the only one that mattered—the world of my fancies and longings. (xlviii)

From time to time in their wanderings through Europe the Pagets and the Sargents met. In 1871 they were at Lake Como together for a few days. The children had outgrown their mischief and their make-believe. John was now as seriously resolved to be an artist as Violet was to be a writer. Strolling beside the lake, they discussed painting and sculpture, pondering the merits of Canova versus the classical Greek, the styles of Guido Reni and Raphael, and relaxing by reading passages from *Childe Harold* to each other (Gunn 60). They met again in Bologna in 1873 when Violet was now totally absorbed in her studies of eighteenth-century music.[5] Mrs. Paget and Mrs. Sargent and their children spent ten days together there. It was autumn: the Pagets were on their way south after summering in Thun or Bagni di Luca; the Sargents were returning to their home in Florence. Bologna had a romantic fascination for them all. "Dusky, many-towered Bologna," as Violet recalled it in an essay forty years later, was "one of those places which exist only in childhood, where, in virtue of some one thing acquiring a supernatural value, all the most ordinary circumstances of life come to partake of its magic" (*Golden Keys* 57). The two families took evening walks through the medieval arcades. The city had not yet undergone the plastic surgery of modernization and, when Violet first saw it, was unchanged from the eighteenth century.

Bologna's principal attractions for her were the Accademia Filarmonica, founded in 1666, where the fourteen-year-old Mozart had been honored on his visit to the city, and the Conservatorio Giovanni Battista Martini, home of one of Europe's greatest music libraries. She spent her days studying the records of eighteenth-century music, emerging late each afternoon to walk through the narrow old streets back to the family's lodgings. She recruited John Sargent to accompany her to the Accademia, where the halls were lined with portraits of "Handel, majestic in blue plush and a many-storied peruke; Gluck, coarse, bright, and flushed in a furred cloak; Haydn, pale, grey, willow-like bending over a meagre spinet; Mozart, sweet and dreamy, with the shadow of premature death already upon him, and their lesser, forgotten contemporaries." These were for her visits of ceremony: "I invariably took a pair of fresh gloves. You could not present yourself badly got up before all those distinguished and delicately dressed people" (*Juvenilia* 1:142). For the aspiring young painter Sargent, the gallery offered challenging subjects to copy. Among others, he did a watercolor of a portrait of the young Mozart.

Another portrait that fascinated them both was of Carlo Broschi, better known as Farinelli, the greatest countertenor of the eighteenth century. Violet had already seen his portrait in Rome and knew from her reading of Dr. Charles Burney's *Present State of Music in France and Italy* (1773) and of Metastasio's letters that Farinelli had been the idol of his age. Wandering through these hallways, peopled by fading images of the dead past, "John and I . . . made ourselves, so to speak, creepily tipsy that last autumn of our adolescence at Bologna." These relics of the past transcended historical research. They existed in the young people's imaginations as ghosts, all the more appealing because this was "unheard" music. "It was a feeling of mingled love and wonder at the miracle of the human voice, which seemed the more miraculous that I had never heard great singers save in fancy . . . which, in the absence of gramophones, was a longing for the unattainable, with the passion only unattainable objects can inspire" (*For Maurice* xxxiii–xxxiv). Obsession with the past, which was to become a major theme of Vernon Lee's later stories of the supernatural, inspired her even this early to sit up late at night some months later, scaring herself by writing a draft of a ghost story, "Winthrop's Adventure," in which a portrait of a great eighteenth-century singer comes alive to sing an aria that the narrator could never have heard in reality.[6]

Those "unheard melodies" of the past had haunted Violet since her childhood in Rome, for the city she came to know and love was not the Rome of the 1870s. In the dust and gravel of Rome's neglected gardens she had found ancient coins and scraps of artifacts of a far earlier antiquity. But it was the closer neighborly past of the eighteenth century that fascinated the adolescent Violet. Its shabby, neglected buildings—especially the empty shell of the old Teatro Aliberti, Rome's principal theatre in the eighteenth century, where audiences had cheered the plays of Metastasio, Goldoni, and Gozzi, and the old concert halls where they listened appreciatively to the music of Porpora, Galuppi, Pergolesi, and to the voice of Farinelli—all these were a palpable presence. "The eighteenth century existed for me as a reality, surrounded by faint and fluctuating shadows which shadows were simply the present" (*Juvenilia* 1:137). Here was an accessible past, not enshrined in museums like the sculpture of ancient Rome and the paintings of the Middle Ages and the Renaissance, but homely, shabby, and dusty, the gardens and statues overgrown with weeds and mold, its undistinguished painting faded and darkened with age and neglect, its music and literature confined to yellowing pages and crumbling bindings.

No one recognized better than the adult Vernon Lee that her passion for the past was an evasion of an unhappy present: her adolescent self-consciousness of her plain if not positively ugly face, her irregular family life, an indifferent father, an ailing half brother, a mother whom she adored but who lavished her affection on her firstborn son. It would not be fair, however, to her candor and to her very considerable engagement in her later years with social and political causes to describe her choice of the past as simply a retreat from reality. She was far too sensitive to the complexity of the subject she was working on to deny its traps for the unwary. She spoke ruefully but humorously of "my foolish passion for the Past" and acknowledged that "the splendour of the Past may be a mere fiction of our own, like the romance of the Past which we say we no longer believe in." The eighteenth century that she explored so enthusiastically in her first book was as much a fiction, a product of her imagination, as it was a fact, the fruit of her conscientious research. Had the past ever really existed? she asked in an essay, "Puzzles of the Past":

> Is not what we think of as the Past—what we discuss, describe, and so often passionately love—a mere creation of our own? Not merely in its details, but in what is far more important, in its essential, emotional, and imaginative quality and value? Perhaps some day psychology may discover that we have a craving, like that which produces music or architecture, for a special state of nerves (or of something else, if people are bored with nerves by that time) obtainable by a special human product called the Past —the Past which has never been the Present? (*Hortus Vitae* 196–97)

An older Vernon Lee could properly ask such questions, but for the Italy-intoxicated adolescent the past was as real as, and infinitely more attractive than, the present. More particularly, she chose the eighteenth century, a less distant but also less appreciated era than earlier periods of Italian history. It was a choice that demanded explanation, an age of little apparent historical or cultural distinction, its physical vestiges unremarkable, its politics insignificant in the grand sweep of war and revolution that transformed the character of Europe, its art and literature vastly overshadowed by the achievements of earlier centuries, its music rarely performed, its civilization altogether, as she writes, "poor, weak, and uninteresting, because in all this it was a mere copy of the English and French Eighteenth Century" (*Studies* 3). In short, it was like the Rome that had at first also seemed to the child Violet shabby and uninviting but became the "other" Rome that was *her* discovery, a private treasury in which her imagination and her scholarship were joined in happy collaboration.

Wisely she confined herself to the arts to which she was most sympathetic—music and drama. As she proclaimed grandly in the introduction to her book in 1880: "Italy in the last century got her philosophy and philosophic poetry, like her dress and her furniture, from Paris and London, but Italy in the last century got her drama and her comedy neither from Paris nor from London, but from her own intellectual soil, where they had been germinating for centuries; and Italy, in the eighteenth century, gave her own spontaneous national music to the whole of Europe." Sweeping generalizations to be sure: a cultural historian barely into her twenties, she summed up the eighteenth century in the rest of Europe as strong in theory but weak in practice, with poetry lacking spontaneity ("mere philosophy decked out in Dresden china pastoral furbelows"), and the plastic arts "dead everywhere." Firm, untroubled by reservations, qualifiers, exceptions, she plunged ahead. Her subject was nothing less than the emergence of a national Italian culture of music and drama: "Not only is this artistic efflorescence the only really national and spontaneous thing which Italy then possessed, she being in all else inferior to other nations, but that artistic efflorescence was the only thoroughly national and spontaneous artistic movement which took place anywhere in the eighteenth century. The other nations had spontaneous philosophical life, but Italy alone had artistic life" (*Studies* 4).

Essentially Vernon Lee was seeking to reconstruct a popular culture, to bring it to life in terms of the people who had created and participated in it. Although the scholarship of *Studies of the Eighteenth Century in Italy* was fortified with diligent research in documents of the past, her writing was inspired by the living Italian present—street fairs and religious festivals, folk literature, commedia dell'arte, and opera. Like Robert Browning, she peopled her vision of the Italian past with sometimes real, sometimes imaginary characters and gave them dramatic life: "Following the sound of the music of Pergolesi and Cimarosa, trying to catch closer glimpses of the Bettinas and Lindoros of Goldoni, of the Truffaldinos and Brighellas of Carlo

Gozzi, we have strayed into the world of Italy in the eighteenth century, the world of fine ladies in stomachers and hoops, of dapper cavalieri serventi, of crabbed pedants, of hungry Arcadian rhymsters, of Gallo-maniacs and Anglo-maniacs—a world of some good, some evil, some folly, and much inanity" (5).

Studies of the Eighteenth Century in Italy is an imaginative travel book; we accompany its author on a journey into the past. We stroll through crowded piazzas "where people are drinking lemonade and coffee, where perambulating booths displayed their wares under the flickering torchlight, where the puppet show stood surrounded by a ring of eager spectators . . . [and] there was music again in plenty." We visit salons where poetasters and genuine poets gather; we attend public concerts in churches, private concerts in the homes of patricians, lavish opera productions, rowdy comedy with slapstick and horseplay, fantasies that blended the comic and the supernatural with dazzling stage sets and mechanical effects. So thoroughly identified is she with her project that she can evoke a living moment from the past:

> As soon as the sun had fairly set and the cool breeze risen, the townsfolk would awake, and having opened shutters, pulled up blinds, and breathed the fresher evening air, they would begin to think of hearing a little music. A little music, nothing grand or tragic, oh no! no great singers who required tremendous applause, something simple, easy, and refreshing. So the men have exchanged dressing-gown for snuff- or puce-coloured light coat, and coloured handkerchief for well-combed little wig, and their wives and daughters having slipped on a tidy gown and a coquettish black veil, the population would slowly wend their way towards the comic theatres, pausing just a little to talk to acquaintances, and breathe the fresh air in the white, pearly twilight. (85)

Although the essays on music in *Studies of the Eighteenth Century in Italy* were written as separate pieces and published first as articles in *Fraser's Magazine* in 1878 and 1879, they have a remarkable unity of effect.[7] The book begins with a quest—a search for the Serbatoio (conservatory) d'Arcadia, the long-forgotten Academy of Arcadians, a literary society that in the eighteenth century emulated those lofty Parnassian centers of literature and art of the Renaissance. In June 1871, when fourteen-year-old Violet was just beginning her eighteenth-century studies, she knew only that the Bosco Parrasio, the Roman headquarters of the Academy, was somewhere on the Janiculum Hill on the road to the Villa Pamphili. The enchantment began with the name itself, the wood of the sacred grove of Apollo where in the seventeenth century Queen Christina of Sweden, self-exiled to Rome, founded an academy to restore Roman poetry to its classical glory. Mrs. Paget shared her daughter's interest enough to accompany her on her first visit. It was an adventure, a climb up a dirty street, a slippery mule path, past some cloth mills and a neglected, overgrown garden. Leaning against the garden gate— an ironic twist on the guardians of gates in mythology—was a slovenly, portly priest who by prearrangement was to be their guide. The once lav- ishly decorated Accademia degli Arcadi was now occupied by peasants who stored their provisions in the stately halls and "hung their hats and jackets on the marble heads of improvisatori and crowned poetesses; and threw their beans, maze, and garden tools into corners of the desolate reception rooms, from whose mildewed walls looked down a host of celebrities—bro- caded doges, powdered princesses, and scarlet-robed cardinals, simpering drearily in their desolation" (9).

It was a scene exactly calculated to seize Violet's imagination: the crum- bling neglect, the shabby living relics of a once sparkling society. She saw in it images of life and death, the profuse vegetation surrounding it and the noisy peasants against a background of faded elegance that was the eigh- teenth century. Her reconstruction of the Arcadians' past is charming; it is also based in sound scholarship. The ignorance and superstition, the affec- tation and rigid social conventions of the time are duly recorded, as are the preciosity and pomposity of much of the literature produced by Arcadians fancying themselves shepherds in a pastoral romance.[8] One contemporary witness was Goethe. In January 1788 he yielded to the persuasion of Italian friends and allowed himself to be introduced into Arcadia "as a distin- guished shepherd." In his *Italian Journey* he describes with obvious amuse- ment the very formal ceremony honoring him, and he reproduces in its ful- some entirety his citation, in the original Italian. "I have not translated it because it would lose its distinctive flavour in any other language" (445).

The Arcadians of the eighteenth century, Vernon Lee observed drily, "were not in the least shepherds, indeed most of them had never possessed a sheep or any animal save a lapdog" (48). Its members were out of step with the emerging trends of European romanticism and failed to keep pace in their own time with Italy's emerging literary masters—Metastasio, Gol- doni, Gozzi, Alfieri. Still the Academy had served a purpose. In the cul- turally barren years of the Napoleonic Wars ("this despicable period of ex- hausted repose"), the Arcadians were a reminder of a once glorious past. Though they were "a mere whimsical congregation of crotchety pedants and blue-stockings" (17), Vernon Lee set them in a larger context as pre- servers and disseminators of a cultural tradition who founded academies all over the intellectual wasteland of the Italian provinces and encouraged writ- ers and artists to practice their skills.

Not the least of the Academy's achievements was its recognition of women both as patrons and as practicing poets in their own right. She recounts with relish the career of Maria Maddalena Morelli, honored by the Arcadians with the name "Corilla Olimpica." A celebrated poet, musician, and hostess, Corilla entertained Dr. Charles Burney on his visit to Florence and once composed a sonnet in honor of the boy prodigy Mozart. Hailed especially as an improvisatrice, a talent much prized in the eighteenth century, Corilla received many honors, the most glorious of them a papal coronation at the Capitol in Rome. Her fame, alas, led to her downfall. Literary rivals ridiculed her and ruined her coronation ceremony. However, Corilla received her share of immortality some forty years later when Madame de Staël apotheosized her as the heroine of her novel *Corinne*.

In her essay "The Arcadian Academy" Vernon Lee sweeps boldly through the political and cultural history of eighteenth-century Italy. It is loosely written, moving forward and backward over the century and interweaving anecdotes and character profiles with innocent disregard for coherence or— since many of her citations are names unfamiliar to nonspecialist readers —clarity. Nevertheless the essay serves well as an introduction to the more sharply focused essays that follow. The best of these is "The Musical Life," a happy blend of musical history and imagination drawn from the travel journals of the eminent eighteenth-century musicologist Dr. Charles Burney. Her chapter on the Arcadian Academy began as a quest for a specific site, then moved swiftly away from its center to ramble over Italy and the whole century. "The Musical Life," on the other hand, moves logically and chronologically, following Dr. Burney in 1770 as he traveled from France through Italy, from Turin in the north to Milan, Bergamo, Brescia, Verona, Vicenza, and Venice, to Florence and Rome, and finally to Naples. Along the way the indefatigable English traveler stopped at many provincial towns, wherever he had reason to believe that he would hear interesting music. All this he recorded in a journal, a "battered volume" that Violet had first read in the library of the music school in Bologna, published in 1771 as *The Present State of Music in France and Italy*. This English music master, like his daughter Fanny, admired France greatly, but he took a dim view of French music. "In short," he wrote after attending all the concerts and operas offered in Paris, "notwithstanding they can both talk and write as well and so much about it, music in France, without respect to the two great essentials of melody and expression, may still be said to be in its infancy" (*Studies* 76). He came to Italy, however, with high musical expectations, and he was not disappointed. While others visited Italy to study ruins of antiquity and art of a long lost Renaissance, "he had come to hear music finer, as he believed, than that of any previous time, to enjoy the fruits of an artistic civilisation while it was yet in its prime . . . he had come to deal not with a dead art but with one which, as he says, 'still lived'" (*Studies* 81).

As Dr. Burney soon confirmed, the music of Italy was a living culture: church music in the morning, theatre music in the evening, street music day and night. It was a people's art: "The shopkeepers, artisans and peasants, while dawdling carelessly about, imbibed music unconsciously; they became critics and occasionally one of their sons or nephews, instead of turning shopman or farmer, would turn composer or performer; and indeed nearly all the great Italian musicians belonged to the humbler, often to the humblest, classes of society" (82). Serious opera in 1770 had not yet reached the lofty heights it was to achieve with Mozart, but the crude comic opera of the *burletta* was gradually refining itself into shapelier lyrical and dramatic form. Burney heard music in the homes of amateur and professional musicians, concerts where the "dilettanti would sit down to their instruments, their silken coat-tails neatly disposed on either side of their chair, their well-starched ruffles carefully drawn out; the ladies would rise, smooth out their dresses and aprons, unroll their scores, and the performance would begin, interrupted only by a few solemn pauses, during which candles were snuffed, violins tuned, bows resined, and snuff-boxes passed around" (90).

Determined to re-create for her readers the sights and sounds of this eighteenth-century world, Vernon Lee explains the differences between these antique musical instruments and their modern counterparts, emphasizing that Dr. Burney and his Italian hosts heard a different quality of sound from what we hear. In Venice particularly he was exposed to all manner of musical sounds: "there were guitars, mandolins, fiddles and voices in the two squares of Saint Mark, among the coffee-house tables and the story-tellers . . . gondoliers chanting Tasso . . . serenades on the canals, which to Burney sounded exquisite, and music issuing from the windows of the palaces" (98). He visited the music schools of Venice where young girls were trained for the grand oratorios and masses. (Here George Sand's fictional Consuelo began her remarkable career under the tutelage of the real Niccolò Porpora.) In Venice too he heard the music of Benedetto Marcello (1686–1739), "the personification, the incarnation, of all that was most original and noble in the music of the Venetian oligarchy, uniting as he did the genius of a great composer with the spirit of a noble of the great commonwealth" (103). For Vernon Lee, though not for Dr. Burney, "who was inconceivably blind to [his] merits" (107), Marcello set the standard for eighteenth-century music in his work—simultaneously eclectic and catholic, commanding both the comic absurdities of opera buffa and "the musically sublime."

Moving on to Bologna, Dr. Burney was made an honorary member of the Accademia Filarmonica. He interviewed the Franciscan monk Giam-battista Martini, "the most learned theoretical musician in Italy," but his most thrilling experience was his meeting with Farinelli, the countertenor whose portrait and history had so fascinated the young Violet and John Sargent in Bologna in 1873. Farinelli, the toast of Europe in his day, had sung to the acclaim of both the masses and the nobility for many years. He was especially esteemed in Spain, where King Philip V, who suffered from melancholia, engaged him to sing to him every night, like the Chinese emperor cheered by the song of the nightingale. By the time Burney met Farinelli he was old, living in retirement in a country house near Bologna, but still capable of charming a visitor with "the dim halo of royalty which surrounded the old singer" (114).[9]

He proceeded then to Florence, "not a particularly musical town in the musical Italy of those days," where he heard many first-rate performances, among them "a weazened, childish little creature, who played the harpsichord astoundingly, had composed an opera, and was being courted by everyone." Dr. Burney had little faith in the future of such infant prodigies, even this one, "Volfango Amedeo, son of M. Mozart, Vice Chapelmaster of His Serene Eminence the Prince Archbishop of Salzburg" (116). He moved on to the center of musical life in his day, Rome, though the city was more remarkable for performance than for creativity. Cutting across all class lines from nobility and clergy to shopkeeping middle class, Roman audiences were noisy and enthusiastic in their approval and disapproval, strikingly different from the decorous upper-class audiences Burney had known at home.

Lively as Rome was, "the most musical town in Italy" was Naples, "the last of the stages of Dr. Burney's musical pilgrimage." Vernon Lee considers it the birthplace of modern music: "It was there that, towards the middle of the seventeenth century, music had ceased to be symbolical, liturgical and scientific, and had become human and humanly excellent" (126). Entertained everywhere by the best local society, he was received in Naples by Sir William and the first Lady Hamilton (not, Vernon Lee hastens to add, "the terrible Lady Hamilton of the year '99"); he interviewed the most celebrated performers and composers—among the latter Piccini, Jommelli, Paisiello —and visited the famous conservatories where boys (not also girls, as in Venice) received the best, and free, musical education. But with all this activity, Dr. Burney shrewdly detected a decline from the high standards of the past. Nevertheless, in the light of the overwhelming glories of the musical scene he had been observing in Italy, he returned to England "highly delighted with Italian music."

"In the second half of the eighteenth century," Vernon Lee writes near the conclusion of "The Musical Life," "music had run through an untroubled course; it was still young, still vigorous . . . men did not yet require dramatic effects or psychological interest, for they could still obtain pure beauty; they did not ask for distinctly marked characters, for historical pictures, for mythological allegories; they asked only for music" (130). Opera, which she, not Dr. Burney, takes as the touchstone of eighteenth-century Italian music, was composed for singers. The libretto was respected and admired, but it was reduced to recitative. The public came to hear the *prima donna* and the *primo uomo.* "The art of singing," she wrote in an article in the *British Quarterly Review* in October 1880, "developed with extraordinary rapidity, and by the end of the first quarter of the eighteenth century . . . it had reached complete maturity; it had attained a degree of perfection absolutely analogous to the perfection of sculpture among the Greeks, and of painting in the Renaissance—a perfection which was maintained until almost the close of the eighteenth century, when it began to decline more and more rapidly as it approached our own day" (166). Nineteenth-century opera— she cites Donizetti, Meyerbeer, and Verdi but identifies as her primary target "the school of Wagner"—is dramatic and "the dramatic declamation of melody is inevitably destructive of its musical shape, since it implies that the accentuation required by the music is to be sacrificed to the totally different accentuation belonging to spoken passion" (174).

The daring and self-assurance of this twenty-year-old amateur musicologist—for Violet admitted that her technical command of music and her musical education were severely limited—are nothing less than astounding. She wrote and published as an authority in a field where trained musicologists tread cautiously. Her contemporaries, however, knew little or nothing of her subject and read her generally with respect and admiration. And indeed her essay on the musical life of the eighteenth century, though full of sweeping and questionable generalizations forcefully argued, is also full of sensitive insights, brilliant guesses perhaps, that reflect not only an uncommon but a complex and sophisticated intelligence. Violet valued eighteenth-century music because it represented the dominance of the intellect over the emotions, the strict practice of emotional discipline and control. These were values that she had absorbed from her mother, whose favorite reading was the eighteenth-century rhetoricians and political philosophers. That these values were easier to profess than to practice Violet was soon to discover.

In 1796, long after he had returned to England, Dr. Burney published a three-volume *Memoirs of the Life and Writings of the Abate Metastasio,* anticipating by many years the ambitions of fourteen-year-old Violet Paget, who bought a copy of the book when she was in Paris in 1870. A year later, on a visit to the Academy in the Bosco Parrasio, she saw Metastasio's portrait:

"reclining on his sofa, fat, easy, elegant, languid with selfish, self-complacent sentimentality" (*Studies* 10). Here indeed was her eighteenth century incarnate. This crafty but also brilliantly gifted poet-dramatist almost single-handedly created eighteenth-century Italian opera by providing literary texts of powerful dramatic structure, works that inspired composers to liberate traditional opera from its rigid formality and give it flexibility, subtlety, and emotional depth. Recitative and arias, until then static set pieces, became expressive and flowed with the dramatic movement of the libretto. Metastasio wrote directly for the Italian opera stage. He knew its composers, singers, and scenic designers. Equally important, he knew his audiences. "The plays of Metastasio," Vernon Lee writes, "are neither fashionable pieces of pseudo-classical work, like those of Voltaire, nor eclectic works of classical imitation, like those of Alfieri; they are a national, spontaneous form, evolved by the artistic wants of a whole nation" (204).

Her essay "Metastasio and Opera," the longest of the eighteenth-century studies, is also the most ambitious. Although Violet heard fine musical performances whenever the opportunity arose—far more, certainly than most of her contemporaries—she had little opportunity to hear or see the eighteenth-century operas of which she wrote so confidently. Pergolesi, Cimarosa, and Mozart were performed, but the vast corpus of eighteenth-century opera—those many works written by Metastasio that she describes with such enthusiasm—were for her musical ghosts. That no doubt added to their piquancy and challenged her all the more. Equally challenging was the long, colorful career of Metastasio himself, which touched upon every major and many a minor composer and performing artist of the eighteenth century. Embodied in one man was everything that had fascinated Violet Paget since her early adolescence. She shared her enthusiasm for Metastasio with Dr. Burney, who had sought him out and had several meetings with him during his visit to Vienna in 1772.

When Burney began collecting and translating Metastasio's letters for his biography, the undertaking was a refuge for the now elderly Burney from the grim news of the French Revolution. He wrote to a friend in 1796, having just completed his book: "Indeed the work was undertaken more to keep off the *foul fiend* Politics, than with any view to fame or profit . . . during so total a revolution in the moral as well as political principles of mankind, when virtues are metamorphosed into vice, & è Contra how can the mild effusions of so tranquil & benignant a heart as that of Metastasio be thought worthy of display and admiration?" (Lonsdale 370). But in Vernon Lee's "Metastasio and Opera," Metastasio emerges as anything but "benignant." In contrast to Dr. Burney's idealized and bland depiction, she offers a portrait of a brilliant, self-serving, and self-centered opportunist. For Burney he was "a Poet of refined taste and sentiments, and a Man possessed of every moral and social virtue that embellished society." He sums up his achievements by linking him with a highly regarded predecessor poet-dramatist venerated by the Arcadian Academy: "Apostle Zeno seems to have been the Eschylus [*sic*], and Metastasio the Sophocles and Euripides of the modern melodrama" (3:326). For Vernon Lee his fame was deserved, but his character was flawed and his biography demonstrated "that a mean man may be a greater poet than a noble one, and that a faulty product of a whole time and nation is more valuable than a faultless fabric of eclectic refinement" (144).[10]

Her Metastasio was "weak and characterless"; as a young man he was "handsome, soft-mannered, and clever. . . . Effeminacy, the absence of strength of character . . . was written in his fair, smiling face." He exploited his benefactors; he had "no interest in life beyond himself" but managed somehow always to surround himself with generous friends. The Abate Gian Vincenzo Gravina, an eminent priest and legal scholar, had found him as a little boy, the son of a poor shopkeeper, singing improvised verses in the streets of Rome. Gravina adopted him from his only-too-willing family and had him educated. He changed his protégé's homely family name Trapassi to the elegantly classical name Metastasio and introduced him into society, where the boy's wit and precocious talents were instantly appreciated. On his death Gravina left him a fortune. Thus generously endowed at twenty, Metastasio continued to ingratiate himself with patrons, especially women, a number of whom appeared delighted to further his career.

Metastasio quickly squandered his fortune and was obliged to turn to the practice of law in Naples. Thanks to the help of an adoring actress-mistress, he became a highly successful dramatist. When he received a lucrative offer to move to Vienna to serve as court poet to Emperor Charles VI, he promptly accepted. Here again he found a protective mistress, and here his career flourished for fifty years. But with success, Vernon Lee points out, also came ennui and melancholy. In the court of Maria Theresa, successor to Charles, he lived largely on his reputation, rising to creative enthusiasm only late in life when he composed cantatas for his longtime friend Farinelli. She paints a grim picture of the now old man, "a hypochondriac, an idle routinist, without the desire or the power to work. . . . He had no interest in life beyond himself, so that himself once provided for he ceased to have any at all." Soon after his death he was almost forgotten by the public that had so idolized him.

"Metastasio and Opera" should not be read as anything more than the kind of fiction Victorians liked to describe as "a tale founded on fact." As such, it is a delightful narrative, strengthened by its learned commentary on eighteenth-century opera, weakened only by some extended summaries of Metastasio's intricately knotted plots. For the first time in her early writing career, Violet let her imagination run freely over her scholarship. Without forsaking the basic facts of her subject's life, she created a character and placed him in the center of a bustling musical society. With the skills of an expert novelist—skills strikingly absent, unhappily, in her first full-length novel, *Miss Brown*—she created a plot that might have intrigued Stendhal.

Her imagination embellished the record—Metastasio's surviving letters, "pruned and revised by those who published them." But his Italian editors had been far less zealous than Dr. Burney to select only those that were models of civility and discretion. In them—and in a terse account in the commonplace book of Gotthold Lessing—she found a record of toadying, family discords, and emotional entanglements. Honesty forced her to admit that much of this was legend, gossip only partly confirmed by the record. But it made a splendid story: the handsome and talented young law clerk sought out by a famous actress considerably older than he. The actress is Marianna Bulgarelli, known as La Romanina. She is married, but her husband is complaisant, and Metastasio is soon comfortably settled in their household. La Romanina was only one of many women in his life, but his liaison with her was the most turbulent. The dramatic climax comes when Metastasio moves to Vienna and finds a new protector in the Countess of Althann. Vernon Lee cannot resist the devices of romantic fiction, including a frantic historical present:

> But the Romanina cannot take things philosophically; she has no future, no present; she has only a blank, a void, an immense bitterness to live upon. And were they not to meet? Was he not to return to Rome after a few years? Does he ever allude to that, the ungrateful wretch? Was there not talk of her joining him in Vienna? . . . Has not the Emperor a chapel, does he not engage all the greatest Italian singers? . . . Metastasio is terrified at the idea. Engage her, an old woman? Never. There is no danger of that indeed. But if she knows there is no chance by this means, who can tell whether she may not sacrifice house, husband, all and come to Vienna, openly, avowedly to see him? He trembles at the thought. (186) [11]

In her 1907 "Retrospective Chapter," an older and more sober Vernon Lee repudiated much of this as lacking "objective historical reality." However, she made no effort to change or modify her account.

The shorter remaining essays that conclude *Studies of the Eighteenth Century in Italy* are more restrained. Their subject is Italian comedy, and they bear immediately on her announced thesis: that Italy's contribution to eighteenth-century European culture was its music and drama. Her essay "The Comedy of Masks" is a succinct history of a genuinely Italian genre, commedia dell'arte, which she traces back to its Roman origins, moving on to its evolution through the Renaissance and its gradual divergence from classical comedy into a unique genre. "The Comedy of Masks was not an invention, not a revelation, it was a natural product; it did not seize hold of national taste, it sprang up and developed everywhere because its seeds had long existed in the Italian mind, and because the intellectual temperature of the latter sixteenth century necessitated its germination and development" (238). Its decline in the seventeenth century, its "dethronement" as a national genre, was simply another step in the evolution of a new national comedy in the eighteenth. This is the subject of her essay "Goldoni and Realistic Comedy."

In Goldoni, Vernon Lee found another colorful personality who stimulated her imagination: "his character and his life resemble nothing so much as his works." Free-spirited, good-natured Goldoni, "amiable, honest, superficial though perfectly sincere in all his attachments, never once, as he himself tells us, lets any misfortune interfere with his supper" (250). His strength was his comic genius, and Vernon Lee portrays him as one of his own creations: "He did not construct his plays, he created them—blew them out like soap bubbles; a drop dilated into a delicate, delicately tinted, winged bubble by the breath of genius" (261). As serious criticism of an acknowledged master of comedy, her essay has the weight of those soap bubbles, but she catches the mood, the essence of his comedy and sets it in the lively context of eighteenth-century Venice, the home of carnival, "the headquarters of Italian gaiety." His comedy is the embodiment of the real, the domestic and daily life of the Italian people—servants and shopkeepers: "the comedy of Goldoni, as the offspring of the comedy of Masks, had its origin in the very heart of the people" (267).

The other side of the Comedy of Masks—clowning and fantasy— found its eighteenth-century incarnation in the magical whimsy of "kindly, idle, half-crazy Count Carlo Gozzi" (275). With her essay "Carlo Gozzi and the Venetian Fairy Comedy" Vernon Lee brings her eighteenth-century studies to a fitting end. Venetian audiences were fickle; they tired of Goldoni's earthy realism. In contrast, Gozzi's *fiabe* or fairy plays, based on tales familiar to us from childhood like his *Love of Three Oranges,* offered escape into the grotesque and exotic, the world of fairyland. Vernon Lee portrays him as she does Goldoni, as a self-created character out of one of his own plays—whimsical, capricious, the total Venetian capturing the essence of his city in his comedies: "strange, weird, beautiful, half oriental, half mediaeval . . . [a] city of gorgeous colour and mysterious shadow" (279).

One of the earliest readers of *Studies of the Eighteenth Century in Italy* was John Addington Symonds, to whom Violet sent a copy as soon as it appeared. Highly ranked among the leading scholars and cultural historians of his age, an expert on the Italian Renaissance, Symonds responded promptly on 23 May 1880. "I found it charming," he wrote, wondering, however, if a public unfamiliar with Italian culture could appreciate the book. "As an older craftsman, may I speak to you, a younger craftsman, frankly? For I think you have a real literary gift. . . . You have the main thing—Love; wh in art of all kinds takes the same place as Charity among the Virtues. You love your subject simply, & you bring to the treatment of it rare qualities—almost too exuberant in their unpruned vigour" (*Letters* 2:635–36).

In seeking his opinion of the book, Violet had asked for candor, and he obliged. He had unmixed admiration for her chapter on Metastasio, where "because the subject itself is simple—you go right."[12] Though generally impressed with her "maturity and grasp of mind," Symonds was troubled by her "want of thinking out" her chapters, her undisciplined prose—"superfluous adjectives, repetitions, & incoherent strings of clauses with a dash to save all at the end"—and her allusiveness, "which cannot fail to confuse people for whom the whole set of musicians & literary people are unknown." He urged her to post over her desk the motto of the composer Sacchini: "Chiarezza, bellezza, buona modulazione" [clarity, beauty, good modulation]. His comments on her writing were echoed a few weeks later by the English reviewers, none of whom knew her age or gender. "Mr. Lee," the *Spectator* (26 June 1880) wrote, "throws plenty of vigour and colour into his portraiture of this life [Metastasio]. His style, indeed, is not very easy, and not without an unpleasing mixture here and there of the 'Carlylese.' But it has a certain robustness; while his criticism is often just, and even subtle." The *Athenaeum* (12 June 1880), while praising her scholarship, pronounced her style "excessive." Some years later, in *The Handling of Words,* Vernon Lee reminded would-be writers of the importance of making every word count. Yet intellectually rigorous as she always was, she could never discipline her prose style. Her mind was so crammed with knowledge that it erupted in her writing in volcanic chunks. Symonds's warning went unheeded, but his evident interest in her work was encouraging, and she began a lively correspondence with him.

In spite of the many reservations about her writing, she had every reason to be encouraged by the warm reception of her book. Although an Italian translation, *Il settecento in Italia,* was not published until 1881, the English edition was reviewed by her friend Enrico Nencioni in *Fanfulla della domenica,* 1 August 1880. His only complaint was that she exaggerated the neglect of the eighteenth century by contemporary Italian scholars and critics. He cited important work in that area by Luigi Settembrini, Francesco de Sanctis, and Giosuè Carducci. Otherwise Nencioni hailed her as "il critico sagace e immaginoso," who knows her subject profoundly and treats

Italy with the artistic insight demonstrated in the poetry of Robert Browning. But it was the English response to the book that most gratified her. As Symonds had anticipated, it was not a best-seller, but she never sought a wide public. Still, in the earnest, aspiring readership of the working and middle classes of late Victorian England there was a hunger for culture that brought writers like Symonds, Walter Pater, Matthew Arnold, and Vernon Lee a measure of popularity unimaginable in the twenty-first century. And to this day, its scholarship superseded and its subject matter, to all but the most passionate of Italophiles, obsolete, *Studies of the Eighteenth Century in Italy* remains a small classic.

3 *BELCARO:* DEFINING A SELF

The myself who had, almost as a child, been insanely bewitched by the composers and singers, the masked actors and pedants, and fine ladies and fops, the whole ghostly turn-out of the Italian eighteenth century; who had, for years, in the bustle of self-culture, I might almost say, of childish education, never let slip an opportunity of adding a new microscopic dab of colour to the beloved, quaint, and ridiculous and pathetic century portrait which I carried in my mind; this myself, thus smitten with the Italian eighteenth century, had already ceased to exist.

Belcaro

☙ By 1880, the year in which *studies of the eighteenth Century in Italy* was published in England, there were important changes in the Paget family. Their wandering life ended in 1873 when they settled in Florence in a house near the Arno at 12 via Solferino. In early 1882 they moved to 5 via Garibaldi, then in the spring of 1889 to a country house, Il Palmerino, in Maiano, a short distance from Fiesole and within easy reach of Florence. This was to be Violet's home until her death in 1935. Mrs. Paget had come into her inheritance at last, and though not rich she was able to provide a comfortable home for her family. But the principal reason for abandoning their old way of life was Eugene. Never happy in the diplomatic service, work he described as routine clerical duties, and bored with his colleagues, he complained increasingly in his letters to his mother of homesickness.

Compounding his unhappiness in his career, he was frustrated in his ambitions to publish. His chosen field was history. While proposing challenging subjects like "the political decline of the Dutch republic" for his little sister's schoolroom exercises, he was himself working on several historical projects for which he received no encouragement. In 1869 J. A. Froude, editor of *Fraser's Magazine,* rejected his article on Pope Sixtus V, designer of the Vatican Library and an urban planner responsible for building one of the central arteries of early modern Rome, the via Sistina.

Nothing daunted, Eugene wrote his mother on 7 January 1870:

> I am a good deal vexed about my article, but I am now again in good spir-
> its . . . I have determined to give up all idea of making my way into litera-
> ture in that way. I mean to devote all my energies (after giving a proper
> share to diplomacy) to the study of history, taking care that general litera-
> ture and philosophy keep pace with it. In a few years I doubt not I shall be
> in a position to make a worthy contribution to historical literature and to
> publish it at my own expense.

Such optimism could not be sustained, and his failing health made it obvious that he could never meet the demands of historical research and writing. He wearied of the travel his job demanded, including an assignment in
Geneva in 1871 during the arbitration between Britain and the United
States over compensation for the Confederate cruiser *Alabama,* which the
British had allowed to escape from one of their ports. He looked forward
only to leaves of absence when he could be with his mother. From Tours in
1870 he wrote: "I wish . . . every hour of the day that I were with thee, for
where thou are I can always enjoy even the most disagreeable places, and
without thee, the most charming is wearisome." From Bordeaux in 1871 he
wrote: "How I long for these weeks to be passed. I am so utterly sick of this
place, and so distressed at the disappointment thou must feel at not having
me already with thee! I think of our walks in the Borghese, in the Volkon-
sky, and try to make the time pass quicker in this gloomy hole by thinking
how happy we shall be when I am with thee" (Gardner 116).

An appointment to Lisbon in 1873 did little to alleviate his unhappiness,
and when he was offered a promotion for transfer to Buenos Aires, he flatly
refused it. Almost simultaneously he began to complain of chest pains, sensitivity to light and sound, and general debility. By February he was confined to bed with a condition his doctor diagnosed as the result of overwork.
An even more alarming symptom developed, a paralysis of the legs and back,
the cause of which baffled medical authorities. They suspected that his illness was more than physical, and for want of a better diagnosis pronounced
it a "cerebro-spinal disease." In light of his later total recovery, there can be
little doubt that his problem was psychosomatic—"auto-suggestion" as even
he came to describe it.

Terrible as its effects were, Eugene's illness served its purpose. It released
him from his professional duties and brought him home, a helpless invalid,
to his mother's care. He lived for nearly twenty years as a virtual paraplegic,
with a male attendant who moved him about on a plank bed and a loving
mother and sister hovering over him. Violet's devotion to her brother was
never for a moment questioned.[1] As her own social and literary life expanded

in the late 1870s, she shared her interests with him. With the passing years, however, she grew more absorbed in her career, and Eugene's invalidism became a heavier burden. It separated her further from her mother, who squandered all her energies on her son, and—because he was now even less a presence to be reckoned with in a household that gave all its attention to Eugene—from her father, who spent most of his time fishing when the weather was good or sitting in the buffet of the railway station in Florence reading his newspaper and watching the passing scene.

By the mid-1870s, while Eugene retreated into invalidism and dependency, a new and exciting world was opening for Violet. The project she had begun so earnestly in 1870 was flourishing. She was writing and publishing not only on the eighteenth century but, having won entry into the *Rivista europea,* on a variety of literary and cultural subjects. Where Eugene had failed to publish articles, his young sister stormed the gates of British periodicals and began publishing as Vernon Lee in *Fraser's* and other prominent British journals. The transformation in the Paget family lifestyle was dramatic and due largely to Violet's rising reputation in Italian literary circles. No longer the rootless wanderers with no society other than the few other English and American self-exiles they met in the spas and holiday retreats of France, Germany, Switzerland, and northern Italy, they now had a home in Florence and a widening circle of British, American, and European visitors. By the end of the decade even helpless Eugene had found a voice and won some recognition as a poet. Physically unable to write, he dictated his poems to Violet and hired amanuenses to read to him.

Eugene Lee-Hamilton's first appearance in print was as the translator of passages of poetry that his sister quoted in her article on contemporary Italian poets in the *Quarterly Review,* October 1877. He included some of these translations in his first collection, *Poems and Transcripts,* published by Blackwood in 1878. Like most first collections it was neglected by reviewers, but it caught the attention of a few discriminating readers, among them John Addington Symonds, who sent his compliments to her brother in his first letter to Vernon Lee in May 1880. In the years and volumes that followed, Lee-Hamilton acquired a small but appreciative readership.[2] The poems are conventional in form—rhymed lyrics, mainly sonnets that he connected in narratives or dramatic monologues. In subject matter they are dark and morbid, gothic in the manner of Edgar Allan Poe, reflecting both his personal condition and his reading of European and English poets of romantic and Victorian melancholy: Leopardi, Baudelaire, Dante Gabriel Rossetti, Swinburne (whom he professed to despise), and, in his dramatic monologues, Robert Browning. Dramatic poetry in particular gave him freedom to indulge in fantasies of cruelty and madness—a nurse who turns into a vampire and sucks the lifeblood of her patients ("Sister Mary of the Plague"), a vengeful Venetian struggling to control his urge to murder a rival who is his double ("Ipsissimus"), a man who murders his mistress after dreaming that her long black locks are writhing snakes ("The New Medusa"). Symonds, absorbed in his own ill health and always fascinated by aberrant states of mind, followed Eugene's work with sympathetic interest and included inquiries about his condition in many of his letters to his sister. In 1892 Symonds wrote a short essay on Lee-Hamilton's poetry for Alfred H. Miles's anthology *The Poets and Poetry of the Century,* pointing out that "his most salient quality appears to be a power of identifying himself through the imagination with abnormal personalities, exposed to the pressure of unusual circumstances or exceptional temptation." In Eugene's poem "Apollo and Marsyas," Symonds suggests that the poet identified himself with the orgiastic satyr-victim: "Of his personal susceptibility to the influence of Marsyas Mr. Lee-Hamilton makes no secret."[3]

There is certainly a large measure of self-pity in Eugene's poems and personal identification with the physical and mental suffering of his characters.[4] One group of these is titled "The Wheeled Bed" and begins, "Hybrid of rack and of Procrustes' bed / Thou thing of wood, of leather and of steel." In another sonnet, "To the Muse," he describes his condition as "the posture of the grave," which denies him the joys of nature and natural activity:

> In summer's heat to breast no more the wave,
> Nor tread the cornfield where the reapers reap;
>
> . . . .
>
> No more to rove where scarlet berries cling
> To leafless twigs, and pluck the ripe blue sloe—
> 'Tis hard, 'tis hard, but thou dost bring relief,
> Fair, welcome Muse, sweet soother of all pain.

How painful it was for Eugene to witness his young sister's thriving health and activity we can only speculate. In the early years of his invalidism she was a sympathetic partner, encouraging his writing, bringing interesting guests home for him to meet, and seeking out publishers for his work. In 1886 she opened her collection of dialogue-essays *Baldwin* with "To my brother Eugene Lee-Hamilton, I dedicate this book of views and aspirations, grateful for all he has done in forming my own." In 1891 he dedicated his drama *The Fountain of Youth* "To Vernon Lee with her brother's love." They collaborated on a collection, *Tuscan Fairy Tales* (most of them Italian versions of the Grimms' stories), published in 1880 by W. Satchel, who had published her *Studies of the Eighteenth Century in Italy.*[5] Any envy or resentment that Eugene might have felt toward Violet would have been miti-

gated by the fact that with the loss of his health he had won his mother's undivided attention. His sister's success was a source of pride to them both,
and as she grew more independent of her family, traveling to France and
England and sending back long letters reporting on everything she saw and
everyone she met, he lived vicariously through her. If anyone was slighted
in the arrangement, it was Violet. With the loss of her childhood and with
Eugene's helplessness she had lost what little claim she had on her mother's
love. Fortunately for her, she was discovering new sources for the love she
so desperately wanted.

In 1907 (Agnes) Mary (Frances) Robinson (Darmesteter) Duclaux published a reminiscential article "In Casa Paget" in *Country Life* about her
early friendship with Vernon Lee and the Paget family. Air-brushed by time
and Mary Robinson's sanguine disposition, it is a near idyllic picture of her
visit to the Casa Paget, then on the via Solferino in Florence, in September
1880. The occasion for the 1907 article was the recent death of Eugene Lee-
Hamilton, but its emphasis was on the happier past, shadowed but not completely darkened by his invalidism, and brightened by the presence of the
"dazzling" Miss Paget, Vernon Lee, "then publishing the first of those brilliant essays . . . in which she loves to track, through all their devious cur-
rents and sudden disappearance underground, the secret founts and unsuspected sources of our aesthetic pleasure."

For Mary Robinson, only a few months younger than Violet and herself aspiring to a writing career, she was an idol. Everything about her, even
her paralyzed brother, glowed in the radiance of a Florentine autumn. Coming from a solidly prosperous family home in London furnished in solidly
Victorian style, she was enchanted with the Casa Paget and its inhabitants:
the high-ceilinged rooms, the tall windows with their "crimson satin hang-
ings," the polished marble floors, the elegant eighteenth-century furniture,
"the roses in quaint old painted pots." It was not Mary's first trip abroad; she
had spent a year (1872–73) in school in Brussels. Unlike most English girls
of her class, she had had an excellent education, including Greek, which she
studied at the University of London. In 1880 she toured Italy with her parents. In Venice they met the archaeologist Henry Layard, whose discoveries
at Nineveh had fascinated her in the British Museum. They also met the controversial Ernest Renan, of whom years later she wrote a very sympathetic
biography.[6] She recalled in the preface to that biography that when she first
met him, "I knew him only by repute, as a heretic (that was attractive) and
a philologist (which seemed less interesting)." The Robinsons moved on to
Florence, where they were welcomed by the Anglo-Florentine colony of
which Violet Paget was by 1880 a prominent member. Violet invited Mary
to stay on as a houseguest when her parents returned to London.

Florence had long been the focal point of cultivated English visitors, many of whom elected to make it their permanent home.[7] From the Brownings, who had done precisely that, to transients like George Eliot and George Henry Lewes, researching historical records for *Romola,* and Henry James, one of the many perpetually returning transients, they flocked to this city, more temperate in climate and less congested than Venice or Rome and always hospitable to foreigners. When Eugene's health failed and the Pagets were obliged to settle down, Florence was the perfect choice. The city offered the cultural ambience that Violet needed for her work. The nearby Tuscan hills made it possible for even Eugene to enjoy the pleasures of the countryside. In her article Mary Robinson recalled morning drives in the country in "a clumsy-looking long landau, so constructed that it could receive the plank bed placed slant-wise from front to back." With Mrs. Paget seated beside him and Violet or Mary opposite and the other up front with the coachman, they rode through what Mary remembered as a pastoral wonderland, the young women stopping to gather armfuls of flowers: "that cypress spinney above Vincigliata, honey-sweet with the yellowish blossoms of the hellebore or wild Christmas rose; or the little farms near Bellosguardo, where for a few soldi the peasants let us pluck anemones to our heart's content. . . . And all the while down in the valley sparkled Florence, a smoke of blue olives, a vision of towers."

For young impressionable Mary, the elder Pagets were equally incandescent. Even the usually invisible Mr. Paget emerged as "a charming person . . . a great hunter, sportsman, walker, Mr. Paget was always out of doors." But he came in from time to time, she recalled, to tell "his long amusing stories, his tales of hair-breath escapes by flood and field, his somewhat incongruous and bantering compliments. . . . weeks would pass and we would hear no more of him, hearing only his voice in the hall where (every evening after dinner) he came to take his wife for a walk." That formidable wife, however, made a deeper and more lasting impression, one that fully confirms Violet's recollections of her mother: "a fragile, dauntless little being, with light soft hair like raw silk (all blonde and silver, curling about her ears), and pale sweet eyes." But even Mary recognized her imperiousness, her "dominating will": "the sweetness in her was tempered by something aromatic, pungent, even bitter, as if uncounted disenchantments, mingling with the kindest disposition, had left her inclined at once to expect the worst and believe the best of human nature." The mature Mary who wrote this article also perceived what might not have been so apparent to outsiders in 1880: "She was proud of Violet; she worshipped Eugene; and, need I say with what absolute and almost despotic oblation she sacrificed her life to his?"

If Violet was sensitive to her now total displacement in her mother's affections, she had much to compensate her in the adoring presence of her English guest. "From early dawn to dewy eve," Mary wrote, "we appeared to exist merely to communicate to each other our ideas about things in general." From his wheeled bed Eugene contributed to and often dominated their conversations: "We were so young—Violet and I—more than a dozen years younger than Eugene—we had mixed so little with life, that he fell naturally into the position of our guide, philosopher and friend." But it was Violet and the shared intimacy of the two young women that lingered most powerfully in Mary's recollection: "She had soft blonde hair, benignant grey-green eyes, which gleamed through a pair of huge, round eighteenth-century goggles; I can see the long column of her throat, the humorous, delicate irregular features which made up such an eloquent and eager face, and especially I see the slender hands, with their fragile *retroussé* fingers issuing from the starched cuffs of her tailored-gown. She looked at once audacious, refined, argumentative, and shy."

For all the dream dust of her memories, Mary Robinson measured Violet well. The impression she made on the literary salon which gathered at the Casa Paget was precisely that mixture of contradictory qualities that Mary noted. As hostess—for Eugene could not perform the duties of host—Violet entertained an interesting assortment of guests ranging from the famous and sometimes notorious to the obscure and now totally forgotten. Mary had come from a family in London who regularly entertained the most distinguished literary society of the day, but even she was impressed with the variety of visitors to the Casa Paget: "How many men and women, of how many types, characters, and nationalities!"

Unlike most expatriate English in Italy, the Pagets were hosts to as many Italian as English and American guests. Violet's essays and book reviews in Italian journals during the late 1870s and early 1880s—*La rivista europea, Domenica del fracassa, Fanfulla della domenica, Cronaca bizantina*—and the Italian translation of her *Studies of the Eighteenth Century in Italy* (1881) introduced her to Italian readers, and she was truly an *inglese italiana,* as Mario Praz described her (*Voce dietro* 40). Her spoken Italian was pure Tuscan. She spoke it, Aldous Huxley recalled, "with the kind of literary perfection which can only be achieved by a foreigner who has completely mastered the language but still speaks it from the outside, so to say, as an artist consciously manipulating his medium" (Cary, "Aldous Huxley" 131). Her fluency in French and German as well kept the guest lists impressively cosmopolitan: Italians like the historian Pasquale Villari, critics and men of letters like Enrico Nencioni and Carlo Placci, the philosopher Giacomo Barzellotti; the Russian poet Peter Boutourline; the German literary critic Karl Hillebrand and the sculptor Adolf von Hildebrand; from France the novelists Anatole

France and Paul Bourget; the English philosopher Alfred William Benn, the astronomer Agnes Mary Clerke, the bold and outspoken novelist and journalist Eliza Lynn Linton, and the English-born but thoroughly Europeanized Louise de la Ramée, better known as Ouida. Violet had little regard for Ouida's novels but shared wholeheartedly her love for animals and her antivivisectionism.[8] In the 1880s Henry James came often. It was at Casa Paget in 1887 that he heard from Eugene, who had heard it from the Sargents, the story of Captain Silsbee, whose pursuit of Shelley manuscripts led him into a compromising situation with Jane (Claire) Clairmont's maiden niece—the inspiration for *The Aspern Papers.*

When she came to Florence in 1880, Mary Robinson was a fully credentialized young poet with a published volume, *A Handful of Honeysuckle* (1878), and a verse translation of Euripides, *The Crowned Hippolytus,* about to be published (1881). Her modest but eminently respectable talent, combined with her learning, her intellectual curiosity, and her sweet, winning personality, had already endeared her to Robert Browning and to John Addington Symonds. According to Emmanuel Berl, a young French admirer who wrote a memoir of her many years later, Mary first met Browning on the Calais–Dover ferry where, seasick, she stood at the rail holding an equally sick cat. Relieved by a seasickness remedy the poet offered her, she replied, "Oh, Poseidon, god of the seas, thanks for having me saved by Browning." Eleanor Frances Poynter, sister of the painter Edward Poynter and a close friend of Symonds and his family, introduced her to him in 1879 while he was living in Bristol. They corresponded regularly after Symonds moved to Switzerland for his health, and Mary visited him and his family in Davos several times. She looked up to him as her master, sent her poems to him for his always generous criticism, and proudly dedicated her *Crowned Hippolytus* to "My friend J. A. Symonds." He in turn was flattered by her admiration and took a warmly avuncular attitude toward her, worrying about her health and advising her on her writing.

After Mary met Violet, however, and began spending much of her time with her, Symonds reacted with something very like jealousy. His biographer Phyllis Grosskurth suggests that "Symonds appears to have been more than slightly enamoured of the tremulously feminine Miss Robinson, who was sixteen years his junior." Bisexual but with a stronger inclination for his own gender, he apparently resented Mary's seeming transference of the hero worship she had for him to Violet. There is no evidence of any lessening admiration on Mary's part, but Symonds was increasingly uncomfortable about her relationship with Violet. His suspicions of Violet, whose work he knew though he met her only once, were obvious. With the ambivalence of many men of the period, he applauded women who had intellectual interests, but he disliked "clever" women.[9] His early praise of *Studies of the Eighteenth Century in Italy* had been balanced with criticism, and his letters to Mary suggest a struggle between his growing dislike of Violet and his fear of offending Mary. As early as 15 August 1880, soon after Mary's first visit to the Pagets, he wrote to Eleanor Poynter: "I should be very sorry to lose Miss Robinson. Nothing yields a drearier sense of failure than the fading out into frigidity of what once had the semblance of vital warmth" (*Letters* 2:646). He did make friendly gestures to Violet. On 25 June 1882, in London to consult Sir Andrew Clarke about his diseased lungs, Symonds invited her and Mary to tea, but apart from this one brief meeting they did not meet again.

On 1 February 1883 he wrote Violet: "I congratulate you & Miss Robinson both on being together. The words she writes of your life make me feel that both are getting good" (2:798). But a few months later, noting one of their brief separations, he wrote Mary: "I do not wonder that you miss Vernon. She must be a most electrical companion, with her strong, swift spirit & illimitable vigour. Good God! How I wish she would but discipline her powers!" (2:812–13). Now openly challenging Mary's loyalty to her friend, he could not resist commenting on "Vernon's stylistic perversities": "the ineffable ugliness & vulgarity into wh she so willingly plunges. Only women seem capable of that stylistic dévergardage." A year later he wrote Mary, hardly consolingly, that the unfavorable reviews of her latest collection, *The New Arcadia,* were not entirely unjustified. "Your last book of poetry reveals an effort, is not quite full & strong in tone." This he attributed pointedly to the stress he thinks she is undergoing. "I am not sure whether you produced it under wholly healthy influence. I dread lest you should be overtaxing your vigour by living at too high pressure." He showed his hand in the last paragraph: "How I should like you to go & live somewhere away from clever women & clever men for some long while! You know I have always desired this for you. But I do not think you will give yourself so excellent a chance. Meanwhile believe me ever yours. / J.A. Symonds" (2:949).

Whether motivated by jealousy, genuine concern for Mary's well-being, or simple curiosity, Symonds consulted his friend the sexologist Havelock Ellis, who suggested that Vernon Lee and Mary Robinson "might serve as a possible case-history for the section on Lesbianism in *Sexual Inversion.*"[10] But others close to the two young women were not disturbed by their relationship. Attachments between single women, sometimes called "Boston marriages"—defined by devoted companionship and often open expressions of affection—were not only acceptable but, because young women could not properly live or travel alone, expedient and even desirable. The guardians of Violet's home life, her mother and Eugene, welcomed Mary as an eminently suitable friend. From a rich and respectable English family with important literary connections, she was cultivated, pleasant company for Mrs. Paget and Eugene as well. Like them she appreciated and encouraged Violet's writing; more important, she filled what even they must have recognized as a void in her emotional life. As Lillian Faderman noted in her study of romantic friendships between women, *Surpassing the Love of Men,* what we now regard as erotic or homoerotic was viewed differently in the past. "These romantic friendships were love relationships in every sense except perhaps the genital, since women in centuries other than ours often internalized the view of females as having little sexual passion" (216). As long as women remained securely fixed in their role as women and did not attempt to usurp men's privileges, they were no threat. Violet of course had early on assumed a masculine pen name and a male persona in her philosophical essays, but this was a common practice among women writers. She also assumed mannish attire—dark, severely tailored dresses, high starched collars, stiff bowler or boater hats. But these were fashionable in the '80s and '90s "Girl of the Period" style. As a plain—in the judgment of some ugly—woman she dressed in an entirely appropriate way. But less acceptable in society was her strong personality. Talkative, argumentative, dogmatic, she insisted on dominating conversations. Good, even brilliant as her talk may have been, it was not always appreciated in company.[11]

Mary Robinson was not the first of the many romantic friendships in Violet's life. Her early attachments to older women like Mrs. Jenkin and Mrs. Turner were poignant expressions of her need for motherly affection. The first of her mature romantic attachments was to a woman closer to her own age of whom little is known. This was Annie Meyer, the wife of John Meyer, who visited Florence sometime in 1877 or 1878 and was introduced to the Casa Paget by mutual friends, the American painter and journalist William J. Stillman and his wife. By 1880, when Mary came to Florence, Violet had quarreled with Mrs. Meyer and the friendship had ended. But she left an indelible impression on Violet. Several years later, in late 1883, Violet learned of her death. From that time until her own death she kept a photo of Annie Meyer over her bed, and she dedicated her *Countess of Albany* to her in 1884: "To the memory of my friend Madame John Meyer I dedicate this volume, so often and so lately talked over together, in grateful and affectionate regret."

In some unpublished "Autobiographical Notes" that she kept from this period, Violet referred to her "still-born" friendship with Annie Meyer, acknowledging that as two strong-willed women they were never likely to have achieved intimacy: "never perhaps to that point of seeing, of being able to touch and embrace the whole personality which, in my opinion, is the only complete friendship." Unlike Mary Robinson, with whom "complete friendship" was achievable, Annie Meyer was too like Violet in temperament: "as passionate, wayward and vain as myself—perhaps I should add as naked?"[12]

Although they were never reconciled, Violet had news of her from time to time from her friend Alice Callandar, who was Annie's niece. When she heard that she was dying, Violet asked Alice if she might see her, but Alice wrote back "telling me not to come, as fixed, that Monday evening because my friend was very, very ill." Shortly after, in January 1884, Violet confided in her "Autobiographical Notes": "She was alive then, still alive, completely, entirely; but death was rushing on her; that those few words represent the brief moment which is still the present, only to become before we know what has happened, the past." It was not until 1885, months after Annie's death, that Alice Callandar coldly informed Violet that her aunt had never returned her love:

> But I went away cruelly dashed. For the thing which resulted from this talk, or seemed to be, that I thought I had been loved, that, alas, this ghost which for eight months had walked by my side, had taken my hand and looked into my eyes, was a mere phantom of my imagination, that I had been mistaken when I said to myself "Nothing can deprive me of that dead woman" —no, indeed, for I was being deprived of her then, being told I had never possessed her. Had this then been an unreality? Have I been describing myself . . . as the dupe of my own vanity and suspiciousness while in reality there was no affection to spurn? I cannot tell.

This unanswered question was one Violet was to ask herself many times in future relationships, and it left her more rueful than embittered. In June 1885 she added a note:

> We can never love one friend so much as when we have been given the cold shoulder by another. The not meeting what one wants arouses our creative powers, makes us create that person of some semi-imagined reality which we desire and strain after. I know how I, for instance, whenever the feeling of being misunderstood or misappreciated come[s] . . . over me, used to seek comfort in the thought of A.M. who very likely, had she been alive, would not have been particularly comforting.

During this period of self-analysis Violet was writing a series of essays which she collected in *Baldwin: Being Dialogues on Views and Aspirations* in 1886. In one of these, "The Consolations of Belief," she introduced Annie Meyer as Agatha Stuart, "that stubborn-looking Scotch girl," who becomes the spokeswoman for absolute faith. Baldwin, Vernon Lee's persona and spokesman, rejects the notion of religious faith but denies that he is an atheist: "I do not say that there was no God; I merely said there was no God with whom religion can bring us into contact" (77). Agatha recoils from Baldwin's refusal to acknowledge a divine power: "The more I think about it the more horrible and incredible it seems to me that a human soul should live in such a nightmare of wickedness as that—should endure the pollution of a belief such as yours" (103). In a later essay in the book, "Of Doubts and Pessimism," Baldwin recalls Agatha as someone he once thought his best friend, but Olivia, Agatha's cousin, tells him that she never really loved him. "She was interested in you not because she wanted your friendship, but because it seemed to her that God was being cheated of you, and you were being cheated of God." It is painful for him to hear this—and here Vernon Lee repeats the revelation of her autobiographical note: "I had not been loved where I thought I had been; and that, alas! this ghost which for months had walked by my side, had taken my hand and looked into my eyes, was a mere phantom of my imagination." Baldwin consoles himself by affirming the only faith left to him—"the terrible doubt of appearances." And when Olivia berates him for his apparent lack of feeling, he replies: "Consider me henceforth a man of cut and dried opinion, the desultory philosopher on the loose" (342–46).

Violet needed no hard shell of defense, no pose of jaded cynic, with Mary Robinson. There was no conflict of ideology between them. If Mary was not as outspoken as Violet in her unconventional views on religion, it was only because of the differences in their personalities. Furthermore, like most of Violet's close friends, she recognized that Baldwin, "the desultory philosopher on the loose," was simply a mask for an idealistic and very vulnerable young woman. Thanks to Mary's forbearing nature, their life together was harmonious. And for a few years, until Mary's marriage shattered it, Violet enjoyed an emotionally and, as far as they allowed it to go, a physically fulfilling relationship.

Belcaro, published in 1881 and dedicated to Mary Robinson, is a collection of essays, some published as early as 1878. The book marks the beginning of Vernon Lee's lifelong effort to describe and analyze aesthetic experience. Although she had launched her career boldly with a brilliant work of cultural history, *Studies of the Eighteenth Century in Italy,* she was a neophyte in aesthetics. Not that her youth inhibited her from making doctrinaire assertions about "poetic morality" and form in art.[13] But *Belcaro* has the balancing virtues of surprise and delight—surprise at her own newly discovered insights into art and delight in the liberation that aesthetics gave her. Cultural history is particularized and confining: "To plan, to work for such a book as that first one, seems to me now about the most incomprehensible of all things; to care for one particular historical moment, to study the details of one particular civilisation, to worry about finding out the exact when and how of any definite event; above all, to feel (as I felt) any desire to teach any specified thing to anybody; all this has become unintelligible to my sympathies of today" (*Belcaro* 4–5).

In the opening essay of *Belcaro,* "The Book and Its Title," Vernon Lee proclaims the birth of a "new myself," no longer magisterially pronouncing on the Italian eighteenth century but "humbly gone to school as a student of aesthetics." This radical transformation from savant to student parallels a similar awakening in her personal life: an open acknowledgment of her attachment to Mary Robinson, her "other self." She pronounces Mary "the nearest, most difficult, most desired convert." The conversion-education process is described lovingly: the memory of a December afternoon drive to Belcaro, "the strange, isolated villa castle, up and down, and round and round the hills of ploughed-up russet earth, and pale pink leafless brushwood, and great green pine-woods, where every sharp road-turning surprises one with a sudden glimpse of Siena, astride, with towers and walls and cupolas, on her high, solitary ridge" (1–2).

That afternoon the idea of assembling her essays in a book was born. Italy of the eighteenth century, on which she had labored so long and hard, "ceased to exist." Foremost now was pure art, transcending time, history, a particular culture. But as she describes her "art philosophy" in the remainder of the essay, it assumes more and more the aspect of romantic love—"entirely unabstract, unsystematic, essentially personal, because evolved unconsciously, under the pressure of personal circumstances, and to serve the requirements of personal tendencies." Long disciplined to methodical study and painstaking detail, she awakened to the joy of simple appreciation simultaneously with her awakening love for Mary Robinson. Her dedication to art had the conviction and total commitment of a passionate romantic encounter: "My own art philosophy is therefore simply to try and enjoy in art what art really contains, to obtain from art all that it can give, by refraining from asking it to give what it cannot" (13).

Art legitimates and justifies itself not on any high moral ground but because it gives pleasure. Although she claims to have read all the philosophers of art "from Plato to Lessing, from Reynolds to Taine, from Hegel to Ruskin," the more she observed art at first hand, the more she was confirmed in "my original childish impression that art was a simple thing to be simply enjoyed." But hers was a far too complex and educated mind to accept a naive romantic notion like this without qualification. She had read and, as she makes clear in the essay "Ruskinism" in *Belcaro,* totally rejected the concept of the morality of art. "Beauty, in itself, is neither morally good nor morally bad; it is aesthetically good, even as virtue is neither aesthetically good nor aesthetically bad, but morally good. Beauty is pure, complete, egotistic; it has no other value than its being beautiful" (210–11).

Vernon Lee did not name Walter Pater in her list of philosophers of art, but she included Plato, his master in aesthetics as Pater in turn was to become hers. They shared a vision of the aesthetic experience as a way of life because it combines pleasure with aspiration, the pursuit of the ideal. Pater's endorsement of art for its own sake inspired her not because of its amoral, hedonistic possibilities but, the reverse, because of its commitment to the Platonic ideals of truth, purity, and beauty. In this respect she was indeed, as some of her contemporaries called her, "Walter Pater's disciple." She also shared qualities of his creative imagination. The best of her short fiction— usually described as ghost stories though more precisely they are stories of psychological possession—show the influence of Pater's *Imaginary Portraits* with his lush incantatory prose and his fascination with the past, pagan myth, and medieval Christianity. Her own extravagant prose often echoes his with long chains of independent clauses weaving sentences so intricate that the reader is forced to go back to the distant beginning of a sentence to bring all its ideas together. As Denis Donoghue writes of Pater's, hers is "a prose nearly independent of syntax" (295).

With Walter Pater as her inspiration, Vernon Lee launched her own philosophy of art and embraced aestheticism as its guiding principle. For her as for others of her generation, aestheticism was a form of rebellion against the older Victorian generation's moralism and its philosophy of Utilitarianism. Even more fundamentally, it was a rebellion against a Puritan-Calvinist tradition that had too long isolated England from the rich cultures of the Continent, particularly of France and Italy. In "the conflict between our moral and artistic halves" that she discusses in "Ruskinism," she enlisted herself on the side of art. Ruskin was part of a past shaped by outmoded notions of virtue and morality: "He belongs, it is true, to a generation which is rapidly passing away; he is the almost isolated champion of creeds and ideas which have ceased even to be discussed among the thinking part of our nation . . . a man left far behind by the current of modern thought" (201). While Pater resolutely assumed the role of aesthetic critic, a classicist even in the modern age, and moved in *Marius the Epicurean* even closer to a spiritual faith not irreconcilable with traditional Christianity, the younger Vernon Lee was proclaiming a new order of "self": "For, just in proportion as the old religious faith is dying out . . . as the old restrictions of the written law are melting away, so there appears the new restriction of the unwritten law, the law of our emancipated conscience; and the less we go to our priests, the more do we go to our inner selves to know what we may do and what we should sacrifice" (199). But at this point her rebellion takes another direction. The "emancipated conscience," however radical a concept, is still a conscience. Even as it rejects traditional values, it creates its own value system, its own moral imperative which "with our daily growing liberty, grows and must grow, to all the nobler among us, our responsibility" (199–200).

It should have been a simple matter, therefore, to dismiss all questions of morality from the appreciation of art. But the strict discipline of aesthetic analysis confined her too narrowly. She wrestled with the issue and made fine distinctions. It was easy enough to refute Ruskin, but to deny the morality of art altogether was a challenge she could meet only with verbal sleight of hand: "In every artist there is a man, and the moral perfection of the man is more important than the artistic perfection of the artist; but in as far as the artist is an artist, he must be satisfied to do well in his art. For, though art has no moral meaning, it has moral value; art is happiness, and to bestow happiness is to create good" (229).

If Walter Pater's *Studies in the History of the Renaissance* had not resolved these ambiguities for her, it had at least pointed a way to a new vocation, one that combined scholarship and imagination in the pursuit of pleasure not for its own sake but for its capacity to enlighten and ennoble the human spirit. She read the conclusion to Pater's book, so widely misread as hedonistic and profane, as the creed of a faith—not Christian, because she remained a free thinker all her life, but aesthetic. Pater offered Vernon Lee a model for the role she wished to assume for herself after *Belcaro*—the "aesthetic critic," whose function, he had written in his preface to *The Renaissance*, "is to distinguish, to analyze, and separate from its adjuncts, the virtue by which a picture, a landscape, a fair personality in life or in a book, produces this special impression of beauty or pleasure, to indicate what the source of that impression is, and under what conditions it is experienced."

The Renaissance was the ideal choice for Vernon Lee at this stage in her career. The eighteenth century caught her attention when she had barely emerged from childhood. Its literature—Metastasio, Goldoni, Gozzi—appealed to her imagination; its relatively unappreciated music was a challenge to her precocious scholarship. Moving back in time to the Renaissance was an even greater challenge not only to her scholarship, in which she now had solid confidence, but to her ambitions as an aesthetic critic. Here, in an age as notorious for its moral corruption as for its artistic splendor, her new "art philosophy" could be tested. She was hardly alone among her contemporaries in being fascinated by so rich a culture. It had already intrigued some of the major historians of the nineteenth century—Jules Michelet, Jakob Burckhardt, Pasquale Villari. Closer at hand were the examples of Pater and John Addington Symonds, whose ambitious *The Renaissance in Italy* was published in seven volumes from 1875 to 1886. They all shared one thesis, that the Renaissance was not an isolated or miraculous phenomenon but a stage in the onward development of human civilization, serving specifically as a bridge between classical antiquity and the modern era. It was a reawakening and liberation of the human spirit, which had long lain dormant under the iron rule of feudalism and the Roman Catholic Church, and in the emergence of poets like Dante and Petrarch and paint-ers like Giotto and Fra Angelico the achievements of the fifteenth and six-teenth centuries were anticipated.

For Vernon Lee the aspiring young critic the Renaissance was an intellec-tual challenge, but it signaled even more for Violet Paget the woman. For her it was a personal liberation from the well-meaning but intellectually con-fining domination of her mother and her brother. Written over a period of about five years, from 1878 to 1883, the essays she collected in *Euphorion: Be-ing Studies of the Antique and the Mediaeval in the Renaissance* (1884), while they have the painting, sculpture, and poetry of the Middle Ages and the Renaissance for their subject matter, are in fact exercises in self-exploration and self-discovery. These years mark her first break with home ties, her first independent travel abroad, her growing attachment, no longer to mother surrogates like Mrs. Jenkin, Mrs. Turner, and Mrs. Sargent, but to women closer to her own age like Annie Meyer and Mary Robinson. The birth of a new self that she announced in *Belcaro* found its parallel in the rebirth of humanistic culture in the Renaissance. Pater, the model of the aesthetic critic, had articulated that liberation of self in his preface to *The Renaissance*: "What is this song or picture, this engaging personality presented in life or in a book, to *me*? What effect does it really produce on me? Does it give me pleasure?" Equally "self"-conscious, Vernon Lee writes in the opening pages of *Euphorion* that "the Renaissance has been to me not so much a series of studies as a series of impressions," and proceeds to emulate the technique of the emerging Impressionist painters: "the only truly realistic art . . . by giv-ing you a thing as it appears at a given moment, gives it you as it really ever is: all the rest is the result of cunning abstraction, and representing the scene as it is always, represents it (by striking an average) as it never is at all" (1:10).

As the opening of *Belcaro* had made clear, Vernon Lee's progress from historical scholar to aesthetic critic was inextricably connected with Violet Paget's emotional involvement with Mary Robinson. Mary offered a release for her long repressed hunger for love and reciprocal affection. That their relationship was and remained nonsexual in the physical sense is beyond doubt. But physical desire was not absent, at least on Violet's part. The art philosophy she had defined in *Belcaro* translated romantic love into aes-thetic terms: the object of love was a work of art; its physical reality was pure form; and it evoked in the lover a pleasure that in itself was neither moral nor immoral. In *Belcaro* she proclaimed "the law of our emancipated conscience"; that law operates not against but outside conventional morality. But Vernon Lee was no more a hedonist than was Walter Pater. For her indeed, as her novel *Miss Brown* attempted to demonstrate only a few years later, the risks of the mindless, irresponsible pursuit of pleasure in art were all too real. The pleasures offered by art can be dangerously perverted unless—and it is the function of the aesthetic critic to make this absolutely clear—the artist (like the romantic lover) strictly preserves "a sense of moral right and wrong."

Vernon Lee makes no allusion to Pater in *Belcaro,* although in the conclusion to his *Renaissance* she found confirmation for everything she had written there. She could embrace aesthetics without rejecting morality, but she had to walk a fine line in loving Mary Robinson. The delicacy of her position was demonstrated in an essay in *Euphorion,* "Mediaeval Love," where she sees the moral ambiguities of the Renaissance implicit in the earlier poetry of chivalric love. These poems celebrated forbidden love. The troubadour who is addressing himself to a married woman must cloak his forbidden desires in such idealized language that what is in reality sordid ("a love steeped in the passion of adultery") transcends lust to become "a morality within immorality . . . purely aesthetic passion," the love that Dante expressed for Beatrice in the *Vita nuova:* "the spark of ideal passion which has, in the noblest of our literature, made the desire of man for woman and of woman for man burn clear towards heaven, leaving behind noisome ashes and soul-enervating vapours of earthly lust" (*Euphorion* 2:125).

Was such a love possible in reality, outside "the noblest of our literature"? With Mary Robinson at her side, there could be only one answer:

> To my mind, indubitably. For there is, in all our perceptions and desire of physical and moral beauty, an element of passion which is akin to love; and there is, in all love that is not mere lust, a perception of, a craving for, beauty, real or imaginary, which is identical with our merely aesthetic perceptions and cravings; hence the possibility, once the wish for such a passion present [*sic*], of a kind of love which is mainly aesthetic, which views the beloved as gratifying merely to the wish for physical or spiritual loveliness, and concentrates upon one exquisite reality all dreams of ideal perfection. (*Euphorion* 2:183–84)

Her feelings for Mary Robinson were to remain "a kind of love which is mainly aesthetic." Whether she could achieve in her own life what she had found in medieval poetry would be, however, uncertain. "Platonic love," she wrote, "was possible, doubly possible in souls tense with poetic wants; it became a reality through the strength of the wish for it" (2:185).

4 THE LESSON OF THE MASTER: PATER AND *EUPHORION*

Some of the intensest romance of Italy was brought to me less by the real places overseas as by Pater's books; their perfume brought Rome, slowly distilled, to just such a North Oxford house as these are. It was in the dining room in Bradmore Road, hung with photographs and pre-Raphaelite pictures, that Novara [a small town in Piedmont], which I have never seen, became a place of enchantment: "Novara, yes, Novara, there was such good bread at Novara," said Mr. Pater, in deep dreaminess.

"Vernon Lee Notebook 1894–1930"

EVEN IN HER SHELTERED EXISTENCE AT THE CASA PAGET, "baby," as her family called her, had been part of a cosmopolitan Anglo-Florentine society that kept abreast of the news from England. Eugene had been at Oxford during the 1860s when the Greats (*Literae Humaniores*) curriculum was significantly altered by Benjamin Jowett, who introduced the study of Plato. With it, as Linda Dowling writes in *Hellenism and Homosexuality in Victorian Oxford,* was also introduced "the spirit of Mill's ringing dictum in *On Liberty*—that one's first duty as a thinker is 'to follow his intellect to whatever conclusions it may lead'" (84).

Both Violet and Eugene read the latest British books and periodicals and probably read Walter Pater's essays in the *Westminster* and *Fortnightly* before they were collected in his *Studies in the History of the Renaissance* (1873). They were certainly aware of the shock with which some of Pater's readers reacted to the book's conclusion, with its admonition to live life passionately, "getting as many pulsations as possible into the given time," and to enjoy art for no other reason than for the experience of art itself: "for art comes to you professing frankly to give nothing but the highest quality to your moments as they pass, and simply for those moments' sake." George Eliot represented a large constituency of readers who found the book, and especially its conclusion, "quite poisonous in its false principles of criticism and false conceptions of life." [1]

Pater prudently excised the offending conclusion from the second edition of the book in 1877, and when he restored it in 1888, he added a cautionary footnote explaining that he had earlier omitted it "as I conceived it might mislead some of those young men into whose hands it might fall." This was precisely John Wordsworth's charge against him in a letter of 17 March 1873. Once Pater's student at New College, Wordsworth (grand-nephew of the poet) was pained to read the conclusion; overall he admired the book for "the beauty of style and the felicity of thought by which it is distinguished." But he was alarmed by Pater's philosophy "that no fixed principles either of religion or morality can be regarded as certain, that the only thing worth living for is momentary enjoyment, and that probably or certainly the soul dissolves at death into elements which are destined never to reunite." Although since 1871 students and teachers at Oxford had been exempted from all religious tests and Pater was free to express his heterodox views, he had special responsibilities of which John Wordsworth reminded him: "Could you not indeed have known the dangers into which you were likely to lead minds weaker than your own, you would, I believe, have paused" (Pater, *Letters* 13–14).

Pater's reputation suffered further damage in 1874 when Jowett, the esteemed and powerful Master of Balliol College, learned of indiscreet letters he had exchanged with a nineteen-year-old student, Walter Money Hardinge, who was a self-proclaimed homosexual. While Pater was a model of discretion in his quiet private life, he became for Jowett "the demoralizing moralizer";[2] if not corrupt himself, he inspired corruption, specifically homoeroticism, in the young students who read him and attended his lectures and tutorials. Until then a leading candidate for the proctorship of Brasenose College, a post that carried a generous stipend as well as honors, he lost the election, ironically, to John Wordsworth. Two years later, largely owing to Jowett's influence, there was so much opposition to him that he withdrew his name from consideration as Matthew Arnold's successor in the Oxford poetry professorship. He continued to pay dearly for that conclusion as late as 1885, when he lost out on the Slade professorship of fine arts to succeed John Ruskin. Notoriously shy and self-conscious about his ungainly physical appearance, Pater reacted to these setbacks by assuming a social pose that his friend Edmund Gosse characterized as "affectation": "It is not to be denied that in the old days, Pater, startled by strangers, was apt to seem affected: he retreated as into a fortress, and enclosed himself in a sort of solemn effeminacy."[3]

Oxford gossip was pretty much confined to the university, but Pater suffered more-open embarrassment in 1877 with the publication of W. H. Mallock's *The New Republic.* In transparent disguises Mallock introduced some of the most distinguished intellectuals of the day—Matthew Arnold as Mr. Luke, Ruskin as Mr. Herbert, Jowett as Dr. Jenkinson, Thomas Henry Huxley as Mr. Storks, and Pater as "the pre-Raphaelite Mr. Rose," whose two topics of talk are "self-indulgence and art." The characters in *The New Republic* assemble for a country weekend and they talk—and talk— and talk. Their speeches are clever and capture with some fidelity both the substance and the style of the speakers. The satire is pointed, but cruel only in relation to Mr. Rose, where it is personal. The consummate aesthete, he pursues "exquisite living, the making of our own each highest thrill of joy that the moment offers." He also pursues young men, making a point of noticing a household page, "a pretty boy with light curling hair," and he lectures the company on "the immortal drama" of history, with "the exquisite groups and figures it reveals to us, of nobler mold than ours—Harmodius and Aristogeiton, Achilles and Patroclus, David and Jonathan, our English Edward and the fair Piers Gaveston" (154).

Whatever scandalous reputation Pater may have acquired, Violet Paget was unperturbed. On her visit to England in the summer of 1881 she and Mary Robinson spent some time in Oxford, meeting the most select intellectual society the university offered. Pater's Brasenose colleague Thomas Humphry Ward and his wife Mary, only then beginning her own brilliant career as a novelist, invited the young women to a supper party at their home. They knew that Pater and his two unmarried sisters were also to be guests. Learning of their plans, their landlady observed: "Ah, Mr. Pater, 'ee as is fellow of Brasenose—'ee lives with his sisters still in the Broadmore Road. Mr. Pater don't seem to be getting married, do 'ee, Miss?" Violet reported this, as well her first impression on meeting him, to her mother and Eugene, not without a degree of relish. Like many first impressions, hers was considerably altered when she became better acquainted with Pater, and even in this early letter she rejected Mallock's portrait of him: "He is a heavy, shy, dull looking brown mustachiod creature, over forty, much like Velasquez' Philip IV, lymphatic, dull, humorless. I sat next him at supper, and then he sat by me all the evening. Of all the people I had met in England, he is the one who has been most civil to me. . . . He is heavy, but to my surprise quite unaffected, and not at all like Mr. Rose" (18 July 1881).[4]

She warmed immediately to Pater's friendly interest. Not only did he flatter her with praise for her book on eighteenth-century Italian culture, but he paid her the supreme compliment of consulting her on his own work. Two days after their first meeting, she and Mary were invited to dine at the Paters', where his sisters, who had struck her on their first meeting as "rather gushing old maids," now appeared charming. "The Paters are all very friendly," she reported home on 20 July:

What strikes me is how wholly unlike Pater is to the Mr. Rose of Mallock, so much so that, in some of Mr. Rose's sentiments and speeches I could almost imagine meant for Symonds rather than for Pater. They have a pretty house, with a great many pretty things in it, aesthetic but by no means affected and cheap, like for instance the Gosses. Pater meditates spending one of his vacations near Rome, in order to work at his new book on mythology, so I suppose we should see him. He seems never to get separated from his sisters.

The letter reveals a genuine respect and admiration for Pater. Close friendships with men were rare in Violet's life. With the exception of Maurice Baring some years later, her intimate friendships were with women, most of them intellectually her inferiors. In Pater, however, she found a master or, as she probably preferred to regard him, a peer. Not only did they share an aesthetics based on Platonic idealism, but there was a more fundamental, though unacknowledged, bond of mutual recognition of their sexual ambiguity. Pater saw no possibility of compromising himself with a young woman as masculine in manner as Vernon Lee. Nor was there any built-in hostility such as she aroused in sexually active men like Bernard Berenson, or any implicit rivalry such as existed with Symonds over Mary Robinson.

In March 1882 Vernon Lee sent Walter Pater a copy of the newly published *Belcaro,* along with an invitation to him and his sisters to visit the Casa Paget if they traveled to Italy the following summer. Pater's response was as cordial as she could have wished. He had high praise for the book, which "as a whole, and almost always in its parts, has left on my mind a wonderfully rich impression of a world of all sorts of delightful things, under the action of a powerful intelligence. The union of extensive knowledge and imaginative power, which your writing presents, is certainly a very rare one." His sole reservation was delicately balanced with praise for her "unusual power of expression, in which, if I might make one exception, there is perhaps at times a little crowding. I think you would find instances when you have admitted alternative images and expressions, the weaker of which might have been dismissed" (*Letters* 42).

In light of the criticism, even by her admirers, of Vernon Lee's prose for its verbosity, Pater's demur is a model of diplomacy. He closed with an invitation to visit him and his sisters on her next trip to England, adding that he doubted that they would "find it prudent to venture to Italy on the summer vacation." Prudence ruled and the Paters remained in Oxford, where she visited them in August.

Their correspondence—all the more remarkable because Pater wrote so few letters[5]—resumed after she returned to Florence. On 18 November 1882 he wrote to thank her for a photograph of a drawing of herself[6] and a copy of *Fraser's Magazine* of July 1882, in which her essay "Apollo the Fiddler" appeared.[7] Like Pater's imaginary portraits of gods of antiquity reappearing in the Middle Ages, "Denys l'Auxerrois" and "Apollo in Picardy," her essay speculates on an anachronism in one of Raphael's frescoes in the Vatican. It depicts Parnassus with poets, the Muses, laurel-decorated youths, and King Apollo seated "with his bow in his hand and his fiddle against his cheek." To modern eyes the fiddle, a medieval invention, is incongruous, but she condemns such a reaction as "logical realism"—a violation of "the inherent organic conditions of art . . . [giving] in exchange for the stability and imperishableness of artistic form, the fluctuating, changing impersonality of scientific fact." No convert to logical realism himself, Pater admired her essay for "its charming portraiture of Italian things and ways, which real knowledge alone could have made possible, and it has many dexterous points which add to its effects of reality . . . like a very good French piece of work. You know that is high approval from me" (*Letters* 45–46).

She had also sent the Paters her brother's latest collection of verse, *The New Medusa,* which, Pater wrote, "we like very much." He especially admired the narrative poems for their "really imaginative boldness which puts them, I think, beside Browning's, but with a simplicity not often his. It is a very real and original contribution to poetry, and I hope your brother may do more. I hope also to make his acquaintance when I come to Florence, as I think we may next year, towards autumn." And recalling her visit a few months earlier, he wrote, most uncharacteristically for the reserved Pater, "What a fund of conversation we had!" (46).

The correspondence continued and the conversations flourished whenever Violet visited England in the following years. In 1884, writing to her Italian friend Carlo Placci from the "Casa Pater" in Oxford, she described "the delicate Morris papers and chintzes and prints and blue china, where between two delightful maiden sisters and two fascinating longhaired cats, the great apostle of quietly engaged beauty is enthroned, fat, sleek, in beautiful broadcloth and silk stockings. Seriously I know no modester man even among those far his inferiors, perhaps because I know no artist in literature equal to him" (Pantazzi, "Carlo Placci" 115).

In the course of writing *Marius the Epicurean,* Pater had read her essay in the May 1882 *Contemporary Review,* "The Responsibilities of Unbelief" (reprinted in *Baldwin*). Written in the form of a philosophical dialogue and subtitled "A Conversation between Three Rationalists," it represents rather daringly for its time and for so young a writer a series of arguments against traditional religion. The speakers are Vere, identified as "an aesthetic pessimist" ("Protestantism . . . may be called the spiritual enfranchisement of the servile classes; it turned . . . a herd of slaves and serfs into well-to-do artizans and shopkeepers" [*Baldwin* 31]); Reinhardt, "an optimistic Voltairean," who ridicules all religious belief ("Do you mean to say that a man in possession of all his faculties, with plenty to do in the world, with a library of good books, some intelligent friends, a good digestion, and a good theatre when he has a mind to go there—do you mean to tell me that such a man can ever be troubled by the wants of his soul?" [21]); and Baldwin, a "humanitarian atheist" and the author's voice, who condemns the idle rich, has compassion for the poor, but rejects socialism in favor of a ruling elite, "a class quite above all necessity for manual labour and business routine, which, while the majority of men are keeping the world going by supplying its most pressing bodily wants, may separate the true from the false, and gradually substitute higher aims and enjoyments for the lower ones" (38). Pater, working out the spiritual quest of his hero Marius through the stages of paganism, Epicureanism, and Stoicism toward, finally, the primitive Christianity of the early converts and martyrs, wrote her on 22 July 1883 that he felt his composition was becoming "a sort of duty," because "I think there is a fourth sort of religious phase possible for the modern mind, over and above those presented in your late paper in the Contemporary, the conditions of which phase it is the main object of my desire to convey" (*Letters* 52).

"The Paters are most kind," she wrote her mother, 20 June 1884. "Each afternoon I have had a long private audience in his study, on account of his lameness, and he has read me part of his philosophical romance about the time of the Antonines." Much as she respected him, however, she detected his limitations. "Fine," she continued, "but I think lacking vitality"[8]—a view more candid than but similar to her published comment on *Marius the Epicurean* in *Juvenilia* in 1887: "It is the morality of all antique art and philosophy, of the teachings of Goethe and Plato, of every blossoming fruit tree and sprouting blade of grass. Unfortunately, it is delusive, and when we come to read 'Marius' a second time we feel a certain sadness" (1:9).

Their friendship continued from the summer of 1881 to Pater's death in 1894. On her annual visits to England Violet never failed to visit the Paters. When he planned a trip to Rome in 1882, she sent him letters of introduction to her friends there. When he and his sisters finally visited Florence in 1884, she was in England. She wrote her mother to ask that she offer a gesture of hospitality: "I am sure they would like to come to tea with you, but you must not be bothered." Evidently uncertain how the strange habits of the Casa Paget would strike the reserved and timid Paters, she proposed instead that her mother send them some wine, fruit, and flowers: "As they have been exquisite to me, I want to be civil."[9] She could not resist, however, catering to her family's taste for gossip. On 20 June 1884 she reported on a tea party given by John Singer Sargent in his London studio. She, Mary, and Mary's sister Mabel were guests, along with Henry James and the Paters—Hester and Clara Pater "in fantastic apple-green dresses," while Mary and Mabel wore "pretty white frocks, myself in high black brocade . . . with Pater limping for gout and Henry James wrinkling his forehead as usual for tight boots." She also noted and duly reported Pater's interest in another guest, Marc André Raffalovich, a young Jewish poet and Catholic convert, "universally rich, lives in London and writes English and French verse—in the English very pretty. Isn't it odd?" [10]

Vernon Lee published *Euphorion: Being Studies of the Antique and the Mediaeval in the Renaissance* in 1884. Most of the essays included had appeared earlier in periodicals, and they all reflected the influence of Pater's *Studies in the History of the Renaissance* more strikingly than that of any other major Victorian writer on the subject. In 1883 she had confided to him her plans for collecting these pieces, and he had written encouragingly: "I am very glad to hear you are going to collect those papers which I have admired so much from time to time. They certainly deserve republication, and I shall be pleased and proud of your dedicating them to me, and thus in a way associating me in your so rapidly growing literary fame. I feel great interest in all you write and am really grateful for pleasure thereby. The title of your proposed volume is I think ben trovato" (50–51). Although the source for the felicitous title *Euphorion* is Goethe's *Faust*, Part 2, she acknowledged John Addington Symonds's use of the name with a direct quotation from his magisterial *The Renaissance in Italy* (2:54):

> Faustus is therefore a parable of the impotent yearnings of the Middle Ages —its passionate aspiration, its conscience-stricken desire, its fettered curiosity amid the cramping limits of imperfect knowledge and irrational dogmatism. The indestructible beauty of Greek art, whereof Helen was an emblem, became, through the discovery of classic poetry and sculpture, the possession of the modern world. Medievalism took this Helen to wife, and their offspring, the Euphorion of Goethe's drama, is the spirit of the modern world.

This citation of Symonds plus a brief mention in her bibliography are the only references to his work. Jules Michelet, she claimed in an appendix, was her inspiration: "how much I am indebted to the genius of Michelet: nay, rather, how much I am, however unimportant, the thing made by him, everyone will see and judge." For general historical information she consulted Burckhardt, Villari, and "Mr. J. A. Symonds," adding that she deliberately avoided reading his volumes 4 and 5 on Italian literature of the period, "from fear that finding myself doubtless forestalled by him in various appreciations, I might deprive my essays of what I feel to be their principal merit, namely, the spontaneity and wholeness of personal impression" (*Euphorion* 2:452).

As promised, Pater received the brief but eloquent dedication of *Euphorion:* "In appreciation of that which, expounding the beautiful things of the past, he has added to the beautiful things of the present." She paid him the further compliment of imitation, at least in the organization of the book, rejecting the chronological approach of a history for a series of separate essays that, like his, range over an eclectic choice of subjects from ancient sculpture and fourteenth- and fifteenth-century Italian painting to medieval love poetry and Elizabethan and Jacobean drama set in the Italian Renaissance. Like other late nineteenth-century writers on the Renaissance, all of them strongly influenced by Hegelian theories of "organic" history, she and Pater shared a vision of "a natural movement . . . to be accepted as an effort of humanity for which at length the time had come, and in the outward progress of which we still participate." (These are Symonds's words, from the introduction to the first volume of his study of the Renaissance, *The Age of Despots.*) For Pater it had been enough to sketch this progression from pagan antiquity to specific works of literature and painting: the charming French romance of "Aucassin and Nicolette," which, as he read it, reveals "the return of that ancient Venus, not dead, but only hidden for a time in the cave of those old pagan gods still going to and fro on earth, under all sorts of disguises"; the recovery of antiquity in the scholarship of Pico della Mirandola; the classical sensibility reflected in the paintings of Botticelli and Leonardo da Vinci and in the poetry of Michelangelo; the literal discovery of ancient Greek culture in the work of the eighteenth-century historian Johann Winckelmann. Pater never deviated from his role of aesthetic critic. Beauty was the object and the end of his quest, and the supreme expression of beauty in the Mona Lisa is enigmatic and subjective, answering to no purpose or function other than its own being.

To measure the distance between the aesthetic critic and the critical role that Vernon Lee assumed for herself in *Euphorion* it is instructive to compare her discussion of "Aucassin and Nicolette" with Pater's. In her essay "The Outdoor Poetry" she cites his "beautiful essay on that story," but only to point out a significant omission there. Pater left out of his summary of the poem the episode in which Aucassin, wandering in a forest in search of his beloved, comes upon a rough-looking peasant, "hideous quite marvellously," who is weeping bitterly because he has lost one of his master's bullocks and has no money to pay for the loss. The noble Aucassin saves his life with a gift of money. That single episode, Vernon Lee argues, strips away the "delicate and fantastic mediaeval love poetry" to reveal "the sordid reality, the tragic impersonation of all the dumb miseries, the lives and loves, crushed and defiled unnoticed, of the peasantry of those days" (1:137). Her focus has shifted from the aesthetic—the beauty of the poem—to a value judgment on the social inequities of feudalism. It is characteristic of the stimulating but exasperating essays in *Euphorion* that they often drift toward polemics, with sweeping judgments on the morality—social or personal— of the Middle Ages and the Renaissance. In the same way, she reads the love poetry of the Middle Ages as a beautiful cloak concealing a reality of oppression and brutality, of forbidden love and adultery. "This almost religious love," she writes in a companion essay "Mediaeval Love," with Tristan and Isolde and Lancelot and Guinevere as examples, "this love which conceives no higher honour than the service of the beloved, no higher virtue than eternal fidelity—this love is the love for another man's wife" (2:139).

Thanks to that "onward progress" of which Symonds wrote in the introduction to his *Renaissance,* medieval love poetry emerged purified of moral ambiguity in poets like Dante and Petrarch, who "made the desire of man for woman and of woman for man burn clear towards heaven." The conclusion to "Mediaeval Love" celebrates a transformation in sensibility:

> The feudal Middle Ages gave to mankind a more refined and spiritual love, a love of all chivalry, fidelity, adoration, but a love stamped in the poison of adultery; and to save the pure and noble portion of this mediaeval love became the mission of the Tuscan poets of that strange school of Platonic love which in its very loveliness may sometimes seem so unnatural and sterile. For, by reducing this mediaeval love to a mere intellectual passion, seeking in woman merely a self-made embodiment of cravings after perfection, they cleansed away that deep stain of adultery; they quadrupled the intensity of the ideal element. (2:216)

As her friend the Italian critic Enrico Nencioni observed, Vernon Lee's confidently asserted moral judgments were sometimes more in the spirit of the Ruskin she had repudiated than the Pater she acknowledged as a master: "a Ruskinian accent sometimes makes itself felt, in spite of the author."[11] Like her contemporaries writing on the period, she had no choice but to confront directly the question of Renaissance morality. What values can we extract today from an age so notorious for evil that nevertheless produced such glorious art? In the opening chapter of *Euphorion* she writes:

> The nations who came into contact with the Italians opened their eyes with astonishment, with mingled admiration and terror; and we people of the nineteenth century are filled with the same feeling, only much stronger and

more defined, as we watch the strange ebullition of the Renaissance, seething with good and evil, as we contemplate the enigmatic picture drawn by the puzzled historian, the picture of a people moving on towards civilization and towards chaos. (1:29)

Ruskin had judged and condemned Renaissance art because it was the product of a corrupt society. The most thorough and comprehensive scholar of the period, Symonds, wavered uneasily between admiration and censure; overall, as a self-professed "historian of culture" he let the record speak for itself: "False political systems and a corrupt Church created a malaria, which poisoned the noble spirits of Machiavelli, Ariosto, Guicciardini, Giuliano della Rovere. It does not, however, follow therefore that the humanities of the race at large, in spite of superstition and bad government, were vitiated" (*Renaissance in Italy* 1:382). Pater, on the other hand, made clear his unqualified admiration for the age:

> The fifteenth century in Italy is one of these happier eras, and what is sometimes said of the age of Pericles is true of that of Lorenzo—it is an age productive in personalities, many-sided, centralised, complete. . . . There is a spirit of general elevation and enlightenment in which all alike communicate. The unity of this spirit gives unity to all the various products of the Renaissance, and it is to this intimate alliance with mind, this participation in the best thought which that age produced, that the art of Italy in the fifteenth century owes much of its grave dignity and influence. (*Renaissance* xxx)

Not by nature given to compromise and mediation, Vernon Lee displays a mixture of judgments in *Euphorion*. She resolved to be an aesthetic critic, announcing in her opening pages that her book, like Pater's, will be unabashedly subjective: "The following studies are not samples, fragments at which one tries one's hand, of some large and methodical scheme of work. They are mere impressions developed by means of study . . . of thought and feeling in myself, which have found and swept along with them certain items of Renaissance lore. For the Renaissance has been to me . . . not so much a series of studies as a series of impressions" (1:16).

There is no question about her revulsion at the depravity of the age. Yet she celebrates the "splendid and triumphant wickedness of Italy." What indeed fascinated her was precisely the paradox of its creativity flourishing in an atmosphere of "moral gangrene" and "moral chaos." Essentially she remained within the value system of her contemporaries: "The Renaissance," she writes in the epilogue of *Euphorion*, "is simply the condition of civilisation when, thanks to the civil liberty and the spiritual liberty inherited from

Rome and inherited from Greece, man's energies of thought and feeling were withdrawn from the unknowable to the knowable, from Heaven to Earth; and were devoted to the developing of those marvelous new things which Antiquity had not known and which had lain neglected and wasted during the Middle Ages" (2:234). On a scale of relative values she finds that the art of the Renaissance far outweighs its immorality. She does not forgive, but she reduces the evil of the period to the level of mere banality. Of "the great criminals of the Renaissance"—the Sforzas, the Borgias, the Gonzagas—she writes: "Most of these men were neither abnormal nor gigantic. Their times were monstrous, not they. They were not . . . at variance with the moral atmosphere which surrounded them; and they were the direct result of the social and political condition" (2:92). With her taste for paradox she reverses the verdict of popular history: "The blindness to evil which constitutes the criminality of the Renaissance is such as to give it a certain air of innocence" (1:102). Yet she reminds her readers in an essay aptly titled "The Sacrifice" that there was a price to pay, a kind of Faustian bargain with Satan. In the long run, Italy lost its health as a society and a culture, but the rest of us were richly rewarded: "That, in short, while the morality of the Italians was sacrificed to obtain the knowledge on which modern society depends, Italy was sacrificed to the diffusion of that knowledge, and that the nation was not only doomed to immorality, but doomed also to the inability to reform" (1:53–54).

Generalizations like these led critics even as sympathetic as Nencioni to pause and respond, "Ma come!" *Euphorion* is replete with paradox, intellectual gymnastics ("ginnastica intellectuale"), and exaggeration. A case in point is her essay "The Italy of the Elizabethan Dramatists," highly praised by reviewers for its sensitivity to the fascination that the Italian Renaissance had for English visitors, themselves steeped in austere Protestantism and distrust of "Romanism." This image of an Italy where crime and corruption lurked in ominous shadows, however false, inflamed the imaginations of Webster, Ford, Tourneur, and Marston. It also gave free rein to her own impassioned prose:

> The world of these great poets is not the open world with its light and its air, its purifying storms and lightnings; it is the darkened Italian palace, with its wrought-iron bars preventing escape; its embroidered carpets muffling the footsteps; its hidden, suddenly yawning trapdoors; its arras-hangings concealing masked ruffians; its garlands of poisoned flowers; its long suites of untenanted darkened rooms, through which the wretch is pursued by the half-crazed murderer; while below, in the cloistered court, the clanking armour and stamping horses, and above, in the carved and gilded hall, the

viols and lutes and cornets make a cheery triumphant concert, and drown the cries of the victim. (1:78–79)

"Ma come!" indeed. But Nencioni had high praise for what he considered her balanced portrait of this era, her emphasis on "the other Renaissance" too often neglected by writers on the period—"the sweet and tender poetry of Bembo and Vittoria Colonna and Tasso . . . the virginal saints and madonnas of Raphael, the joyous angels of Correggio . . . this splendid time of exuberant vitality, of this strong and serene Renaissance," as she puts it (1:80). What was more difficult for Nencioni to overlook were the excesses of her admiration, her attempts to find extenuating circumstances for the evil that flourished alongside the good. Thus she excuses the notorious cruelty of the Borgias as part of the natural order of things: "If Cesare Borgia be free to practise his archery upon hares and deer, why should he not practise it upon these prisoners?" she writes of the "innocent merriment" that he apparently took in using human targets for his sport (1:94).

As Nencioni, a personal friend, wisely perceived, Vernon Lee's problem was that her writing was her conversation put down on paper and transferred to print. He relished its freshness and spontaneity, the large and distinct imprint of her personality, her omnipresent "il proprio io." Reading Euphorion, he wrote, "evokes the lively conversation of a person of rare and varied culture and of even rarer intellect whose diverse arguments have the heat of profound conviction and animated discussion" (Saggi 79). The reader is overwhelmed, half-drowned in the flood tides of her arguments, but these are always presented beautifully, "in a luminous style, picturesque and irresistible." Nencioni's opinions were shared by most of Euphorion's English reviewers, who noted, as the unsigned reviewer in the Athenaeum did (5 July 1884), "a countervailing defect" in the otherwise "conspicuous merits" of the book, "a habit of over-criticizing and over-writing—an inclination to start an argument and raise a distinction at the slightest provocation—an indisposition to let the reader go when once the subject has been propounded." The Saturday Review (6 September 1884) responded in much the same way: "Its merit is that it is not the compilation of laborious learning, but the direct utterance of an individual mind. Its faults lie in the incessant and undue assertion of this individuality, in confusing impressions with ideas, in a wanton riot of needlessly strong language, and in a harassing and vexatious attempt to overwhelm us with tumultuous description."

What in essence Vernon Lee attempted in Euphorion was to amplify and clarify the message of Pater's conclusion to The Renaissance: "For art comes to you proposing frankly to give nothing but the highest quality to your moments as they pass, and simply for those moments' sake." She failed

—partly, one suspects, because of the obscurity of Pater's message—but mainly because for all her reading she lacked the knowledge and the analytical power that aesthetic criticism demands. The success of her cultural history of eighteenth-century Italy had made her overconfident. In *Euphorion* she indulged in all the excesses that Symonds had criticized in her *Studies of the Eighteenth Century in Italy*—overwriting, repetition, careless use of language, dogmatic arguments, and plain illogicalities and errors of fact. In her zeal to refute Ruskin's idealization of the Middle Ages, for example, she argued that "feudalism stamped out civilisation; monasticism warped it"; that the only literature that existed in England was "half-effete and scattered fragments of Chaucer, of Scotus, and Wycliffe"; that the art of Giotto "is an art of mere outline"; that Dürer's is an art of "a stunted, poverty-stricken society . . . [a] mediaeval society of burghers' wives." In the Renaissance, she writes, with apparent indifference to her own remarks on the tyranny of the rulers, "men were free agents, both in thought and in deed. . . . For the first time since Antiquity, man walks free of all political and intellectual trammels" (1:46–47). She draws a tenuous parallel between Renaissance Italy and France in the late eighteenth century: "These two have been the great fever epochs of modern history; fever necessary for a subsequent steady growth. Both gave back truth to man, and man to nature, at the expense of temporary moral uncertainty and ruthless destruction" (1:52).

These egregious passages and others like them Pater chose to ignore. He was impressed with the undeniable if at times misdirected erudition and enthusiasm of this young woman who dared to speculate and generalize as he —ever cautious, ever qualifying in his own writing—rarely did. He paid her homage in a footnote to the third edition of his *Renaissance* where he referred to *Euphorion* as "a work abounding in knowledge and insights on the subject which it treats." In a letter of 4 June 1884 he responded enthusiastically to her gift of the book, with thanks for her "generous and graceful dedication to myself" and a catalogue of its merits. These include "very remarkable learning: by which I mean far more than an extensive knowledge of books and direct personal acquaintance with 'Italy's self'"—learning, in the sense in which it is above all characteristic of Browning . . . evidence of a great variety and richness of intellectual stock—apprehensions, sympathies, and personal observations of all kinds—such as make the criticism of art and poetry a real part of the 'criticism of life.'" He praises her style without qualification: "full of poetic charm . . . justly expressive, sustained and firm—as women's style so seldom is." As a fellow writer on art, he appreciates her ability "to make *intellectual theorems* seem like the life's essence of the concrete sensuous objects, from which they have been extracted . . . it is also an effect I have myself endeavoured after, and so come to know its difficulties." Finally he writes something that her publisher might have used as an endorsement of the book: "I find in it, not merely historical learning dominated by ideas, which is certainly a good thing; but ideas gathering themselves a visible presence out of historical fact" (*Letters* 53–54).

From another writer on the Renaissance, Vernon Lee received a totally different and dismaying response. She had boldly launched her book in a literary marketplace that had already welcomed John Addington Symonds's *Renaissance in Italy.* Symonds, with a university degree and a solid reputation as a scholar-critic, could not have been concerned about being superseded by a still little known and eccentrically educated young woman. He had been generous in praise of her *Studies of the Eighteenth Century in Italy,* though he had even then cautioned her to restrain her exuberant prose. They exchanged letters over their common interests in Italian culture, Symonds's admiration for Eugene Lee-Hamilton's poems, and their mutual friend Mary Robinson, but his opinions of the work she continued to send him were invariably qualified. He read *Belcaro,* he wrote her (28 March 1882), "with sustained interest & a constant sense of its power." Then he noted its defects: "You know my opinion is that you are over-confident in your own intuition & over-hasty in expression." There were also fundamental disagreements on aesthetics, with Symonds arguing as much against Pater as against her that "Art is not Art's end; & Beauty is not its end; Art is the means, & Beauty is the mode chosen for utterance of the Geist" (*Letters* 2:710).

They clashed on religion and ethics. Commenting on her essay "The Responsibilities of Unbelief," to which Pater had given respectful attention, he conceded in a letter of 22 May 1883 that it was "a most brilliant & well-wrought piece of writing," but objected, "The attitude of a dogmatic atheist (as opposed to a simple agnostic) wh you assume & the promulgation of a Nihilistic faith as ascertained truth, wh you insist upon, are however to me incomprehensible" (2:815). Disagreements over philosophical questions strained their friendly relations. On 5 August 1883 he wrote, evidently in response to a letter in which she had complained of his "sneers," that "I do not consider you now at all in the position to instruct the world upon these topics, simply because I see that the most poignant points in them have not as yet occurred to you" (2:841). A year later (4 April 1884) he felt so strongly that he could not resist a personal attack: "I feel that you imagine yourself to be so clever that every thing you think is either right or else valuable. And your way of expressing yourself is so uncompromising that your belief in yourself grates upon my sense of what is just and dignified . . . you miss, according to my notion, the supreme grace of dignity. It is possible to be frank without appearing to have posed as an oracle" (2:897–98).

Symonds's brutal candor reflects on Violet Paget the woman as well as on Vernon Lee the writer, for it was the woman he regarded as a rival for Mary Robinson's affection. That she received such criticism and yet continued to correspond with him, and indeed sent him *Euphorion* a few months later, testifies less to her forgiving nature than to her youthful self-confidence, which survived many blows. With *Euphorion* she had dared to venture into his immediate territory, writing not only on the Italian Renaissance but, in one chapter, on Elizabethan drama, on which he had recently published a book, *Shakespeare's Predecessors in the English Drama*. Although he had responded graciously to her "munificently appreciative review" of that book in the *Academy*, 8 March 1884, he could not restrain his irritation when he acknowledged her gift of *Euphorion* on 20 June 1884. His thanks are icy and edged with sarcasm: "I envy you the freedom of your method; so different from the stiff & hampering method adopted by myself in my book on Itn R, wh you describe by a felicitous metaphor in your opening pages. I admire the imagination, the learning visited with emotion, the originality & audacity of view, even the paradoxes in which you delight" (2:924).

Symonds proceeds to a slashing critique.[12] While he finds a few things to praise in the book, even his praise is calculatedly ambiguous, emphasizing that he had anticipated her on these points in his *Renaissance in Italy*, two volumes of which, he reminds her, she had chosen not to read. With her chapters "The Sacrifice" and "The Italy of the Elizabethan Dramatists," he writes, "I almost wholly concur." But, "The gist of the former article is what I always tried to impress in each section of the book I wrote. You will find the latter in quite remarkable harmony with my chapter on the Drama in Vol 5 of 'R in It,' as well as with the essay on Vittoria Accoramboni & A Cinque Cento Brutus in my 'Italian Byways.'" He feels that she overrated the poetry of Lorenzo de Medici, especially his pastoral "Nencia da Barbarino," which she had hailed as "a kind of little idyll" of peasant life displaying "a heart for the simpler, ruder, less favoured class of mankind": "But I believe you will find that I had in Vol 4 of 'R in It' done justice to the versatility & originality of his initiative." He agrees with her on Boiardo's superiority to Ariosto, but reminds her that his views had appeared nine years earlier in the *Fortnightly Review*. Although he praises her chapter on Italian painting, "in spite of exaggeration & one-sidedness details," he challenges her remarks on Fra Angelico's fresco of the Crucifixion in San Marco. She had judged the work "a juxtaposition of the most conventionally idealistic, pious decorativeness with the realism straight-forward, unreflecting, and heartless to the point of becoming perfectly grotesque . . . artistico-religious prudery." He calls this comment "crudely unintelligent, as it stands." Symonds's most interesting criticism, considering his own homosexual proclivity, is his remark on her argument that adultery was the reality that the poetry of chi-valric love concealed: "Your treatment of the more repulsive side of the sub-ject is pretty much the same as that of a man who, dealing with the real Greek Platonic Love, should insist upon the patent fact that it had more or less of an indissoluble connection with a vice wh bears an uglier name than Adultery" (2:922–23).

Symonds's criticism must have been painful for Vernon Lee. It was barely softened by his summing up: "I wish 'Euphorion,' so rich in literary excel-lence, all success & feel assured that it will be successful." He had touched a nerve. Over the course of their correspondence, invitations to visit had been exchanged between them from time to time, but they met only once and this two years before the publication of *Euphorion,* on her visit to En-gland in June 1882. He had come to London from Switzerland especially to consult his doctors and a repeatedly postponed visit to tea finally took place. Violet wrote her mother: "Poor Symonds looks very ill and is dreadfully de-pressed for he thinks his end is hastening, and that at all events he is con-demned forever to remain at Davos. He is very courteous and sympathetic. Poor creature, I am greatly grieved for him, especially as I think he has little fortitude."

After *Euphorion* the letters ceased altogether. Symonds continued to get news of her from Mary Robinson, but that correspondence too ended after Mary's marriage to James Darmesteter. Nevertheless he retained a grudg-ing respect for Vernon Lee. On 13 April 1886 he wrote Mary that "Miss Pa-get's Baldwin is upon my list to get as soon as it appears. I expect it to mad-den me. Tell her that this is a compliment" (*Letters* 3:133). In a letter of 26 March 1887 he urged his daughter Margaret to read her: "You shall read Miss Paget's *18th Cent. in Italy,* wh is all about Metastasio & the Opera—a most wonderful book for a girl of 22 to have written" (3:214).

Walter Pater died in 1894, a year before Vernon Lee collected another se-ries of essays under the title *Renaissance Fancies and Studies: Being a Sequel to Euphorion.* These pieces were the last substantial writing she was to pub-lish on the Renaissance, in a sense rounding out an era of her work. After the mid-1890s she abandoned the role of art philosopher, acknowledging that her interest lay in other directions. *Renaissance Fancies and Studies* closes with a retrospective essay, "Valedictory," occasioned by Pater's death. It is a farewell and eulogy to him, but it is also a farewell "to some of the ambitions and most of the plans of my youth." In the period framed by her Renaissance studies she had experimented boldly in what she called "art philosophy" and moved formally from cultural historian to aesthetic critic, only to discover that she had achieved neither goal. These were years of both professional and personal frustration. They began with high hopes for her career based on the favorable reception of her eighteenth-century studies. There were also high hopes for her personal happiness and at least partial independence from her family. But by 1894 she was a middle-aged woman sobered by disappointment and a physical and mental breakdown. "Circumstances of various kinds," she writes in "Valedictory," "and particularly ill-health, have put me, although a writer, into the position of a reader, and have made me ask myself, as I collected these fragments of my former studies, what can the study of history, particularly of the history of art and of other manifestations of past conditions of soul, do for us in the present?" (236).

She answers her question by defending such study as personally satisfying, whatever its practical value: "We require, as we require mountain air or sea scents, hayfields or wintry fallows, sun, storm, or rain, each individual according to individual subtle affinities, certain emotions, ideals, persons, or works of art from out of the Past" (240). The intellectual life remained the only possible existence for her. But the historical scholarship and aesthetic criticism that had engaged her for so many years, she now discovered, imposed barriers and distractions to the immediate experience of viewing a work of art itself. The details they uncover are insignificant. "Art is a much greater and more cosmic thing than the mere expression of man's thought and opinions on any one subject. . . . Art is the expression of man's life, of his modes of being, of his relations with the universe, since it is, in fact, man's inarticulate answer to the universe's unspoken message" (253).

The shift in her sensibilities—and, as a consequence, in the direction of her future work—is one she also traces in the career of Walter Pater. Her "Valedictory" is double-edged: a farewell to her youth and its achievements and a farewell to Pater. In him she traces a spiritual evolution akin to her own: "He began as an aesthete, and ended as a moralist." His was not, however, the parochial moralism of Ruskin or of any given society or epoch. "By faithful and self-restraining cultivation of the sense of harmony, [Pater] appears to have risen from the perception of visible beauty to the knowledge of beauty of the spiritual kind, both being expressions of the same perfect fittingness to an ever more intense and various and congruous life." Looking back twenty years to his *Studies in the History of the Renaissance,* she sees a different Pater, who began as "an aesthete of the school of Mr. Swinburne's *Essays,* and of the type still common on the Continent." Like other seekers of aesthetic perfection, he had achieved exquisitely written but sterile results, "a sense of caducity and barrenness, due to the intuition of all sane persons that only an active synthesis of preferences and repulsions, what we imply in the terms *character* and *moral,* can have real importance in life—be, in short, vital" (255–56).

Happily, as Pater developed in those twenty years she notes "an inborn affinity for refined wholesomeness" that saved him from "the cultivation of sensations, vivid sensations, no matter whether healthful or unhealthful" (a fate that awaits her antihero in the novel *Miss Brown*) and made him ultimately "the natural exponent of the highest aesthetic doctrine—the search for harmony throughout all orders of existence." He became, like the Plato he revered, "a teacher of self-discipline and self-harmony." As she wrote several years later in an essay, "The Use of Beauty," "It was Mr. Pater who first pointed out how the habit of aesthetic enjoyment makes the epicurean into an ascetic" (*Laurus Nobilis* 33–34). In "Valedictory" Vernon Lee seeks to correct what she calls "the inappropriate name of 'art for art's sake.'" She could not altogether erase the false impression that his *Renaissance* had left with many readers, but she could clarify that impression by showing the affinity between Pater and Plato and his distance from the flamboyant aestheticism of the 1880s and '90s.[13]

The self-denying discipline of her mother's teachings had long been in conflict with Violet Paget's craving for self-expression and self-fulfillment. Consciously or unconsciously, she recognized something like the same conflict in Walter Pater, "whom I always revered as a master." Her tribute to him in "Valedictory" acknowledged that the conflict remained unresolved, but that he had pointed a way to its resolution:

This which we guess at as the completion of Walter Pater's message, alas! must remain for ever a matter of surmise. The completion, the rounding of his doctrine, can take place only in the grateful appreciation of his readers. We have been left with unfinished systems, fragmentary, sometimes enigmatic, utterances. Let us meditate their wisdom and vibrate with their beauty; and, in the words of the prayer of Socrates to the Nymphs and to Pan, ask for beauty in the inward soul, and congruity between the inner and the outer man; and reflect in such manner the gifts of great art and of great thought in our soul's depth. For art and thought arise from life; and to life, as a principle of harmony, they must return. (259–60)[14]

5 THE TELLER AND THE TALES

WHEN TWENTY-FOUR-YEAR-OLD VIOLET PAGET VISITED LON-
don in June 1881 as a guest of Mary Robinson and her family, her confidence in herself as a writer was solid. In addition to her much praised *Studies
of the Eighteenth Century in Italy,* she had published essays on art, aesthetics, and music in prestigious journals like *Fraser's,* the *Cornhill,* and the *Contemporary Review.* She arrived on the London literary scene as something of
a prodigy, a genteel young woman who wrote and talked authoritatively on
an immense number of subjects. That scene, however, was crowded with
literary celebrities. Her youth and her significant but small reputation were
duly appreciated, but she soon realized that she would have to fight for the
attention she felt she deserved.

One of her missions was to sound out English publishers for herself and
for Eugene. She wasted no time following leads given her in Florence by
Eliza Lynn Linton and other well-established writers, seeking out possible
connections like Richard Garnett, keeper of the printed books at the British Museum; Norman MacColl, editor of the *Athenaeum;* Leslie Stephen of
the *Cornhill,* and the publisher T. Fisher Unwin. But the principal purpose
of her visit was to plant herself firmly in the center of literary society. This
she was able to do, thanks to the hospitality of the Robinsons. George
Robinson was a prominent banker, not a writer himself but a man who enjoyed the company of writers and artists. With his wife and talented young
daughters—Mary, a poet, and Mabel, who later published several novels—
he lived at 84 Gower Street, within easy walking distance of the British Museum and the University of London. He took pride in educating his daughters, traveling abroad with them and entertaining in their London home
with regular gatherings that they called "tertullas" (an English adaptation of
the Spanish *tertulia,* an evening party).

The record of this first visit is in the long chatty letters Violet dashed off
to her mother and brother almost daily. Emerging from the hothouse environment of the Casa Paget in Florence, where the cultivated guests were

mainly expatriates removed from the center of English literary life and where all activity focused on her as hostess, she found herself suddenly in a dizzying round of visits, receptions, tea and dinner parties, theatres, and introductions to all manner of celebrities. Her letters home are a curious mixture of breathless girlish excitement and jaundiced cynicism, a series of hasty first impressions often reversed in later letters, prejudices affirmed and confirmed—all exactly what she knew her mother and brother would relish. They were absolute in their judgments of others. Like the little girl of the nursery rhyme, when they were "good" they were hospitable, generous, and firm in their loyalties. When they were "bad" they were nothing less than "horrid"—ruthlessly critical, implacable, unforgiving. Mrs. Paget, as even gentle Mary Robinson observed in her reminiscence published years later in *Country Life,* balanced her kindness with "a dominating will" and "something aromatic, pungent, even bitter." Violet described her mother as a mass of contradictions: "tyrannical . . . overflowing with sympathy and ruthless unforgiving" (*Handling of Words* 300). Eugene, understandably, was moody and bitter, confined to his couch and struggling to write the poetry for which he felt he was unappreciated.

From childhood Violet had been conditioned to a world of "us" and "them"—ordinary people who lived ordinary lives and toured Europe with their eyes glued to guidebooks. Meeting now a new society of the famous and near famous, she carried with her what her mother and brother liked to think of as their uniqueness and superiority. She entered the Robinsons' drawing room therefore a little apprehensive, appreciative of the opportunities it offered her but zealously guarding her pride. On 22 June 1881 she reported on her debut: "Eugene must not be very angry that I would not be introduced to Mr. [Robert] Browning, who was there, *menant train de grand génie.* I thought it so derogatory to be honored in the way that Agnes Clark [Clerke] was, by two minutes platitude. He is a rather common looking old creature." As with Walter Pater, she reversed her first impression when Browning received her cordially in a private visit later that summer.

She was similarly alienated by the gaucheness of Leslie Stephen, from whom, as editor of the *Cornhill,* where she had been publishing since 1878, she had expected a warm welcome:

Presently in came Leslie Stephen, a tall sort of solemn, scraggy jawed Rubens type, who looked hideously shy, and sat in silence for half an hour. On my taking my departure he shambled forward and stammered inaudibly that he was sorry he had no opportunity of speaking to me! Whereon I departed. Had I come to England to extend my literary connexions I think I might go hang myself for sheer despair on the first peg I met. Fortunately I came to see Mary and I am extremely happy with her and more charmed every minute.

In the same rueful tone she wrote her mother a few days later that "the only two creatures who seemed to have heard of me as a writer were William Rossetti and Oscar Wilde." She had a special affinity for "the wonderful Oscar Wilde! He talked a sort of lyrico-sarcastic maudlin cultschah for half an hour. But I think the creature is clever, and that a good half of his absurdities are mere laughing at people. The English don't see that." In his unabashed flaunting aestheticism she quickly detected the satire he was directing at the humorless aesthetes of Pre-Raphaelitism. By the early 1880s the major popularizers of the movement, like Wilde, George du Maurier with his cartoons in *Punch,* and W. S. Gilbert in *Patience,* were also the chief satirists of its affectations and excesses—surfeits of chintz, floral wallpaper, blue-and-white china, japonaiseries, flowing garments. Not surprisingly, Violet, who defined her own serious aesthetic creed in *Belcaro,* cast a cold eye on the movement, although she admired the Morris wallpaper and the richly colored silks she saw at Liberty's. Aestheticism—she wrote her mother from Oxford, where she had just seen a performance of *Patience*—"(except at Mr. Gosse's who receives his guests in ginger velveteen and red slippers) has well nigh died out in London" (18 July 1881).

When the Pre-Raphaelite painter Evelyn Pickering took her to a gala exhibition at the Royal Academy that summer, she was unimpressed:

> All the exhibition rooms were thrown open & crammed with people more or less artistic or fashionable. I never saw so many shabby or insane dresses & so few pretty women in my life. I was quite astounded coming out, to see so many grand carriages. The dresses didn't look at all on a par with them. There were some crazy looking creatures: one with crinkled gauze all tied close about her & visibly no underclothes (& a gold laurel wreath), another with ivy leaves tied to each others' stalks, on short red hair; another with a trimming and necklace of marigolds & parsley fern on thread, a lot of insane slashing & stomachings. (L. Ormond 136)

Coming from her Florence home with its rich but spare Italian elegance, she found these excesses disgusting. Much as she appreciated the hospitality of the William Rossettis in Hammersmith, she wrote her mother in 1882: "Oh what a grimy, filthy aesthetic house! I shuddered to sit down in my white frock." She judged the furnishings of the Humphry Wards' house in Russell Square "the height of aesthetic desolation" (Ormond 138).

Fortunately for her sensibilities, her visit to London was balanced with happier impressions. Her old friend John Sargent turned up shortly after her arrival and did a quick sketch of her. "Extraordinarily clever and characteristic," she reported home, "it is of course mere dabs and blurs and considerably caricatured, but certainly more like me than I expected anything could—rather fierce and cantankerous. . . . He says I sit very well; the goodness of my sitting seems to consist in never staying quiet a single moment" (25 June 1881). Completed as a portrait in oils now in the Tate Britain (see frontispiece), it captures the vitality and sharpness of her expression, the severity of her dress (black with a small white collar), her short hair carelessly combed, her eyes glittering behind spectacles, and her lips parted as if about to burst into speech, as she probably was.

Violet also met people she considered more substantial than the Pre-Raphaelite circle. These included two German-born women—Helen Zimmern, a writer and translator who remained her friend for many years,[1] and Mathilde Blind, a sister contributor to the Eminent Women Series with biographies of George Eliot (1883) and Madame Roland (1886)—and influential men of letters like Edmund Gosse and Andrew Lang. On 12 July 1881 Mary took her to call on Robert Browning, then staying with his sister in Maida Vale. Without the distractions of other society, Violet received the attention she felt she deserved from the venerable poet. On this first visit she found him amiable, "quite of another sphere from all the Rossettian poeticules" (Cary, "VL's Vignettes" 195). In addition to their love of Italy they had a good friend in common, Enrico Nencioni, the Italian critic who had known both Brownings in Florence and whose translations had introduced Robert Browning to Italian readers. Violet visited Browning several times thereafter, with ever greater admiration for the man as well as the poet. During her visit with him in August 1885 he showed her the Old Yellow Book, his source for *The Ring and the Book.* "It seemed absurd, but it moved me much more to think that this was the book out of which the great poem had come, than that the man who was showing it me had written the poem" (Corrigan, "Vernon Lee" 118).

In 1886 she sent him a copy of her newly published *Baldwin: Being Dialogues on Views and Aspirations,* with a note calling his attention to passages on Caponsacchi and Franceschini: "They are the result of some discussion I had with Enrico Nencioni." Browning had good reason to be flattered by two dialogues in *Baldwin.* In "On Novels" her spokesman Baldwin and Nencioni's Carlo are in full agreement on the brilliance of *The Ring and the Book.* "You will not, I suppose, deny that it is one of the most magnificent and noble works of our day," Baldwin says. Its plot, however, is not one to attract an English novelist: "Mudie would simply refuse to circulate a novel the immense bulk of which consisted in the question, discussed and re-discussed by half a dozen persons: 'Has there been adultery between Pompilia and

Caponsacchi?'" (231). In the other dialogue, "The Value of the Ideal," Baldwin hails Browning's poem as "one of the greatest monuments of ideal art, great in magnitude and completeness of beauty in the same sense as some temple front or fresco decoration on an immense scale" (285). The poem is proof of Baldwin's theory of "the necessity of the ideal," demonstrating the transformative power of literature, which here converts the sordid reality of greed, lechery, and adultery into art.

The Old Yellow Book was not the only prose account of Franceschini's crimes. In her exploration of the bookstalls of Florence, Violet had come upon another and more recent book by Alessandro Admello, *Le giustizie a Roma dal 1674 al 1840* (1881), and she copied out the relevant material for Browning, who had known of the existence of the book but never seen it. She continued to call upon him on subsequent London visits, boasting to her mother in June 1887 that "Old Browning treated me like a long lost grandchild." But the old man was not as doting as she thought. "Dear Vernon-Lee-Violet-Paget treats old R.B. as if he were the philistine he is not, when she plays at supposing he forgets her existence," he wrote her playfully (31 January 1887). The frequently cited reference to her in "Inapprehensiveness," a poem in *Asolando* written in 1889 only a few months before his death, is, with typical Browningesque ambiguity, less a compliment than a dramatic gesture appropriate to the context of the poem. The speaker is reflecting on his inability to communicate his love to the woman standing beside him. As she admires the landscape, a sunset over an old ruined castle, she wonders whether it was Ruskin who had noticed the effect of weeds growing over such ruins. While the lover suppresses his "dominant passion needing but a look / To burst into immense life," she coolly pursues her academic question:

> "No, the book
> Which noticed how the wall-growths wave,"
>   said she,
> "Was not by Ruskin."
>   I said, "Vernon Lee?"[2]

In the opening chapter of *Belcaro* Vernon Lee announced her resolution to abandon history for aesthetics, facts for ideas. Since what she had written as history—her *Studies of the Eighteenth Century in Italy* and her medieval and Renaissance studies in *Euphorion*—was as imaginative as it was factual, her resolution was superfluous. Nevertheless she liked to think that she was moving on to something new, a fiction she could enrich with her copious knowledge of the eighteenth century in particular and of Italian culture in general. She had chosen to write her early histories in the form of topical essays rather than as chronicles. The essay was a genre she

enjoyed because it gave her freedom to move between imagination and reality: "For an Essayist possesses, inasmuch as he is an Essayist, some of the
instincts of the superior creature called a novelist, a certain half imaginative
perception of the past, a certain love of character and incident and description, a certain tendency to weave fancies about realities." This is quoted
from her preface to *Ottilie: An Eighteenth Century Idyl* (1883), a modest but
elegantly written novella set in a picture-postcard eighteenth-century German provincial town. She had been toying with fiction since her childhood
story about an ancient Roman coin. In addition to the anonymous collection of Italian folklore *Tuscan Fairy Tales* (1880), she had published as Vernon Lee a children's fantasy, *The Prince of the Hundred Soups* (1883), inspired
by her research on the commedia del'arte and Gozzi's *fiabe*.

Ottilie was her first attempt at adult fiction. She introduces herself to the
reader as an essayist chafing under the restrictions of that genre: "How
many readers guess at the terrible temptation of the poor Essayist to tell you
some adventures and thoughts and feelings which he feels perfectly persuaded happened in the life and passed through the mind of the historical
character?" Even more troubling for "the unlucky Essayist" is the intrusive
imagination that persists in creating "vague forms of men and women whose
names he does not know, whose parentage is obscure; in short, who have
never existed, and who yet present him with a more complete notion of the
reality of the men and women of those times than any real, contradictory
imperfectly seen creatures for whose existence history will vouch." These
imaginary men and women haunt but so teasingly elude the essayist in *Ottilie* that (s)he transfers the burden of narrator to another, an unnamed traveler visiting a sleepy little German town, who notices a frail, elderly couple
on their daily walks. He learns that they are brother and sister and observes
that after a while the man walks alone because the woman has died. Known
to his neighbors as "The Poet," the old man had published some poems and
stories years before, but they are now forgotten. "People at W—— maintained that in all these productions the sister had done at least half the work;
and indeed the general opinion seems to have been that she was the master
mind of the two." The brother too soon dies, leaving a manuscript, "My
Confession—1809," and it is from this that the story of *Ottilie* emerges.

Peter Gunn cautions against reading autobiography into *Ottilie,* but the
details of the plot parallel so closely the circumstances of the Paget family's
life in the late 1870s that the reader must wonder how Violet dared to write
it. One of her friends during this period, Carlo Placci, immediately made
the identification, writing her enthusiastically in September 1883: "It is perfectly charming and reads so deliciously quaintly and quite carries you off to
another life, to another time, to another way of thought. I think I recognized

the original of Ottilie and I have the greatest admiration for such sisterly dévouement" (Pantazzi, "Carlo Placci" 109). We can only imagine Eugene's and Mrs. Paget's reactions to the book. Even if they failed to recognize Violet's identification with her heroine, if they were distracted by such transparent devices as her making Ottilie Reinhart an older rather than a younger half sister, or even if they preferred to identify Ottilie as the devoted mother Matilda Paget caring for the invalid son Eugene, they must surely have recognized the similarity between the melancholy, irresolute half brother Christoph and Eugene. Both leave university without taking degrees, both fail at careers and, still young, return home to live in passivity and dependency, writing undistinguished poetry. Ottilie, the older half sister, sacrifices her own promising future at court and later refuses offers of marriage because of her brother's selfish demands on her. He, on the other hand, plunges impulsively into marriage with a young woman who is his social and intellectual inferior. The marriage fails, and he once again returns to his sister, who is always ready to receive him with love and forgiveness. After Ottilie's death Christoph acknowledges, in the "Confession" that frames the narrative, the nobility of her character and the weakness of his own: "I had suffered as she had; but alas! while she had suffered from a generous sacrifice, I had suffered from my own selfish wilfulness."

As its subtitle promises, *Ottilie* is consistently eighteenth century in its subject matter, but it is not an "idyl." The first impression of the narrator, who introduces the story, is that in spite of her white hairs, Ottilie "seemed, with her bright serenity, to give life and strength to the weakly, melancholy, and wistful-looking old man." No disguise of fiction could have given Violet Paget "bright serenity," but fiction did supply a medium for freer self-expression than did history. Underlying her fictional heroine's lifetime of self-sacrifice and her half brother's demands is a current of morbid and only partly repressed fear that Eugene was a threat both to her own dependence on her mother and to her independence as a woman. Much as she may have loved him, she could anticipate only that with the aging of Mrs. Paget he would become an increasing burden upon herself, a Christoph to her Ottilie.

Violet wrote *Ottilie* several years before it found a publisher. At 25,000 words it was too long to publish as a short story and, in the judgment of Longmans, where she had submitted it in 1881, too short for book publication or serialization in *Fraser's Magazine*. As Vernon Lee, however, she was able to publish it in T. Fisher Unwin's Pseudonym Library, where it was well received. What reviewers admired most was its evocation of the past, of the romantic charm of the eighteenth-century Germany that had enchanted her in her childhood—memories of little spa towns like Wiesbaden and Baden-Baden, where the Pagets had stayed in their leaner years, and of the dedicated German and Swiss governesses who had regaled her with märchen and the poetry of Goethe and Schiller. *Ottilie* is indeed Vernon Lee's personal reconstruction of the romantic age of *The Sorrows of Young Werther.*

One reader who took special interest in the historical background of *Ottilie* was the German literary critic Karl Hillebrand, who had been a frequent guest at the Casa Paget since 1875 and an admirer of both Violet's and Eugene's work. Although in failing health—he died only a year after the book's publication—Hillebrand was flattered by the author's dedication of the book "To my friend Karl Hillebrand" and wrote her from Vevey on 16 July 1883: "Now let me congratulate you upon the very clever way in which you have woven your story into the historical ground and shewn, without too much emphasis, the action of the general current of thought on the individuals" (P. L. Leighton 187). That "current of thought" was the wave of Sturm und Drang that swept Germany from about 1770 to the end of the century. While Ottilie stays at home engaged in her household duties, like Werther's domestic Charlotte, but also supervising her brother's solidly classical education, Christoph discovers "some of the works of our new literary school"—*Götz von Berlichingen, Laocoön,* the writings of Winckelmann. He goes off to university, a hotbed of Sturm und Drang, where students neglect their academic studies to read Ossian, Klopstock, and Schiller and compose their own romantic tragedies "in which paradoxes, hyperboles, murders, seductions, and abominations of all sorts are heaped together, till it seemed as if a poet was to be valued according to the number of people whom he slaughtered on the stage" (111). Christoph is caught up in this madness and succumbs to fashionable Weltschmerz, finally abandoning his studies to return home penniless and without any prospect of a career.

As intellectual history, Christoph's immersion in German romanticism is lightweight, but Vernon Lee enhanced her story with historical details. Her mastery of the period, like her command of eighteenth-century Italy, was impressive. She was widely read in German literature and comfortable if not fluent in the language. But as with all her historical writing, she was careless of details. For all his admiration of *Ottilie,* Hillebrand could not resist correcting her inaccurate dates. She sends Christoph to university at nineteen in 1788 yet gives his year of birth as 1759. He noted similar inconsistencies, such as her confusion about the publication dates of *Laocoön* and other books cited, all of which she could have corrected in the second edition (1893) but failed to do. Overall, however, he did not challenge the soundness of her history. Ironically, what he considered the chief merit of the book was that "the characters are not psychologically analysed or anatomically described, as is the fashion now a day's, and that no moralizing intention is visible." His only reservation was that the characterization of Christoph comes dangerously close to "the abyss of modern art": "This would be difficult to change now and is besides excused by the morbid habits of introspection which you lend to your hero" (Leighton 188).[3] In fact, Vernon Lee was a pioneer enthusiast of the psychological novel. In her dialogue "On Novels" in *Baldwin* her spokesman argues in direct refutation of Hillebrand that the strength of the modern novel is its power to explore human character analytically and sympathetically and leave the reader with "a moral, a lesson, a something which will be treasured up, however unconsciously, as a generalization" (221).

Vernon Lee is on more solid ground both historically and artistically when she introduces a genuine historical character into *Ottilie*. He is Karl Philipp Moritz (1757–93), a novelist and essayist who rose from humble circumstances to become privy councillor to Prince Karl August in Berlin. He turns up as the darkly handsome Councillor Moritz in the little town where Ottilie and Christoph live, a worldly and somewhat world-weary man. Christoph, at the time only a teenager, is already familiar with Moritz's writings on Italy, where Moritz had met Goethe. The boy is enchanted with the older man, who befriends him and lends him books that feed his romanticism. But when Moritz meets the still attractive and highly cultivated Ottilie and falls in love with her, Christoph becomes furiously jealous: "They were getting nearer and nearer each other, and I proportionately further and further from both." Though Ottilie shows no lessening of her love for her brother, he confesses: "I felt overcome by heart-breaking loneliness. . . . The feeling became insupportable to my excessively sensitive and egotistic nature, rendered morbidly jealous of having been my sister's sole thought, her life, her tyrant. What was I now? Merely her brother" (96).

When Moritz proposes to Ottilie, the boy shouts, "Councillor Moritz, I would rather die than be your son!" (101). The older man realizes that Christoph is selfish and in need of discipline; he urges that he be sent away to school. But there is only one choice for Ottilie. She rejects her suitor, who goes off to Rome, leaving Christoph unchanged in basic character but with a distinct sense of guilt. "I felt sometimes as if I had committed some great crime" (105). By the melancholy conclusion of the novel he has come to terms with his guilt. To the graying Ottilie's observation that she has grown old he replies, " 'So have I . . . but we should not complain of Time and his doings, since he has taught us that we were made only for each other.' And I kissed those few white hairs" (177).

In 1883, the year that *Ottilie* appeared, Mary Robinson published a biography of Emily Brontë in W. H. Allen's Eminent Women Series. It was a short book but an important contribution to Brontë studies because Mary had interviewed Ellen Nussey and several Haworth residents who remembered the Brontës. She managed, therefore, to demythologize the most enigmatic of the sisters without diminishing her genius. Always ambitious for new writing projects, Violet offered to write a biography of Fanny Burney, Madame d'Arblay, for the series. She was especially sympathetic to the subject having been inspired both by Charles Burney's writings on eighteenth-century music and by Mrs. Turner's bequest to her of the watch that had once belonged to Fanny. The publisher had other plans for that book, but he offered her instead fifty pounds for a biography of the Countess of Albany, the Flemish princess who married Charles Stuart, the no longer Young Pretender. Though pressed for time—she was in the midst of collecting her essays for *Euphorion* and completing her three-volume novel *Miss Brown*—she could not resist the opportunity to return to her favorite period and setting, eighteenth-century Italy.

She dashed off *The Countess of Albany* between September 1883 and June 1884. As usual in her work, haste was apparent in the breathless, careless prose, but her scholarship was sound. The book engaged her as a novelist as much as a historian. Working from two major historical sources, a German biography by Alfred von Reumont and a French biography by St. René Taillandier, as well as from archives in Siena, Milan, Florence, and Rome, she imaginatively reconstructed the life of the Princess Louise of Stolberg, who married in 1772, at the age of nineteen, to the middle-aged Count of Albany, no longer Bonnie Prince Charlie but a drunken and dissolute wreck of a man living on the charity of the Church of Rome. Her wretched marriage and her love affair with the poet Alfieri, who in his time was hailed as Metastasio's heir, constitute the historical plot of *The Countess of Albany,* which Vernon Lee enriched with her distinctive knowledge of eighteenth-century Italy. Like her "story" of Metastasio in *Studies of the Eighteenth Century in Italy,* the book portrays a dying society in all its perverse elegance and decay, a Rome "sombre and squalid, . . . with its huge ostentacious rococo palaces and churches, its straggled black and filthy streets, its ruins still embedded in nettles and filth," and its beautiful fountains, its brilliant salons where "daintily embroidered and powdered aristocrats from England and Germany" came to marvel at Italian music: "A large proportion of the best new operas were always brought out in Rome. . . . And the young singers from the conservatories of Naples came to the ecclesiastical city" (29).

The Countess of Albany's story is one in which history begs for the indulgence of the imagination. It begins as pure romance with the journey to Rome of the "beautiful little fairy princess, with laughing dark eyes and shining gold hair . . . a childish woman of the world, a bright, light handful of thistle-bloom" (2). She is coming from Paris, where she has been married by proxy to a man she has never seen. The bridegroom who greets her is more than twice her age, with "a red and bloated face," large coarse features, and "pale blue eyes," and is "gloomy, helpless, vacant and debased in the whole face" (13). By 1772, when the book begins, Charles Edward's claim to the throne of England has become a feeble French and Roman hope for a restored Catholic monarchy. The fairy tale swiftly dissolves into a sordid story of a loveless, politically arranged marriage.

Vernon Lee covers the historical background of her story briskly, almost as if to clear the way for the stormy love affair that is the center of her book. Characteristically, she colors her historical personages with her own strong judgments: "Charles Edward was the victim neither of a hereditary vice nor of a mental disease; drink was in his case not a form of madness, but merely the ruling passion of a broken-spirited and degraded nature" (19). Having worn out his welcome in Rome, the count moves with his young wife to Florence, "where every married woman was furnished, within two years of her marriage, with an officially appointed lover" (51). *Cicisbeism,* a term she uses with particular relish, was all but institutionalized in this society, where "conjugal infidelity was a social organisation supplemented by every kind of individual caprice of gallantry . . . in this world of jog-trot immorality, where jealousy was tolerated in lovers but ridiculed in husbands" (52).

In sympathetically portraying a married woman who takes a lover, Vernon Lee shocked Victorian readers. Eyebrows had already been raised over W. H. Allen's selection of George Eliot for the first biography in their Eminent Women Series. The Countess of Albany, though clearly a victim of the corrupt system that had arranged her marriage, was an adulteress, and Alfieri, though a highly respected poet, was her lover. The American Harriet Preston Walter, in an article on Vernon Lee in the *Atlantic Monthly* of February 1885, worried about "the degrading effects of sensual vice on both the heroes of the story" and judged the countess "not an exemplary character." Although Vernon Lee had been challenged by a few reviewers of *Euphorion* for her ambivalence on Renaissance morality, this was the first time she actually offended some of her readers. With *Miss Brown,* published only a few months later, she offended a great many more. She was mystified by such criticism. Her experience as a historian had taught her that contexts, specifically the manners and mores of other societies, dictate a degree of moral relativism. But she was also a stern judge and outspoken critic of the morality of others. She did not condone the adultery of the countess any more than she had approved the cruelty of Cesare Borgia in *Euphorion.* "The immoral law had produced the moral lawlessness" was her judgment on the erring eighteenth century.

Essentially what engaged Vernon Lee in *The Countess of Albany* was a moral question of a higher order: how the worldly and decadent European high society eroded the ideals of potentially noble characters—the countess, an intelligent and cultivated woman, and her lover Vittorio Alfieri, a talented poet. She dismisses with distinct cynicism the romantic legends that lingered among the loyal Scottish Jacobites of an heir born to the countess: "The Court of Versailles wasted its money; the officially negotiated baby was never born." The novelist in Vernon Lee is concerned with the young woman herself:

> Who can say when Louise d'Albany, hitherto apparently so childish, became suddenly a woman with the first terrible suspicion of the nature of the bondage into which she had been sold? Such things are unromantic, unpoetical, coarse, commonplace, yet if the fears and the despair of a guiltless and charming girl have any interest for us, the first whiff of brandy-tainted breath which met the young wife in her husband's embraces, the first qualms and reekings after dinner which came before her eyes, the first bestial and unquiet drunkard's sleep which kept her awake in disgust and terror, these things, vile though they may be, are as tragic as any more ideal horrors. (46–47)

This is the prose of a writer who had read Ouida as well as George Eliot and Carlyle. But she had also read Stendhal and, however disapprovingly, Flaubert and Maupassant. Her countess is not destroyed. She survives because she is intelligent, tough-minded, "rather deficient in sensitiveness." She finds consolation in intellectual activity: "a creature, so to speak, only half awake, or awake, perhaps, only when she devoured her books and tried to puzzle out her mathematical problems" (53). Spurning the conventional *cavaliere servente,* she establishes a salon to which the handsome and moody young poet Alfieri comes.

Vernon Lee the novelist did not have to invent her hero. Vittorio Alfieri fit the role in every romantic detail—son of a Piedmontese aristocrat, rich, well traveled, interestingly neurotic, even suicidal, a libertine and a veteran of many tempestuous love affairs. Once he discovered his vocation in literature, however, Alfieri had settled down to a serious literary career, writing lyric poetry and tragedies in a style Benedetto Croce described as "passionate oratory." It was his dedication to his art, Vernon Lee suggests, not sexual attraction that first drew him to the young countess. "She was a cold, virtuous, extremely intellectual woman, trying to find consolation for her quietly and bravely supported miseries in study, in abstract interests which should take away her thoughts from the sickening reality of things, a woman who would be valuable as a friend to a poet, and who would know how to value his friendship" (74). With such a woman, Alfieri reasons, he can renounce his self-indulgent past and dedicate himself to his lofty ideals of truth, justice, and the liberation of Italy from its foreign rulers: "He had determined to be the poet who should make men ashamed of being slaves and ashamed of being tyrants" (85–86).

Vernon Lee portrays a hero and heroine on her own, not necessarily history's, terms: "strange, self-modelling, unconsciously attitudinizing lovers," who conduct their love affair "according to the pattern of Dante and Petrarch." Disgusted by the memories of his profligate past, Alfieri welcomes "this strange intellectual passion." His idealism is aroused by the challenge of, Caponsacchi-like, rescuing an abused woman. He arranges for her flight to Rome, where, after much negotiating and maneuvering, he joins her. They maintain separate residences and what Vernon Lee ambiguously calls "a more passionate kind of friendship." Alfieri fills his time writing poetic dramas that are received with acclaim, appealing to the taste of the period, polished in language but, in Vernon Lee's opinion, lacking in genuine poetic imagination, "deficient in the power of suggesting images, of conceiving figures of speech . . . the indefinable something which we call lyric quality" (113). His characters are shallow, with no attempt to analyze their emotions. No matter. The small upper-class audience for whom he wrote, more interested in manners than in morals, in style more than substance, approved his work. When Metastasio died in 1782, his eulogist, addressing the members of the Arcadian Academy, prophesied that in Alfieri "Metastasio had found a successor greater than himself."

The happy-ever-after of the young princess's fairy tale was not to be. Charles Edward consented to a legal separation in 1784 and died in 1788. By then the countess and Alfieri were living together in Paris. Vernon Lee briskly disposes of the inevitable question: "Alfieri and the countess did not get married, simply, I think, because they did not care to get married . . . because marriage would entail reorganisation of a mode of life which had somehow organised itself, because it would give a commonplace prose solution to what appeared a romantic and exceptional story; and finally because it might necessitate certain losses in the way of money, of comfort and of rank" (149). In time the great love story shrank from romance to pathetic domestic drama.

> Mme d'Albany took it all as a matter of course: she was probably no longer at all in love with Alfieri, but she admired his genius and character as much and more than ever, and was probably beginning to develope a certain good-natured, half-motherly acquiescence in his eccentricities, such as women who have suffered much, and grown stout and strong, and cynically opportunistic now that suffering is over, are apt to develop towards people

accustomed to resort to them, like sick children, in all their ups and downs of temper. (173)

After Alfieri's death in 1803 the countess preserved his memory by commissioning Canova to design his tomb in Santa Croce in Florence and arranging for the publication of his complete works in twenty-two volumes (1805–15). She consoled herself with the companionship of the French painter François Xavier Fabre and a salon in Paris, where she entertained a cosmopolitan society of French, English, and Italian guests. She lived contentedly if not happily ever after and died in 1824.

The Countess of Albany is strongest not as a record of the life of its subject but in its descriptions of eighteenth-century Rome. Vernon Lee was never more fluent than in evoking the Rome she remembered from her childhood, and she delighted in "the desolate tracts of the town," the abandoned villas and palazzi overgrown with lush shrubbery, the shepherds herding their flocks through what by the 1880s, when she was writing this book, was a bustling modern city. It is the novelist who surfaces in these evocative passages, which are in themselves irrelevant to the sheltered and circumscribed life of the countess. But elsewhere the novelist has to content herself with historical characters. She cannot control their personalities or their destinies. Compounding her problem was the delicacy of her subject and its fundamental unfitness for the Eminent Women Series. The countess was a passive women, intellectual but in no way of lasting importance, except perhaps as the custodian of a poet of only questionably lasting importance himself. To meet her publisher's requirements of a book-length manuscript, Vernon Lee was obliged to pad it with reiteration of the Platonic nature of the relationship and repeated emphasis on the "immoral law" of the age against which the behavior of the lovers was, even if not innocent, pardonable.

Reviewers were quick to note the repetition and the hasty, careless writing, the long and often confusing sentences, a disregard for the rules of grammar and syntax, and lapses into what they regarded as slang (Prince Charles Edward is described as "tipsy" and "dead drunk" and being "egged on" by France into his marriage). But in the balance they were impressed with Vernon Lee's ability to bring a long dead past to life. The *Athenaeum* (23 August 1884) found the book "totally superior" to the "lifeless" German biography of the countess by von Reumont, and the *Academy* (6 September 1884) had high praise for her portrait of eighteenth-century Italy, especially her vignettes of the salons of Rome and Florence: "definite and brilliant, admirable examples of intense and graphic art." The book was appreciated into the next century; in 1910 the *New York Times* (10 April) hailed the second edition as "an impressionistic biography which holds the imagination better than many novels." Slight as *Ottilie* and *The Countess of Albany* were, they confirmed the promise of Vernon Lee's early work.

Although the writing of novels was never a primary interest in Vernon Lee's later career, she remained attracted to fiction as a vehicle for historical narrative. It challenged her powers of evoking the past, of re-creating scenes she imagined as well as those she knew at first hand, and of imaginatively spinning off characters, real or imagined, from the past. When she attempted contemporary settings and characters modeled on real-life figures—notably in *Miss Brown,* which is set in the heyday of the aesthetic movement of the 1870s and '80s—she failed dismally. Realism as a literary genre eluded her completely, although the social, political, and cultural issues of the day engaged her all her life. She had no genuine talent for the novel, but there was a ready market, growing larger every year. However much she proclaimed her indifference to commercial success, she was human enough to court it from time to time.

In 1903, for example, she published a short novel, *Penelope Brandling: A Tale of the Welsh Coast in the Eighteenth Century.* It had all the elements of popular fiction: the wild rugged coast of Wales, an old castle occupied by rough characters who pose as fishermen but are really smugglers, a brave young heroine-narrator and her husband, a dark family secret. Certainly with an eye to the market, she submitted it to several publishers without success, until T. Fisher Unwin took it for their Pseudonym Library. In her letter accompanying the manuscript she described it as "a virtuous and exciting tale, rather Stevensonian" (5 January 1902).[4] Unwin's readers reported on it favorably but cautiously. One (G. M. English) saw commercial possibilities: "There is a mystery and gruesomeness about it which should attract the general public, and literary people always admire her." Another (H. D. Banning) recommended it with reservations: "This is a good story, but not to our mind anything really first rate. It is of course excellently written and has an admirable atmosphere, but as a story apart from the telling there is nothing very remarkable about it." Reviewers and the public alike confirmed this judgment, and the book was quickly forgotten.

In contrast to her short stories of the supernatural, which have always enjoyed some degree of popularity, turning up in anthologies throughout the twentieth century, Vernon Lee's novels—those, that is, that were written in the popular modes of social realism (*Miss Brown*) and neogothic thriller (*Penelope Brandling*)—deserve the neglect they have received. An exception is *Louis Norbert: A Two-Fold Romance,* published in 1914 when events in Europe overshadowed the publication of even far more significant novels. It is in fact a charming romance, blending history with mystery—its subject a scholarly quest that involves two incongruously matched characters who discover their elective affinities as they attempt to solve a mystery out of the scraps and fragments of seventeenth-century history. As its subtitle suggests, *Louis Norbert* has two pairs of lovers, one long dead and tragic, the other contemporary and lovers only in the sense of uniting in their passion for the past.

The novel consists largely of an exchange of letters over a two-year period, 1908 to 1910, between an aristocratic, middle-aged English widow, Lady Venetia Howard, and a much younger Italian archaeologist, never given a name, who serves as her guide in Pisa. Visiting the Campo Santo, she is struck by a funerary inscription commemorating one Louis Norbert de Caritan who died in 1684. The archaeologist cannot identify him, but the name awakens Lady Venetia's memory of a portrait of a handsome young man that hangs in her family home and bears that name. She had been fascinated by it in her childhood but knew only that the subject was of French birth, adopted and raised by her seventeenth-century ancestors. Her curiosity now aroused, she immediately speculates on the slab's inscription identifying Norbert as a Frenchman who traveled in Italy in the service of the king of England and died of a fever at the age of twenty-four. The slab had been erected by the Abbe Manfredini of Pisa, who identified himself as a dear friend of France. From this scrap of information Lady Venetia spins off a theory that explains everything—that Norbert had been the victim of a conspiracy, murdered by Manfredini on the orders of the French court. The scholarly young archaeologist promptly dismisses her as a self-indulgent, frivolous romantic: "He had a notion that great ladies were all addicted to some form or other of spirit-rapping" (11). Nevertheless, her persistence and her, to him, scatterbrained charm win him over, and he agrees to delve into the local archives while she returns to England to search the long-neglected family archives stored in the muniment room.

Their discoveries, reported in their letters, gradually unfold a mystery involving intrigue in the court of Louis XIV, a story worthy of Alexandre Dumas—disguises, coded messages hidden in books, a secret marriage between the king and the niece of Cardinal Mazarin, the birth of a son who, presumed dead, was smuggled off to England to be raised as Louis Norbert. On his fatal visit to Italy, Norbert falls in love with Artemisia, a brilliant young woman, a poet and musician, who tries vainly to rescue him from the assassins and retreats to a convent when she fails. Artemisia's letters to him tie up the loose threads of the mystery, the solution of which proves that Lady Venetia's spontaneous and unscientific theory had been correct. But Vernon Lee is not writing a defense of romance over history. In the course of her research Lady Venetia has become a conscientious, methodical scholar, and the strictly scientific archaeologist has indulged his roman-

tic imagination. Together they have achieved an ideal. Early on in their quest
she had written him: "You have written me down as a foolish woman with
a hopeless tendency to romancing about everything, what you call a *born
poet or novelist*" (168). Nearing the end, he admits to her: "You are a born
poet and novelist, that is to say, a superlative historian!"

Louis Norbert, the last of Vernon Lee's novels, runs riot with logic and
credibility, but it has a delicacy of characterization that is displayed nowhere
else in her work. The two ill-fated antique lovers are merely conventional
props, but the two modern antiquarians, mismatched in age, background,
and personality, develop a relationship that Henry James might have appreciated.[5] At some subliminal level—perhaps in the ghosts of Louis Norbert and Artemisia—they have become lovers. This is romance. In reality
Lady Venetia, who has been obliged to leave her family home because her
brother has married, marries a much older wealthy nobleman for security
and social position, and the archaeologist will apparently marry a learned
young woman who has assisted him in his research. In her last letter to him
Lady Venetia imagines him and his wife discussing "the strange story which
happened in Pisa in 1684. Or was it rather (the thought suddenly strikes me)
in 1908?"

Matilda Paget. From a
painting by Frank Stone.
(Courtesy of Colby College)

Henry Ferguson Paget.
(Courtesy of Colby College)

Violet Paget, ca. 1870.
(Courtesy of Colby College)

Violet Paget, ca. 1872.
(Courtesy of Colby College)

Vernon Lee, from a drawing by J. S. Sargent, 1889.
(By permission of the Ashmolean Museum, Oxford)

Mary Robinson, ca. 1880.
(Courtesy of Colby College)

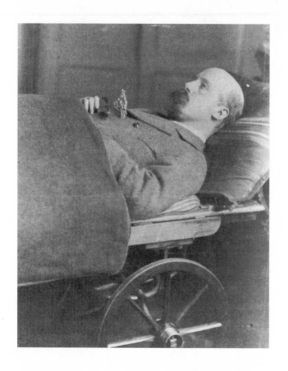

Eugene Lee-Hamilton
on his invalid couch,
Florence, 1880s.

Vernon Lee at Sestri, 1914. Photo by Margery Taylor.
(Courtesy of Colby College)

Vernon Lee in her academic gown as Doctor of Letters, honorary degree from the University of Durham, 1924. From a painting by Berthe Noufflard. (Courtesy of Colby College)

꧁ In the years from 1881 to 1884 violet paget emerged from her sheltered existence in Florence—a life in many ways so purely of the mind that she arrived in London a social innocent. During this period, in addition to writing reviews and articles for English periodicals, she was seeing *Belcaro* through the press, arranging for the publication of *Ottilie* and her whimsical *The Prince of the Hundred Soups*, researching and writing *The Countess of Albany*, collecting her essays for *Euphorion*, germinating the essays that were to appear in *Baldwin* (1886), and writing the three-volume novel *Miss Brown*, published by William Blackwood late in 1884. One theme that dominates almost all this work—history, essays, fiction—is the large and troubling question of the social and moral value of art. It was a question that confronted many of her contemporaries, but few of them struggled with it as long and as energetically as she. From the putatively adulterous relationship of the Countess of Albany and Alfieri to the indisputable corruption of the Renaissance princes to the emergence of literary realism in French novelists like Zola, Maupassant, and Flaubert—everywhere she looked Vernon Lee perceived challenges to the lofty aesthetic principles she had enunciated in *Belcaro*. For her, the moral supremacy of art was not to be questioned, and in her versions of the Italian Renaissance and the eighteenth century, moral issues are irrelevant, eclipsed by the beauty of the art, poetry, and music these periods produced.

In contemporary England, however, a society in flux where traditional values were under constant examination and revision and where science had challenged the very foundations of religious faith, the old certainties were vanishing:

> There is more room for indirect moral perversion . . . than there has been for a good while; for the upsetting of ideas, the infiltration of effete or foreign modes of thought and feeling, is much greater. . . . with our science and our culture, our self-swamping with other folk's ideas, we are infinitely

less morally steady than the good sceptics of the days of Voltaire, who always believed in the supremacy of their own century, their own country, their own institutions, their own conventionalities; who were in danger only from the follies and uncertainties of every past century from which we have inherited. ("A Dialogue on Poetic Morality," *Belcaro* 255–56)

Far more mature minds than hers—Tennyson, Matthew Arnold, even earlier Carlyle—had wrestled with these challenges and left them unresolved. But in her "Dialogue on Poetic Morality" twenty-four-year-old Vernon Lee had the answer. The aim of life, her spokesman Baldwin declares, is "the creation of the good," and the creator of the good "is above all men the artist." With Walter Pater she affirms that "the creation of perfect beauty is the highest aim of the artist." But she had learned from Pater's experience that without qualifications such ideas can be dangerously misinterpreted.

It was against this background of aesthetic and moral confusion that Vernon Lee conceived *Miss Brown*. She chose the genre of fiction for the simple reason that the novel commanded the largest reading public.[1] For the same reason, she chose a contemporary setting, with many of her characters thinly veiled portraits of people she had met in the tertullas of the Robinsons and their friends. To explore profound moral and ethical questions in the genre of popular fiction was hardly unusual in the late nineteenth century. George Eliot had set an impressive model, and in 1889 Mrs. Humphry Ward's *Robert Elsmere,* about the crisis of religious faith that tormented many Victorians, became a phenomenal bestseller in England and the United States. As a critic and historian of Italian culture, Vernon Lee looked down upon popular fiction. In 1881 she wrote her mother that the publisher Longmans had suggested that she write a novel: "Think if I were a novelist! But even had I time, I should shrink from writing what would certainly be vastly inferior to my other work" (Gunn 98). But as the ambitious young Vernon Lee seeking recognition in the literary marketplace, she was tempted. Moving through London society and observing the popularity of French novels like Gautier's *Mademoiselle de Maupin* and Zola's *Nana,* she was gathering material for a novel. Two years later she defended Mary Ward's polemical *Robert Elsmere:* "But she *does not* sell herself; and if she has made more money by her novels than anyone since George Eliot . . . it isn't because she has written down to the public but because, writing her own very serious and excellent but mediocre views of religion, etc. she has happened to meet the wants of the majority" (24 August 1893).

Vernon Lee was loath to "sell herself," but like Mary Ward she had confidence in her convictions. She came increasingly to believe that the aesthetic movement had perverted the nature of art by reducing it to hedonism—art not for art's sake as the realization of the Platonic ideal, but for pleasure's sake, self-indulgence, affectation, and ultimately moral corruption. Baldwin's partner in the "Dialogue on Poetic Morality" says that he finds the whole idea of art for art's sake disgusting: "men who seemed to lose sight of all the earnestness and duty of life, who had even what seemed to me very base ideas about art itself and . . . debased it by associating it with effeminate, selfish, sensual mysticism." He is here somewhat belatedly echoing the charges brought against Pre-Raphaelitism in a sensational article, "The Fleshly School of Poetry," in the *Contemporary Review* of October 1871. The author, who signed himself "Thomas Maitland," was the novelist and playwright Robert Buchanan. He directed his attack principally against Dante Gabriel Rossetti, Swinburne, and William Morris—"the fleshly gentlemen [who] have bound themselves to solemn league and covenant to extol fleshliness as the distinct and supreme end of poetic and pictorial art." [2]

As for "selling" herself with a popular novel, it should be noted that Vernon Lee was not entirely disinterested and she had sufficient confidence in her book to fight for her own terms. The old and distinguished firm of William Blackwood and Son accepted her manuscript with a generous offer: £100 for the first 750 copies and 10s. on each copy up to 1,000, "when I am free to do what I like. I think it's awfully *handsome* and much more than I deserve," she wrote her mother. Her self-confidence was unshaken when, four days later, Blackwood's senior editor, J. M. Langford, "suggested my altering the whole catastrophe of *Miss Brown*—an insane notion. I foresaw that once a week William Blackwood, who had not read the book, would be forwarding similar suggestions and I foresaw that he was far too great of a swell to be thwarted. So I boldly told him that Mr. [Richard] Garnett, who believes in astrology and has made out my horoscope, finds it in the stars that I am 'kittle cattle to drive.' The game was a bold one, but the result is that I have my hands free" (26 July 1884).

With her dedication of *Miss Brown*—"To Henry James, I dedicate, for good luck, my first attempt at a novel"—she was courting the favor of a highly esteemed novelist and friend who was a welcome visitor to the Casa Paget on his visits to Florence. She kept him informed of the progress of her work and proudly wrote to her mother in October 1884 that "he takes a most paternal *interest* in me as a novelist, says that *Miss Brown* is a very good title, and that he will do all in his power to push it." Certainly James acted in good faith. He responded to her dedication gallantly: "To tell the truth it frightens me a little that you should attach to me the honour of your invocation, however casual; it is an honour I am really not *de taille* to carry" (21 October 1884). He did in fact think her a remarkably intelligent young woman and was impressed by what he described to T. S. Perry as her "prodigious cerebration." He was also one of the few who enjoyed her stream of talk. "She is one of the best minds I know," he wrote Edmund Gosse, "is almost worthy to be French and makes one a little less ashamed of the stupid English race. She is disputatious and paradoxical, but really a superior talker" (28 September 1884). Nevertheless, he approached the three volumes of *Miss Brown,* when he received an advance copy, with something less than enthusiasm.

Miss Brown is the story of a poor and uneducated young woman who becomes the protégée of a wealthy painter-poet, Walter Hamlin. He meets her when he visits a painter friend who lives with his wife and children in a country villa near Lucca. Hamlin is suffering from a melancholia that he cannot shake off even in the exquisite Tuscan countryside: "All these things seem to have lost for him their emotional colour, their imaginative luminousness. . . . He and the world had become paler in the last three years" (1:4). He is aroused from his malaise when he sees Anne Brown, the orphaned daughter of a Scottish father and an Italian mother. She is the children's nursemaid, a household servant, not a governess. She is strikingly beautiful, a large "monumental" figure who appears to Hamlin "like some of Michelangelo's women . . . a superb creature . . . a Valkyr or Amazon," with thick, dark, curly hair and "tragic" dark eyes. Hamlin—pale, blond, "effete," with "girlish beauty"—is instantly inspired to paint her. He lends her books, takes her to the opera in Lucca, and resolves to rescue her from her humble circumstances: "Either Anne Brown must turn into a sordid nursery governess or into the avowedly most beautiful woman in England —that is to say in the particular Pre-Raphaelite society which constituted England to him" (1:118). He rents a studio where he paints her as "Venus Victrix":

> Instead of the naked goddess triumphing over the apple of Paris . . . Hamlin made a sketch of a lady in a dress of sad-coloured green and gold brocade, seated in a melancholy landscape of distant barren peaks, suffused with the grey and yellow tints of a late sunset; behind her was a bower of sear-coloured palms, knotting their boughs into a kind of canopy for her head, and in her hand she held, dragged despondingly on the ground, a broken palm-branch. (1:128–29)

By now determined to play Pygmalion and educate his Galatea for a life in London society as his wife, Hamlin makes her a generous and honorable offer. He will send her to school, settle an income on her, buy her a house in London when she has completed her education, and then leave her absolutely free to decide whether or not she will marry him. Even her guardian, her cousin Richard Brown, a hard-working engineer who lives in England, overcomes his suspicions and consents to the arrangement. Deeply moved by Hamlin's generosity, Anne accepts: "I must become worthy of him," she resolves (1:208).

A tabula rasa at the start, within the next year and a half Miss Brown acquires an education at a remarkably progressive girls' school in Germany: "By virtue of her half-Italian nature, Anne required little to make her, in education and manners, a lady. With her wide-open but rather empty mind, her seriousness and dignity of person, extreme simpleness, as the reverse of complexity of character, it was wholly unnecessary that she should unlearn anything, or even that she should absorb anything absolutely new; the only thing was to fill up the magnificent design which already existed in her" (1:209–10). She proceeds to London, where Hamlin, who has kept his distance all these months, has bought and furnished a house for her in Hammersmith. Ever the gentleman, he provides her with a companion-chaperone, his elderly aunt Mrs. Macgregor.

This frail but strongly opinionated and outspoken woman, one of the few admirable characters in the novel, is drawn from the living model of Mrs. Paget: "The old lady was good-natured, garrulous, flighty; but yet, beneath the shiftiness of her exterior there seemed to be something real, something sad and bitter, when you looked at her thin drawn mouth and melancholy eyes." She reads the books that Mrs. Paget read—"a whole library of what were once deemed literary firebrands, but might be described as mild, old-fashioned free-thinking literature" (1:269–70). Twice married—"each time for love and each time to men who . . . had been immediately reduced by her into the most devoted and timid slaves" (2:64)—she is disgusted by the idea of sex (men and women, she believes, "are entirely at the mercy of their animal passions"), regards marriage as a necessary evil for procreation, and finds the art and poetry of her nephew's aesthetic friends "indecent." Nevertheless she tolerates their society for his sake and accepts Miss Brown enthusiastically.

Society accepts Miss Brown even more enthusiastically. She is an overnight sensation. Hailed as "the queen of aestheticism" for her statuesque beauty ("Hamlin looked at her as he might have looked at a beautiful cathedral front" [2:56]), her dignity, and her unusual background, she is invited to sit for paintings and is the center of attention wherever she goes. Though bewildered by her sudden celebrity, she is sensible enough to recognize the artificiality and foolishness of most of the people she meets. Out of gratitude to Hamlin she welcomes his friends and tries to adapt herself to the fashions of the period. But her natural warmth and instinctive intelligence keep her honest and unaffected. Gradually, however, she awakens to what she regards as the pernicious effects of this society upon him. She encourages him to write simple pastoral poetry, but when he reads one of his poems to his friends they scoff at it as "Wordsworthian," complaining that it lacks "that exotic perfume which constitutes the essence of poetry" (2:75). Humiliated, Hamlin rewrites the poem in the style of his friend Cosmo Chough's poetry: "descriptions of the kisses of cruel, blossom-mouthed women, who sucked out their lovers' hearts, bit their lips, and strewed their apartments with coral-like drops of blood" (2:24).

Although Miss Brown drifts away from Hamlin and his circle and acquires new interests and friends of her own, she continues to live chastely with him and do her duties as his hostess. She meets her cousin Richard Brown, now a successful self-made businessman planning to go into Parliament as a liberal social reformer. Physically he is the antithesis of Hamlin — large and muscular with strong features and a heavy dark beard. Anne admires his energy and dynamic personality and shares his reformist ideas. When he introduces her to the philosophy of positivism, she finds "a new belief in the necessity of doing one's duty for the sake of mankind and of progress" (2:333). She begins to read books on political economy, and she attends working-class women's lectures with the idea of preparing herself to teach women and improve their lot in society. Also a positive influence are the Leigh sisters, Mary and Margery, "who existed as it were on the borderland" between society and the real world. Like Mrs. Macgregor, they have real-life models—Mary Robinson and her sister Mabel. They are intelligent young women with serious interests in improving the conditions of the poor. Mary Leigh especially becomes a devoted friend—"in a sort of way in love with Anne Brown." But it is Margery who brings to her attention the misery and squalor in which the tenants on Hamlin's estate live. By now, however, he is so absorbed in the self-indulgent life of aestheticism that he ignores Anne's pleas to improve their lives.

It finally dawns on Miss Brown that she has committed herself to an unworthy man: "And the thought that she would be chained for ever to the side of a man whose whole nature was merely aesthetic, who was wholly without moral nerves or moral muscles, filled her with despair" (3:337). Her only hope now is the sudden appearance in London of Hamlin's cousin Sacha, Madame Elaguine, a widow with a mysterious past. For all her instinctive wisdom, Anne fails at first to recognize a vampire, a "lamia," in this woman who wears heavy makeup, lives on coffee and cigarettes, and reads French novels. So blinded for the moment is she that she is pleased by Hamlin's obvious infatuation with his cousin, reasoning that if he were free of his pledge to marry her, she would be free to go to Girton College and train for a teaching career.

The arrival of a trusted friend of Hamlin's, her former employer in Italy, crushes Anne's hope. He recognizes Madame Elaguine and reveals to Anne the sordid details of her past: "She is the sort of woman who absolutely degrades a man, takes pleasure in turning him into a beast and a madman" (3:246). Anne had earlier suffered a bitter disappointment when Richard Brown, whom she respected and admired, suddenly declared his passion for her: "I love you—I want you—I must have you!" For Anne "it was like the outburst of another nature, a strange, unsuspected ego, bursting out from beneath the philanthropist's cool and self-sacrificing surface" (3:73). These blows bring on an attack of brain fever through which Mary Leigh lovingly nurses her. On her recovery Anne resolves to rescue Hamlin, now debauched by drugs and alcohol, "a poor, weak, sick soul," from his cousin's evil clutches. Although she knows that "marriage without love was a mere legalized form of prostitution," she offers to marry him: "She could not prevent his growing worse, she could not make him grow better; her position would be that of a woman who devoted herself to nurse a person sick of an incurable disease" (3:278). Ironically, it is Madame Elaguine who enjoys the final victory, telling Miss Brown: "I am only surprised and amused, and extremely interested, from the psychological point of view, in finding that a virtuous woman may condescend to things that would turn the stomach of a woman who has no pretense to virtue." There is no denying the truth of her remark. "Miss Brown," Vernon Lee concludes, "had forgotten that ignominy is an almost indispensable part of all martyrdom" (3:313).

The aestheticism that Vernon Lee decried in *Miss Brown* was not, strictly speaking, the Pre-Raphaelite movement, which produced a large body of colorful, highly stylized poetry, painting, and decorative art from the 1850s to nearly the end of the century. Nor was it the Christian aestheticism of John Ruskin or the Platonic aestheticism of Walter Pater. At times in the novel she approaches the broadly caricatured aestheticism of W. S. Gilbert and *Punch,* but there is no sustained humor. Vernon Lee was eclectic and introduced elements of all these, but initially her target was the harmless silliness of what she and Mary Robinson called "high art," what the 1960s called "camp"—the excesses that turn serious culture into vulgarity and banality. In a letter to her mother in 1883 she described a party that she and Mary attended in the Hampstead studio of Henry Holliday ("the funny little aesthetic painter who was at Florence"). There were "weird people, women in cotton frocks of faded hues, made wide at the hips & tight at the feet like Turkish trowsers—and lank draperies of all sorts . . . a youth with anemic face & hair played the piano & someone, in a nasal voice, sang a long, pseudo mediaeval ballad about a King's daughter & a swineherd, with an idiotic & melancholy refrain. It felt so completely high art" (*VL's Letters* 124).

Violet reported these impressions with evident amusement to the Casa

Paget. But somewhere in the course of writing *Miss Brown* her humor darkened, and a potentially clever satire became a moralistic indictment of a
whole society. The more she observed contemporary London, the more art
and literature of the period she absorbed, the more critical she became. In
the summer of 1883 Sargent's portrait of the Pailleron children—the young
boy and his sister gazing solemnly at the viewer—was on exhibit at the Fine
Arts Gallery in London. "It is a splendid work," she wrote her mother,
"which, so healthy and wholesome, does one good to see after all this scrofulous English art. Oscar Wilde, who is lecturing here at 10/6 the seat, calls
John's art vicious and meritricious—I wonder what we should call Rossetti's. What particularly affected me is the frightful discrepancy between
the morbid coarseness of his painting and the Dantesque delicacy of his poems. His picture of the Blessed Damozel is the most marvellous misinterpretation of the poem I can conceive" (11 July 1883). Independent of social
convention herself, indifferent to fashions and trends, she held fast to the
strict code of morality she had learned from her mother, especially in matters of sex.

Violet recognized in her own life as in Miss Brown's a human need for
love and companionship, but she felt only revulsion at the thought of sexual intimacy. In *Miss Brown,* as Léonee Ormond notes, she became "a militant Puritan." Ormond detects precisely the fatal weakness of the novel:
"Vernon Lee was not a prude of the conventional type. She was personally
repelled and obsessed by the whole idea of the love relationship, and particularly its physical side, and this distaste colored her whole attitude to life
and art" (151). This is certainly reflected in Miss Brown's horrified reaction to her cousin Richard's sudden declaration of his passion for her: "The
quiet brotherly and sisterly affection had all been a sham, a sham for her and
for himself. . . . Her cousin had preached against selfish aestheticism, had
talked her into his positivistic philanthropy. . . . What for? that he might
satisfy his whim of possessing her" (3:75–76). And when Walter Hamlin responds "with a long kiss on the mouth" after she offers to marry him, she
recoils with disgust: "She drew back and loosened his grasp with her strong
hands," recalling her similar reaction to a kiss from Madame Elaguine: "It
seemed to Anne as if she felt the throttling arms of Sacha Elaguine about
her neck, her convulsive kiss on her face, the cloud of her drowsily scented
hair, stifling her" (3:298).[3]

Sexuality, however, was not the principal target of Vernon Lee's attack
in *Miss Brown.* What she most deplored was the perversion of aestheticism
that, in her mind, turned the lofty Platonic aestheticism of Walter Pater into
sensuality and hedonism. The statement in her early essay "Ruskinism" in

Belcaro that "beauty is pure, complete, egotistic; it has no other value than its being beautiful" (210) was perverse perhaps, as was Oscar Wilde's declaration in "The Decay of Lying" (1889) that "as long as a thing is useful or necessary to us in any way, either for pain or pleasure, or appeals strongly to our sympathies, or is a vital part of the environment in which we live, it is outside the proper sphere of art" (21). But these are different in their implications from what Théophile Gautier had written in his notorious *Mademoiselle de Maupin:* "There is nothing truly beautiful but that which can never be of any use whatsoever; everything useful is ugly, for it is the expression of some need, and man's needs are ignoble and disgusting like his own poor and infirm nature. The most useful place in the house is the water-closet" (27). It is Gautier as Vernon Lee reads him who informs the aestheticism of *Miss Brown.* One of the most repellant characters in the book, Edward Lewis, recommends *Mademoiselle de Maupin* to Miss Brown, and she indignantly rejects his suggestion: "I have never read it . . . but I have often heard that it is a book which a man does not offer a woman except as an insult" (2:150). Vernon Lee, however, had read the book and found its celebration of the "new paganism," with its emphasis on sexual experimentation and promiscuity, depraved. She perceived a resurgence of this spirit in what, a few years later, Grant Allen labeled the "new hedonism" and Oscar Wilde personified in the moral iconoclasm of Lord Henry Wotton in *The Picture of Dorian Gray.*

At one point in the novel Miss Brown hopefully foresees a change: "The aesthetic school of poetry, of which Hamlin and Chough were the most brilliant exponents of the younger generation, was evidently running to seed. It was beginning to be obvious to everyone who was not an aesthete, that the reign of the mysterious evil passions, of the half-antique, half-mediaeval ladies of saturnine beauty and blood-thirsty voluptuousness, of the demigods and heroes treated like features in a piece of tapestry, must be coming to a close, and that a return to nature must be preparing" (2:71). But with Anne Brown's self-immolation and Madame Elaguine's survival at the end of the novel, Vernon Lee appears to be conceding victory to the enemy and anticipating the Decadent movement that would flourish in the next decade. The end product of this perverted version of aestheticism, she warns in *Miss Brown,* is "the belief in the fatal supremacy of evil and ugliness."

It is small wonder then that *Miss Brown* left its first readers confused, frustrated, and in a number of instances positively offended.[4] Nor could it have been comforting to its author that a novelist like Ouida admired her work: "It both amused and interested me. . . . The book gives me the impression of having been written at a galop [*sic*]; but this is better than weeding and

pruning till all flavour is gone" (Gunn 103). But more-discriminating readers complained of a surfeit of "flavour" in *Miss Brown*—all of it nasty. Nevertheless *Miss Brown* sold reasonably well, and most reviewers were polite,
some even—with reservations—favorable.[5] The unsigned review in the
Athenaeum (6 December 1884) begins enthusiastically: "The readers of Vernon Lee's former books will be quite prepared for the ability shown in 'Miss
Brown,' but they will hardly have expected her to write such a good novel."
The praise is confined to the first half of the novel. "In the second half there
is a perceptible falling off." The reviewer proceeds to undermine the initial
praise with objections to her characterizations (Madame Elaguine is "disagreeable and unnatural," Hamlin "a wretched creature," Richard Brown "a
mere lay figure . . . one of the weak points in the book"), her misleading and
inaccurate picture of the Pre-Raphaelite movement, and her writing style
("better than we expected, but would be much improved by revision").

In the *Academy* (3 January 1885), W. C. (William Cosmo) Monkhouse
generously overlooked her use of his middle name in the character Cosmo
Chough, but he found her attack on the aesthetic movement, with its mixture of real and fictitious names, "needlessly painful and unpleasant," and
the attempted satire heavy-handed: "so unsavoury a theme becomes sickening unless treated with the tact and taste of a Thackeray." Privately he wrote
her, "Whatever made you write about such beastly people, do you want to
rival Ouida?" When she replied that it had never been her intention to be
insulting, he answered, "This shows a want of *rapport* between yourself and
those who you wish to be your readers" (Gunn 102–3). The *Pall Mall Gazette*'s reviewer (13 December 1884), less charitable to the excesses of aestheticism than Monkhouse, dismissed her attempts at satire as "rather a stale
joke now" and complained that "she wants humour, which is indeed obvious enough from the mere fact of her taking aestheticism seriously."

The novel cost her dearly. Whatever Vernon Lee's intentions, *Miss Brown*
was read as a roman à clef. It is more attributable to her naïveté than to malice that so many of her characters were readily identified. Her cousin Adah
Hughes, who had been shocked by the earlier *Countess of Albany,* found details in *Miss Brown* that she thought were based on gossip Violet had heard
and people she had met while her guest in Wales. Accusing her of a "very
great breach of hospitality," as Violet wrote her mother, Adah had complained that the loathsome Sacha had been modeled on some gossip Adah
had reported to her about one Madame Skariatine. More serious was Adah's
charge that Hamlin was drawn from one of her brothers and his name taken
from their grandfather Edward Hamlin Adams. "But the thing is a piece of
the usual ridiculous self-importance and touchiness as if all the world had
heard of Adah and her brothers and cousins. As to *The Countess of Albany,*

I couldn't help laughing when I came to that: what could she have found in *that anodyne* little book?" (15 August 1886).

The most far-fetched identification, but one made by several readers of the book, was that of Walter Hamlin with Walter Pater. She showed shocking insensitivity in many of her characterizations, but she was certainly not portraying Pater in "young Hamlin in his girlish beauty . . . a sort of mixture of Apollo and Eros," a wealthy dilettante mingling in stylish society, dabbling in poetry and painting. There may have been some unconscious impulse in her giving the character the same first name and a two-syllable surname, but she might also have had in mind Walter Hamilton, who wrote a popular book, *The Aesthetic Movement in England* (1882), defending Pre-Raphaelitism against "the affected and superficial Aestheticism which had been forced into a hothouse existence by caricaturists, and fostered by those who mistake slang, and stained glass attitudes for culture and high art" (142). Pater seems to have noticed no personal connection with the novel; he acknowledged the copy Violet sent him with no hint of embarrassment: "Miss Brown arrived safely some days ago, and I have already read the greater part of it with much interest and amusement. I send only brief thanks now in answer to your card of this morning, hoping to write at length before long" (*Letters* 56). There is no record of his opinion when and if he finished the book, nor of his reaction to a review by Julia Wedgwood in the *Contemporary Review* for May 1885 in which she treated *Miss Brown* and *Marius the Epicurean* as companion novels that "paint the confused condition of thought in our day better than any essay or sermon but are interesting only for that."

The Hamlin-Pater parallel is merely clumsy, but other characters managed to offend a number of prominent writers and their friends. Not specifically targeted in *Miss Brown,* William Sharp, the Catholic Revival poet and short-story writer who published under the name Fiona Macleod, apparently felt victimized and never forgave her. Years later Bernard Berenson reported that Sharp's widow, who visited the galleries of Florence with him, "furied against Vernon who fifteen years ago must have been a holy terror— worse far than she is now. Vernonia really had no right to run down poor Sharp's verses so—she who thinks alphabet Robinson so great a poet" (*Letters* 48). Whether real or imagined, the sources for many of these characters were wounded. The fictional Mrs. Argiropoulo, for example, a society hostess celebrated for her high art parties—"a lion-hunting lady . . . extremely vulgar looking"—has a Greek surname recalling the real-life hostesses of the wealthy Anglo-Greek Ionides family, patrons of avant-garde artists like Rossetti. Another prominent hostess who might have figured in Mrs. Argiropoulo was Mrs. Charles Tennant, who entertained in a splendid house in Whitehall where Violet attended "a salon or rather a salle of nothing but rank, beauty, and genius. I was asked in the latter capacity" (Gunn 85). Unfortunately, one of Violet's good friends from Florence days, Mrs. William Stillman, who had been born Marie Spartoli of Greek parents and had sat for a painting by Rossetti, saw some elements of herself in Mrs. Argiropoulo and wrote Violet prophetically, 27 December 1884: "I am sure Miss Brown will cause you many 'dispiaceri' and altho' I know you love polemics and are indifferent to criticism I feel that you have done yourself great injustice and you will one day regret this work."

Others who were embarrassed to find themselves in relatively transparent roles in the novel included William Rossetti, who appears as Mr. Spencer, "a stodgy reviewer" (1:310). His wife Lucy, who had been especially kind to Violet when she first came to London, appears as the shallow Mrs. Spencer, "whose soul was divided between her babies and fierce rancours against all enemies of Pre-Raphaelitism" (2:103). William Rossetti also had reason to resent the early scenes of the novel in which Hamlin's manner of painting and his infatuation with a beautiful but uneducated young woman must have recalled painful memories of his brother Dante Gabriel. He had died only two years earlier, and his wife and model Elizabeth Siddal, whom he had discovered working in a milliner's shop, had committed suicide twenty years earlier.

Also not amused at finding himself in *Miss Brown* was Oscar Wilde, who appears as Posthlethwaite, "an elephantine person . . . flabby, fat-cheeked face," wearing a Japanese lily for a boutonniere and scattering epigrams of not remarkably brilliant wit (2:4). Having already been caricatured in *Punch* as Jellaby Postlethwaite (Vernon Lee added an extra *h* to the name), he avoided meeting her again until about ten years later when, on a visit to Florence in May 1894, he accompanied Mary Costelloe (later Mrs. Bernard Berenson) to the Casa Paget to meet Eugene Lee-Hamilton, whose poetry he admired. According to Mary's account, the meeting "was a great success. Oscar talked like an angel, and they all fell in love with him — even Vernon, who had hated him almost as bitterly as he had hated her. He, on his part, was charmed with her . . . when he met her before he found her restless and self-assertive. But yesterday he admitted that she had grown less strenuous" (M. Berenson, *Self-Portrait* 56).

The most wounding identification was of Jane Morris as Miss Brown. Physically they are mirror images. Jane Morris, the icon of Pre-Raphaelite womanhood, was the wife of William Morris and had been model for and mistress of Dante Gabriel Rossetti. Like Miss Brown she was statuesque, with large dark eyes and masses of curly ("crimped") dark hair. Even more tellingly, she came from a lower-class background and had been introduced to society by her worshiping husband. Most of those who recognized themselves in the novel or were offended by what they perceived as insults to their friends eventually forgave Vernon Lee, but the Morrises never forgot.

When she returned to London in June 1885, fortified by the encouragement she had received from her mother and Eugene, Violet was determined to face down her critics. "I am very glad I have come," she wrote home triumphantly. "I have got the better of any intention to give me the cold shoulder." Mrs. Humphry Ward, though not personally lampooned in *Miss Brown,* was at first chilly, but Violet persisted: "I went up to her as bold as brass; she looked shy; but I wasn't shy; it ended in her being extremely gracious and asking me down to her farm near Guildford." The social slights may have been insignificant, but there were more-painful blows to her self-esteem. Criticism from reviewers could be shrugged off, protests from friends, or former friends, could be rationalized, but the opinions of those few she truly admired and even looked up to as mentors mattered. Walter Pater, though gracious in his few comments, failed to offer the praise he had heaped on her earlier books. And the one contemporary novelist she truly respected remained inscrutable for months after the publication of her book.

Henry James had acknowledged receipt of *Miss Brown* with thanks, and a month later he wrote to explain that the pressure of work prevented him from completing his reading of it. In fact he had read it promptly, but, as he explained to his friend Thomas Perry, he felt compromised by the dedication and by his friendship with her. "But I may whisper in your ear that as it is her first attempt at a novel, so it is to be hoped that it may be her last. It is very bad, *strangely* inferior to her other writing, and (to me at least) painfully disagreeable in tone." Articulate as he was, James was at a loss for words: "I am sadly put to it to know what to write to her. I think I shall be brave and tell her what I think—or at least a little of it. The whole would never do" (*Letters,* ed. Edel, 3:61).

A few months later James had still not summoned the courage to write her. Instead, on 24 January 1885, he sent a thorough assessment of the novel to his American friend Grace Norton:

> Has the fame of the unfortunate "Miss Brown" reached the U.S.A.? Such is the title of a disagreeable and really very unpleasant novel dedicated to me, by Vernon Lee, which appeared here a couple of months since, and about which I haven't even yet been able to bring myself to write the authoress, though my delay, in view of the dedication and the first copy being sent me is scandalous. You probably know that Vernon Lee is the pen-name of

a certain astounding young woman named Violet Paget, who lives in Florence, spends part of her time here, and has written two or three very unperfect, but very able and interesting books on the Italian Renaissance. . . . She has not the kind of ability that a novel requires, and *Miss Brown* is a rather serious mistake (I think) . . . with an awful want of taste, and you will say of *decency*—yet it has *du bon,* and is an interesting failure, if an unsavoury one. I tell you this, however, not that you should read it if it is republished in America, but that you shouldn't! (*Letters* 3:66)

It wasn't until May 10, nearly five months after *Miss Brown* had appeared, that he composed his letter to its author, a masterpiece of discretion and tact but also a sound and shrewd critique of the novel. He began with a profuse apology "for my distressing conduct, my odious, unmannerly and inconceivable delay in writing to you." Then with characteristic delicacy he gets to the substance of the matter. The book is "imperfect" but "interesting . . . bravely and richly and continuously psychological." Miss Brown herself is nobly conceived: "Anne lives in the mind . . . as a creature projected (from your intelligence) in all her strange, original, tragic substance and form, with real imaginative and moral superiority." The *donné* of the novel is "exceedingly in the right direction . . . appealing to the intelligence, the moral sense and experience of the reader." But it is precisely in the moral sense, James perceived, that the novel—or rather the novelist—went wrong. She had been "too much in a moral passion," and in her "ferocity" she has produced "exaggerations, overstatements, *grossissiments,* instances wanting in tact" (*Letters* 3:84–87).

Criticism like James's was all too familiar to Violet by 1885. Five years earlier, commenting on her eighteenth-century studies, John Addington Symonds had advised her to follow the composer Sacchini's motto of "clarity, beauty, good modulation." James advises: "Cool first—write afterwards. Morality is hot—but art is icy!" With the zeal of an evangelicizing Puritan she had allowed no middle ground. As he explains: "There is a certain want of perspective and proportion. You are really too savage with your painters and poets and dilettanti; *life* is less critical, less obnoxious, less objectionable, less crude, more *bon enfant,* more mixed and casual, and even in its most offensive manifestations, more *pardonable* than the unholy circle with which you have surrounded your heroine." As if to soften his diplomatically phrased but deadly accurate criticism, James ends his letter with good wishes. He urges her—one suspects with fingers crossed—to write another novel, more carefully crafted and "less moral," and assures her of his goodwill. Of his goodwill there can be no question. In July 1885 she wrote her mother that James had called on her and advised her encouragingly: "He came to see me again yesterday afternoon. He says his plan through life has been never to lose an opportunity of seeing anything of any kind; he urges me to do the same. He says that chance may enable me to see more of English life, if I keep my wits about me. He is really very kind and wise, I think." They continued to see each other in London and Florence and remained on friendly terms until 1892 when, no longer driven by moral outrage but as oblivious as ever to the sensitivity of others, Vernon Lee introduced Henry James transparently and unflatteringly as a character in her short story "Lady Tal."

However boldly she faced the world, Violet knew that her novel had been a mistake. "Life is too serious to be represented as it is in *Miss Brown*," she admitted to herself in a journal entry in 1890, and as late as 1920 she looked back regretfully: "What a pity I didn't put off writing *Miss Brown* for thirty years!" (Gunn 107). The permanent scar left by the criticism of her novel was less a challenge to her ability to write a novel (she was to publish two more) than a challenge to her moral sense. It was not so much her heavy-handed and mostly wrongheaded satire that had offended readers, but the morally outrageous ending of the novel—Miss Brown's marriage to a man she neither loves nor respects, in the perverse (some would say perverted) belief that although she cannot redeem him, she will nurse him as "a person sick of an incurable disease." James had called her decision "false, really unimaginable." Others professed horror and disgust—none more vigorously than the unsigned reviewer in the *Spectator* (13 December 1884), who struck directly at the heart of Violet's faith in her own moral probity. "We cannot review this book at the length its powers would justify, the subject being too repulsive," it begins. Within a single paragraph Violet's vulnerability was painfully exposed. Only a great poet, the reviewer continues, could represent Miss Brown, a noble heroine, moving like Spenser's Una unsoiled through "the vileness of the London fleshly school." Vernon Lee is not a poet, "only a strong writer overloaded with knowledge, who exaggerates the area of the sexual question in life and who, in long study of early Italian literature and the history of the Renaissance, has lost touch with English feeling, and does not always know what is good to say or leave unsaid." As a writer who had dedicated herself to the higher aestheticism, Vernon Lee had assumed the moral superiority of art, transcending physical beauty and the demands of the flesh. But to her dismay, the *Spectator* implied what Henry James later confirmed, that the novel *Miss Brown* (and hence its author) was obsessed with sex: "Zola would have shrunk from some touches [in it] . . . not so much bad or vicious as putrescent."

In the reflective quiet of New Year's Eve 1884, only a few weeks after she had read that review, Violet confronted the alarming possibilities and confided to her journal:

> It strikes me now, perhaps all those people are right, perhaps the British public is right; perhaps I have no right to argue on the matter, because I may be colour blind about the data. Here I am accused of having, in simplicity of heart, written, with a view to moralise the world, an immoral book, accused of having done more mischief by setting my readers' imagination hunting up evil, than I could possibly do good by calling on their sympathies to hate that mischief: accused, in short, of doing, in a minor degree, the very things for which I execrate Zola or Maupassant. . . . I say to myself, "What if these people were right, or at least nearer the truth than I?" . . . I, who have written so many fine things about the complexity of our nature, the surprise at the deceptions to which these complexities subject us, the extreme difficulty of knowing one's self—am I not perhaps mistaking that call of the beast for the call of God; may there not, at the bottom of this seemingly scientific, philanthropic, idealising, decidedly noble-looking nature of mine, lie something base, dangerous, disgraceful that is cozening me?[6]

She had much to learn, and the experience of *Miss Brown* was only the first in a series of painful lessons.

Ah! well for us, if even we,
Even for a moment, can get free
Our heart, and have our lips unchained;
For that which seals them hath been deep-ordained.

Matthew Arnold, "The Buried Life"

As one who goes between high garden walls,
Along a road that never has an end,
With still the empty way behind, in front,
Which he must pace for evermore alone—
So, even so, is Life to every soul,
Walled in with barriers which no Love can break.

. . . .

For ever, irremediably alone,
Not only I or thou, but every soul,
Each cased and fastened with invisible walls.
Shall we go mad with it? or bear a front
Of desperate courage doomed to fail and break?
Or trudge in sullen patience to the end?

Mary Robinson, "Personality: A Sestina"

THE JOURNAL ENTRY THAT CLOSED THE MOMENTOUS YEAR 1884 was the first open expression of a fear that was to plague Violet Paget for the rest of her life. It was not mistrust of her ability to observe, interpret, and report correctly and, by her lights, eloquently on all manner of subjects. Although *Miss Brown* had failed, she had no doubts of her vocation as a writer or of her power to command an audience of educated, thoughtful readers. But for the first time she confronted the possibility that her moral judgment was fallible and that its principal victim might be herself. The resilience that had carried her triumphantly through her youth—this plain-

looking, socially awkward young woman who wrote and talked so brilliantly
—was losing its elasticity. In itself the painful confession of New Year's Eve
1884 was no more significant than the transitory end-of-the-year melancholy common to most of us. It was confirmed, however, by a new note of
nostalgia that came increasingly to dominate her writings of the later 1880s
and the 1890s. The familiar dogmatism and self-assurance were still conspicuous, but along with these there is an uneasy sense of loss. What, until
she wrote *Miss Brown,* had seemed so absolute—the moral transcendence
of beauty whether in nature or in art, music, and poetry—was now exposed
as merely another theory, a hypothesis that demanded repeated testing and
even possibly modification or, worse yet, rejection. Suddenly the certainties
were only possibilities. Aesthetics was not enough, not adequate to shape
and condition our moral judgments on others or on ourselves.

There were, as we have noted, conjectures about the real-life inspiration
for Miss Brown. To outsiders the most likely model was Jane Morris. To
those more intimately connected with Violet there was in the large striking
presence and strong moral fiber of Anne Brown something of Annie Meyer,
for whom Violet had had the first of her adult attachments. Two strong-
minded women, each outspoken and convinced of her own beliefs, they
were not destined for happy intimacy and had quarreled some years before
Mrs. Meyer's death in 1884. Violet may have exorcised Annie Meyer's ghost
by introducing her in the philosophic dialogue "The Consolations of Belief" in *Baldwin* as Agatha Stuart, but she never forgot her. But a more
likely source lay closer at hand, although apparently only Mary Robinson's
shrewd and outspoken sister Mabel perceived it.

The Robinson sisters enjoyed a private joke about Violet's pen name—
one that was less than flattering but taken in good spirit by her—calling her
"little vermin flea." In a letter to Violet, then back home in Florence, on
14 December 1885, Mabel reported Mary's idea that the aesthete Walter
Hamlin "is a true portrait of that said flea as seen by itself." Mabel herself,
however, brusquely rejected the suggestion of Hamlin as the author's self-
portrait. Instead she wrote that Miss Brown "in all her sudden impulses and
tricks of expression reminds me of a certain animal (not without piquancy
and charm) familiarly known as the 'little vermin flea.'" Any overt resemblance between Violet Paget and the beautiful Anne Brown is too far-fetched
to contemplate, but the novelist Vernon Lee had created a character out of
her imagination. She had modeled her heroine physically and to some degree circumstantially on Jane Morris. But her beauty is only an excuse for
the plot. Anne Brown's singularity is an otherworldly quality. She is a char-
ismatic figure, with a power to inspire and spiritually ennoble those who

respond to her, as Hamlin was inspired until he yielded to the temptations of fashionable "high art." She is superior to mere mortal appetites, a transcendent asexual creature:

> Some few women seem to have been born to have been men, or at least not to have been women. To them love, if it come, will be an absorbing passion only of brief duration, the mere momentary diversion into a personal and individual channel of a force which constitutes the whole moral and intellectual existence, whose object is an unattainable ideal of excellence, and whose field is the whole of the world in which there is injustice, and callousness, and evil. . . . Masculine women, mere men in disguise, they are not; the very strength and purity of their nature, its intensity as of some undiluted spirit, is dependent on their cleaner and narrower woman's nature, upon their narrowness and obstinacy of woman's mind; they are, and can only be, true women; but women without women's instinct and wants, sexless—women made not for man but for humankind. Anne Brown was one of these. (2:307–9)

As Mabel Robinson came close to guessing, Anne Brown is the Vernon Lee that Violet Paget longed to be. Her sexuality is idealized into some Shelleyan abstraction of womanhood. The first inkling of her genuine power comes not in Hamlin's infatuation with her but in a schoolgirl's hysterical grief when Anne leaves the school in Germany: "She ran to the window and seized the struggling small creature in her powerful arms, and knelt down before her, clasping her round the waist: 'Oh, forgive me! forgive me!' cried Anne, as the consciousness of the girl's love, which she had never before perceived, came upon her" (1:239). At that point in the novel we are reminded, "But she was already thinking of Hamlin." By volume 3, however, Anne has lost her illusions about her benefactor, as she has also about her cousin Richard Brown. But she is now beloved by another who, like the poet in "The Buried Life," cannot express that love. Mary Leigh, who had nursed her through a near fatal illness, idolizes her:

> She had often longed to tell her so; she longed at this moment to put her arms round Anne's neck, and say quite quietly—'I love you, Anne'; but she had not the courage. How much may this sort of cowardice, called reticence, cheat people of? The knowledge that there is a loving heart near one, that there is a creature whom one can trust, that the world is not a desert,—all this might be given, but is not. And the other regrets, perhaps throughout life, that word which remained unspoken, that kiss which remained ungiven, and would have been as the draught of water to the wearied traveller. (3:10–11)

This is as public a declaration of her feelings for Mary Robinson as Violet ever dared to make. Transferred to a minor character and safely disguised as fiction, it passed unnoticed, publicly at least. There was no murmur of disapproval from the Casa Paget in Florence, where Mary continued to pass some months with Violet every autumn. The Robinsons, however, were becoming uneasy about the intimacy of the two young women. They also had reason for irritation at their guest's only too obvious interest in promoting herself. Thanks to them she was meeting the most influential publishers, editors, and writers in London. Her bold assault on these people and her rebarbative comments about them—which she apparently did not confine to her letters home—could not have pleased her hosts. And she did indeed monopolize the attention of their daughter.

Mary and her younger sister Mabel had accompanied her in July 1881 on her first visit to Oxford, where the Humphry Wards introduced her to a wide circle of their friends, among them Walter Pater; she was guided around the colleges and the neighboring countryside and saw a performance of *Patience,* which delighted her. However, when she returned to London, again a houseguest of the Robinsons, the petty frictions between her and Mr. Robinson, whom she described to her mother as "an extremely hard and tyrannical little man," exploded. It was Violet's intention to spend some time in France on her way back to Florence, stopping in Brittany to visit her cousin Pauline, who had refused Eugene's marriage proposal years before and was now Madame de Cargouet. Violet planned to have Mary accompany her on this visit. Although Mary had been invited, Madame de Cargouet neglected to write her parents for permission, and Mr. Robinson, more irritated by Violet's cool assumption that she could take Mary along than by the absence of a formal invitation, forbade her to go.

A minor rift, all soon healed, and Mary was again a guest at the Casa Paget in the autumn of 1881. The following summer Violet returned to England once more to stay with the Robinsons in London. On her way she stopped in Paris to see her childhood friends Emily and John Sargent, who had already won distinction as a painter and was exhibiting at the Salon. Once settled in Gower Street, she resumed her busy social life. Humphry Ward had just been appointed an editor of the London *Times* and had moved with his family to a house in Russell Square. Transplanted from Oxford to the lively London scene, Mary Ward, now herself launched on a writing career, was a generous hostess.[1] At the Robinson tertullas, at Mrs. Ward's parties, and at those of the journalist and psychical researcher Edward Gurney and of her old friend Mrs. Stillman, Violet made new acquaintances. She visited the William Morrises in their "aesthetic house" in Hammersmith, the Alma Tademas in a house in Regent's Park crowded with his decorously

Victorian paintings of pagan Roman life, and the William Rossettis with
their collection of his brother's work. Unfortunately, Violet could not confine her acid-edged and sometimes cruel observations to her family, who
were amused by them. Except when writing about Mary, she never failed to
balance her neutral comments with nasty ones. Gurney is handsome "but
is more like a butler with a dash of guardsman"; Thackeray's daughter Anne,
married to Richmond Ritchie, twenty years her junior, is "a sentimental,
leering, fleshy, old person who would marry her godson, and who seems
quite brimming over at the idea of having babies at an age when she ought
to be ashamed of it"; Richard Garnett, who gave her sound advice on placing her work, is "blinking, smirking . . . very obsequiously & shyly civil"
(Gunn 84–85; Cary, "VL's Vignettes" 182).

Violet may not have expressed herself quite so candidly to the Robinsons, but she was incapable of repressing her strong opinions. She became
increasingly irritating to the family—to Mabel, who felt slighted by her devotion to Mary; to Mr. Robinson, who sensed a rival for his rule over his
household; and to Mrs. Robinson, who sympathized with Mabel and must
surely have been concerned about Mary's attachment to Violet. A petty misunderstanding over an invitation to a Royal Academy reception led to an
open quarrel in which Mrs. Robinson declared that Violet was upsetting
the peace of the family. She complained, Violet wrote home, "that until I
came there had never been a happier house . . . that since I had come there
had been nothing but disagreeables . . . that I had ruined their family peace,
and that for her part she thought that if I couldn't agree with people I had
better go." She left a few days later with Mary, writing her mother: "You see
the outburst might have been pardoned, but I can never pardon not being
thought worthy of a word of apology when I alone was the injured person.
Mary, darling, acted very well, with perfect respect towards her mother, but
with perfect firmness in asking for reparation and determining to stick by me.
Indeed I love her more than ever, and feel more than ever that we couldn't
give each other up" (20 July 1882). Planning her battle strategy with care,
Violet enlisted sympathy from her mother and Eugene and a promise that
Mary would always be welcome at the Casa Paget, a refuge from her philistine family who failed to recognize and foster her literary talent. With a
comfortable income of her own, Mary "is determined not to let herself be
separated any more from me." Violet had rescued Mary from the tyranny of
her family and was confident of the support of her mother and her brother:
"I feel at the same time a certain relief that now matters lie much more exclusively between ourselves and Mary."

A few days after the quarrel in Gower Street, the two women rented a
secluded country cottage in Sussex where Violet could resume her writing

in peace. They read, worked, and lived in idyllic domesticity. She wrote her
mother that Mary "is a most excellent housekeeper and she is so sweet and
cheerful when she has nothing but me and a few books and the country to
amuse her" (Gardner 165). She added that because she was disturbed by bugs
in her room, she had begun sleeping in Mary's bedroom. At the end of July
they separated, friends as ever. Violet spent a few days in Oxford as a guest
of the Paters, then went to Llanfair in Wales to stay with her cousin Adah
Hughes. Here she took the opportunity to see her mother's girlhood home,
Middleton Hall. It was now out of the family's hands, but she was given
permission to visit the house, where the portraits of her mother and grand-
parents were still hanging on the walls. The English summer was drawing
to a close, but before leaving she spent a few more days with Mary in the
country. She returned briefly to the Robinsons to pick up her luggage and
apparently to make peace with them. Her journey back to Italy was leisurely
with a few days in Belgium and a boat trip on the Rhine, which disappointed
her because the scenes of the German legends she had so loved in childhood
lost their enchantment in modern reality. By the end of August she was with
her family, back at work and looking forward to Mary's autumn visit.

The winter passed busily and uneventfully in Florence, and the following summer, 1883, she returned to London. On this visit she stayed in lodgings in Kensington with Bella Duffy, another of her literary women friends
whom she had first met in Florence in 1880.[2] She saw a good deal of Mary
of course and spent the month of August with her in the country. There
were old friends to visit and new people, like the painters G. F. Watts and
Sir Frederick Leighton, whose remarkable house in Kensington she described to her mother: "This is quite the 8th wonder of the world, including a Moorish cupola place, with a fountain, all lined with precious Persian
tiles and mosaics by Walter Crane, as good almost as a Ravenna church. Sir
Frederick is a mixture of Olympian Jove and a head waiter, a superb deco-
rator and a superb piece of decoration, paints poor pictures of correctest
idealism, of orange tawny naked women against indigo skies" (Gunn 88).
By now her exposure, or overexposure, to fashionable art was producing the
raw material for *Miss Brown*. Her reaction was less one of aesthetic distaste
than of moral outrage. Visiting the private collections of Sir Frederick Ley-
land, including Whistler's famous and controversial Peacock Room, she saw
a portrait of her friend Mrs. Stillman painted as "Veronica Veronese"—"a
vile caricature, with goitry throat, red hair and German housemaid sentiment," and another of Jane Morris "making her look as if her face were covered with ill-shaven stubble and altogether repulsive . . . [all] not merely ill
painted and worse modelled, but coarse and repulsive; and to make mere

painted diseased harlots of women like Mrs. Stillman and Mrs. Morris requires a good deal" (Gunn 88).

The pattern of summers with Mary in England and autumns with Mary in Florence continued unbroken until 1887. Having resumed reasonably friendly relations with the Robinsons, who had moved to Earl's Terrace in Kensington in 1883, she stayed with them from time to time. Their house continued to be a center for literary social life. Walter Pater, who had resigned his tutorship at Brasenose College in 1883, moved with his sisters to London in 1885, and they became the Robinsons' neighbors in Earl's Terrace. The tertullas were flourishing. Violet met the Irish nationalist and novelist Justin McCarthy and his son Justin, also a novelist and historian; she met George Moore and Edmund Gosse and renewed her friendship with Henry James. She visited her old friend John Sargent in his studio in Chelsea and his country retreat in the picturesque village of Broadway in Oxfordshire. In 1884 she traveled in the north of England, observing, as only a foreigner could fully appreciate, the dramatic contrast between the still beautiful but shrinking pastoral landscape and a rapidly growing industrial economy. Her condemnation of the self-indulgent and self-centered Walter Hamlin in *Miss Brown* was influenced by the degrading conditions of the laboring classes that she observed in Leeds and Newcastle. Her hostess in Leeds was Emily Ford, of a family rich enough to be philanthropic and cultivate a social conscience. Through them Violet was introduced to new forms of political activism, as Miss Brown would be by her friends the Leigh sisters and her positivist cousin Richard. She attended meetings where the idealistic rich, avowed radicals, and men and women simply interested in social reform listened to lectures by the socialist William Morris, the Marxist H. M. Hyndman, and the Fabian Annie Besant.

At this stage in her life Violet Paget was a sympathetic observer rather than a social activist, curious but not committed to any political philosophy. Much of what she observed at these meetings struck her as well intentioned but silly: the prosperous upper classes vicariously thrilled by the oratory of radicals and nihilists prophesying their doom. A faithful reporter, she described these audiences to her family in Florence as "mainly women, with a sprinkling of aesthetic men" and society hostesses like Lady Dorothy Nevill eager to have "ardent agnostics" (to use R. H. Hutton's phrase) like Cotter Morison and radical trade unionists like Henry Hyde Champion (in Violet's words "a tall young-looking man, very beautifully dressed, with a carnation in his button hole . . . a sort of St. Just le Vertueux, with a head ripe for the guillotine") at their dinner tables (Gunn 117).[3] Violet had come to England without any ideological baggage. From her mother, "a mass of contradictions" as she described her, she had acquired a residual eighteenth-century Enlightenment humanitarianism, a distrust of established authority, a *de haut en bas* sympathy for the poor. Mrs. Paget's only passionate social commitment—which her daughter shared wholly—was antivivisection-ism. Both were outraged by the often cruel treatment of their working animals by Italian peasants but relatively indifferent to the harsh conditions of the lives of the peasants themselves. In her essay "Of Honour and Evolution" (*Baldwin*), she outlined her political philosophy as a latter-day version of Plato's *Republic* with governance by philosopher-kings, not royalty but an aristocracy of the morally and intellectually elite. She envisioned an "evolutionary morality . . . our new creed of the perpetual development of the nobler by the perpetual elimination of the baser motives of their nature" (183).

In practical terms Violet was happy enough to associate with the social elite, accepting but not necessarily ignoring their intellectual and moral limitations. At the dinner tables and receptions of Mrs. Charles Tennant, Lady Dorothy Nevill, and Lady Jeune she felt herself in the center of English society. Much as she ridiculed her hostesses and their guests in her letters home, she was flattered by their attention and she respected their power. Lady Dorothy Nevill and her "frumpy" daughter Meresia may have been "quivering with political fervour," but as the equally patrician Lady Jeune recalled, "Lady Dorothy's house was a sort of whispering gallery; all her friends were *dans le mouvement,* and she knew everything that was going on."[4] Violet's friend Alice Callandar, Annie Meyer's niece, who became a lady-in-waiting to Queen Victoria, introduced her to her sister-in-law, the beautiful Lady Archibald Campbell. In 1885 "Lady Archie" invited her to an outdoor production of Fletcher's *The Faithful Shepherdess* at Combe Park, in Surrey, and insisted on using her influence to help Violet publish her impressions of the play. Lady Archibald's efforts were not successful, but Violet had no trouble placing her essay, "Perigot: Random Notes on the Dramatic and Undramatic," in the *Contemporary Review* for August 1886. (It was later collected in *Juvenilia*.)[5]

In all these activities Violet Paget was gathering ideas and material for her writing. Essentially art and aesthetics, not social problems, remained her dominant interest throughout the 1880s. It was their vulgarization in "high art" that she deplored in *Miss Brown*. Increasingly she detected in herself and in the world around her the vanishing of the ideal of pure beauty, the loss of innocence and the spontaneous appreciation of the beautiful and therefore of the good. Addressing her friend Carlo Placci, to whom she dedicated the essays in *Juvenilia* in 1887, she wrote almost envyingly as an older woman to a young friend emerging from "intellectual boyhood": "The Beautiful, you will say, the Beautiful thus contemptuously classified under the head of 'Juvenilia,' is the beautiful not merely of material objects but of the soul. We, who are young . . . are not mere fiddle-faddle dilettanti, adorers of roulades and Japanese lacqueur and 'Odes Funambulesques.' We are serious; and seriously seeking for the beautiful, and for what is the same as the beautiful, the good" (1:5–6).

For Violet Paget in 1887 the beautiful and the good were receding. This was an aesthetic crisis, but it was also becoming a personal one. She had recovered from the wounds to her self-esteem inflicted by the reception of *Miss Brown*, but a more serious threat was emerging in the possibility of estrangement from Mary Robinson. Although their attachment to each other remained strong, they were now often separated. Violet was determined to advance her career by traveling as widely and observing as much as possible, since in Florence for half the year she lived an enclosed life in the family nest. There were, to be sure, guests from the outside world. Among them was the young Jewish poet and novelist Amy Levy, who stayed at the Casa Paget in 1885, four years before she committed suicide; she paid her host tribute in a poem, "To Vernon Lee":

On Bellosguardo, when the year was young,
We wandered seeking for the daffodil
And dark anemone, whose purples fill
The peasant's plot, between the corn-shoots sprung.

Over the grey, low wall the olive flung
Her deeper greyness; far off, hill on hill
Sloped to the sky, which, pearly-pale and still,
Above the large and luminous landscape hung.

A snowy blackthorn flowered beyond my reach;
You broke a branch and gave it to me there;
I found for you a scarlet blossom rare.
Thereby ran on of Art and Life our speech;
And of the gifts the gods had given to each—
Hope unto you, and unto me Despair.[6]

There were also side trips to Tuscan towns, which inspired some of Vernon Lee's best travel essays. But as Henry James and other visitors observed, the Paget household was airless, centering on the invalid Eugene. In contrast, her long summers abroad in Germany, France, and principally England were crowded with new experiences and new people.

Mary Robinson too was pursuing her writing career. Encouraged by favorable notices and a surprisingly good sale of her first collection of verse, *A Handful of Honeysuckle,* she worked seriously—perhaps too seriously for some, like the reviewer for the *Spectator* (4 October 1884) who dismissed her next volume, *The New Arcadia,* as "the elaborate work, not of one who feels but of one who is trying to feel and to make others feel."[7] Her poems have an undeniable flavor of the library and a too studied earnestness, but they are graceful lyrics, free of the emotional excesses characteristic of much poetry of the 1880s and '90s. Mary herself described her poetry as the product of a life of "tranquil sequences"—"My life has been an Ode, of which these pages are the scattered fragments."[8] Not without reason, Arthur Symons called her a "spoilt child of two literatures," French and English, the languages in which she wrote;[9] and her very sympathetic French critic Sylvaine Marandon called her "mignardaise." If this sweetness and delicacy weakened her poetry, it also disarmed most of her critics and endeared her to her friends.

Violet, not herself drawn to writing poetry, respected Mary's poetic sensibility, as she also respected her brother Eugene's. She encouraged her to write and to share her own enthusiasm for medieval and early Renaissance lyric poetry and folk ballads. As Mary transferred mentors from the classical of John Addington Symonds to the Italian of Vernon Lee, she began writing her "sober little songs" in new poetic forms—Italian sonnets, *rispetti, stornelli, strombotti.* In all these forms she showed competence; a few have a Browningesque cadence:

> Flower of the vine
> I scarcely knew or saw how love began;
> So mean a flower brings forth the sweetest wine!

> ———

> Love is a bird that breaks its voice with singing,
>   Love is a rose blown open till it fall,
> Love is a bee that dies of its own stinging
> And love the tinsel cross upon a pall,
> Love is the Siren, towards a quicksand bringing
>   Enchanted fishermen that hear her call.
> Love is a broken heart,—Farewell,—the wringing
>   Of dying hands. Ah, do not love at all!
>   "Stornelli and Strambotti" (*Collected Poems*)

The 1880s were productive years for Mary Robinson. Working often side by side with Violet, she published *The New Arcadia* in 1884, *An Italian Garden and Other Lyrics* in 1886, and *Songs, Ballads, and a Garden Play* in 1888. She also contributed two volumes to the Eminent Women Series— *Emily Brontë* in 1883 and *Margaret of Angoulème* in 1887—and published a collection of historical essays, *The End of the Middle Ages,* in 1889. Her one distinct failure was a two-volume novel, *Arden,* in 1883, about a young English girl who is brought up in Rome, then transplanted to the English countryside in Warwickshire, where, after a series of misadventures, she marries a farmer. George Saintsbury, who reviewed the book for the *Academy* (12 May 1883), was kind but candid: "We cannot honestly say that *Arden* discovers much vocation for novel-writing." The *Athenaeum* (19 May 1883) gently dismissed the novel: "One is frequently struck by the grace of a metaphor and the aptness of a simile, but there is a lack of force in Miss Robinson's delineation of character which it may be hoped will be supplied by experience."

Of all Mary's writings, one volume of her verse proved the most personally rewarding. In 1886 a distinguished French philologist and orientalist, James Darmesteter, came upon a copy of her *Italian Garden* while on a research trip to India. He read the volume in an exotic garden in Peshawar and was so impressed with this work of a poet unknown to him that he wrote her for permission to translate it into French. In his introduction to the translation, published in 1888, he hailed the "mood of the ardent feeling which suffuses this eager mind" and the "classic purity" of her style: "Neither in England nor abroad has the poetry of idealism shown itself more penetrating or profounder." [10] After corresponding for a few months, Darmesteter and Mary met in August 1887, appropriately at the British Museum. On their third meeting they became engaged.

Darmesteter was thirty-eight, eight years Mary's senior, but age was not an impediment. He was a professor of language and literature at the Collège de France, with a doctorate in letters awarded in 1877 and a reputation as the foremost scholar of ancient Persian in Europe. In 1893 he published a French translation of the most sacred of Persian religious books, the *Zend-Avesta.* He was also a student of English literature, a translator of Shakespeare and Robert Browning, and an author of essays on the romantic poets and on George Eliot. Mary, who was born for intellectual discipleship, having already looked to John Addington Symonds and Violet as masters, was understandably attracted to a man like Darmesteter; under his influence she later studied Persian and Eastern religious thought. But the announcement of their engagement was received with horror and dismay by all who knew her, first because he was, as Marandon put it, "un homme contrefait," dwarfed and crippled by a childhood spinal disease. And he was a Jew, of an educated but impoverished family who had emigrated to France from Darmstadt (Hesse) in the eighteenth century. His father, a Hebrew scholar once intended for the rabbinate, was obliged to support his family as a bookbinder and bookseller. His mother, who came from Prague, traced her ancestry to the medieval rabbi Akiba ben Joseph. Poor as the family was, the elder Darmesteter managed to educate his three sons, one of whom, Arsène, became an eminent scholar of Hebrew and biblical exegesis. James too had a traditional Talmud-Torah early education, but he won a scholarship to the Lycée Bonaparte and went on to the University of Paris; in later life, while he did not practice the Jewish religion, he never denied his heritage.[11]

Violet had been separated from Mary during much of the summer of 1887, traveling in the north of England while Mary remained in London to look after her ailing mother. Among Violet's many women friends in England was Susan Muir (Maia) Mackenzie, at whose home in Surrey Violet met a young Scotswoman, Clementina Anstruther-Thomson. They had friends in common, among them Violet's old friend Alice Callandar. Physically they were opposites. Violet was short and slight; Kit, as she was known, was large, hearty, and athletic, strikingly different from the daintily feminine Mary Robinson. Violet described her in a letter to her mother as "a semi-painter, semi-sculptor, handsome creature."[12] Since she planned to travel to Scotland that summer, she welcomed her new friend's invitation to visit her at her home, Charleton, in Fifeshire. In the society of articulate and independent women where Violet was now very comfortable, Kit's attention and evident attraction to her were flattering. There is no evidence that she felt in any way disloyal to Mary by accepting the invitation. But it came at an a crucial moment—only a few days before she learned of Mary's engagement.

On 20 August 1887 Violet wrote her mother an account of her first visit to Charleton. It was English country life as novelists depict it—a large, rambling, old-fashioned house in the Lammermoor hills. Kit's country squire father ("a funny, quaint but decidedly nice old Bracebridge") and his daughter shared "horsey" interests; Violet reported on Kit's theory

> about how a galloping horse ought to be painted, for this great, swagger, groomily dressed creature cares only for painting and books . . . really a very enchanting creature; under a childish affectation (she is very shy) of ultra [Alice] Callandarian-swagger, manner and slang; she has a delightful original, discussing, picturesque, extremely intellectual mind, and a very simple, refined, dignified sort of temper. . . . She is also very beautiful to my mind, at least in the evening, when she isn't rigged out in ill-fitting masculine shirts and coats and petticoats a great deal too short.

She was struck particularly by Kit's resemblance to Annie Meyer: "This girl has a very great charm and goodness and intelligence, and rather odd, half fashionable and half ramshackle manners, something simple and childish and at the same time grande dame . . . she constantly reminds me of poor Mme Meyer, but with all the things that made Madame Meyer difficult to tackle, entirely removed."

In these first days of what was to be their long relationship, Kit Anstruther-Thomson appears to have been the more aggressive. On August 24
she placed a rosebud on Violet's pillow, a gesture that under other circumstances she might have appreciated and forgotten. But because that very day
she had heard the devastating news from Mary, she preserved the flower in an
envelope on which she wrote, some time later, "neue Liebe, neues Leben."
Her initial reaction to Mary's letter was one of numbed shock: "A sudden
blow—almost physical—the sense of the necessity of holding on as I read
the letter: incredulousness then, the vague notion of a joke, at all events a
mistake, something that would be explained away (I remember feeling this
when Annie died), a dull resignation, seven years of being mutually the most
important item in my life; is this all the result on my part?" ("Commonplace Book" III). On August 25 she wrote her mother: "My plans are shattered for the moment by a rather astonishing occurrence." She gave no further details, adding only that she had not been directly involved. She did,
however, beg her mother for permission to invite Miss Anstruther-Thomson
to Florence for a visit, "to repay (if such things can be repaid) a great debt
for most timely kindness." And she concluded almost desperately: "I ask
you this as a very great favour at a moment when, if I could explain everything to you, I don't think you would refuse me any request."

The Casa Paget had to remain in the dark for further news until Violet
wrote them on August 30: "Last week I received half a sheet of notepaper
from Mary telling me that she had engaged herself to marry James Darmesteter, a Jewish professor at the Collège de France, whom I had seen once (he
brought a letter three or four days before I left town) and she had seen *thrice,*
including the occasion upon which she asked him (for she says she asked him
rather than he her) to marry." She then repeated her plea to invite Kit: "You
will understand now why it would make me utterly miserable if I were not
permitted to have this woman in Florence." The bluntness of Mary's announcement was matched only by the promptness with which Kit sprang
to comfort her. "I don't know how I should have felt that evening and the
following days," Violet continued, "if good luck had not put me in the
house of one of the most wonderfully good, and gentle, and strong and
simple of all created things, namely this big Kit Thomson."

Shaken as she was, Violet was not ready to accept the engagement as final. Nor, for that matter, was anyone else.[13] The house in Earl's Terrace was
in disarray. Sir John Pollock, who knew the Robinson family in his youth,
wrote in his memoir *Time's Chariot* that when she announced her engagement, her mother said, "Mary, how can you? How can you love him? He's
a Jew! He's almost a dwarf!" To which Mary replied, "When I look at him,

I don't see it" (106). The reaction of the Robinsons was mild compared to the consternation in the Casa Paget. Mary had been a part of their household, virtually a member of the family, for close to seven years. Unaccustomed to change, Mrs. Paget and Eugene had assumed the permanence of the relationship between Violet and Mary. They had also assumed that they knew Mary's character as intimately as they thought they knew Violet's. The idea of a marriage to anyone, let alone a man like Darmesteter, was incomprehensible.

Mary Robinson announced her engagement to Darmesteter in August 1887. They married a year later, in March 1888. In that interval a battle raged in which ultimately the chief victim was Violet, who suffered a nervous collapse that weakened her health for the next two years. The initial shock of the news was followed by a period of relative calm in which she, and presumably the Robinson family, tried to reason Mary out of her resolve to marry, but gentle and pliant as she seemed to be, Mary was firm. She had earlier clung loyally to Violet when her family quarreled with her, and no amount of pressure from them would persuade her now. Still, she was conflicted. Violet reported that she appeared ill and worn "by the opposition she meets everywhere," less worried, one suspects, about her family than about her sense of disloyalty to Violet. She knew only too well how deeply she had wounded her friend and how painful any separation would be, and she sought to console Violet by insisting, from her first letter, that they continue their relationship and that Violet "consider me in the light of a sister."

Violet planned to return to Florence in the autumn. As soon as she was well enough to travel, she went for a short visit to her cousin Pauline in Brittany. Mary meanwhile had gone to Paris, her fiancé's home. Violet joined her there, and they traveled down to Italy together. "Of course this will be the last time," she wrote her mother. "She wishes our relations to continue as before and I, God knows, will stick to her always. But of course everything will be quite different" (*VL's Letters* 272). They stopped briefly in Piedmont for a visit with the Marchesa Alfieri di Sostegno, a relative of the poet who had figured so prominently in the life of the Countess of Albany. Almost as if to delay their confrontation with the Casa Paget, they spent some time in Venice, where Violet met the notorious writer and womanizer Gabriele d'Annunzio. She had published articles in a journal he edited, the *Cronaca bizantina,* and she respected his position as a man of letters. But he did not impress her personally: "rather like an inferior Boutourline," she wrote her mother, referring to the young Russian poet who was a frequent visitor to the Casa Paget. "He is not at all coming on, and has good manners. Still I suspect him rather of being—well, a Neapolitan" (Gunn 119).

Violet correctly anticipated trouble when they reached Florence. Much as she cherished Mary's company, her trip home was filled with anxiety about her family's reaction to the engagement. The opposition Mary had encountered in England was mild in comparison with the reactions of Mrs. Paget and, especially, Eugene. Mrs. Paget was opposed to the whole idea of marriage, confident that she would never have to face the prospect with her own children. Mary, who had been so intimately a part of the family in recent years, was now threatening the tranquillity of their household, the very fabric of their lives. Eugene was especially vocal in his opposition, and as Violet and Mary slowly made their way south to Florence, he heaped advice and dire warnings in his letters. Violet had, perhaps unintentionally, aroused their opposition with her description of Darmesteter in her first letter about him (30 August), describing him as

> a dwarf, a humpback, a cripple from birth, in so grievous and horrible a way that one can scarcely look at this quivering, suffering mass of distortion when he is quiet, still less when he drags himself across the room. He looks as if all his misshapen little body (he is the size of a boy of ten) would fall to pieces, and his hand, even on a hot day, was cold like a snake. . . . How could he . . . accept such a sacrifice? Really, two centuries ago this Quasimodo would have been burnt for less.

This hysterical outburst had obviously been her initial reaction to the shock of Mary's news. Violet was never again so uncontrolled. By early September she was cool enough to acknowledge to her brother that though Mary's motives were "inexplicable," Darmesteter "is very good, no doubt, and very learned." She transferred her objections from the physical man to the intellectual: "But he is dull, totally inartistic (has never looked at a picture or read a line of verse). . . . He says he wants to be Lewis [*sic*] to her George Eliot; but fancy if Lewis had been a French Jew . . . hating novels. Well, well. I feel quite dazed with it; and all I know for certain is that Mary is very good to me" (12 September). Clearly she had not yet cooled enough to measure Darmesteter objectively and to recognize how she was misjudging him. Dominating everything was her revulsion at the thought of a physical relationship between someone like him and a woman as attractive as Mary. She blamed herself for leaving London during the summer when Darmesteter had appeared, and she attributed Mary's feelings for him to her innocence, unaware that it was her own innocence of human sexuality that made such a union inconceivable to her.

A physical union, however, never seems to have been contemplated by either Mary or Darmesteter, and by mid-September Violet was reconciled to the idea that theirs would be a platonic relationship. Having lost first claim to Mary's affections, she consoled herself with this. "I see that this marriage

offers her a better chance than any other. For I think that marriage in the
normal sense, would be suicidal and wicked for her" (14 September). With
the prospect of Mary unhappy, torn between the wishes of her friends and
family and her love for this brilliant but misshapen man, Violet could find
comfort only in her concern for Mary's future happiness. Without the interference of her mother and Eugene she might have resigned herself quietly to the inevitable. But her family persisted in their opposition, bombarding her with letters as she made her way back home. Mrs. Paget was simply
and implacably opposed to marriage. Eugene, however, took it as a personal
obligation to stop or, if that failed, to dictate the terms of the marriage. He
had no designs on Mary himself, nor did he express any concern that his sister was losing a devoted companion. But he was morbidly and obsessively
preoccupied with the sexual nature of such a marriage, and in urgent letters
to his sister he insisted that she do everything she could to prevent it.

Darmesteter was evidently fully conscious of the opposition he faced.
He had seen Violet in London before she left for Italy in early September.
To her objection that Mary was "quite unfit for ordinary marriage," he
made it clear that it would indeed be a platonic marriage. "[Mary's] affection," she wrote her mother, "is of a very curious order. It is love; I don't believe she has pitied him once. . . . He himself seems to dislike any sort of
love making very much. [He is] very good, true, kind and upright; I really
like him; and I am touched by his confidence in me. I am touched and astonished also that in the midst of all this dear little Mary seems to care for
me just as much as ever" (8 September).

In spite of these reassurances the campaign from the Casa Paget continued hot and furious. On September 11 Eugene sent his sister an extraordinary message that betrayed his own frustrated sexuality: "With respect to
the marriage business, the platonic promise seems to me almost as nasty and
unnatural though less immoral than the converse. If the man has the irrita-
ble temper which is usually attributed to cripples, it will not be improved
by his being made to play the part of a dog on whose nose you put a biscuit
while forbidding him to eat it; and she will find herself in a very false position, especially in a country of *Cruelles enigmes et crimes d'amour*" (11 September).[14] Still the baby sister in the family, Violet found herself wavering
painfully. She insisted that Mary's happiness was the only issue, but she admitted to bewilderment over where that happiness lay. Eugene, on the other
hand, had no doubts. Anticipating a crisis when Mary came to Florence
prepared to introduce her fiancé to the Paget household, Violet appealed
to her mother to intercede: "I do implore Eugene to hold his peace, whatever provocation Mary may give him. He has no tact, and she has no sense,
and I really foresee only misery unless this subject is kept absolutely in the

background. Why do you not say anything on the subject, Mama? I feel a wretched, helpless idiot" (14 September).

Mrs. Paget could not have exerted much energy in silencing Eugene, but three days later he did write to say that he would not bring up the subject when Mary came to Florence. He had not, however, given up the cause or released Violet from what he regarded as her duty to prevent the marriage:

> A woman who is capable of engaging herself *unconditionally* to marry a ricketty cripple whom she has seen only three times is, as far as that action goes, immodest and unmoral. It will be no thanks to her but to others if she do not become the mother of some scrofulous abortion. . . . As I say there is nothing now to be done and your attitude is the only possible one, but I am not sure that you did not miss an opportunity when you were in London and had them both face to face. The very conditions of Platonic relations which the man proposed gave you I think an opportunity of summoning them both to break off the match as an unnatural one and shaming them out of it—I may be mistaken in this idea and the experiment might have been too dangerous, but it *might* have succeeded *with a tongue as eloquent as yours*. This is all I find to say or ever shall say on the topic. (17 September)

Like many pledges, Eugene's was only half honored. He did not thereafter write of the matter to Violet, but he kept the subject alive with his mother and remained a source of anxiety to his sister. His assumption that Violet was somehow responsible for Mary's behavior and should have made even greater efforts to influence her and Darmesteter was very troubling. "Eugene is quite mistaken in supposing I could have shamed them out of anything," she wrote her mother.

> I might perhaps, though I doubt it, have bade her choose between him and me, by picking a violent quarrel with him. But such a course would have been a wrong one, certainly. One can't make people do this or that, not legitimately at least, I think; one can only try and make them see what they ought to do. This I have done all in vain. I wrote to Mary again from Brittany, expressing violently my sense of the unnaturalness and danger of the situation; but all my remarks ran off like water from a duck's back, without even hurting her feelings in the very least. (20 September)

It had become by now a matter of principle with Violet to act correctly regardless of her own feelings. She was trying to translate the abstract aesthetic "good" as she understood it into the conduct of practical morality and ethics. "What Eugene is apt to overlook in the situation is the foundation of real worth in the individual," she continued. Darmesteter is "a very distinguished and worthy man, though how he can have done such a thing with a good conscience I can't understand." Even more mystifying was Mary's attachment to him and, though it remained unspoken, her alienation from Violet. "As regards Eugene," she concluded, "I greatly fear his exploding when Mary talks about her man, which she does constantly."

She turned to her mother again with a plea for support, "Don't you think so, Mamma?" explaining that she was only trying to prepare Mary for the inevitable problems of marriage (24 September). But from Casa Paget there came repeated warnings of the terrible consequences of a sexual union. It was Eugene who had first proposed the possibility of a "scrofulous abortion," a monstrously deformed offspring. An alternative to such a prospect —and Eugene was worldly enough to suggest it—was artificial birth control. To this Violet reacted with horror:

> I consider all the French and Mrs. Besant's practices as an abomination bringing marriage to the level of prostitution. . . . Mary and her man have no right to tie themselves together; but if they insist upon doing so (recognizing as they do openly that they would be criminal in producing children) let them honourably bear the difficulties and bitterness of their false position, without giving way to instincts whose natural results would be criminal. I warned Mary of the probability of a Frenchman who said he wished to have no children resorting to such methods, but he seems to have no idea of the kind. . . . I would far rather see Mary unhappy than dishonoured by what I consider an abominable practice. (27 September)

Mary and her fiancé showed remarkable forbearance in the face of this debate raging in the mails over the intimacies of their coming marriage. Violet could not resist observing to her mother that Darmesteter "must be an astonishing greenhorn, a sort of seminarist without a notion of the flesh and the devil, or with astonishing belief in his powers of settling all things right." Under these pressures, however, Mary began to weaken. Violet wrote her mother with some satisfaction that "as a result of a lecture of mine," Mary had written her fiancé "telling him she positively would not incur the crime of having children (he has always from the first insisted on the Platonic plan) and telling him she was warned he might be preparing misery for himself and that he was therefore at liberty to give her up. She is now very wretched, poor thing, but of course he won't take her at her word" (27 September). There is no record of what must have been a painful meeting at the Casa Paget between the engaged couple and their hosts sometime in October.

Whatever pressures Mrs. Paget and Eugene had exerted, they had no lasting effect—except upon Violet's health. In November she collapsed and was ill for several months. Mary, meanwhile, had returned to England still conflicted between her love for Darmesteter and the many obstacles that had been placed in their way. She was determined to preserve her friendship with Violet, but the bitterness of the last months had chilled them both. Kit wrote consolingly to Violet:

> I still hope you won't break off with Miss Robinson. People have got tired of me and dropped me on several occasions, and I have always accepted the situation as the fortunes of war—quite philosophically. [I have] gone out of my way, gradually learning to "sit quite tight" to people and things, liking them very much, but not depending on them the least . . . and then one beau jour I came across you and found you really mattered to me and that I couldn't "sit tight" to you and there it is. (19 February 1888)

Kit's profession of affection, her obvious readiness to take Mary's place, must have been comforting to Violet. As early as 19 September 1887, in the heat of the Pagets' campaign to stop the marriage, she had been offering herself: "I'm taking it almost for granted that you care more for her than for your own skin; but then I think you do, don't you—you see it would be horrid for her if you drifted away from her and got 'out of touch' so to speak; judging by how I should feel if you did it to me. What a kind chap you are Vernon. You are always doing kind things." With Mrs. Paget's approval she came to Florence in March 1888 to nurse the ailing Violet, who recovered slowly and only partially. Years later, in her introduction to *Art and Man,* Vernon Lee recalled: "Kit at once took the measure of my depression and restlessness and understood that, in a household composed of my prematurely old parents and my chronically invalided brother, it needed someone from outside to take my case in hand and pull me through" (16–17). By late spring Violet was well enough to resume her work. "I have succeeded in completely starving out the unreasonable affection I had for this nice woman," she wrote Kit (13 June 1888), who had returned to Scotland. Mary and Darmesteter were married, and Kit obligingly took her place in Violet's life. For the next ten years theirs was in every sense but the physical a devoted lesbian relationship.[15]

8 "THIS CLEVER WOMAN WHO CALLS HERSELF VERNON LEE"

Kit came to stay with us in Florence after leaving Paris at Easter, 1888. The precise date has been fixed in my mind less by the importance it later showed itself as having in my life than, oddly enough, by the recollection, as vivid as their own colours, of putting scarlet and purple anemones in her room; and also of our first walk, of which I seem to see in my mind as clearly as I can in daily reality the hundred yards or so of the old road to Fiesole, where it ascends between steep olive yards and big black cypresses against the blue. And bells were ringing that morning. "Bells are always ringing," Kit used to remark all through her life, "whenever we two meet." And if not in the body, at least in the spirit.

Vernon Lee, introduction to *Art and Man*

ALTHOUGH MOST OF THE ESSAYS COLLECTED IN *JUVENILIA* were written sometime before the book was published, Vernon Lee's introduction, dated New Year's 1887, offers a prophetic framework for the stormy events of that year. The title itself is dismissive: the work of her youth, whatever its merits, is finished, labeled, and put away. Something new must replace it, and the title implies that what follows will be different in spirit, work of sober maturity. Like the writings of the romantic poets, these essays plangently record a loss. Compensations are granted, but they can never replace the loss. Vernon Lee uses Pater's *Marius the Epicurean* as a frame for her own passage from youthful idealism to mature realism. She recalls the joy with which she first read the book, in "those aesthetic, classic Goethean days . . . a sunny scene, [a] bracing Florentine spring." At that time just emerging from her teens, she was convinced that the Good and the Beautiful were one, that Art and Morality coexisted and flourished equally. But returning to *Marius* in 1886, a woman of thirty, she feels "a certain sadness." She perceives that "there are ugly things in the world" and "ugly things within ourselves . . . apathy, selfishness, vice, want." The ugliness is even reflected in the natural landscape—both in England, which "shows its evils

grimly," and in Italy, which, "thanks to climate, beauty, and a certain dignified stagnation, hides them." More than simply the ravages of the Industrial
Revolution she sees erosion in the human spirit. In living as she has most of
her life "with the beautiful serenities of art," she has ignored "the dreadful,
messy, irritating, loathesomeness of life." With her maturity has come an
awakening sense of humanity. Like Dorothea Casaubon's epiphany after her
dark night of the soul in *Middlemarch,* Vernon Lee has emerged from her
self-absorption to discover "a great living mass, travelling and suffering on
its onward path; and it makes me feel less isolated, in a way, to recognize all
round, among creatures of different habits and views from one's own, and
profoundly unconscious of one's existence, the companionship of the desire
for good" (1:20).

The public Vernon Lee was announcing the awakening of a social conscience. The private Violet Paget, however, was awakening to a harsher personal discovery, not only that a purely aesthetic life is a delusion, but that
the certainties by which she had lived—the devotion of an intimate friendship and the loving support of her family—were also delusory. Aesthetics
had not failed her, but life had betrayed her. "Beauty, whether of nature or
of art is simple, harmonious, complete," she wrote in the epilogue to *Juvenilia,* but "the human element, *the world,* full, even at the best, of disso-
nance, imperfection, complexity, and enigma, that awaken suspicion and
evil thoughts, [leaves] us, even where it shows handsomest, with a notion
that under the surface all is far from beautiful, that there are mixtures of motives, and motives and motors hidden away—drains and dustbins of the
soul" (2:211).

In her pain at the loss of Mary Robinson, Violet perceived for the first
time how her family had failed her. Their pettiness and relentless criticism,
their failure to offer her the sympathy and support she desperately needed,
were only too apparent. Fortunately Kit Anstruther-Thomson was at hand
to offer just that. And Kit offered more. In her relationship with Mary, Violet had been the dominant partner, strong and decisive, but with Kit the
roles were reversed. In contrast to Mary's soft, delicate, feminine beauty, Kit
was a handsome woman, tall, athletic, a take-charge person ready to nurse
the now physically as well as emotionally ailing Violet. Kit did not condemn
Mary but humbly offered herself in her place.

Curiously enough for a woman notorious for her social liabilities—argumentative, abrasive, dogmatic, pedantic, so self-absorbed that her conversation (as Coleridge's was once described) was "one-versation"—Violet Paget
had as many loyal friends as she had enemies. When her unguarded tongue
and hasty temper offended, she was usually contrite and apologetic. Her
generosity in reading and commenting frankly on the writings of others was

sometimes misconstrued as patronizing or insulting. Her unattractive appearance and peremptory manner instantly chilled casual acquaintances. And by the 1890s her open relations with women and her circle of admiring women—what Ethel Smyth called her *"cultes"*[1] and Bernard Berenson, who often attended her salons, dismissed as "a flock of women . . . all striking more or less Botticellian poses, all breathing an aura of acute Renaissance" (Morra 92–93)—caused some of the more conventional society matrons to shun her. Nicky Mariano recalled in her memoir *Forty Years with Berenson,* for example, that the socially prominent Mrs. Janet Ross issued "lugubre warnings" to her young niece "that friendship with Miss Paget implicated the most horrible danger" (102).[2]

There were painful quarrels to be sure, many of which she regretted, especially her loss of Henry James's friendship in 1893 over her story "Lady Tal." But most of these wounds healed in time, even the bitter quarrel in 1897 with her neighbor in Fiesole Bernard Berenson, which was not forgotten until they were reconciled in 1920. Her separation from Mary Robinson was of a different order. Theirs had been a relationship so sympathetic that it transcended the ordinary patterns of anger and forgiveness. Blissfully happy in her marriage to James Darmesteter, Mary nevertheless worried about its effects on Violet. In order to keep peace she ignored the ugly intrusions of Mrs. Paget and Eugene Lee-Hamilton into her personal affairs. In June 1888 she wrote to Eugene asking him "to lessen the anxieties of Mrs. Paget whose kindness to me in her house and throughout many years is always present in my mind. Give her my love and assure her I will seek no interview with Vernon." In the years that followed, they met from time to time as friends, but it was Mary rather than Violet who made the overtures.

She wrote her, for example, in April or May 1894 to express her embarrassment over the publication of Anatole France's novel *The Red Lily,* in which she and Violet were actually named. Drawing loosely on his visit to the Casa Paget some years earlier, France introduced a character, Vivian Bell, an English poet: "Miss Bell lived in Fiesole, an aesthete and philosopher, while in England she was renowned as the favorite English poetess. Like Vernon Lee and Mary Robinson, she had fallen in love with Tuscan life and art; and, without staying to complete her *Tristan,* the first part of which had inspired Burne-Jones to paint dreams in water-colours, she was expressing Italian ideas in Provençal and French verse." France described Miss Bell as "pleasant and plain, with short hair and slim, flat figure, almost graceful in her tailor-made coat and skirt of masculine cut" (7). She is given to long gushy speeches about art and nature, and she has a handsome admirer, Prince Albertinelli, but "he seemed too matter-of-fact and commonplace to please an aesthete for whom love would have something of the mysticism of an Annunciation." How Violet reacted to this portrait we do not know, but Mary apologized because *The Red Lily* had originally been published in the *Revue de Paris* under James Darmesteter's editorship. "He [France] seems to have made a bizarre melange of your house and a little of your name, of the history of Ouida and of my verse and conversation in the portrait of Miss Vivian Bell" (Marandon 39).[3]

On the whole her Italian friends—all of them highly cultivated, many of them titled and well-to-do—were more generous in overlooking her flaws than were the English. They tolerated her excesses as harmless eccentricity, a quality they had long associated with the English. But they also recognized that if she could never be one of them—her spoken Italian too precise to be native and her moral judgments too inflexible—she was nevertheless the most knowledgeable and enthusiastic of Italophiles. They opened their homes to her. She was a frequent visitor to the English-born Baroness Elena French Cini's villa just outside Pistoia. Count and Countess Pasolini, to whom she dedicated *Renaissance Fancies and Studies,* and the Countess Maria Gamba welcomed her to their palazzi in Rome and introduced her to other interesting and influential Italians. Among them was a pioneer woman psychologist, Donna Laura Gropallo, of whom Mary Berenson wrote in 1901: "But (though I don't like her) I can't help remembering that she had very good brains and uses them too. I have not often met a woman so intelligent, nor so intellectually perverse when she gets an idea into her head" (98).[4] It was a judgment many would have pronounced equally on Vernon Lee.

The most rewarding of her Italian friendships were with the literary critic Enrico Nencioni (1837–96) and with Carlo Placci (1862–1941), who wrote little but had impressive social and literary connections. Nencioni first visited the Casa Paget in 1881. A longtime admirer and translator of English writers, he had met the Brownings years earlier and translated Robert's poetry into Italian. Impressed with Violet's knowledge of Italian literature, he reviewed her books enthusiastically in the *Nuovo antologia.* At the Casa Paget, Nencioni widened his circle of English friends. In February 1887 Violet introduced him to Henry James, some of whose work he had already translated into Italian. Nencioni's relations with Violet were always cordial, but, a devout Catholic, he strongly disapproved of her religious "unbelief." They shared antivivisectionist views, however, for which he was evidently ready to forgive even her excesses of literary style. He figures as Carlo in the discussion of *The Ring and the Book* in *Baldwin* and as the professor in her philosophical dialogues in *Althea,* "with his thin Tuscan face, in which, as in his gentle and fiery soul, his friends are apt to trace a likeness of St. Francis" ("The Spiritual Life" 233).

Carlo Placci, son of an Italian banker and a Spanish-Mexican mother, is better remembered as a social gadabout than as a man of letters. An ardent Anglophile, as fluent in English as in Italian, Placci had the means to travel freely and meet some of the most important thinkers and writers in Europe, among them Pareto, Rilke, Romain Rolland, Paul Bourget, Anatole France, and Daniel Halévy. Placci came early to the Casa Paget as an admirer of the work of both Violet and Eugene. Though only a few years older than Placci, Violet assumed an affectionate, almost motherly attitude toward him. She introduced him as a speaker in *Baldwin* and *Althea* and addressed her introduction to *Juvenilia* to him. He first met Bernard Berenson at the Casa Paget, an occasion that Berenson described in his characteristic acerbic manner: "When in came Carlo Placci, a sleek, and fearfully unpleasant person. Vernonia seemed queer, excited like a girl when her sweetheart is unexpectedly announced. I retired quickly" (Samuels 178).[5] Berenson soon revised his first impression and the two men become lifelong friends; they frequently quarreled but just as frequently reconciled. Violet too had her disagreements with Placci, but they remained friends for many years.

It was to Placci in August 1894 that Violet confided her awareness of the psychological damage her family had done her (see chap. 1, p. 2): "I now see that one should get to know oneself (since others don't take the trouble) and particularly to know . . . one's parents and one's own childhood." The mother who had calculatedly shaped her daughter into the rigid mold of pedant and bluestocking, the brother who had aided and abetted her in the process, the father who was simply indifferent, all of them were revealed to her now as "neuropathic and hysterical." After Mary Robinson's marriage Violet suffered a series of breakdowns. To the outside world she appeared still vigorous and self-assured, a prolific writer with a small but appreciative readership. But to Placci she revealed her terrible despair and loneliness: "One of our worst sufferings is the sense of isolation, of being left behind, like ship-wrecked people, by the great moving bulk of activity."

Her recuperation from the first breakdown was slow. In the summer of 1888 she was in England and Scotland. She suffered a relapse in August and remained in Kit's care at Charleton until November, when she decided to return to Italy slowly by way of Tangier and southern Spain. She traveled with another friend, Evelyn Wimbush, who paid a substantial part of the expenses of the trip.[6] The change of scene failed to relieve her depression. She returned to Italy by sea, stopping in Naples and Rome, where she was a guest of the Pasolinis. Her Italian friends were supportive, but her anxiety increased as she thought of returning home. On 29 January 1889 she released her feelings in a letter to her mother. She felt guilty for having imposed the burden of her ill health on her aging mother. "Dearest Mamma," she wrote while still on shipboard, "How often have I not thought how cruel your position is, with him [Eugene] so miserably ill on your hands, and me ill at a distance, indeed, indeed. I wish I may ever be of some sort of comfort to you. I shall get all right with time and care, and this illness has been a great lesson to me not to strain after the impossible, but to do what lies at hand. So much love, yr, V."

But only three days later, having landed in Naples, she turned on her mother with almost hysterical bitterness. For some time she had been urging that the family move out of congested Florence to the neighboring countryside. All such decisions of course were in the hands of Mrs. Paget, who had never objected to leaving Florence during the hot summer months. But possibly considering the social advantages of town life for the homebound Eugene, she had steadfastly refused to live in the country. Violet's patience was exhausted. Until now, while she had complained to her mother of Eugene's criticism of her failure to stop Mary's marriage, she had never directly confronted her:

> Considering how much fatigue every letter to you has cost me, I expected they would have been read more carefully. So that when, after writing me that you were "willing to move to a villa at Bellosguardo or Colli but not further from town" you write that you can't think of it "except for the summer," I feel what a difficult, difficult task is before me not merely in trying to get well, but in making others understand that *I am ill* and that I shall in future, if my life and work are of any value, have requirements as distinct and necessary as a ground floor and a carriage are to Eugene. They are, heaven knows, not very excessive, and I have explained them often enough: sunshine, the possibility of getting easily into the open air (a garden) and quiet both from visitors and such noises as are inevitable in town. (29 January 1889)

There is a note of desperation in her plea: "Please think about this. I see that you have never realised that, for some time to come at least, I have a broken constitution. It is now nearly a year since I fell ill; I have given up all work, all society, everything that could make me ill; but I am as ill as ever."

Self-pity occurs in much depressive illness, but there is more to her complaints than the cries of a sick woman. Belatedly perhaps but clearly, Violet was growing up. The hothouse world of the Casa Paget, ruled so imperiously by her mother and centered so exclusively on Eugene, was no longer tolerable. With the status now of invalid herself, Violet had her own demands. It is significant, however, that she never seriously considered leaving her home and living independently in England, as many women her age and with her reputation as a writer were doing. But her ties to her mother would never be broken.[7] Moreover, Italy was her home. No place in the world was so congenial to her. Her roots were there. It was her refuge from the ugliness of the present and the center of everything she valued. Evidently Mrs. Paget at last recognized the urgency of her daughter's pleas. There were many attractive and affordable houses in the hills within a short distance of Florence. Bellosguardo was the most popular with the Anglo-American colony, but Fiesole offered a wide choice of houses too. In the spring of 1889 Mrs. Paget rented a modest but comfortable villa, really a gentrified farmhouse, Il Palmerino, in the village of Maiano, on the hill of Fiesole. By the time Violet rejoined her family in April they had moved in. She took an immediate interest in the management of the property. Her letters to her mother during her travels abroad in the early 1890s are sprinkled with instructions for cultivating the fruit trees, making jam, and planting and pruning the garden. Some years later, after the deaths of her parents, she bought Il Palmerino, and it remained her home until her death.

In the troubled years from 1887 to about 1896, Violet did not write with the facility and exuberance of her earlier work. There were long periods of ill health and inactivity. During her slow recovery she recognized that writing was her salvation, the therapy that could release her from morbid self-absorption. The three books she produced in this period—*Juvenilia* (1887), *Althea* (1894), and *Renaissance Fancies and Studies* (1895)—are collections of essays, several of them published first in periodicals. They are, for her, curiously subdued, with none of the egregious historical generalizations of *Euphorion* or the unblushing dogmatism of *Baldwin*. On the whole they received better, or at least cautiously favorable, reviews. After the debacle of *Miss Brown*, it must have been a relief for her to read the *Spectator's* praise of *Juvenilia* (28 January 1888): "She unites feminine suppleness of intellect with a considerable mastery of her subject. Her learning sits lightly upon her, and her erudition is rarely aggressive. She is at once subtle and audacious, engagingly frank in proclaiming her likes and dislikes, agreeably discursive, though never wantonly irrelevant." *Althea,* a collection of philosophical dialogues less controversial than those in its predecessor *Baldwin,* was admired for its seriousness, its "grand idealism" (*Athenaeum* 13 December 1893), and its "honesty of thought" (*Saturday Review* 16 April 1910). *Renaissance Fancies and Studies,* by far the best of the three, was compared favorably with the work of Walter Pater, whom she eulogized in the closing essay of the book.

By 1895 the critical consensus was that Vernon Lee was not a major aesthetic critic nor an especially felicitous stylist, but an extremely well-educated and "clever" woman—*clever* carrying with it the faintly disparaging Victorian connotation of superficiality or glibness. (Charles Kingsley advised his young lady readers, "Be good, sweet maid, and let who will be clever.") Whatever satisfaction she might have taken from these reviews was tempered by her disappointment in the shrinking size of her audience as reflected in the sales of her books. In 1893 she wrote to Eugene from London: "At thirty-seven I have no public," but the old self-assurance had not vanished. "On the other hand," she consoled herself, "I am singularly far from being played out and crystallised, as I see most writers become even before that age." She was not writing for money or easy fame, but only for the satisfaction she derived from "the determination *never* to write a thing which did not happen to interest me at the moment, and with the desire to prevent myself getting into intellectual ruts." Mary Ward had urged her to undertake regular critical writing:

> She thinks I ought to have a position like Matthew Arnold's or St. Beuve's. She wants me to engage to furnish, say every two months, a paper to some big review, so as to get a clear identity before the public. The advice is excellent and I have pondered over it. But I find that I should have to write on actualities, new books, new editions, at the choice of an Editor. . . . I cannot sacrifice all intellectual private life to reading up for articles. As a human being I feel bound to get information on a great many subjects, and the subjects increase the more I know. So I am determined [I] will not read a book unless it conduces to my education as a human being or to my pleasure, which comes to the same. (30 August 1893)

Whether Vernon Lee rejected paid critical writing out of such high principles, or whether she simply never had an attractive offer, we do not know. She did not reject the opportunity to give public lectures, however, because she regarded these as an extension of her "conversations" with her *cultes*. She could choose her own subjects, ranging freely among her many interests, and publish the lectures afterward as essays. But the free, improvisatory nature of conversation, she soon discovered, did not suit the lecture platform. "Kit has very wisely persuaded [me] to write all my lectures, and that takes time," she wrote her mother in June 1894. "I found on the first occasion that I have no faculty for keeping my subject in hand. I am clear, I believe, and I think (and one or two people seem to agree) more impressive when I speak. But I am literally improvising much beyond the words—new ideas come up and I cannot restrain myself from going after them, with the result of confusing and spoiling the proportions of the whole." A few days later she reported that the second lecture "was a great success" with about forty people in attendance. After the expenses of advertising the lecture and renting the hall and chairs, she realized about thirty-five pounds. Although she wondered why people "prefer reading out loud to speaking," she concluded that "it was rather good practice putting down my thoughts in the order in which I should have wished to speak them."

The self-restraint demanded by public lecturing never extended to her writing. She once proudly quoted Walt Whitman: "Do I contradict myself? / Very well then, I contradict myself." In *Althea* her spokesman Baldwin ("employed merely to express a portion of my own notions") is considerably less dogmatic than in the earlier volume that bears his name. "A reader of my earlier dialogues," she writes in her introduction, "will find in these new ones a good deal which directly contradicts them . . . the difference there must necessarily be between the attitude of youth and the attitude of maturer life." In *Juvenilia* the "aesthetic critic" who had earlier repudiated "Ruskinism" now feels a moral imperative to serve humanity: "But this seems certain: in order that the great mass of mankind, which has neither peace nor dignity, nor beauty of life, should obtain a small allowance of any such qualities, it becomes necessary that we, who happen to possess thereof, should deprive ourselves of a portion for their benefit" (1:11–12). Although the essays in this collection revert to familiar themes—eighteenth-century Italy, the natural beauties of Tuscany, frescoes in country churches, the living presence of the past, the assaults of modernism on her sensibilities—the voice is less strident, sobered by a sense that the beauty she celebrates cannot be enjoyed by everyone and is increasingly jeopardized by modern industrial society. Nevertheless, she does not despair. Rather she looks to extending the appreciation of beauty to an ever widening public: "But there is an artistic possession more valuable than any picture, statue, cathedral, symphony, or poem whatsoever—indeed, the most precious artistic property that we possess. It is the power, the means, the facility, due to the condition both of our minds and of works of art, of assimilating art into life" (1:105–6).

For all her expressions of social conscience, her insistence on the duty of the fortunate to uplift others, the business of "assimilating art into life" is for her a condition of the individual mind, not a program of social action. Her struggles with depression and her attempts to trace her neurasthenia to its roots in her family and her childhood inevitably reshaped her approach to art. As earlier she had moved from history to aesthetics, she was now moving from aesthetics to psychology or, more precisely, to a study of the relationship between the mind and art. Why, she asks in *Juvenilia,* do our responses to a work of art or a scene in nature alter over time if beauty itself is timeless and unchanging? Why, for example, did the banks of the Rhine, which gave her such pleasure in her childhood, seem so drab on her recent journey? Something has been lost: "Whither is fled the visionary gleam? / Where is it now, the glory and the dream?" For Wordsworth, the answer was the Platonic notion of the soul's prior existence. Living in the modern scientific age, Vernon Lee answers with a psychological theory. The pleasure we take in the experience of beauty comes from the connections we make in unconscious memory. The child remembering the legends of the Rhine that her governess had told her associated the scene with happiness, her state of mind conditioning her aesthetic response. "Association means the investing of one object, having characteristics of its own, with the characteristics of some other object; the pushing aside, in short, of reality to make room for the fictions of the imagination or memory." To objections that association reduces concentration on the work of art itself by distracting our attention, she replies that in fact association enriches our perception:

> Without association, I say, no art. In the first instance, every modern psychologist who has studied the origin of our aesthetic faculties, will tell you that one half, and that in far more complex of the instinctive preferences which are the rudiments of all our aesthetic feelings, is referable, not to the simple kind of such rudimentary instincts of beauty, to the greater physical comfort which the eye and ear experience in the perception of certain relations of colour and sound; but to the habit . . . of associating material pleasure, safety, or usefulness with certain aspects rather than with others. (1:56–57)

Association then is an act of mind, but the mind, as Violet had learned from her own breakdown and even more obviously from Eugene's paralysis, has profoundly mysterious connections with the body. Our pleasure in beauty is not merely a matter of intellect or memory but of feelings, reactions in the body as well. A few years later, collaborating with Kit Anstruther-Thomson, she would work out her own version of "psychological aesthetics" by connecting aesthetics to its elemental bodily reactions—eye movements, pulse and heartbeat, muscle tension. In *Juvenilia*, however, she was not seeking to push the question beyond the general sense of pleasure and well-being given by the experience of beauty.

In more immediate terms, she writes in the essay "Signor Curiazio: A Musical Medley" that the function of the critic is to expose the looseness and vagueness, the speciousness and most particularly the formlessness of any work of art that fails "to increase our power of coping with the difficulties and agitations to which our soul is exposed." This essay, like the others in *Juvenilia*, is unabashedly personal, an indulgence in her own taste. She confesses her preference for a forgotten opera of 1796 by Cimarosa, *Horatii e Curialii*, to Wagner's *Tristan und Isolde*. Acknowledging that Wagner's music is appreciated by far larger audiences, she argues that the grand passion of his lovers has no power to move *her:* "That passion, without object or motive, blind, if passion ever was, deaf and sterile, communicated to our soul by the mysterious passion of Wagner's music, shakes and unsettles it, weakens our mental and moral muscle, making it incapable of resistance in the present, less capable of resistance in the future" (2:175).

All the essays in *Juvenilia* share this subjective indulgence. Some of the pieces are pure whimsy: "Apollo the Fiddler," a mere footnote on an anachronism in a painting by Raphael; "Don Juan (con Stentorello)," a report on a puppet show of *Don Juan* staged in a little Tuscan town, to which she appends a ghost story about a less notorious Spanish rake who reforms when he discovers that his current mistress had died some time before their recent rendezvous; "The Immortality of Maestro Galuppi," another of her imaginative reconstructions of the musical life of eighteenth-century Venice; "Perigot: Random Notes on the Dramatic and Undramatic," an argument for the superiority of naive pastoral drama to the sordid realism of modern drama. Others are reminiscences of her childhood in Germany, her ardent youthful studies of old music in Bologna, her discovery of frescoes by Botticelli in a shabby farmhouse in the hills above Florence. Everywhere these essays echo the sense of loss—a shining past, a lusterless present redeemed only by memory and the imagination. The mood is summed up best in the last lines of the essay on Galuppi, where, as she sails back to Venice from Burano, she recalls a long-forgotten melody, not of Galuppi's but of some unknown composer: "I alone know it. And I let it sing through my memory, while watching the faded rose colour that dies in the greyness of the lagoon; the colour, as I said, of the forgotten songs" (2:233).

The essays in *Juvenilia* range speculatively over a miscellany of topics treated for the most part lightly in the manner of sketches or, as Nencioni put it after Thackeray, "round-about papers." Nencioni compared them to her conversation—"fireflies at noon" (*lucciole a mezzogiorno*). In contrast, the essays she collected in *Renaissance Fancies and Studies* are more studies than fancies. The subtitle announces a sequel to *Euphorion,* and in her preface she acknowledges not only several scholarly books but also the conversation of friends—Eugenie Sellers (later Mrs. Arthur Strong), an expert on ancient sculpture who became head of the British School of Archaeology in Rome; "my friend Mrs. Mary Logan whose learned catalogue of the Italian paintings at Hampton Court is sufficient warrant for the correctness of my art-historical statements, which she had the kindness to revise"; and "Mr. Bernhard [*sic*] Berenson, author of *Venetian Painters* and a monograph on Lorenzo Lotto." Mary Logan was the pen name of Mrs. Mary Smith Costelloe, not as yet married to Berenson, who was himself in 1895 only beginning to emerge as the dominant figure in European art connoisseurship.[8]

Although fortified with such scholarly support, Vernon Lee was far more cautious in her judgments in *Renaissance Fancies and Studies* than in its predecessor. There is an almost chastened note in her recollection of her earlier high-handed dismissal of Renaissance morality in *Euphorion:*

> The conscience of writers on history and art has long become quite comfortable about the Renaissance; and the Websterian (or in some cases John Fordian) phenomenon of twenty years ago has been forgotten as a piece of childish morbidness. Does this mean that the conscience has become hardened, that evil has ceased to repel us, or that beauty has been accepted calmly as a pleasant and necessary, but somewhat immoral thing? Very far from it. Our conscience has become quieter, not because it has become more callous, but because it has become more healthily sensitive, more perceptive of many sides instead of only one side of life. (248–49)

Unlike her earlier collections, these essays share a theme: the primacy of art as perceived in pure form, its power to exalt and ennoble its appreciators. Fittingly the book ends with her "Valedictory" for Walter Pater, "the natural exponent of the highest aesthetic doctrine—the search for harmony throughout all orders of existence." Fittingly too her prose is more measured and controlled than in her earlier writings. Vernon Lee remains the subjective, impressionistic critic, but with fewer eccentricities. Her historical generalizations are less outrageous. The Middle Ages, judged so severely in *Euphorion,* now emerges as an age of growth, not merely a bridge to the Renaissance but its seedtime. In the Gothic convolutions, the gloomy interiors, the gargoyles and grotesque sculpture, the crude images of pain and suffering decorating medieval churches, she reads the history of plague, terror, the persecution of heretics. But she also notes the softening presence of "the love of the saints" inspired by St. Francis of Assisi with his devotion to all living things, human and animal. The crumbling ruins of old churches and houses that she sees in the backstreets of Florence are "all signs, poor primitive rhymes and primitive figures that the world is teeming again, and will bare, for centuries to come, new spiritual wonders" (3).

This is less the tendentious Vernon Lee of her earlier books than the sensitive observer, recording as she does so brilliantly in her travel writings sights and sounds filtered through her unique sensibility. The best essay in the collection is "The Imaginative Art of the Renaissance," in which she describes an *Annunciation* by Signorelli in the Uffizi:

> In it the Virgin is seated beneath a portico, breathing, as such creatures must breathe, the vast greenness, the deep evening breeze. And to her comes bounding, with waving draperies and loosened hair, the Archangel, like a rushing wind which the strong woman is quietly inhaling. There is no reli-

gious sentiment here, still less any human: the Madonna bows gravely as one who is never astonished; and, indeed, this race of giants, living in this green valley, looks as if nothing could ever astonish them—walking miracles themselves, in constant relation with the superhuman. (88)

Without flippancy she reads Martin Schongauer's *Rest on the Flight into Egypt* as a charming domestic idyll:

> a delightful oasis: palm and prickly pears, the latter conceived as growing at the top of a tree; below, lizards at play and deer grazing; in this place the Virgin has drawn up her ass, who browses in the thistles at his feet, while St. Joseph, his pilgrim bottle bobbing on his back, hangs himself with all his weight to the branches of a date palm, trying to get the fruit within reach. Meanwhile a bevy of sweet little angels have come to the rescue; they sit among the branches dragging them down towards him, and even bending the whole stem at the top so that he may get at the dates. (119–20)

And her sense of humor has full play in her summary of the series of paintings of the Griselda legend doubtfully attributed to Pinturicchio and now in the National Gallery in London. She reads these like a comic strip: the humble peasant father ("Bless my soul! the Lord Marquis!"), the proud marquis "with pointing finger" ("Where is your daughter?"), the marquis bringing Griselda rich garments ("Would you mind, dear Grizil, putting on these clothes to please me?"), the marquis later "standing hand on hip" confronting her father ("You see, after that I really can't keep her any longer"), while "several small dogs sniff at each other in the background" (109–10).

The longest essay in *Renaissance Fancies and Studies* is a narrative, "A Seeker of Pagan Perfection: Being the Life of Domenico Neroni, Pictor Sacrilegus." Like several of Walter Pater's *Imaginary Portraits,* her piece was inspired by the notion, popularized by Heinrich Heine in *Die Götter in Exil* (1853), of the displaced pagan gods returning to a medieval Christian world. In two of Pater's portraits, "Denys L'Auxerrois" (1886) and "Apollo in Picardy" (1893), innocent Christians possessed by pagan spirits suffer terrible fates. Vernon Lee's Neroni, "a contemporary of Perugino, of Ghirlandaio, of Filippino Lippi, and of Signorelli," whose life story she tells in the straightforward manner of Vasari's lives of the painters, is a Faustian figure. He is an artist obsessed with the pursuit of pure form. He rejects sculpture for painting because "a figure must needs look real when it is solid and you can walk round it, but to make men and women rise out of flat canvas or plastered wall, and stand and move as if alive, is truly the work of a god" (174). But he fails. "Too much of a seeker for new things, for secret and complicated knowledge, to undergo a mere widening of style like his more gifted or more placid contemporaries, he fell foul of his previous work and his previous masters, without finding a new line or new ideals" (185).

One day in Rome he sees an ancient statue of Bacchus and a young satyr in which he finds perfect form: "a sense of ease, of suavity, of full-blown harmony." Soon after, he meets a humanist scholar, widely traveled, an expert in the lore of paganism. Together they begin to practice secret rites in an abandoned church built on the fragments of a pagan temple on the Aventine hill. Though he knows that the pagan gods are damned, he is willing to risk his soul to learn the Greek sculptor's formula for perfect proportion and harmony: "convinced that this secret could be communicated only by a Pagan divinity, just as certain kinds of mysteries, such as the use of the rosary, had been revealed to the saints by Christ or the Virgin." He and the scholar are discovered in the midst of their pagan ritual, condemned as heretics, and burned in the public square.

This gruesome and rather pointless story nevertheless has its place in a book dedicated to the memory of Walter Pater, "the natural exponent of the highest aesthetic doctrine—the search for harmony throughout all orders of existence." Like Neroni, Pater began his career with total dedication to aesthetics, "art for art's sake." But unlike Neroni, he moved from the search for aesthetic harmony to "the knowledge of beauty of the spiritual kind." Having denied earlier in *Baldwin* that religion is the source and inspiration of morality, Vernon Lee shared with Pater a kind of secular idealism. She never denied the existence of the soul, the source of our capacity to perceive and appreciate beauty in nature and in art. But precisely how aestheticism could stretch to ethics and morality, to human conduct, remained unresolved. The youthful Baldwin had argued in "The Responsibilities of Unbelief" that God (she did not deny the existence of God, only the possibility of knowing God through religion) is unknowable. In "The Consolations of Belief," still an "unbeliever" in conventional religion, Baldwin says: "I think that morality is a necessity grown out of social life, that the only duties of man are towards the mortal creatures of the present and the future, and the highest possible conception of mankind is the man who enlarges the sphere of its moral obligations" (*Baldwin* 117).[9]

Eight years later she returned to these arguments in another collection of philosophical dialogues, *Althea: A Second Book of Dialogues on Aspirations and Duties.* The alteration of the subtitle from *Baldwin*'s "Dialogues on Views and Aspirations," with its new emphasis on *duties,* signifies a profound change in outlook. After a long period of grief and introspection, she was ready to offer the world the results of her reflections. As she described her work to her mother in July 1893: "It is far the most important book I have so far written, and a great immeasurable advance on *Baldwin.* . . . It is a study, on the whole, not of everybody's duty, but of the duties of those who have spiritual conceptions and compensations, and, being freer than others from the ties of the world (desire for pleasure, prosperity, ambition, vanity) ought to act as pioneers for those far more numerous persons whom circumstances and temper render less free."

The genre of the philosophical dialogue is didactic by its nature, but as Plato used it there was a genuine element of dialogue involved. Socrates questioned and gradually evoked from his pupils the wisdom they presumably possessed innately. The problem with the essays in both *Baldwin* and *Althea* is that, while philosophical, they are not truly dialogues. They are monologues interspersed with passages of descriptive writing—her speakers walk in the country or on the seashore, commenting on the scenery and the changes in weather, or they visit churches and art galleries that serve merely as background for their talk. Their responses have no element of spontaneity, no suggestion of intellectual exchange and growth. Oscar Wilde used the same genre in "The Decay of Lying" and "The Critic as Artist" (1891–92) with infinitely more wit but with the same results—an extended essay arguing the author's thesis, broken into parts that keep the discussion going without challenging the reader to examine her own thinking on the subject.

The "C.A.T." to whom *Althea* is dedicated is Kit, who participates in all the dialogues as Althea. The book is a gallant but curiously ambivalent tribute to her devoted friend:

> Althea is naturally the pupil of Baldwin; for, being all she is by the mere grace of God, she is, at first, inarticulate, unreasoning, ignorant of all why and wherefore, and required to be taught many things which others know. But, once having learned the names, so to speak, of her instincts, the premises of her unconscious argument, she becomes, as necessarily, the precursor of Baldwin's best thoughts, the perfecter of most of them. (xvii–xviii)

That Kit was not an intellectual she would have been the first to admit. An upper-class country girl with a hearty constitution and enormous physical energy, she grew up in the home of a father whose two-volume autobiography records his military, hunting, and equestrian achievements in loving detail but barely mentions his family and gives no inkling of any cultural interests. Although in the role of Althea Kit calls herself "rude . . . selfish and stupid . . . [I] have never been taught anything except to ride," she was in fact not "ignorant of all why and wherefore." She had studied at the Slade School of Art in London and taken painting lessons in Paris in the studio of Carolus Duran, John Singer Sargent's teacher. Her principal talents, however, seem to have been directed toward more physically demanding activities like nursing the sick and managing a household. She gave Violet generously of her strength as a supportive friend as well as an attentive disciple.

Althea is a sincere tribute to her, and to the extent that Althea responds with unfailing interest and intelligent (i.e., leading) questions to Baldwin's pronouncements, she is an ideal companion. She is also a strikingly handsome woman; Vernon Lee describes her as a combination of the classical beauty of Venus de Milo and a child of nature out of Rousseau, "with her large, calm, blond beauty, and that mixture of moral gravity and unconscious poetical vision, of being in some odd way closely akin to the trees and grass, and clouds and sea, the real things of the world as she called them" (4). But Kit was also a physical being with whom Violet was by now in love, extending the Socratic spirit to the worship of a beautiful body, "like that of some antique youth in whose marble effigy we fancy we recognize one of the speakers of the *Phaedo* or the *Euthydemus*" (7).

Other speakers introduced in *Althea* are good friends. Donna Maria, who shares Baldwin's views on the morality of art and his suspicions of modern music like Wagner's "Liebestod" ("unholy . . . suggests all the wild beasts in mankind" [85]), is either Maria Pasolini or Maria Gamba. Carlo, the young cosmopolitan realist and enthusiastic defender of modernism in all the arts, is Carlo Placci. Signora Elena, a wise woman who detects Althea's "stoical sense of duty" and Baldwin's "aesthetical pessimism" and reminds them both of "the simple, commonplace thing called love," is Baroness Elena French Cini, a lifelong friend. The young Russian Boris is Peter Boutourline, an impassioned antisocialist who nevertheless agrees with Baldwin's views on the unequal distribution of wealth and the social obligation of the upper classes to assist the poor. The professor, a defender of religion and the nobility of the soul "because it can be united to God," is Nencioni.[10] Althea listens and reacts in all these dialogues: "Althea had been following the discussion with that intent, rather puzzled look of hers, earnestly separating the grain and the chaff." But Baldwin is the center of every dialogue. When the professor comments to her, "What a disciple Baldwin has found in you!" she replies, "I cannot understand why he hasn't found many more . . . I had never heard about such things before I met him; but when he told me, it seemed wonderful that I could have lived so long without finding it out for myself" (256).

By 1890 Kit had established herself firmly in Violet's home and heart. Mary Robinson had been replaced by a woman in many ways better suited to Violet's needs. While both Mary and Kit had friends and family ties in England, separating from Violet part of every year, Kit was far more committed to their relationship than Mary, with her many admirers both male and female and her own thriving literary career, had ever been. Violet knew even in the years of their closest relationship that Mary was as much a peer as a disciple. Her affection had been offered generously because she respected Violet's learning and shared many of her interests, but she never subordinated herself to her companion. In James Darmesteter, Mary had found a man of even greater learning, of wider and more solid intellectual achievements. When he died in 1894, she remained in France, cherishing his memory by translating a collection of his essays (*English Studies,* 1896) and supporting the Dreyfusard cause. In 1901 she remarried, this time to a man of even higher reputation than Darmesteter, Emile Duclaux (1840–1904), a prominent scientist.

Kit had humbly offered herself with the flower she left on Violet's pillow that August day in 1887 when Mary announced her engagement to Darmesteter. She waited patiently during the following months while Violet and her family struggled to prevent the marriage. When in her despair Violet felt herself abandoned both by Mary and by her own family, stolid Kit took over. But in 1898 she too broke away. While Violet grieved at her loss, it was not the emotional crisis she had suffered over Mary. Rather it was the simple recognition of the inevitable—that she could love but she could never make, nor expect from another, the total commitment of a fulfilled sexual relationship. On 18 August 1904, six years after Kit had returned to England, she wrote to her recalling her first visit to Charleton:

> I got the news that the first great friendship and love of my life had come to an end; next evening when the little white rose on my pillow told me that a new, greater, eternal (I think, dear Kit) one had begun . . . and every turn of the road tells me of those strange dream-like months of illness and hopelessness, of misery and of such enveloping happiness out of which your patience and loving kindness drew me, a new creature. You have made whatever there is of humanly decent in me, Kit; and that alone will make you care for me.

It was not until 1924, three years after Kit's death and a quarter century after their amicable separation, that she publicly expressed her appreciation of Kit's discipleship. Under Violet's tutelage Kit had written some short pieces on art appreciation that she now collected in *Art and Man: Essays and Fragments,* to which Vernon Lee added a long introduction. In Kit she had found a "natural"—unsophisticated and malleable, with a spontaneous reaction to art that Violet, with her highly developed tastes and sensibility and her vast knowledge, lacked. "She was always *seeing,* asking herself *what,* or rather *how* she saw. And, becoming aware that, in her sense of *seeing,* I saw half nothing, I tried to learn a little *to see,* looking at her way of looking at things. This, when it was successful, meant that I was learning to see a little with my own eyes and my own reactions" (*Art and Man* 30).

Kit was probably less influential in the development of her aesthetics than Violet credited her. But she was useful in a way that Mary Robinson was not, and Violet was genuinely grateful to her. Kit was at her side for much of the time in the difficult last years of her parents' lives. In November 1894 when Henry Paget died suddenly following an attack of asthma, Kit was in England nursing a sick friend, Mona Taylor. As soon as she learned of his death, she wrote Violet offering to come at once to Il Palmerino, but Violet did not ask her to come. Her father had been too little a presence in the lives of his family to be much noticed, dead or alive. He had requested that he be cremated, although he knew that Mrs. Paget owned a family plot in the Allori Cemetery in Florence. Sensing no doubt the appropriateness of her father's wish—for Violet had deep though unexpressed feeling for him— she arranged a private cremation. Her mother, by then in failing health herself, never knew. In early 1896 she became critically ill. Fortunately for Violet, Kit was then with her at Il Palmerino, and they shared the duties of nursing the dying woman. In the early morning hours of March 8, sensing her exhaustion, "Kit sent me to bed. And when she woke me at dawn it was to say that my mother had died in her arms" (*Art and Man* 18).

Matilda Paget's death released Violet at last from the ties of family obligation. For years Violet had been consulting specialists in London and Paris about her brother's paralysis. They all agreed that his condition was neurasthenic. Some recommended massage therapy, some hypnosis, all predicted that recovery, if it came, would be gradual, as indeed it was. In a letter to Eugene of 31 August 1893 from London, she wrote: "How wonderful to get a whole letter in your handwriting." She also observed that with his improvement he would soon have the energy to read with greater concentration—presumably relieving her of the responsibility of recruiting the secretary-amanuenses he required. With Mrs. Paget's failing health she was increasingly aware of the burden of caring for her brother. She commiserated with her friend Elena French Cini, who had suffered a nervous illness from nursing her invalid son, and she wrote to Kit: "I remember when I was young the extraordinary feeling of being squeezed out like a lemon by the mere fact of sitting constantly in the same room and under the eye of my brother" (24 June 1902). By 1895, however, he was walking, and immediately after Mrs. Paget's funeral he announced that he was leaving the Casa Paget. In a full recovery that would have seemed miraculous were it not for the obviously psychosomatic nature of his invalidism, Eugene Lee-Hamilton went forth into the world. He traveled, often by bicycle, in Italy and England and in 1897 ventured across the Atlantic to visit Canada and the United States. Edith Wharton, who entertained him at her home in Newport, remembered him as a delightful guest, "rejoicing in his recovered vigour, and keeping us and our guests in shouts of laughter by his high spirits and inimitable stories" (*A Backward Glance* 132). Even more remarkable was his trip to Neosho Falls, in southeastern Kansas in midsummer for a week's visit with a fan, Florence L. Snow, who had read some of his poems in American periodicals in 1889 and started a correspondence with him. He addressed a sonnet to her (published in his *Wingless Hours*). Miss Snow, a local literary celebrity herself, reported in her memoir *Pictures on My Wall: A Lifetime in Kansas* (1945) that he was delighted with everything—fried chicken suppers, buggy rides over the prairie, and Methodist church socials.

In 1898 Eugene married Annie Holdsworth, a feminist and modestly successful novelist. They settled in a hillside villa in San Gervasio, not far from Il Palmerino, where they had a lively social life and collaborated on a volume of verse, *Forest Notes,* in 1899. In 1903 he published his first and only novel, *The Lord of the Dark Red Star.* According to Florence Snow, the publisher, Walter Scott, failed to promote the novel and it "added little if anything to his previous standing." Over the years he also undertook a translation of Dante. He had completed the *Inferno* and was working on the *Purgatorio* at the time of his last illness.

For Violet liberation from her family came late, perhaps too late for her to savor it. She maintained a distant relationship with Eugene, attending his wedding in England, receiving the couple at Il Palmerino when they settled in Italy, and visiting them at least once in San Gervasio. She reported to Kit on that visit in October 1898: "My brother has much improved since his marriage. They very kindly met me at the station. My sister-in-law has made me a nice birthday present and seems dreadfully anxious for good terms. But oh! oh! They dined here on my birthday. And the dulness [*sic*], the want of manners, the perpetual saying of things (on her part) that made one hot— platitudes." A distinct coolness arose between them when her sister-in-law became pregnant in 1902. "Nannie, I feel sure, longed for a child; they are both in 7th heaven. It wasn't, I think, an accident. Only she'd given up hope, I fancy." Violet confided to Kit, however, that her readings in psychology convinced her that "E. has *no* right to have children. It isn't the individual child, it's the *taint* communicated to the race. Of course he considers himself quite sound, or affects to. I think that as is usual in such cases, there is the saving grace of not realising anything except one's inclinations" (13 December 1902). And in a letter to her brother that ironically recalled their correspondence years earlier over Mary Robinson's impending marriage, she could not resist a personal thrust:

> I have long come to the conclusion that, in matters where public opinion is not decided, each individual must act according to his own conscience and experience and that it is no one's business to be the keeper even of their nearest and dearest's notions of right and wrong, still less to judge of their application in concrete cases. You think one way, I another. I only regret I had not arrived at this attitude when Mary married James Darmesteter, and that I let you override my acquiescence. (Gunn 163)

To the inconsolable grief of her parents, the child, a daughter named Persis, died in less than a year. Eugene never forgave his sister for her disapproval, and a few days after the baby's death he acknowledged her letter of condolence bitterly: "I am grateful for your kind words. But had you given her a single smile or penny toy while she was alive, it would have been more to the purpose, and would have left you none the poorer—perhaps even a little the richer" (Gunn 164). The charge was unfair, but Eugene was not aware that Violet had provided generously for her niece. She had written to Kit (7 January 1904) that "after much deliberation and not without considerable bitterness (for I know well how I should like to employ my money) I have settled £2000 on my niece. She will have another five or so from her father. They must not know it, because my sister-in-law is a spendthrift. But I want you to know. The poor wretched child is the least attractive figure on God's whole earth to me!"

With his wife Eugene wrote a poem eulogizing their child, "Mimma Bella: In Memory of a Little Life," published in the *Fortnightly Review* in November 1907 and, along with some other poems, as a book in 1909. According to his widow, he never recovered from the loss: "The child filled her father's life; it was almost as if she gave him back something of what he had lost."[11] His physical health began to fail, and in June 1905 Violet wrote her friend Maurice Baring that she planned to accompany him and his wife to Switzerland, where he was to undergo surgery. During this period she was supportive, but—as she confessed in a letter to Kit—uncaring. "Ever since this illness began, even when apparently much better, life seemed a mere worry and dreariness to him. I am very sorry for my sister-in-law, who is very gallant about it all. But, although I know how bad things are, I seem unable to feel anxiety. I have worn out my capacity for anxiety, if ever I had one. I really am very hard hearted" (25 November 1906).

If indeed Violet's reaction to what was to be her brother's fatal illness—a combination of kidney disease and arteriosclerosis—was hard-hearted, it was the result of the years of attrition in what had once been her warm affection for him. Some months before his death she wrote Baring that he had lapsed into a coma:

> I pray and implore fate it may end soon; it is horrible seeing him reduced bodily and mentally to the state of a very, very old man, or rather, of a baby. . . . So, dear Maurice, wish with me that when you receive this it may be over. And yet one clings to him when one sees him sleeping quietly, looking so like what he did when you saw him first on his sofa, and when he smiles and says dear, childish, half-intelligible things.

And as she had so often done before, she questioned her own feelings:

> Could I have abridged his first illness if I had more knowledge and more courage? Been gentler (alas, I was ill and impatient) during his recovery when my father and mother died? One wants to blame somebody or something; for such a sad, sad story—and perhaps there is no one. (7 January 1907)

Eugene survived until September 1907 and was buried alongside his mother and his child. The "sad, sad" story did not end there. Violet had apparently lent him money for the purchase of his villa in San Gervasio, and the question of its disposal arose immediately. On 14 September 1907 she wrote to assure her sister-in-law that there was no need for her to leave immediately, but she made it clear that she could not afford to buy the property "as a speculation": "You have til February to make up your mind about the house; please, please do not talk to me about it til you can listen without wincing and I can speak without disgracing myself."

It is apparent to any student of human nature that Violet's hard-heartedness was a defensive weapon. Her close friend Irene Cooper Willis recalled her once saying: "I *am* hard. I *am* cold. . . . Liking people does not mean for me devotion: it means only my answer, as it were, to qualities in them which please or charm me. Loving them in the way you speak of, in the way of being willing to do anything for them, is *intolerable* to me. I *cannot* like, or love, at the expense of having my skin rubbed off" (Gunn 203). Having deep and passionate commitments to other people, she was vulnerable to every slight — of which, largely due to her own actions, she received many. Her skin had perhaps too often been "rubbed off." Ethel Smyth, so forthright and uncomplicated in her own relationships, went directly to the heart when she described visiting Violet in 1900, soon after she and Kit had separated:

> Myself, I believe the tragedy of her life was that without knowing it she loved the *cultes* humanly and with passion; but being the stateliest, chastest, of beings, she refused to face the fact, or indulge in the most innocent

demonstrations of affection, preferring to create a fiction that these friends were merely *intellectual* necessities. . . . The thought, say, of a good bear-hug would have been, I fancy, as alien and would have seemed as vulgar to her as much mild slang we all indulge in now and then. One day in an extra-expansive mood I gave her a parting hug myself, and though she bore it with kindness and courtesy, I felt I had committed a solecism. (Gunn 167)

Compounding the problem, as the century ended Violet Paget faced the challenge of separating herself the serious writer from her public image of pundit—"this clever woman who calls herself Vernon Lee." [12] Like many of her middle-aged contemporaries who crossed the millennium into the twentieth century, she carried what the younger generation regarded as the burden of Victorianism. Cleverness no longer gave a woman distinction, at least not in the fields where she sought distinction: aesthetics, cultural history, social reform. Never merely clever, Vernon Lee had yet to establish herself as an authority on anything except an obscure area of Italian cultural history, and even here she had been superseded by more academically trained scholars. But she was still a presence, a personality in English and in Anglo-Italian society. This celebrity, although she enjoyed it, was not enough for her still burgeoning ambition. The time had come for solid and substantial achievement, and this Vernon Lee, with the willing and adoring Kit still beside her, set out to accomplish.

9 AESTHETICS AND THE HEALTH
   OF THE SOUL

*There are almost as many books written by women now as men . . . it is certainly
true that women no longer write novels solely. There are Jane Harrison's books
on Greek archaeology; Vernon Lee's books on aesthetics; Gertrude Bell's books on
Persia.*

Virginia Woolf, *A Room of One's Own*

🖋 AESTHETICS IN LATE NINETEENTH-CENTURY ENGLAND WAS
largely appreciative and descriptive. Much as they differed in their approaches, Ruskin and Pater shared a vision of art as the noblest expression
of which humanity was capable, uplifting and therefore beneficial to the individual as well as to society as a whole. Although the conflict between art
and morality had not been resolved, and "art for art's sake" remained a slogan for several generations of young iconoclasts, the common ground had
been firmly settled in midcentury when Baudelaire denounced "the childish utopianism of the school of art for art's sake in ruling out morals." [1]
When Vernon Lee resolved in *Belcaro* to become an aesthetic critic, she had
no problem reconciling her convictions about pure beauty and perfect form
with her earnest belief in humanitarianism and the moral obligation of the
educated and affluent to work for social reform. She was not the first, though
she may have been among the last, of the puritan aesthetes, those who felt
the need to justify on moral grounds the pleasure that art gives.

More troubling for her and many of her contemporaries was accommo-
dating pure aestheticism with the scientific advances of the age. An aesthetics based in descriptive, appreciative art criticism was inadequate to explain
the individual's experience of art. What was now required was analysis. Why
and how do we respond to a painting, a work of sculpture? We recognize a
subject, we appreciate the technique of the artist. But we do not merely *read*
a work of art, nor are we merely observing the emotions depicted in that
work. For example, we respond to the *Laocoön* with fear and horror because
we know the story it represents. But even if ignorant of the subject, even if

the educated intellect were not engaged, would we not react with similar sensations? Analysis extends and enlarges the experience of art because, beyond the intellectual, it seeks out the natural, instinctive responses that are physiological and psychological.

In April 1896 Vernon Lee reviewed a book by a young American, Bernard Berenson's *Florentine Painters of the Renaissance,* for the journal of psychology *Mind.* She acknowledged at the outset that this was a book "destined for a very different public" from the scientific community who read *Mind:*

> That Mr. Berenson is not a student of mental science . . . that his book shows no traces of psychological training are circumstances which . . . enhance rather than diminish the interest of his work in the eyes of psychologists. . . . It comes not as a result of philosophical speculation on the connection between art and other mental phenomena, but in the course of an attempt, on the part of an already distinguished connoisseur and art-historian, to make others share the aesthetic emotions of which he is himself aware. (270)

Though she expressed reservations about Berenson's limitations as a student of aesthetics ("essentially a connoisseur, a professional expert rather than an engaging [engaged?] aesthete"), she endorsed his thesis that "the aesthetic phenomenon has a very distinct *raison d'être* in the fact that it represents a direct increase in vitality or, as Mr. Berenson expressed it, that 'art can give us the life-enhancing qualities of objects.'" Furthermore, he defined "life-enhancing" very much as Vernon Lee would have defined it—as offering a moral as well as a physical benefit: "By 'life enhancement,'" he wrote, "I mean the ideated identification of ourselves with a person, the ideated participation in an action, the ideated plunging into a state of being, or state of mind, that makes one feel more hopefully, more zestfully alive; living more intense, more radiant a life not only physically but morally and spiritually as well." [2]

Having been herself for years a student of "the how and why of the perceptive and emotional phenomena connected with art and the Beautiful," Vernon Lee welcomed a fellow student of the relationship between mind and body in our responses to art. Impressions received by the eye are converted into "bodily activity" and have "tactile" values. She quotes Berenson: "Unless my retinal impressions are immediately translated into images of strain and pressure in my muscles . . . of touch all over my body, it means nothing to me in terms of vivid (visual) expression" (271). The connection that Berenson made between "tactile values" and "life-enhancing qualities" confirmed her long held conviction of what she called "the general wholesomeness of art." Her essay "Beauty and Sanity," published only a year earlier in the *Fortnightly Review* of August 1895 (collected in *Laurus Nobilis*), had argued that beauty in art or in nature alike "has moral worth . . . even mere bodily sensations, of pure air, bracing temperature, vigor of muscles, efficiency of viscera, accustom us not merely to the health of our body, but also, by the analogies of our inner workings, to the health of our soul" (*Laurus Nobilis* 119).

Like many of her contemporaries, Vernon Lee had moved from the subjective aesthetics of German romanticism to an aesthetics that could be quantified and analyzed by observing the spontaneous responses of the body to a work of art. As early as 1880 she had been pronouncing magisterially on "comparative aesthetics" in the *Contemporary Review*, criticizing the major writers on aesthetics from Winckelmann, Lessing, and Hegel to Taine and Ruskin for suggesting that art is "a shapeless, lawless fluid which has no shape of its own but assumes the shape of the vessel wherein it is contained." Rather, she argued, art "is an organic physico-mental entity, whose forms depend not upon coercion from without, but upon growth from within." Central to all appreciation is form: "the mental combination of lines, colours or sounds of which the concrete works of art are but the visible and lifeless image." In *Belcaro* a year later she reaffirmed that "the work of art exists in the lines, tints, lights and shades of the picture or statue, in the modulations and harmonies of a composition, and . . . all the rest is gratuitously added by ourselves" (66).

The proper study, therefore, is "absolute aesthetics," which isolates art from its social and historical contexts and examines solely "the relations between the work of art and the mind which perceives it." In William James's celebrated *Principles of Psychology* (1890) she found scientific corroboration for the connection of mind and body: "A disembodied human emotion is a sheer nonentity . . . emotion dissociated from all bodily feeling is inconceivable." James allowed for the physiological responses that she and Kit Anstruther-Thomson had been observing: "All mental states," he wrote, "are followed by bodily activity of some sort. They lead to inconspicuous changes in breathing, circulation, general muscular tension, and glandular or other visceral activity" (*Briefer Course* 28). But James, who dismissed aesthetics as "the study of the useless," had less to offer the student of aesthetics than did a large number of German psychologists, among them Theodor Lipps, whose theory of *Einfühlung* (roughly translated as "feeling into" or "empathy"), published in his *Raumästhetik* in 1896, provided a scientific basis for the appreciation of art. "As the *word* sympathy is intended to suggest, this subduing yet liberating, this enlivening and pacifying power of beautiful form over our feeling," Vernon Lee wrote in another essay, "Art and Usefulness," "is exercised only when our feelings enter, and are absorbed into the form we perceive; so that (very much in the case of human vicissitudes) we participate in the supposed life of the form while in reality lending *our* life to it" (*Laurus Nobilis* 239–40).

In trying to reconcile the artist/poet and the scientist, Vernon Lee leaned heavily on the romantic concept of the creative imagination while simultaneously absorbing the theories of psychologists like James, Lipps, Carl Lange, Théodule Ribot, Karl Groos, Oswald Külpe, and Giuseppe Sergi. She confessed in her preface to *Beauty and Ugliness* (1912) that "my aesthetics will always be those of the gallery and the studio, not of the laboratory. They will never achieve scientific certainty."[3] In various places in that volume and, years later, in her introduction to her collection of Kit's writings, *Art and Man* (1924), she supports her argument with quotations from Wordsworth ("Tintern Abbey" and *The Prelude*), Shelley (from "Ode to the West Wind": "make me thy lyre . . . Be thou me, impetuous one!"), and in more than one passage Coleridge's "Dejection: An Ode"—"Oh Lady! We receive but what we give, / And in our life alone does Nature live," which "sums up the fundamental principles of modern psychological aesthetics." But she also looked to the scientists who gave empirical support to what she called "aesthetic empathy." "Will art ever become the object of a science not less antiquarian and scholarly but more informed by the facts and methods of psychology and biology?" she asked. Her unique contribution, she felt, would be a synthesis, applying the methodology of science—close observation, experimentation, and minute analysis of the viewer's physiological and emotional reactions to the experience of art.

Early on, Violet decided that in Kit Anstruther-Thomson she had found the ideal instrument for her investigations. Though trained in art and skilled in simple drawing, Kit had little initial knowledge of or interest in classical sculpture or medieval and Renaissance painting. As early as 1892 she had given up the idea of becoming a painter, but as an eager pupil of her master Vernon Lee she became a student of aesthetics. They traveled about Italy with Kit sketching and Violet making notes on landscape, gardens, churches, museums. From her master's pronouncements on political economy Kit also absorbed a sense of social responsibility, a duty to educate the less fortunate. Accordingly, in London she volunteered to teach drawing classes for workingmen and -women and to introduce East Enders to the galleries and museums of the West End. In the winter months that she spent with Violet in Italy from 1889 until 1897, she was her devoted amanuensis. In training, as it were, to serve Violet she read art history and Berenson's master Giovanni Morelli, "the rather enigmatic master of the new study called connoisseurship." Never a systematic student, "Kit simply walked from subject to subject and back again as she walked from picture to picture, from statue to statue, and from church to church, according as it offered itself on her path or came up in conversation" (*Art and Man* 28).

For Violet, Kit's fresh innocence of the arts opened new areas for investigation. "Until then I really knew of works of art only that much which can be translated into literature." For years she had written about art by describing it, a method that in some instances, notably Walter Pater's essay on La Gioconda, produced literary masterpieces but that more often missed the essential question, What is the work of art doing? Observing Kit observing a picture and reporting her changes in respiration, muscular tension, and posture, was a revelation for Violet. "It was not she, but I myself, who discovered that I had written about art without really seeing it" (29). When Kit reacted instinctively and spontaneously, she was "furnishing a psychological framework for observations and experiments." These were "the distinct pre-Freudian days [when] the word *psychology* meant nothing very definite for either of us . . . it had never yet occurred to me that such high philosophical topics could be dealt with as a part of the science of Mind and Mind's relation with Body" (46).

Many years later she looked back at those exciting days of discovery with a mixture of sober realism and humility:

> Like, no doubt, many other over-hasty discoverers, we believed ourselves to have found one of the Keys to the Universe, a key which would instantly turn in the lock and reveal all the mysteries of art psychology to every observer. . . . For when two people work together in complete mutual agreement they are apt to shut out from their view all the rest of the world. Quite natural and proper, and perhaps we should not have achieved as much as we did had we suspected from the first that our achievement was not final, but required the help of a lot of other people, and more especially their criticism and discouragement. (*Art and Man* 49)

Criticism and discouragement came quickly enough when they published their first collaboration, the two-part essay "Beauty and Ugliness," in the *Contemporary Review,* October–November 1897. They announced their thesis boldly: "Aesthetics, if treated by the method of recent psychology, will be recognized as one of the most important and most suggestive parts of the great science of perception and emotion" (*Beauty and Ugliness* 157). Equally bold was the fundamental aesthetic question they raised: "Why should the perception of form be accompanied by pleasure or displeasure, and what determines the pleasure in one case and the displeasure in another?" The essay proceeds to record a series of Kit's experiences (set off in bracketed passages initialed "C.A.T."), followed by Vernon Lee's interpretations. The premise behind their experiments was to demonstrate the correlation between the spontaneous physical reactions of a viewer to a work of art and that viewer's conscious appreciation of aesthetic form.

The experiments began with simple experiences, like the observation of a chair, a blank wall, a jar. Recording in detail so minute that at times it borders on the ludicrous, C.A.T. writes, for example:

> The chair is a bilateral object, so the two eyes are equally active. They meet the two legs of the chair at the ground and run up both sides simultaneously. There is a feeling as if the width of the chair were pulling the two eyes wide apart during the process of following the upward line of the chair. Arrived at the top the eyes no longer pulled apart; on the contrary they converge inward along the top of the chair. (163)

C.A.T. also notices that the lungs, like the eyes, seem to "pull apart" at the bilateralness of the chair, at which point the breath is exhaled. Changes in respiration, circulation, and muscular tension are all carefully recorded. Extending this method of observation to a work of art, C.A.T. discovers its pure form, which draws her into the depth and dimensions of the picture or the piece of sculpture; its balance is realized in the balance of her body, the tension or relaxation of her muscles, the rate of her pulse. At this point Vernon Lee introduces the aesthetic questions: "Why should the perception of form be accompanied by pleasure or displeasure, and what determines the pleasure in one case and the displeasure in the other?" (170). Using as an example Titian's *Sacred and Profane Love,* with its balance of the two allegorical figures and their accompanying imagery, she suggests that viewers unconsciously imitate the inner movement and balance of the painting and experience a pleasurable sensation of harmony and increased vitality. "This supreme quality, which has its analogous one in every department of art, constitutes the picture into such a whole that we, in beholding, are not only made happy, but enclosed, forbidden to escape or lapse, and forced to move through every detail of a mood of happiness. Life outside seems obliterated, and the moment of consummate, self-effacing feeling to have come, and, as in the case of Faust, to have been fixed" (235).

The collaborators concluded that the body reacted to art by unconsciously imitating the form implicit in the work. This was not a discovery but an extension of the theory of empathy—"the unconscious attribution of our own modes of activity to visible forms." To illustrate, Vernon Lee cited the passage from *The Prelude* where the boy who has stolen a boat for a nighttime ride on the lake suddenly sees a mountain looming up in the darkness: "As if with voluntary power instinct / Upreared its head." Empathy, she explained, is "a mental process by which we attribute a movement not to the really moving object [the boat] but to the object which most attracts our attention [the mountain]" (*Art and Man* 72). Thus she enlists a work of creative imagination in the service of psychology, which by the late nineteenth century was recognized as a science. "The science of art," the German psychologist Ernst Grosse wrote, "is in the same position as all the other sciences. . . . The truth finally emerges out of the patient comparison; of numerous and various facts" (Gilbert and Lang 524).

Vernon Lee was soon to discover that the leap from art to science was not as easy as she and Kit had made it appear. Lipps himself reviewed their essay "Beauty and Ugliness" in the *Archiv für systematische Philosophie* and challenged the notion that the body has any part in "the phenomenon of Aesthetic Empathy." A psychological observation, he argued, is not a physical fact. Empathy is not a matter of physiological reaction but an emotional and subjective response. It is not a literal mimicry like C.A.T.'s experiences but an inner mimicry, a feeling of identity, the projection of one's self imaginatively into the object viewed. Over the next decade Vernon Lee altered and revised her views. When she reprinted the 1897 article in her collection *Beauty and Ugliness* in 1912, she added a footnote: "I must apologise to all readers versed in psychology for the cocksureness of extreme ignorance" (162). Her contrition was sincere, but it emerged not so much from the faulty logic and hasty conclusions of the earlier work as from the knowledge that the article had severely damaged her happy relationship with Kit. Ironically, it was Bernard Berenson who initiated the rift.

Vernon Lee was only beginning to explore psychological aesthetics in 1889 when she first met Berenson, whom she regarded as a kind of junior colleague. Given two such strong egos, however, both convinced of their omniscience, a constructive and harmonious association was not even remotely possible. They were too much alike in temperament—volatile, argumentative, sensitive to every slight real or imagined, dependent on the devotion of others.[4] Though of vastly different backgrounds, both had been youthful prodigies—Berenson less productive in his early years but brilliant enough to convince others of his promise. Though not rich, both lived sheltered lives, free to indulge in study and travel in the Europe of pre-1914, a cultural Eden for those with the means to enjoy it. Both were passionate in their dedication to their work and in their love for Italy, especially the Tuscan hills, where they lived as neighbors for most of their mature lives.

Like many students of Italian culture, Berenson made his pilgrimage to the Casa Paget on his first visit to Florence in the spring of 1889. Fresh out of Harvard with no publications except some pieces in the *Harvard Monthly*— among them a review in July 1886 of Vernon Lee's *Baldwin* which criticized that book's "fog banks of metaphysics, theology and economics" but offered praise for her *Studies of the Eighteenth Century in Italy, Belcaro,* and *Eupho-*

rion—he appeared one evening with a letter of introduction. To his dismay he found the salon crowded with members of Vernon Lee's *culte*. "What was I going to do in the midst of them?" he recalled years later. "I had to interest them and stupefy them with something which they would never have thought of. I know a little bit of Arab poetry, and I spoke about that" (Morra 93). At this stage of their relationship, the rivalry was on one side only. Violet was the senior in years and in experience of art, secure in her authority and unchallenged by her associates. Without deferring to her erudition, Berenson acknowledged her generosity and her usefulness to him:

> Then [January 1892] I went to call on Vernon Lee. She lives not far from S. Gervasio, whence to her house is a very pretty walk along the heavily shaded Africo. I was received by Miss Thomson, and a little later Vernon Lee came in in riding costume. She found us plunged in talk already, and when she joined us, she monologized. I never heard such *spropositi* as she aired for an hour. I was scarcely polite in my stern dissent—when I got the chance to cry out a word. Perugino had a great influence on Botticelli she vowed. I begged for proof. He never would have painted scarves as he did if it were not for Perugino. . . . Then she came out with a theory that between creative process and creative process there was greater affinity, than between creative process and anything that is not creative. Now she was creative. Therefore she knew more what was in Botticelli's mind than I possibly could, for I was not creative. . . . Miss Thomson looked bewildered— not by her friend's *spropositi* I am sure, but by my bold dissent. I fancy she is not used to hearing Vernon Lee discredited. I enjoyed the call *quand même*, for it is a pleasure to talk with people who cerebrate, no matter how.[5] (*Letters* 11–12)

Accompanied by the ever present Kit, Violet would sweep through art museums with Berenson, infuriating him with her absolute and impregnable pronouncements yet winning his grudging respect. On one occasion they met at the Uffizi:

> They were there already and we pitched in at once, Vernon Lee talking like a steam engine, and neither of them looking at anything. I can't remember a tenth of their jabber, and most of it is too sickening, and too banale to be repeated. Vernon at any rate could see what you mean, if she could stop to [do] it, but Thomson is profoundly stupid. She makes an overwhelmingly stupid impression. (Berenson, *Letters* 14–15)

At times the "Palmerino Sibyl," another of the epithets he invented for her, came close to charming him:

I walked out nevertheless to Vernon Lee's this afternoon [January 1892]. She
was not at home, but I met her a little way down the road driving jauntily,
sandwiched in between Thomson and another female [Flora Priestly]. They
had been to the woods to gather herby smelling things which are very nice
for the fire. I turned back, and Vernon was excessively affable, seemed very
much more natural, or perhaps I have got used to her manner. She pulled
out the book of the Suardis [the *Oratorio Suardi* in Trescorre near Bergamo]
. . . and insisted on my taking and keeping it until she gets one for *me*. She
is sure she can. So she seems to be fair. I brought out some of the Lotto photos and she enjoyed them. She somehow makes you feel that she is intelligent. (*Letters* 24)

Confident as he was about his own expertise in art, Berenson never pre-
tended to be a good writer. Writing, he confessed in *Sketch for a Self-Portrait*
in 1949, "came hard . . . [it] was the only activity I could call work. For that
I seldom felt disposed and have not yet overcome this reluctance" (31–32).
In 1893 he asked Vernon Lee for her opinion of an essay he was writing on
Renaissance churches. She replied with a long critique, acknowledging his
"very rare" appreciation of art but noting also his weakness in "literary
expression." She offered to go over his essay point by point: "I am so confident of your future that I should be delighted to take a hundred times more
trouble than this would imply." She spared him nothing. On reading the
manuscript of his monograph on Lorenzo Lotto, she wrote that his introduction was "virtually an onslaught on archivists and documentary criticism [that] entirely fails to make the reader feel the immense gifts he is to
receive from the new school of criticism. . . . That is why I want you to learn
to write. You do not do justice to yourself, your conversation, your demonstrations in the gallery are full of suggestiveness and grip; your writings are
almost empty of them" (Samuels 26).

Berenson winced but swallowed her criticism along with his pride. In
the preface to his *Lorenzo Lotto: An Essay in Art Criticism* (1895) he thanked
"Miss Paget" for "suggestions while reading the manuscript." But he could
not have forgotten her censure, in a 1894 review in the *Academy* of his *Venetian Painters of the Renaissance,* that "Mr. Berenson has done rather badly
what so many essayists from Pater downwards have done very well." Even
here, however, she conceded that under the influence of Giovanni Morelli,
Berenson had discerned "the reality of artistic form" (Samuels 183). Nevertheless she believed that his vocation was connoirseurship not aesthetics.
She could have had no notion when she sent him the galleys of "Beauty and
Ugliness" in August 1897 that she was igniting a deadly fire.

Over the years a host of petty irritations built up in Berenson—his resentment over Violet's domination of all conversations, her refusal to accept him as a peer in art knowledge and give him the respect of colleagueship he demanded. An unknown young American in old Europe, he felt himself battling the art world establishment. In 1892 he had written Mary Costelloe from Florence that people never truly listen to what one is saying: "They pounce on some strongly accented word, and hear nothing else. It is because this is so true that such as Ruskin, Symonds, and Vernon Lee have their use. They shout a lot of nonsense at the public, and all the public gets out of it is the monosyllabic *art*. But once the public gets the ring of this monosyllable they will follow anybody who shouts it at them, you and me if we shout loud enough, as much as Ruskin and Co." (*Letters* 20).

Vernon Lee was the only one of this trio whom he knew personally when he wrote this letter, and he resented her. Gossip exacerbated his resentment. He had heard from Mary Costelloe, for example, that while lunching with his American patron Isabella Stewart Gardner in Venice, Violet had "uttered all the evil she could of you, how you were a dreadful poseur, always flitting about" (Samuels 286). He also suspected, not without some basis, that she regarded his connoirseurship as demeaning because he made his living by advising wealthy collectors. The suspicion rankled. More than half a century later he wrote in *Sketch for a Self-Portrait*: "A famous writer on the Renaissance, Vernon Lee, thought it was close and even mean of me not to let her share the secret [of his authority on art]. Finally it degenerated into a wide-spread belief that if only I could be approached the right way, I could order this or that American millionaire to pay thousands and thousands . . . for any daub that I was bribed by the seller to attribute to a great master" (39).

At the heart of Berenson's hostility to Vernon Lee, however, was something more than her abrasiveness and what he regarded as her often wildly erratic judgments on art ("For Vernon, Manet was a man utterly devoid of brains. Rossetti—that's the intellectual painter. You think he is no painter; oh, never mind, he is intellectual" [*Letters* 15]). What he could not conceal was his antipathy to Violet's asexuality. His resentment of her intimacy with Kit and the adoration she received from her *cultes* no doubt reflected his prejudice against lesbianism, but it went further. In January 1896 he wrote to Mary: "Veronia is still neighing contempt at art and aesthetics. Poor female to think at 40 of still pulling things to pieces—*er liebt mich, er liebt mich nicht.* Miss C [Maud Crutwell] thinks V. by nature very passionate and that her, V.'s, sourness is due to her never having had a man's love. As a little girl V. used to stay away when company came for fear people should ask 'Who is this frightful child?'" (*Letters* 37). Since Berenson considered Maud Crutwell, author of several respectable monographs on Italian painters and several novels, "stupid" and "a lineal descendant of Miss Bates [in Jane Austen's *Emma*]," his willingness to circulate her unconfirmed and unlikely story about Violet's childhood suggests a fundamental hostility, a prejudice so deeply rooted in his unconscious that it could find expression only in an explosion over a petty misunderstanding.

In the long run the plagiarism charge that Berenson raised against Vernon Lee and Kit Anstruther-Thomson had little basis, as he later admitted himself. The dispute was simply another teapot tempest over nothing more than some looseness of language. In what was certainly intended as a friendly gesture, Violet had sent galleys of "Beauty and Ugliness" to Berenson in August 1897. He was vacationing in St. Moritz, separated temporarily from his companion Mary Costelloe, who was in England visiting her family, the Pearsall-Smiths, formerly of Philadelphia. Mary, a Quaker by upbringing and a woman of good sense, tried to be a peacemaker. She admired Violet, enjoyed her hospitality at Il Palmerino, and had entertained her in 1894 at the Smith family home in Surrey, where she met Bertrand Russell, soon to become Mary's brother-in-law. Mary's first reaction to the article (as it was reported to her by Berenson) confirmed his charges, but she cautioned him against an open rift: "It would be a mistake for us to quarrel with Miss Paget . . . a person accusing another of stealing his ideas and printing them is always in a ridiculous position. It is true, it is certainly what she *has* done, she and the Anstruther, even to the very phrases, and the only recognition she makes is in a snubbing little note where she carefully omits giving the name of the book" (M. Berenson, *Self-Portrait* 72). The offending footnote—to a comment in the text that "aesthetic pleasure in art is due to the production of highly vitalising, and therefore agreeable, adjustments of breathing and balance as factors of the perception of form"—reads:

> In his remarkable volume on Tuscan painters (1896) Mr. B. Berenson has had the very great merit, not only of drawing attention to muscular sensations (according to him in the limbs) accompanying the sight of works of art, but also of claiming for art the power of *vitalising* or, as he calls it, *enhancing life*. Mr. Berenson offers a different and more intellectual reason for this fact than is contained in the present notes. In a series of lectures on Art and Life, delivered at the South Kensington [*sic*] in 1895, and printed the following year in the *Contemporary Review*, one of the joint authors of the present notes had attempted to establish that the function of art is not merely to increase vitality, but to regulate it in a harmonious manner. (*Beauty and Ugliness* 224–25)

Mary Costelloe concluded her letter by advising that he ignore the whole matter: "But I am sure *thy* best pose is a dignified approval of their work, a sort of taking-it-for-granted that these are commonplaces of aesthetic criticism—for so they are." Mary's letter was written on August 20 and probably did not reach Berenson in time to cool his feelings. On August 24 he addressed to "Dear Miss Paget" a long letter intended, presumably, to be bitingly witty but proving to be bitterly sarcastic. The tone was set in the mock courtesy of the opening:

> I fully appreciate yr. kindness in sending me the proof of yr. articles. I am sure you intended to give me a taste of that pleasure which the blessed gods used to take in first fruits. I have just had my first "read off" yr. paper & it certainly will not be the last. For where else shall I find such perfect distillations, such delightful reminders of numerous conversations I have [had] with you at the Palmerino & of even more numerous visits with Miss Anstruther-Thomson to the galleries? And here I must make the *amende honorable*. Do you remember my sustaining [sic] that Miss Anstruther-Thomson was quite without a memory, while you opposed that she had a memory superhuman, incapable of forgetting? I see from yr. paper that you were right. Her memory is indeed startling. I confess it inspires me with a certain awe; it is too much like conversing with a recording angel, I must add, a benevolent recording angel, one who stores up nothing against one, but takes the whole burden upon his own shoulders. (Berenson, *Letters* 55) [6]

Berenson continues in the same vein, praising the ideas in the essay as "familiar, cherished friends": "How can I sufficiently thank you!" With labored subtlety he praises the coauthors' "gift of putting things freshly, with the illusion of lucidity that I envy," and cites as "the one fatal drawback to this gift" their apparent unconsciousness of what they have done. "To people of my stamp, consciousness in every form, even under its ethical aspect of conscience is after all the one humanizing thing—that which distinguishes man from the brutes on the one hand, & the gods on the other." He ends with a thinly veiled threat of exposure: "Then as luck would have it a number of our common acquaintances have been here. We have been discussing art a great deal, so that they will be well prepared to appreciate the originality of your method & results in aesthetics. I am sure they all would be sending you their regards if they knew that I was writing."

For Violet the unkindest cut in this letter was not the plagiarism charge but his casual aside: "I am very sorry to hear of Miss Anstruther-Thomson's breakdown & anxious for her recovery. I am glad to know that she is better. Pray convey to her my thanks & kindest remembrances." Kit had fallen ill during the writing of "Beauty and Ugliness." Strenuous physical life had never damaged her splendid constitution, but for months she had been engaged in the most strenuous mental activity she had ever undertaken. She was by no means "stupid," "bovine," or "an ass," as Berenson had judged her, but she was not prepared intellectually or psychologically for the demands of this work. Mona Taylor, who had known Kit since her girlhood in Scotland, cautioned Violet in May 1897: "I think you entirely over-rate Kit's power of serious work. *She has not got it and will never have it except by killing her* [emphasis in original]. I say the last four words advisedly. You do not I think realize her physical or mental constitution. Having lived a desultory life for over 30 years, her mental muscles can't stand any steady strain." Writing about Kit years later in *Art and Man,* Violet acknowledged her failure to recognize the strain she was imposing on her devoted friend—the long hours in museums, the intense scrutiny and analysis of works of art, the effort of matching the pace at which Violet was accustomed to work. "Alas! I fear our actual collaboration over 'Beauty and Ugliness' was needlessly difficult in Kit's already overwrought condition" (54).

Berenson's expression of solicitude about Kit was an especially cruel thrust, more wounding than his sarcasm, and it provoked a long and angry reply from Violet on 2 September:

> I feel obliged, after some days of repugnance, to take notice of certain statements and implications contained in your ostensibly very friendly and courteous letter, lest you should, perchance, misinterpret my silence as much as I still hope I may be misapprehending your words.
>
> First let me thank you for all the fine things you say about my powers of expression. They are the more welcome because, as three quarters of the essay are written, with scarcely a word of alteration, by Miss Anstruther-Thomson, it would appear that she participates in a quality which you find rarer than I do.

Mincing no words, she takes his letter as an accusation of plagiarism:

> For the plain English of your elaborate ambiguities . . . the plain English of all this equivocating sarcasm is that Miss Anstruther-Thomson and I have stolen the larger part of our essay from our conversations. I set it down in all its crudeness, because I believe that whatever mean and absurd things your tendency to exaggeration and your pleasure in complicated utterances may have hurried you into writing, you will recoil from acknowledging that a thought so ludicrous and so detestable ever seriously formulated itself in your mind.

The essence of Violet's defense is simply "the fact that we were both of us looking for the secret of aesthetics in the same direction and with the same methods." Apart from this general similarity, she insists that there are vast distances between them. She had acknowledged these differences in her review of his *Florentine Painters* in *Mind* and in their many discussions. Choosing the high road, she writes: "I as yet decline to hold you responsible for the charge of wholesale robbery which constitutes the gist of your letter; a charge which, had you seriously and deliberately maintained, your own manliness & good sense would have couched in the form of a straightforward & specified statement, rather than in semi-jocular ambiguities." She closes in a spirit of forgiveness—but cannot resist a personal thrust: "I have the greatest admiration (I have shown it in writing twice about you and in helping you in yr tongue-tied days) for your talents."

Violet's efforts to protect Kit by concealing Berenson's charges from her were not successful, and as she feared, Kit's sense of honor precluded any easy resolution. "To her rather military notions of honour, PLAGIARISM, if she had ever heard of it, was akin to cheating at cards, the kind of offence for which men are expelled from clubs, to wander outlawed ever after" (*Art and Man* 56). Vernon Lee was accustomed to criticism, and she was prepared for the cool reception of their article by Lipps and others. But Kit, still ailing, insisted on a full airing of the charges. She felt that the burden of defense was on her shoulders and refused to be satisfied with Mary Costelloe's report in a letter to Violet 7/8 November 1897 that "Mr. Berenson confessed that he made a mistake in proffering an actual charge of plagiarism against you and Miss Thomson and that as he was not able to prove it, he would not repeat the accusation. . . . He asks me to send his regrets and apologies and to tell you that he will say the same to the two people with whom he talked it over [probably Carlo Placci and the Countess Maria Pasolini]" (Samuels 289). For her part Violet would have accepted this apology—though at secondhand through an intermediary—but she was sensitive to her responsibility to Kit and her responsibility for Kit's illness.

Mary Costelloe became the referee, then, in a dispute in which the two principals were no longer actively involved. Violet invited her to Il Palmerino for a "thorough hearing" of the case before witnesses—Maud Crutwell and Evelyn Wimbush. As Mary recorded it in her diary for 26 November, Kit emotionally defended herself, saying, "If I stole my ideas from Mr. Berenson, how is it I am now suffering from brain-exhaustion?" Violet, on the other hand, cited her many writings on aesthetics over the years, all of them emphasizing the importance of form and the vitalizing effects of beauty. Mary's conclusion was that she liked Violet "better than before," but that her "bad opinion" of Kit had "deepened." Berenson was satisfied to wash his hands of the whole affair. On 28 November he wrote his sister Senda, with a particularly nasty allusion to Kit, that his "acquaintance [was] diminished by the whole Vernon Lee clan, her brother, her ass, her manservant, and all that is hers" (Samuels 290).

It was not so easy for Violet, however. Not only was Kit's unhappiness a painful reminder, but she was also having second thoughts about the thesis she and Kit had argued in their essay. Lipps's criticism that they had reduced aesthetics to physiology—summed up in his remark that "it is impossible to be aware of bodily sensations while absorbed in the joyful contemplation of a Doric column"—and her continued investigations into aesthetic experience led her within the next decade to repudiate the whole idea that aesthetics could be treated as a science based on objective phenomena. As she wrote in the introduction to *Art and Man* in 1924: "I do not know whether Kit ever completely grasped the psychology of that *Empathy* which she had helped to discover. Nor whether she even admitted unreservedly that the bodily reactions, sensations of altered breathing and balance and muscular adjustments, to which she owed her first ideas on the subject, were not inevitably present in everyone who really took stock of the shapes and colours of works of art and felt their emotional effects" (74).

Nevertheless she persisted in her investigations into empathy. She circulated questionnaires among her friends, measuring their reactions to art, only to discover that their responses were subjective, unpredictable, and of little value in judging a work of art. She kept her own records in a series of "Gallery Diaries" from 1901 to 1904, from which she concluded: "As regards myself at least, aesthetic responsiveness is an essentially active phenomenon, and one subject to every conceivable cause of fluctuation in our energy and variation in our mood" (*Beauty and Ugliness* 344). None of this involved a repudiation of psychology as the study of our mental states as they affect our responses to beauty and as they are affected by beauty. Empathy—our sympathetic identification with form (line, shape, balance) as we perceive it in art or in nature—produces within us a sense of harmony that is vitalizing: "Our aesthetic preference," she wrote in the conclusion to *Beauty and Ugliness* in 1911, "is at once emotional and lucid, by its very essence contemplative rather than active, and it vents itself in action, expressing itself not in passing gestures and untraceable practice, but in the most stable register of human feeling: the forms visible, audible or verbal, of the work of art" (365).

It took years of painstaking effort for her to clarify her thinking on empathy, but she had the honesty to admit that her, and Kit's, efforts had been misdirected. "I now believe," she wrote in 1924, "that the alleged 'mimicry' of a work of art's movement of lines and balance is a great deal more inner than we first imagined, being primarily inside our mind or imagination, and only secondarily in any part of our body (except the organs of whatever our mind or imagination may prove to be)" (*Art and Man* 34–35). Looking over Kit's notes after her death, she also recognized that her friend had apparently drawn more from Berenson (his examples from paintings of movements like "pushing" and "pulling" felt in the viewer's muscles) than she had realized.[7] But, as she correctly observed, the ideas were in the air: "We were part of a mutually, perhaps unconsciously, collaborating band of enquirers." Berenson had not read so widely in German psychology as she had, but he was familiar with the work of William James and the James-Lange theory. He had also read two books that Violet knew well—the German sculptor Adolf von Hildebrand's *The Problem of Form in Painting and Sculpture* (1893), a study of the aesthetics of pure form ("the architectonic conception"),[8] and Edmund Gurney's *The Power of Sound* (1880). Gurney, neither a professional musician nor a psychologist and interested primarily in extrasensory perception, had concentrated on what he called "the aesthetics of hearing." Disclaiming any knowledge of German writings on psychological aesthetics ("many of which are confessedly in the clouds"), he argued that the perception of form in melody "consists in the combination of a number of sense impressions." He also anticipated Berenson by at least a decade in noting the "interplay of muscular and tactile sense with appreciation of art" and suggesting that "the tactile and muscular senses . . . agree with those of sight and hearing" (79).

Vernon Lee made no major contribution to psychology or to aesthetics, although her writings on empathy are not without significance, particularly in her literary criticism collected in *The Handling of Words* (1923). Psychology remained a lasting interest of hers, largely for personal reasons as she struggled to understand her own dark nights of the soul. But her early and unhappy experiments with Kit left her wary of easy solutions to the problems of mind and art. When she reviewed her career up to 1903 in an article for the *Revue philosophique,* she expressed distinct doubts: "I tried to disentangle the origins of art, its influence, the vicissitudes of schools, the evolution of forms, and for this I approached art with an absolutely objective attitude. . . . Alas, this purely scientific interest, for which most of my friends reproached me as a sort of apostasy, determined the direction of my aesthetic life" ("Psychologie d'un écrivain" 236). In 1923 she wrote, in a long introduction to a book on memory and association, Richard Semon's *Mnemic Psychology,* a candid summation of her efforts: "But aesthetics, alas, are the most God-forsaken little corner of mental science, avoided equally by psychologists who have no aesthetic perceptions and by art critics who have no psychological education" (37).

Ultimately she dismissed the whole Berenson affair as "a mere boutade [whim],"[9] but its immediate consequences were serious and painful for both her and Kit. There was no dramatic rupture as there had been with Mary Robinson. Rather there was a gradual erosion of their mutual attachment. Temporary separations grew longer, until by 1904 these became permanent.

What had begun so romantically—the flower on the pillow, Kit's devoted nursing during Violet's breakdown, her hand-stroking and adoring glances, the affectionate letters they exchanged—ended in quiet resignation to the inevitable. As Kit slowly recovered from her breakdown in the summer of 1897, she withdrew from intellectual work altogether and busied herself with building sets for puppet shows and fairy plays that their friends were putting on for children.[10] Her principal mission in life seems always to have been service to others. Even in the years when she devoted herself to the family in the Casa Paget, she had gone to England from time to time to nurse ailing friends, ready to return to Italy, however, whenever Violet needed her.

Kit had always been the more demonstrative in her affection, but Violet was the more deeply dependent, unable to separate her personal need for love from her intellectual work. On 13 June 1895, when Kit was off on a brief trip, Violet wrote her:

> I feel very curiously at a loose end without you. I don't think it is mere affection of me . . . in the ordinary sense for heaven knows I've done that often enough before. This is a sense of enforced silence and at the same time of a sort of deafness, which really comes, I feel sure, of the fact that so many of my thoughts and feelings now-a-days are connected with yr. discoveries, that your ideas have come to form a sort of living atmosphere for me. I find I cannot give my real reactions for so many things to others, and that life, which is so synthetic, seems all in bits.

After the deaths of her parents and Eugene's startling declaration of his independence, she became even more dependent on Kit, unable apparently to imagine a future without her. On 15 September 1896 she sent Kit a full financial disclosure with an unabashed offer to share her worldly goods with her:

> I find it isn't worth while buying much annuity at my age. I am buying annuities with 6000£ and buying debentures worth 10,000£. This will give me about 650£ a year, quite an indecent amount for a woman alone, but I won't suppose being alone, dearest. At present I am very well off, having 500£ in the bank till the April dividends; so you must come and sit on my carpet, and fly off to see Amiens and Reims and St. Mark's and get any book you may need.

Violet knew perfectly well that Kit's affection was not to be bought. Her letter was a love offering and a confession of her need for Kit. But Kit's friends apparently had more compelling needs; and the disappointments on Violet's part and the humiliation that Kit suffered over her collaboration on "Beauty and Ugliness" were signals to them both that their relationship was fragile. Kit visited friends in England and in Italy while she was convalescing. Violet made no secret of her unhappiness to her close friends. Mona Taylor, who knew them both well and was herself recovering from an unhappy affair with another woman, wrote her candidly: "I know you don't want or wish for passion in love. But apart from [t]his, there is a warm[th], a depth, a wholeheartedness of love . . . that you *do want* and Kit can't I fear give you, simply because she has not got it to give." The failing, however, was not Kit's, according to Mrs. Taylor, but Violet's: "If Kit were to take off her skin for you it would not do any good! She has . . . proved over and over her love and care for you. No one could do more—and you simply want it always. *It is not fair. It is not possible*" (19 November 1898).

Violet did not let go easily. In 1898 Kit left Il Palmerino to nurse an ailing friend, Mrs. Christian Head. She still had a strong sense of loyalty to Violet: "I'm literally the only person who can be of any use to her [Mrs. Head]," she wrote apologetically, "for I don't get on her nerves." Kit begged Violet to "lend me to her . . . you will, wont you dearie, but if I get a telegram from you saying you want me at once I will come, for you stand before anything." On 6 March 1899, after visiting Mrs. Head herself, Violet wrote Kit: "Personally, after 20 years of hysteria on my brother's part, I shall always be suspicious of patients who look well and act like well people but tell one of bad symptoms which cannot be seen by the outsider . . . a case for Charcot but *not* for sympathy and ordinary treatment." As late as 7 October 1901 she was still not reconciled to Kit's absence and wrote an almost desperate plea for her return:

> This day week [is] . . . my forty-fifth birthday, and I feel I must organize my work if I am not to let year follow year without a sufficient result. I cannot carry on aesthetics unhelped; I have neither the eye nor the training to continue the analytical work (I mean the analysis of the work of art, *not* introspection) which you began so splendidly in Beauty and Ugliness . . . hoping that the moment will soon come when you will once more give your magnificent intellectual powers to the work which you, perhaps alone in our generation, are able to accomplish. . . . Your doing so *with me* would be the crowning of my life.

At best she was left with a temporary compromise. Kit agreed to spend part of the year with Mrs. Head and part with Violet. It became increasingly obvious that their interests, once so closely interlocked, had diverged. There still remained a bond of loyalty between them though they lived apart, but it was Violet who guarded the flame. When Mary Robinson married, Violet had insisted upon a complete and clean break. Although she later visited her in France, she had no illusions about mending old ties. But she had never shared her work with Mary as she had with Kit, nor depended on her for steady companionship. One was a romantic interlude, the other in all but a literal sense a marriage. And because Kit remained emotionally uninvolved with other women—though she had many women friends—it was years before Violet gave up hope of winning her back. Her letters over the next decade, roughly 1898 to 1908, are curious mixtures of pleas for her return and resignation to their separation. They are also exercises in self-analysis as she struggled with irresolution—her need for Kit, her determination to live independently. As years earlier she had confronted the possibility that her love for Annie Meyer had been one-sided, so she confided to Mona Taylor: "Thinking over the what-she-hasn't-been able to give makes me appreciate what she has given. In seeing that there was no penny for me in her pocket, I have recognized with admiration how comparatively empty that pocket has been all the time she has continued to give me so much merely a widow's mite" (19 March 1899).

Such outbursts of hopelessness were rare on Violet's part; she was too sensitive now to the risks of mental breakdown to allow herself free indulgence in despair. And Kit, though resolved to live independently, maintained her loyalty and interest in her friend's well-being. She responded sympathetically to Violet's letters, which detailed her efforts to find consolation with other women. One of these was Lady de Vesci (born Evelyn Charteris), whom Violet visited in September 1898 at her home, Abbey Leix, in Ireland. The purpose of her visit, she wrote Kit, was to discover "whether or not it had become impossible for me to care about anyone new." Recalling the rose that Kit had left on her pillow in Scotland in 1887, she confessed, "Until now I have never felt anything like this. I love Lady de Vesci so deeply. . . . You see, I have been feeling such a wanderer, so out of everyone's life this summer" (13 September 1898). But three months later she reaffirmed her devotion to Kit: "I don't know what would happen if I thought you were going to marry or even to go off for six months around the world! I can't do without you, dear" (4 December 1898).

By 1900 Violet had come to terms with their permanent separation, but she continued to plead for frequent and longer visits:

> Your rooms are always kept ready and it would be the greatest joy to have you, if I were sure that you come solely to please yourself. But quite apart from your illness last year and before it began, I felt that you came here as a duty and that life here no longer satisfied you, however much you tried to hide it from me and from yourself. It may be a result of your illness here or of disgust with art, the Berenson folly, or it may be that you have reverted to your habits and tastes of before we met. Anyhow there it is, and inevitable, I suppose. The gradual understanding of this change did to me a little

what I suppose people mean when they speak about hearts breaking. But it is over now, and I can think of it quite calmly. I have taken my life in my hands to make the most of, and if it is less hopeful than it used to be, it is very quiet and happy and may perhaps be fruitful. Also, rereading what you have written and thinking daily over your ideas, I cannot easily believe that you will not return someday and bring your own share to the work which I am continuing. (13 December 1900)

She clung to this frail hope of collaboration even as she was rethinking her whole approach to psychological aesthetics. "The method to employ in future is what I should call *the interrogation not of the spectator's consciousness, but of the work of art itself. It is in the work of art that we shall find, more or less clearly registered, the laws, if there be any of aesthetic activity* [emphasis in original]." To Kit she gave credit for establishing "that the laws of aesthetic activity are dependent upon vital physiological conditions." But the focus of their studies in future would be on form; she wrote that she depended on Kit for spontaneous and accurate perception of form. Their goal, she concluded, "is one of the most important steps in modern psychology: the bringing of aesthetics within the pale of the intelligible" (29 May 1901). Her most poignant appeal was in a letter of 12 December 1903. Violet was planning a trip to Venice the following autumn and proposed that Kit join her:

Dear Kit, we are neither of us very young now, and now that you have acquired the sense that you are absolutely free from all obligation or duty to me, does it not seem a pity, and in a way tempting of providence, to waste the years in which we might be something to one another? You and I, since we have ceased living together, have both of us had great friendships, even absorbing ones. And yet we seem, when we have met these last two years, to have recognised that (so far as I am concerned at least) old friendship of you and me was the most satisfying. Do not let us by inadvertence or inertness waste any of its goodness; we are too old to waste anything, my dear, or at least I am.

Kit never renewed her active discipleship, but she did not abandon her interest in art. She drew upon her experiences with Violet in the adult education classes and gallery tours for working-class women that she conducted in England.[11] In 1904 they collaborated on an essay, "Michelangelo's Medicean Tomb: A Study in Artistic Psychology," published in the *Architectural Review* and reprinted in *Art and Man.* Kit continued to write fragmentary notes on sculpture, painting, and architecture using the same technique of recording her physiological responses. Violet collected these after her death in *Art and Man.* Some of Kit's observations are interesting, and they all emphasize the idea of the salutary effects of the contemplation of beauty in nature and in art. For example, she has a note in her diary for April 1906 that, "feeling very sad and harassed" one afternoon in Paris, she stopped to look at the facade of Notre Dame: "At last, as it was getting dark, I turned to go home. And as I walked away I found, to my surprise, that something had changed in me, and that a spirit of high peace had taken possession of me. I could not feel sorrow any more. . . . I walked all the way home (though I don't like walking) for fear of losing this precious sensation of being borne up on to a plateau of high serenity" (200–201).

They continued to correspond, and they met occasionally on Violet's visits to England. But having drifted so far apart intellectually as well as emotionally, they both knew that there was nothing to hold them together in a relationship. As she had often done before, Violet healed herself with work. She also had the distraction of new and interesting friends—Ottoline Morrell, Edith Wharton, Maurice Baring, and the women who continued to enlist themselves in her *culte*. Increasingly, too, she became interested in social causes; to her ardent support of antivivisectionism she added pacifism, taking strong and often unpopular stands on the Boer War, the Italian war with Turkey in 1911 (in which she opposed Italy's expansionist aims), and later World War I. But mainly it was her writing that absorbed her—books, articles, lectures on a dazzling variety of subjects. Keenly aware of the fragility of her own psyche, of "the neuropathic and hysteric" character of her family background, she knew that her future was in her own hands.

The world is overstocked with mixed natures, and one of the great wearinesses,
one of the great pains of spiritual life, is the perception that we can never rest
satisfied with any individual, that we must forever see faults, inconsistences [sic],
must forever take exception; that we cannot give up our soul to absolute reverence,
love, satisfaction. Hence the poignant desire to obtain from art what we cannot
obtain from reality, to create beings whom we can understand without criticising,
without sorting good from evil; to create friends whom we can love completely.

Vernon Lee, "Autobiographical Notes," 19 January 1884

THREE TIMES IN VIOLET PAGET'S LIFE SHE EXPERIENCED THE emotional trauma of rejection a by woman she loved. The first of these, the quarrel with Annie Meyer provoked by the stubborn and impetuous natures of both women, left sad memories but no permanent scars. Violet had the benefits of the natural resilience of youth and the timely entry of Mary Robinson into her life. When Mary abandoned her for marriage, she was more deeply wounded than she would ever again be, but another timely appearance, Kit Anstruther-Thomson, helped to restore her mental health. In the end, it was her dedication to work that proved her salvation. On 17 March 1899, having still not lost hope that Kit would return, she wrote Mona Taylor:

> The value of my friends, practically to me, has been that they have by their good qualities reinforced mine, been atmosphere to me . . . Kit will never understand that the good she did me, specially during my illness, was not fetching and carrying (though she did much of that) but just *being herself* and making me love her. The break with Mary Darmesteter . . . and the agony it cost me 11 years ago damaged my health (already bad, it is true) and made me for years into an uncontrollable invalid. There is no chance of that nowadays, for I am far stronger, more lucid, less selfish and more intellectual. Still, 'tis a sanitary dread. Whether my work is worth anything or not,

I must see to its being as good as it can possibly be made; and at the base of all my work is serenity and buoyancy . . . Labora et noli contristari: work—live, feel, think, enjoy, understand, express.

In 1899, with a new century looming, she needed all the resolve she could muster to work confidently and joyously. Vernon Lee's career had come to a turning point. If she did not realize it, others—friends and critics alike—were beginning to perceive that her ambitions as a writer were sadly misdirected. Determined to be a polymath, to speak and write authoritatively on every conceivable subject, she had scattered her talents. She was not satisfied to be a sensitive, articulate critic of the arts: she had to master the fundamental principles of art and aesthetics, to penetrate the science of psychological aesthetics without having even established that such a science existed. As a result she squandered her energies, and Kit's, on jejune studies written in technical language that alienated the very public, small as it might have been, who relished her short stories and travel essays. In 1902 her devoted admirer Maurice Baring wrote to Henry Brewster, a less devoted admirer but a man who found her interesting "in spite of her capacity to irritate": "You would surely agree with those of Vernon Lee's friends who urge her to write fiction in preference to psychology" (Brewster 282–83).

As she had misdirected her writing, so she also misdirected her friendships. The separation from Kit and, of lesser importance but regrettable, her rift with Bernard Berenson were the most dramatic of her failed or flawed relationships. Her cousin Nena Sturgis complained of her "prickly pear" disposition but remained a friend. Alice Callander, Annie Meyer's niece, compared her to "a porcupine in the spininess of [her] nature"; there were several periods of coldness between them, but they were eventually reconciled.[1] Violet Hippesley, Ethel Smyth's sister, wrote her candidly, 30 August 1900: "I am tempted to think it is impossible that you shouldn't know that you have a great power of attaching people to you, and that your rather cold, stiff manner is a puzzling contradiction to those in whom you have produced warm feelings of affection." Violet must have taken this comment to heart because some time later she wrote Kit: "She [Hippesley] is always saying that I have no notion of the 'warm atmosphere' I create in others. Do I? Is that what I would call warm? Or is it that I remain cold? Certain it is that there is in my experience a greater and greater gulf fixed between what Lady de Vesci distinguished so carefully: liking and loving. And the latter, warm atmosphere, I have done not ten times in my life, and have certainly not been conscious of in others—well—half that number!" (12 December 1903).

Kit Anstruther-Thomson was not the only woman who wore the mantle of disciple to Vernon Lee. Whatever disappointments Violet had in her personal life in this period, she had the satisfaction of an ever widening circle of women admirers who looked to her as a mentor in all matters intellectual and aesthetic and who listened raptly to her stream of talk at social gatherings and at her public lectures in England. These lectures were attended mainly by women denied higher education and eager for self-improvement. They also attracted a small group of privileged women (and some men) who cultivated witty conversation, good food and wine, and called themselves "The Souls." Her friend Maia Mackenzie commented on a lecture she gave in the summer of 1893 on the psychology of writing: "I have heard that your lectures were a social success—that 'Souls' flocked to learn at your feet and that you and your faithful Kit had been visiting all Beaux-Esprits and fine folk" (Smith 98).[2]

Even in rural Fiesole she attracted many visitors. Travelers to Florence from Henry James and Edith Wharton to enthusiastic but undistinguished English and American visitors sought her out. Unmarried women in particular, usually of some economic means and intellectual pretensions, were inspired by her example and her presence.[3] Her flow of talk, rarely interrupted by her guests, her self-assurance and authoritative opinions on English, French, German, and Italian literature, painting, sculpture, architecture, politics, and anything else that came to her mind had something of the quality of revelation for many of them, in some instances (as with Kit) actually changing the direction of their lives. "I met a girl today at Mrs. Humphry Ward's," Kit wrote Violet from London in 1895. "I don't know who she was but she said: 'I went to Vernon Lee's lecture and it was like a new world to me. It has made things look quite different,' this with a little gasp of enthusiasm. I think this is what you wanted to do isn't it?"

Long before she was introduced to Vernon Lee, Nicky Mariano, who was later to become an invaluable aide to the Berensons, noticed Violet and her admirers. "Sometimes when the Fiesole train stopped in San Gervasio, it was boarded by several manly-looking women. One of them seemed to be the central figure. Her face in spite of its snout-like ugliness was fascinatingly witty and intelligent. Somebody told me that her name was Violet Paget and that she wrote books as 'Vernon Lee'" (3). Both Irene Cooper Willis and Ethel Smyth, severe critics as well as lifelong friends of Violet's, noted her power over women. One of these, Evelyn Wimbush, whom Bernard Berenson rather cruelly described as looking like "Oscar à Rebours" (*Letters* 48), was deeply attached to her for years in spite of receiving little encouragement. She accompanied her on the trip to Tangier and Spain in late 1888, paying most of the expenses, and remained a devoted friend despite Violet's coolness. Years later Wimbush wrote her: "You make me care for you, for I truly care for what you give as ideals of thought and life, but not in a cold intellectual way. You make me alive and warm and stir the best part of me . . . I know you like me to look at everything from a more intellectual point of view" (Gardner 293).

Ethel Smyth, who had a stormy friendship with Violet, was perhaps the most reliable and sympathetic of her critics. Referring to the *cultes,* the "aesthetic women" as Berenson described them sitting in Botticellian poses at Violet's feet, Smyth wrote:

> But the hardest to bear was the tone of the house, in which every afternoon a symposium raged. Kit was just a nice strapping handsome girl who went well to hounds. But if Vernon was seized with one of her *cultes* for anyone, that person was firmly manipulated into an expert on art, and incidentally into Vernon's slave and familiar friend. When no symposium was on, Kit spent her time stroking Vernon's hand, and symposium or no symposium, in stroking her vanity. (*What Happened Next* 26–27)

Smyth observed a pattern in the *culte* relationships:

> The story of Vernon's many *cultes,* which succeeded each other all down her life, was always the same. Each of them was at first deeply flattered at finding herself treated as an authority on aesthetics. . . . But Vernon Lee was a tyrannical task master, and the *culte* gradually discovered she was being lovingly and tightly bound by unbreakable cords to OUR WORK. In the end of course there came a moment of violent disruption, and Vernon suffered deeply. Her lesbian tendencies were repressed; the most a *culte* could expect was a kiss which one of them, unnamed, described as having been of the sacramental kind. You feel you had been to your first communion. (*As Time Went On* 241–42)

One young woman who flirted briefly with the *culte* was Ottoline Cavendish-Bentinck, who later became the literary hostess Lady Ottoline Morrell. In 1899, at the age of twenty-five, she was recovering from a love affair with Axel Munthe at his beautiful villa, San Michele, in Capri. On her way back to England she stopped in Florence, visited Il Palmerino, and was instantly fascinated by Vernon Lee. Miranda Seymour writes in her biography of Lady Ottoline: "The food was a disagreeable change . . . Vernon's cook specialised in tongue stewed in chocolate and birds claw omelettes, but Ottoline never cared what she ate. She feasted instead on the afternoon symposiums. . . . When Vernon retired to write, she was sent off to the Uffizi gallery with one of the *cultes,* a stout and lively young art historian called Maud Crutwell . . . Ottoline was startled by her fondness for wearing men's clothes and smoking cigars in public" (38).

Though devoted to the arts even that early in her life, Ottoline had no intention of taking Kit's place as a *culte*. On 18 October 1899 Violet sent her a letter of invitation:

> I have often had a little passing dream of trying to give you the benefit (for you to amalgamate with your own personal views and traditions) of my additional twenty years of reading, thinking, and in practical life. I should like to talk to you about psychology, which is in great measure my study, and political economy, of which I know a little. I can teach you infinitely less than any person at Oxford, but I think we might *think* things out together, which is sometimes quite as fruitful. (Seymour 39)

Ottoline politely declined, but they remained friends. During the war years Violet was a frequent guest at her country home, Garsington—not necessarily to the pleasure of other guests, including Lytton Strachey and Bertrand Russell, who disliked her intensely.[4]

Kit Anstruther-Thomson's place was never filled. The closest Violet came to replacing her was Marie Krebs, a young German girl, daughter of her beloved governess Marie Schülpach. In February or March 1903 she wrote Kit that Marie had left after a three-month stay at Il Palmerino. She had proved a promising pupil, and Violet offered to send her to Berlin or Munich for further training. Anticipating a visit from Kit, she asked if she would be willing "*to teach her everything you possibly can* during your stay here, with a view to her continuing your and my work [emphasis in original]." In December Violet wrote her enthusiastically that the "Krebslein" had returned to Il Palmerino: "I am very pleased to have her; she is so quick at understanding and has such delightful intellectual *joie de vivre,* intellectual spirits as well as animal." A month later she wrote: "The Krebslein is a great blessing. The child is not only interested in your and my work, and capable of continuing it, but is, the more I know her, a most unusually charming creature, the product of a very perfect and happy family and education: sensible, serious, and with a charming delicacy of feeling." Fond as she was of her, Violet was careful to assure Kit that the young girl was not replacing her in her affections: "Also she is *not* devoted to me, which is a blessing, and I am very dispassionately fond of her. A woman my age has no right to attach herself to a creature twenty years younger, for both their sakes." Since there is no further reference to Marie Krebs, one must assume that she did not advance beyond her apprenticeship.

As Ethel Smyth had observed, no one could long endure the demands of rigorous intellectual work in subordination to a woman like Violet. But she continued to have many close friendships with women—some of greater emotional intensity than others. What seemed to matter most to her was the offering of but not necessarily the gift of love. She had long since aban-

doned hope of Mary Robinson, who was widowed in 1894. Mary remained
in France and in 1901 married Emile Duclaux, a close associate of Louis Pasteur and a founder of the Pasteur Institute. He was a widower with two
grown sons. At Mary's urging Violet visited them at their summer home in
the Auvergne. She was much impressed with M. Duclaux—a freethinker
and supporter of the Dreyfus cause—"the man, of all my dear French
friends, who represented to me the inner soul of his country." Some years
after his death she wrote an essay in tribute to him, "In Memoriam Emile
Duclaux," recalling their walks together in the rugged Auvergne countryside: "It was the first time that I satisfied my old longing (ignorant but not
profane) for walks with some one who should tell how a country has come
to be. The Doctor, in his reserved way, rejoiced in that thought of that making: fiery hills upheaving, flaming streams descending, thickening into liq-
uid embers, and stopping, as they touched the sea-plains, cooled into ba-
salt" (*Sentimental Traveller* 180).

From the Duclaux' she went on to Gascony to visit the Delzants, a literary couple who knew and admired her work, at their home in Paraÿs. Ali-
dor Delzant was a lawyer, a bibliophile, editor of the journal *Le revue idéa-
liste,* and author of books on Paul de Saint-Victor and the Goncourts. But
it was Madame Delzant, a highly cultivated woman and student of Pascal
and Jansenism, who won her affection. "Gabrielle Delzant has taken away
my sense of loneliness," she wrote Kit in December 1902, "by giving me the
sense that I make a difference to her. It is strange how it changes my life"
(Biron 123–27). Unfortunately their friendship was brief. In February 1903
Madame Delzant died after a lingering illness. Violet had spent several weeks
visiting her in the autumn before her death and shared with her the essays
she was preparing for her *Hortus Vitae,* published later that year. In a dedi-
catory preface to that volume she recalled the hushed but not melancholy
afternoons in the sickroom when Madame Delzant practiced her English by
reading Violet's essays aloud: "I liked what I had written when she read it"
(vii). Though a devoutly religious woman, Madame Delzant never challenged Violet's unbelief as Annie Meyer had done years earlier. Rather, in a
curious way, her courage in the face of death gave Violet new insight into the
power of faith. "To me [she] revealed the reality of what I had long guessed
at and longed for aimlessly, the care and grace of art, the consecration of religion, applied to matters of every day" (xiv).

Like Mary Robinson, Gabrielle Delzant offered the kind of idealized
relationship that eluded Violet most of her life. Though surrounded by
friends, she was fated to remain alone. Approaching her forty-seventh birthday, she reflected sadly in a letter to Kit: "I believe that when . . . one is solitary as I, 'tis because there is a screw wrong in one, and because one is unfit

in some mysterious way for close contact with others. It's sad; but the conviction is growing strong in me. I have worn out the patience of all who have to do with me, yours, dear Kit, first and foremost; that means that I must not try to have close intimacy, well, *love,* with anyone" (7 October 1903). In 1904 she formed an attachment to Augustine Bulteau, known to her friends as Toche, a worldly French novelist and journalist who wrote under the name of Femina for *Gaulois* and *Le Figaro.*[5] She was divorced from the novelist Jules Ricard and maintained a salon in Paris where she entertained many people from politics and the arts. She also surrounded herself with young women whom she called "Mes Vampyres" and Ethel Smyth described as "a crowd of women of all ages, whose lives she more or less directed" (*Memoirs* 262). Toche offered Violet consolation after Gabrielle Delzant's death, telling her, as she confided to Kit, "that I was to care for her *more than I had ever done for anyone* and that she would transform my life and give me complete peace of mind and happiness." Much as Violet longed for a new relationship, she was sophisticated enough to suspect and reject sexual overtures, although she was confident that Toche would make no such demands on her. "*Her* need of me," she wrote, "which is purely intellectual and moral, is the best part of her, as distinguished from her habit of domination and the not very justifiable means she employs to that end" (17 April 1904).

Close personal relationships failed, but society remained important to Vernon Lee. As Enrico Nencioni had observed years earlier, Vernon Lee's writing was her conversation on paper. She needed an audience—ideally of one devoted companion, but also of a group of listeners—to persuade, educate, entertain. Work was her safety net, her guarantee of mental health, and her work was an ongoing dialogue (too often, alas, a monologue) with an audience. Because the nature of that work was intellectual, confined mainly to the arts, literature, and travel, her audience was confined to women and some few men with cultural interests and the income to support those interests—the "Beaux-Esprits" and "fine folk," as Maia Mackenzie had described her London followers. And indeed the names of her many correspondents and acquaintances over the decades of the turn of the century, roughly 1890 to 1910, constitute a roster of the intellectual and social elite of the period. Titles range from Lady, Marchesa, Contessa, and Gräffin (Irene Forbes Morse, born Gräffin von Flemming)[6] to Empress (Eugénie, widow of the deposed Louis Napoleon of France) and Ranee (Margaret Brooke, wife of Sir Charles Brooke, who succeeded his uncle James, the first white maharajah of Borneo).

She did not seek out the privileged for social advantage (although there is a note of satisfaction in her early letters home to Florence reporting on the socialites she met in London). Like many other intellectuals, she perceived that the gap between the classes in England was widening even while the opportunities for economic and social advancement were also increasing. As a result she had little firsthand knowledge of any society outside her own. Mainly these were people with genuine humanitarian sympathy for the poor and downtrodden. Vernon Lee had represented them in the awakening Miss Brown, her cousin Richard, and her friends the Leigh sisters. In her own life and in many of her essays she vigorously supported social reform, equal rights for women, and a broadly socialist ideology. Along with her friends in France she was a declared Dreyfusard, and at the risk of losing friends in France, England, and Italy she was an outspoken opponent of colonial wars. But like the generous-spirited Schlegel sisters in E. M. Forster's *Howard's End,* who are daringly liberal in their lifestyle yet still view Leonard Bast *de haut en bas,* she was firmly fixed in a social elite. "I am liberal by conviction," she wrote in "Psychologie d'un écrivain." "I have a horror of privilege, luxury, everything that supports mindlessness, the misery of others, but the egalitarian idea chills me. I like certain aristocratic sides [*côtés*], and with a faith in the future, I am attached to the past" (249).

Her circle was a cultural elite. Wealth and title were not criteria for membership unless accompanied by a demonstrated taste for literature and the arts. Lady Mary Ponsonby, Lady Ottoline Morrell, the Ranee of Sarawak, the Empress Eugénie, though not writers or artists themselves, were hostesses to the world of the arts. Initially, Ethel Smyth wrote, Vernon Lee regarded the aging but still beautiful Eugénie as "frivolous," but when she visited her at Farnborough Hall and found her conversing easily with English, French, and Spanish guests, she was impressed. Eugénie was much less impressed with her. "Like Queen Victoria, the Empress hated having speeches made at her. . . . Vernon's oracular ways and the impossibility of getting a straight answer to a straight question out of her irritated the Empress, though from her manner you would never have guessed it" (Smyth, *As Time Went On* 243). She fared better in the salon of the Ranee of Sarawak, who entertained such literary lights as Swinburne, Oscar Wilde, Paul Bourget, and Henry James. The ranee was a loyal friend who visited Violet at Il Palmerino and took a lively interest in her work. One of her warmest admirers was Lady Ponsonby, in her younger years a lady-in-waiting to Queen Victoria, and the wife of Sir Henry Ponsonby, the queen's private secretary. Devoted to music and art and a great reader, one of the founders of Girton College and a friend of George Eliot's, she first met Violet when she visited Florence. She invited her, in turn, to visit her at Norman Tower, formerly the ancient prison wing of Windsor Castle. Lady Ponsonby confided to Ethel Smyth that she was somewhat overwhelmed by the avalanche of Violet's talk: "She says excellent things *à bâtons rompus,* but the wealth of her ideas when she develops a theory makes her, not confused, but so elaborate as to be difficult to follow" (*As Time Went On* 214). Lady Ponsonby reacted in similar fashion to her books: "Let me tell you the deep pleasure *Euphorion* has given me," she wrote her, "but do you know your powers of imagination almost frighten me. . . . I have just begun *Baldwin* and have to re-read *Miss Brown*" (Ponsonby 186). She wrote more candidly to Ethel Smyth:

> Vernon Lee is riveting me at this moment with her books, sayings and letters; and she is one of the very few people whose individuality is worthwhile to study and understand apart from her works. . . . She has such a great literary gift and such a subtle imagination that when I am pondering over a passage in one of her books, I do not know where I am, whether she is forcing me to see things through her spectacles, so that she may be clothing fact and person with qualities derived entirely from her imagination or really if they ever had a separate existence of their own. (183)

It was at one of Lady Ponsonby's luncheons in Norman Tower in the summer of 1893 that Violet and Ethel (later Dame Ethel) Smyth were introduced. They were not immediately drawn to one another—both being strongly outspoken and opinionated—but they became lifelong friends. Smyth (1858–1944) was a remarkable woman, a gifted singer and composer, a world traveler, sportswoman, militant suffragist (she composed the anthem of the suffragist movement, "Shoulder to Shoulder," and served two months in prison for her activities in the cause), and the inspiration for the character Edith Staines, the temperamental composer, in E. F. Benson's once popular satiric novel *Dodo* (1893). A handsome woman, she nevertheless resembled Vernon Lee in dress and manner. Mary Berenson described her years later, in 1934: "Her clothing was a man's soft shirt and tie, and a reach-me-down of rough tweed." She talked in "a loud emphatic voice . . . [and] is deaf, like Vernon. . . . Not quite so deaf, and infinitely more vigorous—a dynamo of energy" (*Self-Portrait* 294). Unlike Violet, she was almost totally uninhibited. "Ethel has just turned up," she wrote Kit, "in wilder form than ever. Yesterday, bicycle in hand, she kept Maria . . . and all a half hour in the yard singing a rather macabre ballad out of her new opera at the top of her voice, till all the windows were black with astonished heads; the less Maria understood of it all, the louder Ethel sang and the more her eyes blazed. . . . It was funny and almost frightening" (29 February 1904). Smyth was bisexual, openly in love with the American expatriate writer Henry Brewster, who was married, and she had once been briefly engaged to William Wilde, Oscar's brother; but generally she was more attracted to women than to men. Late in life she wrote: "Let me say here, that all my life, even when after years had brought me the seemingly unattainable, I have found in women's affection a peculiar understanding, mothering quality that is quite a thing apart. Perhaps too I had a foreknowledge of the difficulties that, in a world arranged by man for man's convenience, beset the woman who leaves the traditional path to compete for bread and butter, honours and emoluments" (*Memoirs* 113–14).

Ethel Smyth understood better than any other of her close friends Violet's repressed lesbianism, recognizing it not as aloofness and lack of feeling for others but as a shield to protect her emotional vulnerability. She had visited Violet at Il Palmerino while her parents were still alive and her brother an invalid and realized that having been brought up "in an atmosphere of fantastic prodigy-worship . . . [she] had had but slight chance of becoming a normal human being" (*What Happened Next* 50–51). Her obsession with her work, her rigorous demands on her *cultes,* her dogmatism and loquaciousness—all revealed to Smyth her insecurity and pathetic need for approval and reassurance. Shortly after they met, Violet spent two days at the Smyth family home in Frimhurst. As Ethel recalled:

> "I believe in you," she wrote after that visit. "I wish I believed in myself half as much." And it is a fact that though convinced that no one but herself knew anything about literature, to my mind she undervalued herself as a writer. By the same token where she admired she was supremely generous. True, if such a one bore away the conversational palm when she herself had intended to shine (which was always the case when there was a gallery) she could not help trying to score off her rival, but once the door was between them she would pay a noble tribute innocent of the faintest flavour of acidity. (*As Time Went On* 241–42)

With the years Violet's affection for Ethel Smyth increased. As other friends died or drifted away, Violet was grateful for Ethel's loyal if erratic friendship, and she learned to tolerate her mercurial disposition. In the summer of 1929 she asked another friend, the writer who published under the pseudonym Elizabeth, if she would invite Ethel to the Chalet Soleil, her home in Switzerland. Ethel came and was charmed by her. In England the following year Elizabeth drove to Richmond to fetch Ethel to her summer home for tea. As Elizabeth recalled: "We hadn't arrived home five minutes when Vernon arrived, gracious and sarcastic, and I thought very amusing to Ethel, who however got into a wild rage and, while V. and I were in the garden, got into V.'s car and went off to the station and home. I was astonished when I found her gone. Vernon merely said, still gracious and serene, 'Characteristic,' and talked delightfully of other things" (De Charms 327).

Elizabeth, who was born in Australia as Mary Beauchamp and was a cousin of Katherine Mansfield, shared with Violet and Ethel Smyth a deep affection for prewar Germany. Ethel had studied music there in her girlhood. Elizabeth's first husband was Count Heming August von Arnim, who owned a large, run-down estate in East Prussia. Her efforts to adapt to a lonely and demanding country life with five children and a strong-willed husband who was often absent are the subject of her first book, *Elizabeth and Her German Garden* (1895). Widowed in 1910 she moved to England and wrote a number of popular novels; best known of them are *The Enchanted April* (1923) and *Mr. Skeffington* (1940). A beautiful woman, she numbered among her lovers Bertrand Russell and H. G. Wells. In 1916 she married Bertrand's older brother John Russell, second Earl Russell, but they were divorced three years later. On the surface she would seem an unlikely candidate for friendship with Vernon Lee, but in fact they were good friends from 1912, when Elizabeth was introduced to her while traveling in Italy with Wells, until Violet's death. Elizabeth saw her for the last time in Florence on 28 December 1934 and reported in a letter: "Vernon delightful, caustic and enchanting me as she always does. She was very funny about *Jasmine Farm* [Elizabeth's latest novel], administering salutary and just pills first, then covering them up with the most delicious jam" (De Charms 356).

In the light of these and other long lasting friendships, it is difficult to credit Irene Cooper Willis's comment to Burdett Gardner that "Vernon Lee was lacking in human affection . . . I never met anyone whose gestures—a hand on one's arm or a holding of one's hand—were so void of warmth" (470). Cooper Willis had a quarter century relationship with her and saw her in a variety of moods. She began as another of the many candidates for Kit's place—a secretary and research assistant, not a lover. She was attractive, intelligent, and loyal enough to endure what Ottoline Morrell considered Vernon's bullying, but she was never a *culte*. Though she remained a steady friend and became, after Vernon's death, her executor, she maintained an independent career as a lawyer and writer, producing books on a number of literary figures including Elizabeth Barrett Browning, the Brontës, and Montaigne. She also published *A Vernon Lee Anthology* (1929) and in 1937 a privately printed collection of her letters (up to 1898).[7]

People who met Vernon Lee rarely had neutral reactions to her. Lytton Strachey, who found her "slightly boring at times," conceded in a letter to Ottoline Morrell (21 August 1916): "Tastes differ, some like coffee, some like tea: / And some are never bored by Vernon Lee" (Holroyd 2:206). Some, too, recognized beneath her starchy manner and her pedantry a warm and generous spirit, an eagerness to share her knowledge and her pleasure in discovering beautiful and interesting things. One of these, an American writer of impressive talent who loved Italy and old Europe almost as much as she did, was Edith Wharton. Their friendship began in March 1894 when Edith Wharton, on her "annual pilgrimage to Italy," called at Il Palmerino to leave a letter of introduction from Violet's old friend Paul Bourget. She approached the Casa Paget timidly, forewarned by Bourget that "Miss Paget [was] so much taken up with her invalid brother Eugene Lee-Hamilton, who lived with her, that she saw very few people, and those only her intimates." But Violet responded immediately with an invitation, adding that her brother, who had admired a poem by "one Edith Wharton" in *Scribner's Magazine*, was eager to meet her. She was warmly received by both Violet and Eugene, although he seemed at that time at the nadir of his illness, capable of only a few minutes of conversation. After the first visit Edith Wharton returned to Il Palmerino many times, enjoying "two of the most brilliant minds I have ever met" (*A Backward Glance* 131).[8] Much as she admired Eugene's poetry, however, it was Vernon Lee, the authority on all things Italian and most especially on the Italian eighteenth century, who held her attention. She had already read her *Studies of the Eighteenth Century in Italy, Belcaro,* and *Euphorion,* and when she resolved to try her hand at a novel, she chose eighteenth-century Italy for its background. Her "Italian novel" became *The Valley of Decision,* published in 1902.[9]

Now all but forgotten and certainly overshadowed by the brilliant novels that followed it, *The Valley of Decision* impressed contemporary readers with its meticulous research for its setting in eighteenth-century northern Italy in the throes of political unrest. Its hero, Odo Vansecca, inherits a dukedom with which he hopes to put into practice the liberal, freethinking ideas he has acquired from his education in Turin. He reads Voltaire and Rousseau, abandons the Jesuitical Catholicism of his family, dabbles in Enlightenment science, and falls in love with a beautiful young woman, Fulvia Vivaldi, who shares his ardor for political and intellectual reform. But when Fulvia is killed by a rioting mob, Odo loses his zeal for the struggle and goes off to an uncertain fate in southern Italy.

The Valley of Decision is by no means a powerfully plotted novel; its strength lies in its evocation of the intellectual spirit of the age, the shaking off of centuries of domination by the clergy and aristocracy, the awakening of a liberal, humanitarian conscience. Edith Wharton paid her highest compliment to Vernon Lee by using her as a source for much of her information on Italian cultural life in the late eighteenth century. In the course of his intellectual development Odo meets Vittorio Alfieri—whom Wharton had read about in *The Countess of Albany*—and accompanies him to the theatre, where they see a performance of Metastasio's *Achilles on Scyros,* to which Vernon Lee had devoted several pages in her *Studies.* Wharton describes the performance in glowing detail—the classical subject matter, the elegant style, the lofty poetry. But as Vernon Lee had earlier pointed out and as Wharton's Alfieri observes, classical Italian theatre, like much else in Italian culture, was in decline by the late eighteenth century: "Metastasio might have been a great tragic dramatist if Italy would have let him. But Italy does not want tragedies—she wishes to be sung to, made eyes at, flattered and amused! Give her anything that shall help her to forget her own abasement" (100).

Edith Wharton frankly admitted her indebtedness to Vernon Lee, but she never overestimated her authority as a cultural historian and critic. In *A Backward Glance* she praised Pater, Symonds, and Vernon Lee for discovering "a field of observation wherein the mere lover of beauty can open the eyes and sharpen the hearing of the receptive traveller," but these are "cultured amateurs," not specialists. Her judgment was no doubt influenced by her close friend Bernard Berenson, whose expertise in Italian art she never questioned. But she was her own woman, independent and basically fair. In 1904 when she was preparing a series of articles on Italian villas and gardens for the *Century* magazine, she could find no more knowledgeable authority than Vernon Lee, whose

> long familiarity with the Italian country-side and the wide circles of her Italian friendships made it easy for her to guide me to the right places and put me in relation with people who could enable me to visit them. She herself took me to nearly all the villas I wished to visit near Florence, and it was thanks to her recommendation that wherever I went, from the Lakes to the Roman campagna, I found open doors and a helpful hospitality. (*A Backward Glance* 134)

Collected with photographs and drawings by Maxfield Parrish, *Italian Villas and Their Gardens* was published in 1904 with a dedication "To Vernon Lee who, better than anyone else, has understood and interpreted the Garden-Magic of Italy."

There is no reason to doubt Edith Wharton's sincerity when she summed up Vernon Lee as "the first highly cultivated and brilliant woman I had ever known." For that reason Wharton not only tolerated but apparently enjoyed her company. "I stood a little in awe of her as I always did in the presence of intellectual superiority, and liked best to sit silent and listen to a conversation which I still think about the best of its day" (132). And no wonder that even the sophisticated Mrs. Wharton was awed by her. Percy

Lubbock recalled in his *Portrait of Edith Wharton* that in the setting of an old Italian garden Vernon Lee, "angular vestal in her stiff collar and her drab coat," bloomed as luxuriantly as the plants themselves:

> She pondered, she reconnoitered as she talked, she wound her way through suggestion, sensation, speculation—she threaded a labyrinth. It all took time, but it was worth while to wait for her. . . . Who will say, listening to Vernon Lee, that a thing of beauty is ever finished or an hour of time accomplished? . . . Most surprising, most interesting, most exasperating of women, in her power and her humour, her tenacity and her perversity— Vernon Lee holds her ground. . . . What a figure!

Lubbock concludes his hyperbolic account of that afternoon, "It was impossible to control or civilise Vernon Lee" (118–19).

Something of that same ambivalence characterized Edith Wharton's attitude toward Vernon Lee over the remainder of their long friendship. Her letters became increasingly affectionate over the years, with salutations and closings warming from "Dear Miss Paget" and "very truly yrs, Edith Wharton" to "My dear Vernon" and "Dearest Vernon" and "yours affectionately, Edith." In early 1903 she was busy with arrangements for Violet to visit the United States, subsidized by lectures she would give at women's colleges. Wharton mentioned specifically Barnard and Radcliffe, where she had connections through Barrett Wendell and Charles Eliot Norton. She gently suggested that Violet's choice of aesthetics as a subject for these lectures might be less attractive than more-colorful topics from Italian art and history. The visit never materialized, but the correspondence continued, full of expressions of mutual admiration.

Edith Wharton's letters to Vernon Lee follow a curious pattern of invitations issued, plans made, invitations withdrawn because of overcrowded schedules, bad weather, ill health, emergency house repairs, missed connections both literal and figurative. Indeed there are so many missed connections that one wonders how the friendship survived for so many years. Wharton was frequently in the neighborhood of Il Palmerino, usually visiting the Berensons at I Tatti, but her heavy social obligations often prevented her from actually meeting Violet. There is no reason to doubt her sincerity, yet one detects a certain reluctance to inconvenience herself for the sake of Violet's company.

The rift between Violet and Bernard Berenson, which lasted for more than twenty years, probably created an obstacle to the Wharton–Vernon Lee friendship. They did meet occasionally on friendly terms because they had friends in common. One such occasion was in the summer of 1912 when they were guests for tea at the Ascot home of the Ranee of Sarawak—

an awkward moment because Henry James, long alienated from Violet, was also there. During the war years there was little opportunity for socializing, especially since Edith Wharton was active in French relief work while Violet, living in England during that period, was an ardent pacifist. But they resumed a fairly regular correspondence after 1920. Again there seem to have been more visits canceled than actually made. Wharton was by now living permanently in France when she was not off on her many trips to England, Italy, Greece, America, and North Africa. Her "little house," she writes Violet from Hyères in the French Riviera some time after 1920, "has only 3 small spare-rooms, two have been filled since I arrived, & a great friend from America sailed this morning to take possession of the third!" Still she urges her friend to "fit yourself in between comings and goings here." Many other visits are canceled for reasons of health. Both women, now in their sixties, were frequent victims of "grippe" and "flu," and Violet was now quite deaf and suffering from heart disease.

But their interest in each other's work never flagged. In March 1925 Edith wrote to acknowledge Vernon Lee's collection of travel essays, *The Golden Keys*, a book that "lets me most smoothly and swiftly into those magic gardens of yours & the delight of my walks there makes me wish more than ever that I could have shown you some of our beauties—you would have given them that light that never was, so they wd not have died when my eyes close on them." In July 1928, again having failed to arrange a meeting, Wharton writes that Mary Berenson had brought news of her: "But I wish I could have verified with my own eyes, and talked the sun down with you, in the good old fashion." They continued to exchange and praise each other's books. Wharton concludes the same letter with thanks for Violet's appreciation of *Twilight Sleep:* "Since the days when you wrote that beautiful wasted introduction to the Italian 'Valley of Decision' I have always treasured your praise—so give me all you can!" In January 1930 she sent her her ambitiously conceived *Hudson River Bracketed:* "I rather particularly want you to like 'Hudson River Bracketed.' I have carried in my mind for many years the image of the young artist struggling with his Daemon (of course, inevitably, *my* Daemon!) & I hope I have been able to convey to my readers something of my inward vision."

Edith Wharton's friendship was unique in Violet's experience. It was uncluttered with the emotional baggage of so many other of her friendships and based purely on mutual respect and admiration. Clearly a better and more successful writer than Vernon Lee—a fact Violet recognized without envy—Edith Wharton was nevertheless a kindred spirit, a peer in dedication to work, to the craft of literature. Her biographer R. W. B. Lewis reported on what may have been their last meeting, in November 1934, when

she spent an evening at Il Palmerino during which Violet, with her characteristic bluntness, berated her for producing so much inferior fiction in recent years. "Next morning," Lewis wrote, "Vernon Lee sent a letter around
to I Tatti by hand":

> What you told me yesterday at the gate, about having to make money for
> your sister-in-law, has left me bitterly ashamed for the unjustifiable words I
> had just said. Please forget them. And remember only the very real admi-
> ration I have for so much of your work, and my gratitude for so much kind-
> ness. (508)

11 HANDLING WORDS: FROM PRACTICE TO THEORY

The great Writer or artist is a creature who lives in a way more intense and more unified than the rest of us, in those fields, at all events, which specially concern him. And hence he can lay hold of our perception and emotion, make it move at a pace surpassing our own, and compel our labouring thoughts, our wandering attention, our intermittent feelings, into patterns consistent, self-sufficing, vigorous, harmonious, unified; in the presence of which all else dwindles and is forgotten.

Vernon Lee, *The Handling of Words*

☙ APOLOGY CAME AS SPONTANEOUSLY TO VIOLET PAGET AS THE wounding thrust. Her last encounter with Edith Wharton, which left her "bitterly ashamed" for her "unjustifiable words," was part of a lifetime pattern of behavior. Quick to speak (and write) and even quicker to judge, she had since her youth caused embarrassment and sometimes pain to others. It was neither malice nor hot temper that provoked these outbursts so much as sheer obtuseness, an innocence all the more astonishing in light of her long exposure to a worldly European society. But the peculiar hothouse atmosphere of her childhood, the social and emotional isolation imposed by her mother and half brother, left a mark on her that was apparent not just in the failure of her most cherished personal relationships but in her literary career as well.

How could Vernon Lee have been so oblivious to the pain she inflicted with the heavy-handed satire of *Miss Brown*? When she examined her conscience in her journal for New Year's Eve 1884 (see above, chap. 6), she acknowledged the possibility that she might indeed be "colour-blind," that her moral certainties might have misled her, that truth was not necessarily absolute as she had conceived it. Ironically it was Henry James who most tellingly brought this to her attention: "Cool first—write afterwards. Morality is hot—but art is icy!" She respected his advice but rarely followed it. And James, who had so gently pointed out her weaknesses as a novelist and continued to admire the spontaneity and sparkle of her nonfiction, became himself the victim of another of her misguided attempts at realistic fiction.

Her short story "Lady Tal," first published in *Vanitas: Polite Stories* in 1892, has none of the fierce moral indignation and crude characterization of *Miss Brown,* but it suffers from the same clumsy literalness. When writing about a society she knew at first hand, Vernon Lee suffered lapses of the creative imagination that gave so much vitality and color to her travel essays, her studies of the Italian Renaissance and the eighteenth century, and her stories of the supernatural. Her imagination, which soared when she confronted the past and its vestiges in modern-day Europe, sank dismally in the immediate present. Not that the stories in *Vanitas* are lacking in interest. There is real humor in "Lady Tal" and a general competence in the other stories in the collection. Two of them had been published first in periodicals —"The Legend of Madame Krasinska" in the *Fortnightly Review* (March 1890) and "A Worldly Woman" in the *Contemporary Review* (October– November 1890). But it was "Lady Tal" that once again betrayed its author's innocent intentions and left two victims—Henry James, who felt himself caricatured, and Violet Paget, who lost a friendship she valued deeply. The only good that came of the story was that she finally learned never again to write fiction with characters modeled on real-life figures.[1]

The stories in *Vanitas* were written during a period of intense activity following Violet's recovery from her nervous breakdown. Accompanied by Kit, she traveled around Italy visiting old Italian friends and newly made British and American ones. Among these were the American expatriates Mrs. Daniel Curtis, mistress of the Palazzo Barbaro in Venice, and Mrs. Katherine Bronson, whose Casa Alvisi on the Grand Canal fronted Santa Maria della Salute and provides the setting for the opening scene of "Lady Tal." She had been introduced to Mrs. Curtis by John Singer Sargent, who some years later painted the Curtis family in their elegantly appointed salon (*An Interior in Venice,* 1898). She was introduced to Mrs. Bronson by a letter from Henry James.[2] He thought highly enough of her, even after the awkward business with *Miss Brown,* to call at the Casa Paget whenever he was in Florence. Here, in spite of his distaste for the other members of her family, he enjoyed Violet's company. "I saw a good deal of Vernon Lee, who has always lived there," he wrote Sarah Butler Wister (27 February 1887), "and though very ugly, disputatious and awkwardly situated *comme famille* (a paralyzed sofa-ridden brother always in the parlour and grotesque, depressing, irrelevant parents) possesses the only mind I could discover in the place" (*Letters,* ed. Edel, 3:169–70). During Violet's visits to London in the summer they met frequently at social gatherings, and in 1886 he entertained her at lunch in his London flat.

When she sent him a copy of her *Hauntings: Fantastic Stories* in April 1890, he acknowledged the book with unqualified praise. He found the stories ("your gruesome, graceful, *genialisch Hauntings*") "ingenious, full of imagination," and in his loftiest Jacobean prose hailed "the bold, aggressive, speculative fancy of them . . . the redolence of the unspeakable Italy, to whose infinite appetite you perform the valuable function of conductor or condenser. You are a sort of reservicer of the air of Italian things, and those of us who can't swig at the centuries can at least sip of your accumulations" (Weber, "Henry James" 679). In September 1891 he gave her tickets for the London production of his dramatization of *The American*. Her enthusiastic reaction to the play comforted him for the chilly reception it had from the critics: "Many thanks for your very interesting note—or rather your generous and glowing letter—of the subject of which we shall have more to say when next we meet. . . . A thousand thanks for your delightful good words" (Weber 680).

Although by this time absorbed in her studies of aesthetics, she neither wanted nor could afford to neglect the subjects on which her reputation was based—Italian culture, travel impressions, and fiction. For all its problems, *Miss Brown* had had its admirers, and there was still a market for her fiction. The British magazines particularly welcomed stories of the supernatural, which, thanks to her rich European background, she produced with considerable success. Editors also welcomed stories of cosmopolitan British and European society, and by 1890 Violet Paget had ample experience of social life in England as well as on the Continent. Still strongly judgmental, she had acquired a sophistication lacking when she wrote *Miss Brown*. Whether it was Henry James's advice about cooling before writing or simply the maturity of middle age, she was no longer writing fiction with the purpose of criticizing and reforming society. She had read enough James by now to recognize the importance of subtle character analysis and the complexity of human relationships. But she remained at heart a moralist. Putting together four stories (originally three; another was added in the second edition, 1911) under the title *Vanitas,* she imposed a unifying theme on them: "sketches of frivolous women." The added story, "A Frivolous Conversion," centers not on a woman but on a young man, an aristocrat with a prejudice against "socialists, Jews, and journalists," who becomes a martyr to his pride and impulsiveness. Under the influence of an elderly Russian woman, a believer in "Tolstoian Christianity," he begins to see that his life has been a pursuit of "worldly vanities," but, unable to control his temper, he fights a duel in which he is killed.

Vernon Lee states her serious moral intention in her preface to the original three stories:

> For round these sketches of frivolous women, there have fathered some of the least frivolous thoughts, heaven knows, that have ever come into my head. . . . Indeed, how can one look from outside on the great waste of precious things, delicate discernment, quick feeling and sometimes stoical fortitude, involved in frivolous life, without a sense of sadness and indignation? Or what satisfaction could its portrayal afford, save for the chance that such pictures might . . . show to men and women who toil and think that idleness, and callousness, and much that must seem to them sheer wickedness, is less a fault than a misfortune?

What she promises in *Vanitas* is remote from what in fact she offers. One of the stories, "The Legend of Madame Krasinska," does indeed introduce a wealthy and beautiful young widow who thoughtlessly mocks a pathetic old mad woman by dressing like her at a costume ball. But immediately her frivolous act begins to prey on her conscience, and after suffering temporary madness and a suicide attempt, she renounces society and becomes a nun. The other two stories, "A Worldly Woman" and "Lady Tal," are lighter and might be described as "Jamesian" comedies of manners. Though announced as stories about women, they have "Jamesian" men as central characters.

The mistitled "A Worldly Woman" is about an idealistic young man, Leonard Greenleaf, an expert on pottery, whose socialist and aesthetic principles are challenged when he meets a charming and unaffected young woman, Val Flodden. She is uneducated in the arts or in literature ("Some books seem so awfully interesting, you know; but there are such a lot of others that one would just throw into the fire if they didn't belong to Mudie" [148]) but eager to learn. Physically she might have been modeled on Kit Anstruther-Thomson—tall, with "chiseled features" and "a rigid, undeveloped sort of grace." She comes from a socially prominent family with no pretensions to culture, but she resists their pressures to conform to the conventions of high society. It is immediately apparent to the reader, though not to Greenleaf, that she is attracted to him and that he can save her from a shallow life. But like Henry James's Winterbourne, who fails to offer himself to Daisy Miller when he might have saved her, Greenleaf cannot commit himself to a relationship with Val: "His life must always be a solitary one with his work."

Henry James is introduced by name in "A Worldly Woman." While Greenleaf is staying at the Flodden family's country house cataloguing their pottery collection, he rereads *The Princess Casamassima* and begins to identify himself with the innocent lower-class Hyacinth Robinson and Val with the frivolous princess, toying with art, social reform, and his affections. Though she claims she is not a reader, Val too has read James's novel. When Leonard condemns the princess for the idleness of her life, Val defends her: "She is merely a clever woman who is bored by society and who wants to know a lot of things and people." The story ends ten years later with Val a prominent society hostess, clearly bored and unhappy in her marriage to a rich and socially ambitious man, "an odd sample of Jewry acclimatized in England."[3] Recalling their conversation of years past, Val says, "It was quite natural on your part to take me for a Princess Casamassima." But he had misjudged her: "I wasn't a worthless woman then; and I haven't really become a worthless woman now. . . . You slammed in my face the little door through which I had hoped to have escaped from all this sort of thing" (217, 219). She urges him in the future to "be a little more trustful to other people who may want your friendship."

Henry James is introduced again by name early on in "Lady Tal" in a reference to the character Jervase Marion: "There is something in being a psychological novelist, and something in being an inmate of the world of Henry James, and a kind of Henry James, of a lesser magnitude, yourself: one has the pleasure of understanding so much, one loses the pleasure of misunderstanding so much more" (194).[4] The problem is that the fictional Jervase Marion is not simply compared to the novelist Henry James, but in a number of details he is the man Vernon Lee knew and valued as a friend. Marion is a middle-aged expatriate American writer whose books "turned mainly upon the little intrigues and struggles of the highly civilized society." He is "a dainty but frugal bachelor," with "well-adjusted speech," "a precise mind," and a habit of "studying human nature." He is also heavy, balding, and his boots are painfully tight. In his life as in his fiction he holds strictly to "the position of dispassioned spectator of the world's follies and miseries." As a result he has sacrificed popular success as well as intimate human relationships to his lofty ideals of art. He has come to Venice on a holiday after completing a three-volume novel for Blackwood. And he has made three resolutions which inevitably in the course of the story he will break: "Not to be enticed into paying calls . . . Not to drift into studying any individual character . . . Never to be entrapped, beguiled or bullied into looking at the manuscript of an amateur novelist" (207).[5]

In "Lady Tal" Vernon Lee produced a reasonably good imitation of a Jamesian character and a Jamesian plot. There is something of the same irony—the speculation, in lightly comic overtones but with deeper implications, about the price one pays for total dedication to the life of art. Marion is neither a fool nor a hypocrite; he is the victim of an artistic credo so rigid and demanding that it leaves him unprepared for the challenges of real life. Having been the detached observer of others for so long, he has lost touch with humanity: "To be brought into contact with people more closely than was necessary or advantageous for their intellectual comprehension; to think about them, feel about them, mistress, wife, son, or daughter, the bare thought of such a thing jarred upon Marion's nerves" (221). He has made the ultimate sacrifice for his art: "For Marion, although the most benevolent and serviceable of mortals, did not give his heart, perhaps because he had none to give to anybody" (223). His plan to use Lady Tal as a character in a novel is foiled because, ironically, she uses him in infinitely more practical ways.

Lady Tal (Atalanta) Walkenshaw is a wealthy young widow with literary aspirations. Physically she is a towering figure: "she looked three times as strong, both in body and mind, with her huge, strongly-knit frame, and clear pink complexion . . . well-cut, firmly closing mouth." She leaves the impression on Marion "of being able to take care of herself to an extent almost dangerous to her fellow-creatures" (210). Worse yet, he breaks his holiday resolution to resist character study and finds himself again the victim of his "demon of psychological study." This time, however, his demon meets its match in "an equally stubborn though less insidious demon apparently residing in Lady Atalanta, the demon of amateur authorship" (221). Even as she bullies him, she fascinates him with her "want of soul," and he studies her as a character for his next novel. The reversal of the story is neat because of course, as he gradually realizes, she is using him. He also discovers in her, in spite of the crudeness of her writing, "the indications of a soul, a very decided and unmistakable soul." At the inconclusive end of the story he confesses to her that his next novel will be about a middle-aged artist "who was silly enough to imagine it was all love of art which made him take a great deal of interest in a certain young lady and her paintings." When Lady Tal asks what happens then, he replies, "What happened? Why—that he made an awful old fool of himself. That's all" (261).

In spite of the clumsy shifting of point of view from omniscient author to the consciousness of the principal characters and the resulting ambiguities, "Lady Tal" is a clever little human comedy. It was unfortunately read as a roman à clef by everyone who knew Henry James and also knew Vernon Lee's propensity for tactlessness. Once again she had written with no thought of how she might be read and certainly no notion of how painful the story would be for James. In all probability he never read "Lady Tal." Had he read it with the close attention he gave to most fiction, he might have perceived that there was no malice in Vernon Lee's portrait of Jervase Marion. If anything, she was, in her characteristically perverse fashion, paying him a compliment. She endowed Marion with a sensibility so delicate that he finally recognizes beneath Lady Tal's battering-ram personality a woman who has suffered an unhappy marriage and the death of an invalid brother whom she had nursed devotedly, and he is ashamed that he had wanted merely to use her as a character in a book: "That gift, a rare one, of seeing the simple, wholesome, and even comparatively noble, side of things; of being, although a pessimist, no misanthrope, was the most remarkable characteristic of Jervase Marion; it was the one which made him, for all his old bachelor ways, and his shrinking from close personal contact, a man and a manly man, giving this analytical and nervous person a certain calmness and gentleness and strength" (232).

Only a woman as oblivious to the sensibilities of others as Violet could have failed to see the damage that "Lady Tal" would do her. No amount of praise of Marion's sensibility could balance the cruel ridicule of Lady Tal's "tomboy cousin" who pronounces his name "Mary Anne." Nor could a reader overlook the slapstick comedy of a scene in which he is browbeaten by Lady Tal into carrying bundles for her along the Rialto and chasing the oranges he has dropped from one of them: "a small number of spectators, gondoliers and workmen from under the bridge, women nursing babies at neighbouring windows, and barefooted urchins from nowhere in particular, starting up to enjoy the extraordinary complicated tricks which the stout gentleman in the linen coat and Panama hat had suddenly fallen to execute" (227).

What would have embarrassed Henry James, had he read the story, even more than such tactless references to his personality and appearance is the implied identification of Lady Tal and Vernon Lee. It is absurd to suggest that in the ambiguous ending of the story, with its hint of a closer relationship between Lady Tal and Jervase Marion—a literary partnership at least if not a marriage—Vernon Lee was declaring a personal interest in James. But the forthright, aggressive Lady Tal, who wants to dedicate her first novel to Marion as Vernon Lee had dedicated *Miss Brown* to him and who has cared for an invalid brother, invited identification. She must have had some uneasiness about the story herself, for she did not send James a copy of the book, as she had with her earlier works.

From early reports he had of it, one can readily understand why James spared himself the pain of reading "Lady Tal." On 16 January 1893 he wrote his young friend Morton Fullerton, an American journalist, commenting more in exasperation than anger on "the irrepressible Vernon Lee":

Excuse me if I don't enter into your bright allusion—but you have more than once found me, I know of a strangely gelid wit. I think there is an initiation that I lack—but please don't give it to me. I believe (as I have been told) the said Vernon Lee has done something to me ("Lady Tal") but I don't know what it is and if I should know I should have to take upon myself the burden of "caring" in some way or other established of men, or of women—and, oh, I don't *care* to care. (*Letters,* ed. Edel, 3:399)

But he cared enough to warn his brother William, who was in Florence at the time and planning to call at the Casa Paget. On 20 January 1893 he sent William "a word of warning about Vernon Lee":

she has lately, as I am told (in a volume of tales called *Vanitas* which I haven't read) directed a kind of satire of a flagrant & markedly "saucy" kind at me (!!) exactly the sort of thing she has repeatedly done to others (her books—fiction—are a tissue of personalities of the hideous roman à clef kind) & particularly impudent & blackguardly sort of thing to do to a friend & one who has treated her with such particular consideration as I have. (James and James, *Selected Letters* 276–77)

There is no doubt that he was deeply wounded. He wrote William Dean Howells a few days later, surely with "Lady Tal" in mind, "I have a morbid passion for personal privacy and a standing quarrel with the blundering publicities of the age" (*Letters,* ed. Lubbock, 1:198). In James's estimation Violet had committed not only a personal offense but an offense against art. As he wrote William:

She is as dangerous and uncaring as she is intelligent—which is saying a great deal. Her vigour & sweep of intellect are most rare & her talk superior altogether; but I don't agree with you at all about her "style" which I find *insupportable,* & I find also that she breaks down in her books. There is a great second-rate element in her 1st-rateness. At any rate draw it mild with her on the question of friendship. She's a tiger-cat! (*Selected Letters* 277)

Enjoying his role of protective older brother, William James ignored Henry's pleas "not to respond to her any further than mere civility requires" and rushed to his defense. He promptly got a copy of *Vanitas,* read the offending story, and wrote "Miss Paget" brusquely that "seeing the book has quite quenched my desire to pay you another visit" (11 March 1893). Violet's response unhappily does not survive, but she must have been contrite enough to satisfy William, for he wrote her on 18 March: "My dear Miss Paget, A woman in tears is something that I can never stand out against! Your note wipes away the affront as far as I am concerned, only you must never, *never,* NEVER, do such a thing again in any future book! It is too serious a matter" (Weber, "Henry James" 684).

Grateful as Henry James was for his brother's outrage, he was, as he wrote William and his sister Alice a few days later, "partly amused and partly disconcerted by the William-Paget correspondence." One suspects that he was more disconcerted by William's gratuitous interference than by Violet's apology. If he could not forgive, he was eager to forget: "Her *procédé* was absolutely deliberate, & her humility, which is easy & inexpensive, after the fact, doesn't alter her absolutely impertinent nature. *Basta! Basta!*" (*Selected Letters* 284). It was not, however, enough for Violet. She long regretted the loss of James's friendship and never gave up hope for a reconciliation. In July 1900, through the good offices of their mutual friend Lady Mary Wolseley, she wrote him a note asking for a meeting. James's reply was gallant but off-putting. He sent her

> recognition, greeting, thanks. . . . I may well have regretted to have failed of late years, of sight and profit of one [of] the few most intelligent persons it had ever been my fortune to know—and as to whom you are right in supposing that my interest hadn't dropped. I hold that we *shall* meet again— let us by all means positively do so at some time of full convenience. That occasion will turn up—in Italy if not here—and will give great pleasure to
> Yours, dear Violet Paget, always
> Henry James (Weber, "Henry James" 685)

Except for an accidental meeting at the home of the Ranee of Sarawak in 1912, the occasion never turned up. Many years later Violet admitted in a letter to Maurice Baring: "I have myself put a full-length description of Henry James into a story, but as, although it was funny, it was also kind and respectful, and I considered William James's attack and H.J.'s years of resentment as very absurd and unjust" (28 March 1926).

There was an element of poetic justice in Vernon Lee's use of Henry James in "Lady Tal," which Mary Berenson was quick to notice. In March 1893 she wrote her mother a lively account of the brouhaha. On arriving in Florence, William James had called on Bernard Berenson, and when she returned the visit, Mary reported that she found him "simply furious" over "Lady Tal":

> Prof. James says it is the most indecent, indelicate, utterly incomprehensible affair imaginable, for his brother and Miss Paget have been very good friends —or at least seemed to be. Yet all the while she was taking the cool impersonal notes upon all his peculiarities and little habits and ways of thought and life. William James considers her a "most dangerous woman," and he is going to write and tell her that after this book she must not be surprised if he declines to continue the previous friendly relations.

Mary could not resist observing, however, that Henry James's *The Bostonians* contains "an evident study—even caricature—of dear old Miss Peabody, who was the James's dear old family friend during Henry's youth. Yet he declared that he did *not* mean Miss Peabody, and on the whole I can believe him, as I understand how readily a novelist can forget the individual who suggested the type to him. In the same way I have no doubt, Vernon Lee is half unconscious of having drawn Henry James to the life" (*Self-Portrait* 52).[6]

Mary Berenson's conjecture is reasonable. Of course Vernon Lee, if only "half unconscious," was also half-conscious of what she was doing. But there is a certain naïveté, even innocence, in her portrait of Jervase Marion that is strikingly different from other works of fiction that introduced Henry James as a model for a character—H. G. Wells's *Boon* (1905), Max Beerbohm's brilliant parody of his style in "The Mote in the Middle Distance" (1912), and a particularly mean-spirited portrait of him by the American Gertrude Atherton in the title story of *The Bell in the Fog and Other Stories* (1905). Though Atherton dedicated her book "To the Master Henry James," there is a personal animus in the story quite absent from Vernon Lee's story, and it is badly written, in a style comparable to the first clumsy efforts at a novel by Lady Tal. As a self-confident professional writer, Vernon Lee did not identify herself with the ambitious tyro Lady Tal, nor was she using Jervase Marion as a vehicle for any personal ill will she might have had toward James. Yet there is a distinct possibility that she connected James's long delay in commenting upon *Miss Brown* with Marion's reluctance to read the manuscript that Lady Tal thrusts upon him:

> Jervase Marion was a methodical man full of unformulated principles of existence. One of these consisted in always doing unpleasant duties at once, unless they were so unpleasant that he never did them at all. Accordingly, after a turn or two more up and down the room, and a minute or two lolling out of the window, and looking into that kitchen on the other side of the canal, with the bright saucepans in the background, and the pipkins with carnations and sweet basil on the sill, Marion cut the strings of the manuscript, rolled it backwards to make it lie flat, and with a melancholy little moan, began reading Lady Tal's novel. (211)

The sample of Lady Tal's novel that Vernon Lee provides—a breathless single-sentence-long paragraph—leaves Marion utterly bemused: "Bless the woman! . . . What on earth is it all about?" Marion decides diplomatically to focus his criticism on her indifference to punctuation, and he recommends that she study Blair's *Rhetoric*. But Lady Tal is too clever to be satisfied with that and finally draws the truth out of him: "Your novel, if you will allow me to say a rude thing, is utterly impossible. You are perpetually taking all sorts of knowledge for granted in your reader. Your characters don't sufficiently explain themselves; you write as if your reader had witnessed the whole thing and merely required reminding. I almost doubt whether you have fully realised for yourself a great part of the situation; one would think you were repeating things from hearsay, without quite understanding them" (217).

This is no longer Henry James speaking in the persona of Jervase Marion but the critic Vernon Lee, who even at the time she was writing "Lady Tal" was germinating a theory of prose style to be fully developed in 1923 with the publication of *The Handling of Words and Other Studies in Literary Psychology*. As early as December 1891 she published an essay, "Of Writers and Readers," in the *New Review* in which she reminded a would-be author to be ever conscious of "how entirely he depends upon the contents and movements of the reader's mind." On 21 February 1896 she wrote her friend Lady Jeune:

> I have been trying to teach some clever young people how *to write,* that is to say how to put together books or articles a trifle less difficult to read than they wd otherwise have been; and I have been so struck, once my attention was drawn to it, with the marvellous lack of a *school*—of all that can be taught and learned, among living English writers, that I feel greatly tempted, when I come to London, to give a series of lectures on the art (or rather the craft) of writing.

Somewhat disingenuously—since she had already been lecturing in London for several years—she asked for Lady Jeune's assistance: "As I am totally in the dark where, when or by what means one does give lectures, I want you to be so very kind as to give me advice on the subject. As everybody who does anything comes to yr house, you are the very person to enlighten my ignorance."[7]

If, in fact, Vernon Lee had followed her intention as stated to Lady Jeune, her lectures on the craft of writing would have followed Jervase Marion's initial advice to Lady Tal to learn grammar and punctuation in order to produce "books or articles a trifle less difficult to read than they would otherwise have been." But to a mind as complex as hers, the craft of writing demanded more than a mastery of mechanics; pedantic as she was, she would never have stooped to a "how to" textbook.[8] She had no more expectation of turning her readers (or listeners) into writers than Jervase Marion had of making a novelist, by his standards of novel writing, out of Lady Tal: "Lady Tal had read other people's books, and had herself written a book which was extremely like theirs. It was a case of unconscious, complete imitation." Nevertheless Marion takes a hand in the revision of her manuscript, impelled by "energy and determination on the part of Lady Tal, and of kindness, more correctly designated as feebleness of spirit, on the part of Marion" (220).

There was no such personal motivation for Vernon Lee. She lectured and she wrote to enlighten her audience on the finer points of literary criticism, to show them how writers achieve their effects. The "variously dated essays and notes," as she described them in her preface to *The Handling of Words,* constitute not an exposition of a specific literary theory or a sustained program of instruction in the craft of writing, but—typical of all her collections of essays—a series of freewheeling ideas and impressions about English prose and its practice. Her essays on style, literary construction, and the aesthetics of the novel are perceptive and, for their time, pioneering.[9]

Written over a period of some thirty years, these essays reflect not so much her development as a writer as her development as a student of psychological aesthetics. She had emerged from the romantic-subjective appreciation of beauty, her creed in *Belcaro* and *Baldwin,* to a quasi-scientific, analytic approach to the experience of beauty in nature and art. As David Seed pointed out in his introduction to a 1992 reprint of *The Handling of Words,* she anticipated the writings of I. A. Richards, the Russian formalists, Mikhail Bakhtin, Wolfgang Iser, and Roland Barthes.[10] On 25 October 1902 she wrote Kit Anstruther-Thomson that she hoped to devote the coming winter "to more scientific work—trying to find 'the reason why' for literature, counting adjectives and verbs and making statistics of sentences." *The Handling of Words* is thus an extension to narrative prose of the psychological aesthetics she had worked on with Kit in the 1890s. The latter part of the title, "Other Studies in Literary Psychology," directs readers to its central issue—how the writer's craft affects the conscious and unconscious mind of the reader and determines his response to the text. Long before the phrase became current, she was studying "the dynamics of reading." "The writer's craft," she argues,

> is based upon the psychological fact that to a greater extent than in other arts, the literary work of art is dependent on two persons, the one who speaks and the one who listens, the one who explains and the one who understands, the Writer and the Reader. And this resolves itself into the still more fundamental one, that the words which are the Writer's materials for expression are but the symbol of ideas already existing in the mind of the Reader . . . the Reader's mind is the Writer's palette. (41)

Vernon Lee's studies in aesthetic psychology had demonstrated that a work of art can stimulate the viewer's nervous and muscular systems, the "tactile imagination," as well as the conscious intelligence. A literary work can in similar fashion make the reader respond exactly as the author intends: "A page of literature, whatever its subject-matter, gives us the impression of movement in proportion as it makes *us* move: not forwards merely, but in every direction; and in such manner as to return back on the parts and fold them into unity" (232). She calls this process "imaginative realization," a phenomenon she had identified in her writing on psychological aesthetics as *Einfühlung* or "empathy." But the presence of beauty, central to the appreciation of painting and sculpture, is irrelevant in literature, especially in prose, on which she concentrates in *The Handling of Words*. The novel in particular, she writes, "has ample resources for fascinating our attention without the help of a very special quality called beauty" (66). These resources are words and, in their combinations, statements. There is no easy formula for "fascinating" the reader. Rather the writer must draw on all the resources buried in the reader's psyche—impressions, memory, association of ideas.

> It is the business of the Writer to awaken in such combinations and successions as answer to his own thoughts and moods—these, which you must allow me to call, in psychologist's jargon, *Units of Consciousness,* have been deposited where they are by the random hand of circumstance, by the accident of temperament and vicissitudes, and in heaps or layers which represent merely the caprice or necessity of individual experience. From the Writer's point of view, they are a chaos; and what is worse for him who wishes to rearrange them to suit his thought or mood, they are chaos of living, moving things. (53–54)

The challenge to the writer is to bring order out of this chaos, "to rearrange the Reader's mind" with what she calls "the signalling word," exploiting "connotative values determined by the combinations in which we place them [words]" (58). When she comes to the principal matter of her book, in chapter 5, "Studies in Literary Psychology," she uses what she and Kit considered a scientific or empirical method of analyzing the aesthetic experience. But instead of noting pulse rates, heartbeats, and muscle tension, she analyzes the effects that writers achieve with language. What follows is the study of the syntax and rhetoric of a group of passages from an apparently random selection of prose writers: three early nineteenth-century essayists (De Quincey, Landor, Carlyle) and six fiction writers from the second half of the century (Meredith, Kipling, Stevenson, Hardy, Henry James, and Maurice Hewlett). Her aim is to show how "every such pattern of words exerts its own special power over the Reader, because it has elicited in that Reader's mind conditions, or rather activities, similar to those which have

produced that pattern in the mind of the Writer" (189). All this is a matter of the writer's "craft." From page one of *The Handling of Words* she
uses the word *manipulate* or its equivalents unapologetically. "The craft of
the Writer consists, I am convinced, in manipulating the contents of the
Reader's mind. . . . What are the mental attitudes which the Writer forces
upon the Reader? What are the mental movements he compels him to execute in the process of evoking and re-arranging those past images and feelings?" "Forces," "compels"—the passage continues with her own emphasis
and italics: "What . . . is the Reader *made to think about* by that particular
Writer? . . . HOW is he made to think of it?" (190). The answer to her question is style, which is "nothing but the Handling of Words," and this, one
infers, is the handling of readers. Manipulating implies that the reader is
passive, but in her choice of passages for close analysis Vernon Lee assumes
an intelligent reader, alert enough to respond to the effects the writer is
seeking and to become, in effect, a collaborator in the act of reading.

The opening essay in *The Handling of Words,* "On Literary Construction" (originally a lecture delivered in 1895), examines a passage of about 150
words from Robert Louis Stevenson's *Catriona* which describes the young
hero David Balfour's encounter with a gibbet as he walks along a lonely
country road. Hanging from the gibbet and twisting in the wind are two
corpses. The grisly scene does not advance the plot. It serves simply, she
says, as "a qualifier of something else . . . an adjective on a large scale." Its
importance is its effect upon the reader, foreshadowing the dangers the hero
will confront in the course of the novel. She uses the episode as a lesson in
construction: "It means thinking out the results of every movement you set
up in the Reader's mind, how that movement will work into, help, or mar
the other movements that are there already, or which you will require to set
up there in the future" (6). This is followed by other devices of literary construction: the setting up of characters as foils to each other (she cites the
scoundrel Anatole and the loyal Dologhow [Dolokov] in *War and Peace*);
the use of diagrams and patterns in constructing the plot—all this with an
eye on how the reader will react—"if you confuse his ideas or waste his energy, you can no longer do anything with him" (10); the careful selection and
management of literary point of view: "This supreme constructive question
is exactly analogous to that question in painting. . . . But once you get a psychological interest, once you want to know, not merely *what* the people did
or said, but what they *thought* or *felt,* the point of view becomes inevitable,
for acts and words then come to exist only with reference to thoughts and
feelings, and the question arises, Whose thoughts or feelings?" (20–21).

Vernon Lee appears to be moving toward the ideal that Henry James was
to achieve with the writer's complete absorption into the consciousness of

his characters. Her highest admiration was reserved for omniscient novelists like Stendhal, Thackeray, and Tolstoy, because in the hands of less skillful writers the collaborative or dialogic relationship between reader and writer is lost. The reader is passive, is *told* a story or *told about* a character, at the sacrifice of his active intelligence. When the writer is, to use her favorite pejoratives, "slack" or "slovenly," the reader responds in kind. Therefore the writer's goal must be to engage the reader's mind in collaboration. The extent to which the writer does this is, for Vernon Lee, the measure of his success.

Among her prose essayists Carlyle fares best, not only because he readily engages the reader with his language—specifically his use of the historical present in *The French Revolution*—but because he transcends the melodrama of Dickens and attains in prose something close to poetry, "the lyric of prophecy" (180). We must take her thesis largely on faith because the essay on Carlyle is the shortest of her studies and the least supported by word counts. Instead she offers two passages from *The French Revolution* on the assassination of Marat in which she changes his present into the past tense. The present, she reminds us, "abolishes the fact of narration . . . doing away with the sense of cause and effect" (176). Transposed into the past tense the historical events become simply a given, a narrative account of a series of incidents: "For we cannot feel any causal connection without projecting ourselves into the past or the future" (176). In Carlyle's use of the historical present, however, there is "realization . . . organic synthesis of co-ordinated detail" (177). "What the present tense does here is to transport us perpetually, to hustle us unceasingly, into the presence of Carlyle himself" (181). But when Dickens uses the historical present we are merely spectators experiencing not realization but "sham belief," dramatic illusion, melodrama. All art, Vernon Lee could recall from Pater, "aspires to the condition of music." For her all great prose aspires to the condition of poetry:

> The present tense, therefore, which is a rough and ready dramatic trick in the ballad, and a vulgar dodge for realization in a Writer (for all his genius) of the superficial psychology of Dickens, the present tense is also the natural form of the lyric or prophecy. For men like Shelley, Browning or Carlyle, it is the tense of the eternal verities, which, from their very nature, have not *been* but, like all divine things, always *are*. (186)

Happily for the reader who approaches *The Handling of Words* expecting solid analysis of the art of prose, her other examples are less subjective than Carlyle. For "The Syntax of De Quincey" Vernon Lee counted verbs, adjectives, nouns, pronouns, and participles to produce an interesting demonstration of how the writer communicates the nightmare effects of opium-induced dreams. Taking a passage from his *Confessions of an En-*

glish Opium-Eater in which the wretched narrator comforts an abandoned and starving child in an empty house, she cites the strong concrete nouns and adjectives with which De Quincey re-created the scene: "Was ever such catalogue of suggestions of gloom, terror and misery? . . . What *a study in black and wretchedness,* as Whistler would have put it!" (140). His relatively infrequent use of verbs suggests "his indifference to action," the helpless, paralyzed condition of the opium eater. Similarly, his reiteration of pronouns and auxiliaries suggests "the infirmity of the opium-eater's will." These are all examples of De Quincey's mastery of his prose. But in other passages she finds serious weaknesses—redundancy, shifting point of view, the arbitrary mixing of elegant diction with vulgar language. In contrast to the order and harmony that Carlyle achieved in *The French Revolution,* she concludes that De Quincey's prose reveals "a strange, ill-balanced mortal. . . . And yet with such subtlety of thought, such tragic depth of feeling, and, occasionally, such marvellous power of seeing and saying!" (157).

She judges Walter Savage Landor more harshly. Carlyle had achieved presence with his reader by his skillful use of the historical present; De Quincey had established empathy with his reader by his subtle variations of substantive parts of speech. But Landor's celebrated "classical prose" emerges, in her analysis, as lacking in substance, offering "high triumphs of literary craft" but empty of feeling. "All this is due, I think, to the fact that Landor did not really care for what he was writing about, but only for the fact of writing. This is proved by his metaphors being not expressive, but explanatory . . . trite or slackly expressed" (167). She makes no attempt to analyze Landor's rhetoric but simply cites passages that in her opinion are ineffective. For example, she finds "empty, transparent words" in Landor's sentence (her emphasis) "When he is present I have room for none [no re-flections] *besides what I receive from him*" (165). She quotes a sentence from his *Leofric and Godiva,* "The beverage of this feast, O Leofric, is sweeter than bee or flower or vine can give us; it flows from heaven; and in heaven will it abundantly be poured out again to him who pours it out here abundantly," as an example of "the rhetorician's indifference. He is so little wrapped up in the dramatic situation that he wanders off after any pretty detail which is trailed across the path" (169). She sums up: "Landor, even the mighty, severe demi-god of classic prose, has appeared to me in the semblance of a boy provided, by heartless teachers, with a theme, and obliged to produce a given number of lines thereon" (170).

Vernon Lee does not make any stronger a case for Landor's failures than she does for Carlyle's success. For all her claims to objective scientific analysis, she leaves her reader with a series of impressionistic judgments. Nevertheless her methodology is sound and serves her far better in the discussions of her immediate contemporaries, writers distinguished not for rhetoric but for the psychological effects they produce in their readers. Here her statistical tabulations, her "little heaps" of nouns, pronouns, adjectives, and so on, begin to cast light on the uniqueness of each writer's relationship with his readers. Her 500-word passage from Meredith's *The Adventures of Harry Richmond* has 159 nouns and pronouns, 66 verbs and verbal participles, 25 adjectival participles, 1 *but*, 12 *ands*, 2 semicolons, and 30 sentences. These figures are sheer pedantry until Vernon Lee shows how the limited number of connectives and the preponderance of substantives serve to keep the reader challenged: "The Reader finds himself called upon to synthesize, to judge and decide; more so, very often, than the less intellectual Reader at all cares to do. . . . It is this odd selection of what he tells and does not tell, this omission of links, which makes Meredith a sealed book to careless or unintelligent readers." He challenges his reader to participate with him in the activity of a complex mind, "perpetually forcing us to spot and to conjecture. We are made to be intellectual in default of himself: to supply what his impatience and impulsiveness denies" (196).

The antithesis of this intellectually challenging prose is Kipling's. Five hundred words from *Kim* (the episode in which Kim is discovered hiding under a table in the British mess hall) reveal "faulty construction . . . slackness and poverty of the thought" (208). The point of view shifts arbitrarily from subjective to objective. Even when we are inside Kim's consciousness, Kipling lapses into observations the boy could never have made; and the reader is constantly distracted by "changes of grammatical direction" and shifts from active to passive voice. A passage from Stevenson's *Travels with a Donkey in the Cévennes,* however, offers a veritable textbook example of harmony and control. Stevenson is describing Sunday dinner in a public house, noting the appearance and the character of the guests and of the woman who is serving them. He moves, Vernon Lee points out, from an impersonal, deliberative prose ("All was Sunday bustle in the streets and in the public house, as all had been Sabbath-peace among the mountains") to himself as observer ("after I had eaten and drunken, and sat writing up my journal"), which prepares the reader for the "give and take between the told thing and the teller, which is very characteristic of Stevenson's mode of exposition" (215). He moves easily back and forth in time: "These changes in tense are, so to speak, *dimensional movements in time,* and their variety and intricacy enlarges it, as variety of movement in space enables us to feel an object as cubic." When he shifts from present to past tense, he gives the impression of "the presentness of the past" (216). Everything is under the writer's control. "No exaggeration, no watering down; no false starts, no loose ends. A humane, many-sided, well-compacted, singularly active, willing and unegoistic personality: a creature in whose company our soul loves to dwell, because we receive much, and are made to give more and better than usual" (221–22).

With her evaluation of Thomas Hardy's prose that follows, Vernon Lee again shifts from a positive to a negative appraisal, from a writer in full control to one who, in her judgment, is careless of logic and consistency, indifferent to his dialogue with the reader. Of a single page of his prose—a passage from *Tess of the D'Urbervilles* describing Tess's first view of the valley of Blackmoor—she writes: "This page is so constructed, or rather, not constructed, that if you skip one sentence, you are pretty sure to receive the same information in the next; and if you skip both, you have a chance of hearing all you need later on. This makes it lazy reading; and it is lazy writing" (230). Her word counts show that Hardy uses fewer nouns, substantives, and more adjectives than any of the other writers she discusses: "We are being *told all about* the locality, not what is necessary for the intelligence of the situation" (224). Worse yet is Hardy's figurative writing. "Not sure of her direction," he writes, "Tess stood still upon the hemmed expanse of verdant flatness, like a fly on a billiard-table of indefinite length, and of no more consequence to her surroundings than that fly" (223). "Hemmed expanses," Vernon Lee notes, imply limits, but the billiard table is unlimited —"of indefinite length." She piles up examples of Hardy's "slackened interest"—irrelevant details heaped one on another, none of them contributing to the effects he was apparently trying to achieve.

Strategically Vernon Lee follows Hardy with a passage from Henry James's *The Ambassadors,* one of the many in the novel that explore Strether's state of consciousness. In contrast to the looseness of Hardy's descriptive prose, James challenges his reader's attention with pronouns: "he must remember what the pronoun stands for . . . the Reader will have to be spontaneously, at full cock of attention, a person accustomed to bear things in mind, to carry on a meaning from sentence to sentence . . . an intellectual, as distinguished from an impulsive or *imageful* person" (244). *The Ambassadors* is a model of authorial control. When James uses a metaphor he sustains it. For example, Strether finds himself in a moral dilemma over Chad Newsom's character; he envisions himself swimming past Chad, caught in an eddy, trying to get to the bottom, seeing Chad as a "fathomless medium," passing him "in their deep immersion, with the round impersonal eye of silent fish." Vernon Lee observes: "Of course it only *felt* like this to Strether. But it feels like this to the Reader; and this thoroughly carried-out picture is probably what enables the Reader to live on through more abstraction" (247). For her it is "a master stroke [that] has awakened a sense of the concrete." Everywhere in the passage under study she shows James in control of

his language and therefore in control of the reader: his use of abstract pronouns, his variations of sentence length, "the splendid variety, co-ordination
and activity of the verbal tenses" (249). Vernon Lee had concluded her thoroughly negative appraisal of Hardy with, one suspects, an obligatory sentence of praise: "And the very faults of Hardy are probably an expression of
his solitary and matchless grandeur of attitude" (241). She has no need for
gratuitous praise of Henry James; indeed, she admits to being troubled by
Chad's relationship with Mme de Vionnet, but she appreciates how James's
art transcends conventional morality:

> With what definiteness this man sees his way through the vagueness of per-
> sonal motives and opinions, and with what directness and vigour he forces
> our thought along with him! This is activity, movement, of the finest sort,
> although confined to purely psychological items. And it is in virtue of this
> strong, varied co-ordinated activity forced on to our mind, that we fail to
> feel the otherwise degrading effect of what is, after all, mere gossip about an
> illicit *liaison*. (250)

Maurice Hewlett's *The Life and Death of Richard Yea-and-Nay* (1900), a
long-forgotten historical novel, provides Vernon Lee with a final example of
a seemingly straightforward passage that is in fact complex and ambiguous.
Narrating a scene in which the treacherous Prince John is suspected of con-
spiring against his brother Richard, Hewlett intrudes with asides—"as I
suppose," "but let me tell you this," "it is believed." These serve to enlist the
reader with the author in a prosecutorial case against John. The apparently
objective narrative is in fact a subtle presentation of the mixed motives of
the characters. Vernon Lee juxtaposes this "violent tragedy" out of history
with Henry James's "teacup storms taking place in well-bred and peaceful
modern souls" (255) to make the point that both writers "catch us in the
meshes of the Writer's and the various personages' views, which become our
own by our effort to follow them" (257). She does not suggest that Hewlett
is a writer of the stature of Henry James. The comparison is simply one of
technique. "The drama for both novelists is an *inner* one," but where James
achieves his effects solely through the medium of Strether's consciousness,
Hewlett describes his characters physically and controls the reader's responses with "physiological peculiarities"—John is "a creeping youth,"
"writhing," motivated "from fear or from love of his own belly," while Richard has "a sensitive gorge" and "loved his royal head." Hewlett does not trust
his reader's intelligence as profoundly as James does, but, she concedes, his
reader is made "to exert himself, to live actively . . . with his brain." Hewlett
packs a single five-hundred-word passage with action. Characters come and
go; they act upon others and react to the actions of others. He "takes sides"

not by explaining the actions of the characters but by directing the reader to his own judgments. As with James, "the reader is drilled to infer rather than to accept. He is ordered to put two and two together and draw conclusions . . . to exert himself, to live actively and attentively" (264–65). But where in James she finds "the unity between subject and style" complete, in *Richard Yea-and-Nea* "no such unity could be discovered" (272).

"All writing," Vernon Lee concludes in her essay "On Style," "is a struggle between the thinking and feeling of the Writer and the thinking and feeling of the Reader. The heaven-born Writer is he whose thoughts, by some accident of his constitution, tend spontaneously to arise in his *own* mind in the order and values in which these thoughts are most easily communicated to other minds" (64–65). For "heaven-born" writers, that process remains mysterious. Literature is "a construction entirely unlike anything in real experience; a construction answering not to the necessities of outward things, but to the needs of the inner nature, the microcosm, the soul" (78).

In the passage cited above alluding to the "illicit liaison" in *The Ambassadors,* as in many other of her comments on the novel, we are reminded that for all her independent and often unorthodox thinking, Vernon Lee remained an aesthetic puritan. She condemned English and French novels alike—the French for their exploitation of "the nasty side of things," and the English for "refusing to admit that things can have certain nasty sides" ("On Novels," *Baldwin* 224). She was suspicious of "all such art as Nietzsche aptly called *Dionysiac*" (258). Living into the mid-1930s, she was alert to the radical transformations in literature and art taking place around her. She knew from firsthand experience the devastating effects of World War I on the European culture in which she had been born and bred. Her essays in *The Handling of Words* span the advent of modernism in the 1890s to its full flowering in the 1920s. She grew with the times intellectually, but personally and emotionally, as she makes clear in "Can Writing Be Taught?," an essay written more than twenty-five years after the first essay in the book, she never outgrew the lessons taught her by her mother, who was her first and only writing teacher. Reflecting on Percy Lubbock's *The Craft of Fiction* (1921), she borrows a phrase from a Victorian she had once repudiated but later came to admire, John Ruskin. In her essay "Imagination Penetrative," she recalls that in her youth she had preferred the carefully plotted "novel of situation" to the looser "novel of character." Later she discovered that the so-called reality of the well-made novel was artificial, the situations contrived, the characters invented to fulfill preconceived notions. Such novels, she now argues, lack depth, dimension—what Ruskin meant when he spoke of the importance of the "imagination penetrative" in painting—vision, the ability to create in depth, to see and project beyond the object.

For Vernon Lee the problem with much contemporary writing was its emphasis on perfection of design, where "everything thus behaved according to definition and programme [when], as a matter of fact, none of it had ever happened at all; the exquisite fitness of such representations of human existence being referable to the same cause which makes clothes sit accurately, with never a crease or a bagging on the dressmaker's doll" (278–79). To illustrate her point she discusses a work by "a noble and exquisite Master," Henry James's *The Turn of the Screw:*

> Only the inveterate habit of working out situations as if they were chess-puzzles can account for the anomaly of a man so tenderly and reverently decorous having come by the abomination of such a story. The very title of it seems to hint at a sense of having put himself into the grip of a logical mechanism every turn of whose relentless winch forced him deeper and deeper into hideous innuendo. For once that situation hit upon, it could be made plausible only by suggestions he would never have entertained had he shrunk from the first contact of those obscene ghosts of servants and of that (one hopes) neurotic governess. That he did not shrink came of the lack of *Imagination Penetrative,* such as reveals the further potentialities of whatever the artist looks at, and thereby stirring his irresistible human preferences and aversions, preserves him from the temptations which beset mere constructive ingenuity in the novelist. (280)

This extraordinary criticism of a writer she otherwise venerated cannot be read as a personal attack. But it reveals once again the burden of Puritanism that Vernon Lee carried with her. And it betrays the ultimate dilemma of her aesthetics, from *Belcaro* to her last works. She remained firmly a disciple of Paterian-Platonic idealism, determined to equate beauty with moral good. "The lewdest and most brutal literature is always the least excellent. . . . Hence, we should not lose patience even with prudishness; and, on the whole, sin rather in making literature too much of a church than in letting it become a free space for processes best performed in private and for proceedings best not permitted at all" (101). In the conclusion to *The Handling of Words,* after acknowledging that in the modern postwar world "we high-minded" readers must recognize and tolerate the cathartic nature of much popular literature, a necessary relief to "the misery of life [and] life's legal sluggishness," she still clings to the hope that the writer can transmit to the reader an Apollonian vision, "an instrument of lucid truthful vision, of healing joy, and perchance even of such prophecy as makes itself come true" (315). With the same faint trust in the larger hope she dedicated *The Handling of Words* to "The many Writers I have read and the few Readers who have read me."

12 MUSIC: THE APOLLONIAN QUEST

It is the art of music which most completely realises the artistic ideal, this perfect identification of matter and form. In its consummate moments, the end is not distinct from the means, the form from the matter, the subject from the expression. They adhere in and completely saturate each other, and to it, therefore, to the condition of its perfect moments, all arts may be supposed constantly to tend and aspire. In music, then, rather than in poetry, is to be found the true type measure of perfected art.

Walter Pater, *The Renaissance*

VERNON LEE NEVER COLLECTED HER WRITINGS ON MUSIC IN a single volume as she did her essays on writing in *The Handling of Words.* Her only book devoted to the subject is *Music and Its Lovers,* her last major publication, in 1932. Based on more than twenty years of research, it is the least interesting of her works because it deals neither with the history of music and its performance nor, except in the most abstract and subjective manner, with the aesthetics of music. Intended originally as an extension of her work with Kit Anstruther-Thomson on psychological aesthetics, it would have applied the same methods of psychophysiological analysis they had used to study the viewer's response to art, but this time to analyze the listener's response to music.

Long before the publication of their collaboration in *Beauty and Ugliness* in 1912, however, Vernon Lee was beginning to doubt their methodology. Therefore she approached music with what she thought was a more scientific methodology, sending questionnaires (in French, English, and German) to 150 people, some personal friends, others chosen at random, seeking information on their backgrounds and training in music, their listening habits, and their reactions to a variety of musical forms and genres. By the early 1920s when she began assembling her data she had no assistant handmaiden like Kit. Seven years later she wrote wearily to Maurice Baring that she hoped to finish the project in another year, "to get rid of my dreadful old-man-of-the-sea book on *Hearers and Listeners* (Lord why did I ever begin it!) which was interrupted by the War and then other things and takes all my remaining strength. When—if—that's off my back I shall dedicate Bossuet's *Reste d'une ardeur* to literary psychology" (26 November 1927). It was not "off her back" for another five years, completed and published as *Music and Its Lovers* thanks to Irene Cooper Willis, who came to Il Palmerino to help analyze the data and finally saw the book through the press. "A huge book on other people's listening to music is going to press this autumn," Violet wrote Baring, "*very* dull and the kind which Ethel [Smyth] and J.S.S. [Sargent] used to open grand eyes of indignation at. I mention it lest it belie all I have told you about my writing days being over; I want you to know that I have been twenty years writing it and broke down two years ago over it, so that it's being *edited* by my friend Miss Cooper Willis and isn't a new Vernon Lee" (5 April 1933).

Although it received a several respectful reviews, *Music and Its Lovers* served only to confirm her complaint that her work was doomed to neglect.[1] She was not a musical theorist or an expert musician.[2] She was, however, an excellent musicologist, a historian of music with a rich, highly specialized knowledge of eighteenth-century music and a wide range of interest in the music of the nineteenth century. Writing under no constraints of editorial discretion and no pressure to meet deadlines, she compensated for her lack of technical expertise with her broad-based knowledge of the arts and her sensitivity to the nuances of interpretation. Even while she insisted on the preeminence of form, on music's independence from "non-artistic interests," and as much as she agreed with Walter Pater on the purity of musical form ("All art tends to the condition of music") and dismissed as dangerously misleading "the literary interpretation of music," her best writings on music place it in the context of the society that produced it. From her adolescent fascination with the operas for which Metastasio wrote libretti through her mature fascination with the power of music to enchant and delude (reflected in her stories like "Winthrop's Adventure" and "A Wicked Voice") and her revulsion from the emotional excesses of Wagner, music was for her not an abstract form but an expression of the health or malaise of its society.

Even more particularly, music was the vehicle that could most immediately restore the ailing soul. She was, in Nietzsche's scheme of the arts, an Apollonian. But in Nietzsche's scheme music was Dionysiac, and there existed a "yawning abyss between the Apolline plastic arts and Dionysiac music." Nietzsche wrote this, it should be noted, in his *Birth of Tragedy* (1872) while serving his discipleship to Richard Wagner, whose music evoked the passions of tragic drama and was therefore judged by Vernon Lee to be irrational and self-destructive. Dionysiac music, she writes in *Music and Its Lovers*, is "excited, overwhelming, spiced with pain, exhausting." Apollonian music, in contrast, is "calm, lucid, serene, bracing" (235)—"healing joy" as she calls it in her conclusion to *The Handling of Words* (315).

It was not Vernon Lee's intention in *Music and Its Lovers* to reduce music to mere therapy. Hers is "a book on aesthetics, but aesthetics as a branch of psychology . . . the study *not* of behaviour, but of feelings and thoughts in themselves" (13). Her method, she insists, is descriptive not prescriptive: "a study of what is, not what ought to be; of why style in composer A is good for 'Listener' or 'Hearer' A; while style or composer B is more to the taste of 'Listener' or 'Hearer' B; not which style or composer is good for all musical mankind and for all ages of music's future existence. In short I have tried (with however small a success) to explain tastes, but not to prescribe them" (544). In constructing questions she was measuring "affective memory" (*mémoire affective*), "the theory broached by my master on psychology, the late Th. Ribot." Question 14, for example, candidly labeled "Quite apart from music," asks: "(A) have you at all, much or little, the power and habit of living over again the emotions of your past life as distinguished from (B) knowing in a historical way that at a given moment you have had an emotion describable as so and so and as distinguished from (C) remembering the circumstances and places connected with past emotion without feeling the emotion itself?" (219). Another question, number 6, "Does music (always without words or suggestive title) . . . ," offers as possible answers:

> (A) put you into emotional conditions or moods different from the one you happen to be in? Or (B) does it merely intensify already existing moods or emotions? Or (C) do you merely recognise, without participating, that music *represents* varieties of human emotion and mood? (D) which of these ways of responding to the emotional character of music is the most common in your case and can you give any reasons (difference of composer, or, of your own condition) which account for such different response? (217–18)

With such an approach, music becomes a medium for psychological study but also remains a subject for aesthetic appreciation. *Music and Its Lovers,* unfortunately, is unrewarding because her vaguely worded questions invite only the most subjective responses. Elsewhere, however, Vernon Lee demonstrates her thesis clearly and effectively. In a passage from her essay "The Use of Beauty" (1896) she is at once subjective and analytical:

> I was seated working by my window, depressed by the London outlook of narrow grey sky, endless grey roofs, and rusty elm tops, when I became conscious of a certain increase of vitality, almost as if I had drunk a glass of

wine, because a band somewhere outside had begun to play. After various indifferent pieces, it began a tune, by Handel or in Handel's style, of which I have never known the name, calling it for myself the *Te Deum* Tune. And then it seemed as if my soul, and according to the sensations, in a certain degree my body even, were caught up on those notes, and were striking out as if swimming in a great breezy sea; or as if it had put forth wings and risen into a great free space of air. And, noticing my feelings, I seemed to be conscious that those notes were being played *on me,* my fibres becoming the strings; so that as the notes moved and soared and swelled and radiated like stars and suns, I also, being identified with the sound, having become apparently the sound itself, must needs move and soar with them. (*Laurus Nobilis* 14–15)

On the surface it would seem that Vernon Lee was reacting to this musical experience with the same degree of empathy she had ascribed to the experience of seeing a painting or sculpture, projecting herself into the work and thus transcending the pain and anxieties of her immediate existence. But empathy is not an act of mind; it is a spontaneous psychological reaction not significantly different from the spontaneous physiological reactions to art that she and Kit had described in *Beauty and Ugliness.* By the time she was ready to analyze the results of her questionnaires, she was herself convinced of the uniqueness of the musical experience. While the other arts, including literature, can evoke emotions, they cannot reproduce them. "Now it is different with music," she explained in the essay "Beauty and Sanity": "Its relations to our nerves are such that it can reproduce emotion, or, at all events, emotional moods, directly and without any intellectual manipulation. We weep, but know not why" (*Laurus Nobilis* 139). The "Te Deum" tune she heard on that dreary London day had the same salutary effect on her that seventeenth- and eighteenth-century music—Handel, Bach, Gluck, Mozart, and to a lesser degree Carissimi, Scarlatti the elder, Marcello—had. "The chief, the never varying, all-important characteristic is the beauty; the dominant emotion is the serene happiness beauty gives; happiness strong and delicate; increase of our vitality; evocation of all cognate beauty, physical and moral, bringing back to our consciousness all that which is at once wholesome and rare" (*Laurus Nobilis* 153)

It was just such effects of music on others that Vernon Lee was investigating with her questionnaires. She knew well enough that others would respond differently from herself. She quotes a friend in "Beauty and Sanity": "You see, there is a fundamental difference between us. You are satisfied with what you call *happiness;* but I want *rapture and excess,*" the sublime but destructive passions of *Tristan and Isolde* (155).[3] A quarter century later, compiling the results of her questionnaires and now far more widely read in psychology than she had been in 1895, she recognized not only that she was investigating "what music does in the mind of the hearer" but also that the mind of the hearer is many minds, all bringing to the experience of music a kaleidoscope of impressions, memories, associations, and emotions. Hence her first group of questions concerns the musical education and musical memory of the respondents, for example: "Can you sing or whistle fragments of things you have heard?" "Can you 'turn on in memory' long fragments (whole movements) of concerted music?" The next group questions the spontaneous reactions of the respondents to a given piece. "Does music (always without words or suggestive title) seem to have a meaning or a message or something beyond itself?" (vii). She moves on to query music's effects: "Does the hearing of music facilitate trains of thought, work, or the seeing of works of art?" (x). Only one question involves musical taste: "How do your preferences stand with reference to Bach? Mozart? Beethoven (state whether earlier or later)?, Chopin? Wagner? Does Wagner seem to you to stand in any way apart, appealing to and producing emotional effects different from those of other musicians?" (viii).

Apart from singling out Wagner for special attention, Vernon Lee betrays no musical prejudices. Even when she analyzes specific answers she makes no judgments on the musical tastes of her respondents. Principally her conclusion is a classification: "But at the bottom of all these varieties of experiences and of the many subdivisions and crosses thereof, lies the question of musical attention." She divides her respondents into two groups: "Listeners," whose response to music "implies intellectual and aesthetic activity of a very intense, bracing and elevating kind," and "Hearers," whose response to music consists "largely of emotional and imaginative day-dreams, purified from personal and practical preoccupations and full of refreshing visions and salutary sentimental associations" (33). Hearers seek "meaning" in music—images, stories, emotional expression. They are Romantics, "more often 'Dionysiac,' or at least highly emotional" (496). For Listeners, whatever meaning exists is intrinsic to the formal structure of the music. "*Listening* implied the most active attention moving along every detail of composition and performance, taking in all the relations of sequences and combinations of sounds as regards pitch, intervals, modulations, rhythms and intensities, holding them in the memory and coordinating them in a series of complex wholes" (31). They are the Formalists, the Classicists, the Apollonians. Although the Listeners (Vernon Lee identifies herself as one) are obviously the more thoughtful and intellectual group, she resists rating them as superior to the Hearers. Her study, she says in the conclusion to this chapter whose title, "Varieties of Musical Experience," echoes William James, shows "how these two main modes of responding to music overlay and enrich one another; it may even suggest how the desire for music as something to be listened to has gradually evolved out of a primitive need for music as something to stir inert, or release pent-up emotions and to induce such day-dreams as restore and quicken the soul" (34).

After devoting more than four hundred pages to detailed analyses of individual responses, Vernon Lee turns finally to "Myself as *Corpus Vile.*" This chapter consists of notes on her own reactions to specific pieces of music she has played or heard performed over the period from 1906 to 1927. For her, "heard" implies not only the literal hearing of a piece but also what she calls "chant intérieur," music that one hears in memory. Musical memory was especially precious because of her hearing loss, and she was fortunate at least that she retained the ability to "hear" music by reading a score or picking out the notes on a piano, "thinking the music":

> (March 18, 1922). Yesterday, playing (after some years) Mozart's G Minor quartet with four hands with E.W. [Evelyn Wimbush?], I had one of the rather rare experiences of complete musical absorption and (despite bunglings) enjoyment. I really did not think of much except the music, though that I *did* is proved by my having at *the time* been struck with the fact, and saying to myself "Am I the least interested in the expression?" No, only in the play of notes, rhythms and intervals. (493)

This is the Formalist speaking. But in these notes Vernon Lee reveals her own attraction to romanticism and the Dionysiac. She refuses to read meaning into a musical composition, but more often than she realizes, her emotions deflect her attention from the purely formal aspects of the piece. In December 1906 she listens attentively to the tempo and the notes in a performance on the piano of Beethoven's Quintet in F Minor: "I was aware all through it of an objective expression of moods in very rapid succession and close relation." But a moment later her mood shifts:

> The notes broke off and brooded, resolved and flung aside; the notes hesitated and decided; the notes finally jubilated and were too happy for it to last; the notes were imparadised. Never once did all this minute and coordinated drama suggest any other actors besides these notes: no human being, no *me,* no *thou,* no *he;* nothing visible or thinkable except the notes themselves. And if I participated in this emotion, it was, most distinctly, as the confidant of these notes, the witness of their wonderful ways.

Playing the slow movement of Beethoven's First Quartet in January 1927 she is bored and depressed, a reaction she never has to Mozart's most solemn and serious music, "which veils itself or shows respect for the world's happiness" (499). Her mind darts to Michelangelo—an artist for whom she has only qualified admiration—whose dark solemnity, curiously enough, does not depress her as Beethoven's does. "Whatever the worth or not of such comparisons, they show that to me there is distinct human reaction on my part. Is this at all of the same kind?" (500).

Music, like the other arts, becomes for her a medium for self-analysis. What she seems to be seeking constantly in her written notes is to discover why she responds emotionally rather than rationally to the music. "By what mechanism does a certain phrase of Mozart [she is referring to the Quartet in C Major] come to have affinity with, to corroborate and unite with, a particular emotion of mine, sometimes at the moment of the emotion existing for other causes, more often merely when the music awakens that emotion or the name thereof?" (506). She can trace her reaction only to a distant memory of playing the piece with a friend who was going away, as a "pièce d'adieu." Was the emotion, then, in her memory or in the musical notes themselves? As a Listener she is less likely "to think of music in terms of human emotion." But as a psychologist she must acknowledge that "something besides the music may go on, may play itself over and over again, in memory: the massive emotion, the bodily and imaginative symptoms and concomitants, which the music has set radiating to wider and fainter circles, though a whole personality. And when that happens the most heaven-born 'Listener' may cease being a mere 'Listener,' may become a 'Dionysiac,' or, with luck, a Composer" (509).

The struggle to be an Apollonian when by instinct one is drawn toward the Dionysiac is a metaphor for Vernon Lee's lifelong struggle for the health of the soul. Of all the arts, music brings us closest to the ideal state of harmony—happiness not as a condition of material fulfillment but as a state of mind.[4] Musical imagery dominates in her description, in "Beauty and Sanity," of the ideal of mental health: "The life which vibrates forever between being better and conceiving of something better still; between satisfaction in harmony and craving for it. The life whose rhythm is that of happiness actual and happiness ideal, alternating for ever, for ever pressing one another into being, as the parts of a fugue, the dominant and the tonic. Being, becoming, becoming being; idealising, realising, realising, idealising" (*Laurus Nobilis* 113). This was a lesson she learned from Socrates and the medieval mystics, the German transcendentalist philosophers like Hegel, and among her contemporaries Walter Pater. In her dialogue "Orpheus in Rome," her persona Baldwin, recuperating from an illness that has left him depressed, is advised by his wise friend Donna Maria to visit the sculpture galleries in the Vatican Museum and to listen to Gluck's *Orfeo*. "I haven't brains like you, and can't explain *why* one ought to love classic things, and

be, in a way, classic in one's life; but I'm somehow constituted in such a way
that classic things please me, and I prefer being healthy-minded and natural; and I feel that those ancient people and Goethe were right, that they
were going with the grain of Nature, doing like the trees, and the sunshine
and the wind—do you understand?" (*Althea* 62). Donna Maria character-
izes the beauty of classic sculpture and of *Orfeo* as "hygienic" and explains
that while Wagner's *Tristan* is beautiful ("as beautiful as Orpheus"), it is "a
beauty that makes one feel not well, but vaguely ill" (72).

The young Violet Paget, whose musical taste was shaped principally by
eighteenth-century Italian composers, felt a unique responsibility for restor-
ing to Italy its pride in its musical heritage. One of her earliest publications,
in the Italian journal *La revista europea* (November 1875), had deplored the
present-day Italian taste for light opera and the neglect of composers like
Pergolesi and Marcello. She was so determined to restore Italy's musical
prestige that, in an essay on Mozart for *Blackwood's,* she claimed Italian "artistic nationality" for the great foreign composers: "Mozart, although a German as a man, was an Italian as an artist, as Handel and Bach and Gluck,
German as much as himself, had also been Italian musicians" (649). Never
given to understatement, she wrote, "The whole really living musical art of
the eighteenth century was Italian . . . Italians composed and sang for all the
other nations" (638).

In 1877, still signing herself "H. Vernon Lee," she had written "Musical
Expression and the Composers of the Eighteenth Century" for the *New
Quarterly Magazine.* Her argument even this early was that "the proper mission of art is to raise us by showing us beautiful forms" and that when music
is written to serve dramatic purposes, "the general object of art is thwarted
. . . the special laws are set at defiance" (187). Her target here is Wagner because his operas, all carefully constructed as musical drama, exploited human emotions in a dangerous way. Eighteenth-century song and opera, on
the other hand, were formal, classic, emotionally controlled. The voice was
everything, the instruments merely provided the support.

What is most remarkable about Vernon Lee's theories of music is how
little they changed over the course of her life. Her views on the aesthetics of
art evolved slowly from her early rejection of Ruskin for his moral condemnation of the Renaissance, through her discipleship to Pater's classical paganism, her rediscovery of Ruskin and recognition of the social and moral
function of art, and her studies in psychological aesthetics. But in her writings on the aesthetics of music and in her personal tastes in music, the Vernon Lee of 1932 is essentially the same as the Vernon Lee of the 1870s. *The
Magic Flute,* the *Jupiter* Symphony, indeed anything by Mozart, "remained
for me exactly what it was since adolescence," she wrote in her "Psycholo-

gie d'un écrivain sur l'art" (228). She was receptive to the work of some nineteenth- and early twentieth-century composers (even Richard Strauss), but her Apollonian ideal was enshrined in the classically pure eighteenth century, when music was "the very archetype of self-concentrated art unconnected with reality and life."

Writing as a psychologist preoccupied with the question of mental health while simultaneously writing about the aesthetics of music posed daunting problems of which Vernon Lee was herself aware. Nowhere is this more apparent than in her attempts to define musical form. In an essay review of Edmund Gurney's influential book *The Power of Sound* in the *Contemporary Review* of December 1882, half a century before she published *Music and Its Lovers,* she attempted to produce a coherent definition of musical form, acknowledging frankly that there is no vocabulary for musical description. The result is a series of incomprehensible, if not incoherent, passages:

> By musical form I mean the equivalent of pictorial, plastic, or architectural form—that combination of merely sensorily or emotionally perceptible single elements of art which can be perceived by the mind as a separate entity, and which can awaken the specific aesthetic sense of beauty or ugliness. . . .
>
> [Musical form] is that which exists actually in our mind before it becomes audible to others. . . .
>
> Musical identity and resemblance reside neither in the rude scientific and mechanical accessories of the art, nor in the emotion suggestions of its mere brute materials, but in that musical form which does not merely please the nerves and excite the emotions, but which exists and persists in the mind. (850–52)

At the end of the essay, entitled "Impersonality and Evolution in Music," she admits defeat. Appreciation of the visual and plastic arts can be enhanced by critics: she cites Ruskin on Turner, Pater on Giorgione, Sainte-Beuve on Pascal. But "in the case of music, only the humming or the playing over of a phrase, the pointing out its parts on the score, can bring home to us any beauties we have failed to perceive, and the attempt of the writer to explain . . . results merely in occupying our minds with irrelevant thought. . . . The literary interpretation of music . . . little better than an unconscious, but not less vexatious hoax" (877).

Fascinated with the art of singing, Vernon Lee was also fascinated by the singers who were themselves creative artists. In *Studies of the Eighteenth Century in Italy* she draws heavily on Dr. Charles Burney's recollections of the celebrated tenor Farinelli (Carlo Broschi). His ghostly image returns later in her stories "Winthrop's Adventure" and "A Wicked Voice," which tell of a fictional voice as capable of destroying sanity as Farinelli's actual voice once preserved the sanity of King Philip V of Spain. Another great counter-tenor, Gasparo Pacchiarotti (1740–1821), inspired a thinly veiled essay, "An Eighteenth-Century Singer: An Imaginary Portrait," published in the *Fortnightly Review* in 1891. Her less-than-imaginary portrait covers Pacchiarotti's life from boyhood to his death at the age of eighty-one. In the essay she calls him Antonio Vivarelli, but this fictitious life is so close to its real-life model that one wonders why she disguised the name. The answer is probably the freedom it gave her to write a composite portrait, incorporating details from the careers of other castrati. Vernon Lee's imaginary Vivarelli (she specifically dates him to a slightly later generation, born in 1756 and dying on the eve of romanticism in 1827) trained in Ravenna and like his real-life model was a spectacular success everywhere he sang. He was warmly welcomed in England, where he became a friend of the Burneys, William Beckford, and (probably her invention) Garrick, Reynolds, and Dr. Johnson. In his honored retirement he was visited by Stendhal, who left an entry in what she calls "an unpublished Venetian diary" that though Vivarelli was of unattractive physical appearance, "no creature has ever possessed such a magical charm."[5]

Her intention in this essay, however, was not to celebrate a fictitious artist. Rather it was to expand in ever more emphatic terms her attack on nineteenth-century music, especially opera, that she had published in 1880 in an essay review called "The Art of Singing, Past and Present" in the *British Quarterly Review*.[6] There her thesis, argued passionately and at length, was that great singing had declined in the present age. With the emergence of the full orchestra, the prominence of the voice as the interpreter of music was reduced, subordinated to the emotion or, in the case of opera, the dramatic content of the piece.

The result, Vernon Lee argues, is that the art of singing declined, "refining itself away into nothingness," while major composers like Beethoven, Cherubini, and Spontini "were tending more and more to orchestral supremacy and dramatic effect" (173). Not only is such a development detrimental to musical form, but at its most extreme—in the operas of Verdi and Wagner—it is damaging to the listener's psyche:

> Expression in the days of good singing was enclosed in the music itself, it was the very ripeness of the forms themselves, the flower, the perfection of their development: let only the piece be phrased rightly, the notes swelled and diminished, the ornaments delicately marked, the whole artistically graduated, and the greatest amount of expression of which the piece was

capable had been attained—pathos emanating directly from the music itself; for we must remember that, as we have before noticed, the music of the
eighteenth century was eminently musical, not dramatic; it was not like so
much of our operatic composition, the unmusical cries of passion tuned
down into uncouth melody. (170)

Although she decried "the unmusical cries of passion" and "uncouth
melody," the Dionysiac frenzy, of much nineteenth-century music, Vernon
Lee found herself attracted to certain works that were unabashedly romantic. A performance of Boito's *Mefistofele* struck her as "an aesthetic experience such as presents itself rarely," and the opening scene with Mefistofele
boldly defying God evoked a most un-Apollonian reaction: "That blast of
the seven trumpets, those strange shivered chords, the earthquake rumble
of all that orchestra, and the anthem which issues out of all . . . this cosmic
or seraphic drama, fitter for Dante than for Goethe, goes to my brain as
goes only one other thing—a fragment of a poem by Benedetto Marcello,
poet and composer, imaginative and aristocratically eclectic artist, artistic
ancestor of Arrigo Boito" (*Juvenilia* 1:153). She also admired, though less
extravagantly, Schubert's *Die schöne Mullerin* and *Winterreise,* all of Brahms,
and some Chopin and Robert Schumann ("Psychologie" 238). Music, she
wrote, "is *the* romantic art above all others . . . the art where the concern for
the subject, for the poetical suggestion, for what the Germans call *Inhalt,*
entirely lords it over any concern for the mere form" (*Juvenilia* 1:161). Citing the authority of Hegel, "a sort of Council of Trent in all aesthetic matters," she argues that when music becomes the aesthetic equivalent of poetry, it has the same uplifting effect. It becomes "audible form" (*Beauty and
Ugliness* 238) and bridges Nietzsche's "yawning abyss" between the Dionysiac and the Apollonian.
    The risks of indulging in what she calls "the intellectual opium of ro-
manticism," however, are considerable. She offers the example of E. T. A.
Hoffmann's musical genius Kapelmeister Johannes Kreisler, "the first of
musical romanticists" as she called him in an essay in *Fraser's* in 1878 (reprinted in *Belcaro*). Like other unlucky Hoffmann heroes, Kreisler becomes
obsessed with a passion to the point of madness. He invites some friends
to hear a demonstration of his art. In an unfortunate accident, one of his
guests breaks half a dozen of the strings of his pianoforte. Kreisler assures
his friends that they can still hear his music, and accompanying himself only
by striking a few bass chords, he improvises a spoken text: "a strange nightmare pageant . . . beautiful and ghostly, like a mad Brocken medley of the
triumph of Dionysos and the dance of Death." But his friends are disappointed. They had come to hear the measured, harmonic sounds of pure

music. They did not want to hear outbursts of wild emotion. Kreisler was offering his listeners only the first unrefined stages of the art of music, which, she writes, is "an elaboration of the human mind, only inasmuch as those sensuous brute elements are held in check and measure, are made the slaves of intellectual conception" (*Belcaro* 117). In Kreisler the intellectual conception (the Apollonian) is sacrificed to the "sensuous brute elements" (the Dionysiac). "Yet," she reminds us, "the crazy musician of Hoffmann is but the elder brother of all our modern composers" (113).

Perhaps not all, but certainly and preeminently Wagner. While Vernon Lee's musical tastes were broad enough to embrace a considerable amount of nineteenth-century music, they could not stretch to Richard Wagner. In this respect she was only one of many mid- and late Victorians who responded with dismay and alarm to his operas. For them his work was more than a musical abomination. It was an expression of a new radicalism, breaking with the traditions and conventions of early nineteenth-century opera defined by Bellini and Rossini, Meyerbeer and von Weber, and indulging in what Nietzsche called "immoderation and glorified unrestraint" (Hollinrake 188). As such, it threatened not only the cultural status quo but the mental health of its audiences. Nietzsche observed that it is in the nature of tragedy to appear "in times of the greatest prosperity and health" but also "in times of nervous exhaustion and overstrain" (*Nervenerschöpfung* and *Überreizung*) (Hollinrake 69). As early as 1852 the music critic of the *Athenaeum*, Henry Fothergill Chorley, referred to "the disease of Wagner's music," and by the 1860s he linked Wagner and Robert Schumann as both responsible "for infecting European music and audiences with the unwholesome music of the future" (Bledsoe 266).

Vernon Lee argues a specific charge against Wagner in her essay "Beauty and Sanity":

> I was listening, last night, to some very wonderful singing of modern German songs; and the emotion that still remains faintly within me, alongside of the traces of those languishing phrases and passionate intonations, the remembrance of the sense of—how shall I call it?—violation of the privacy of the human soul which haunted me throughout that performance, has brought home to me, for the hundredth time, that the Greek legislators were not so fantastic in considering music a questionable art, which they thought twice before admitting into their ideal commonwealth. (*Laurus Nobilis* 137)

For her, Wagner was the consummate violator of "the privacy of the human soul." To the degree that his music exposed forbidden passion—the adultery of Tristan and Isolde, the lustfulness of the unredeemed Kundry, the depravity of Tannhäuser while he was enslaved to Venus—it stirred emotions she had long suppressed. Even if she ignored the sexual implications of many of Wagner's libretti, she could not ignore the turbulent nature of the music itself. It exposed passions she had struggled vigorously to subdue and pain she had buried deep within "the privacy of the human soul"—Annie Meyer's curt repudiation of her affection, her humiliating loss of Mary Robinson, the gradual erosion of Kit Anstruther-Thomson's devoted attachment. Recalling and reliving memories like these imperiled her mental health and well-being. "It is the long, horrible, hysterical attack put into music," she wrote of *Tristan and Isolde,* "the furies of speechless sobbing, writhing, murderous passion. . . . Whenever art plays the savage within us, rouses these primaeval passions, it attains perhaps its most potent emotional effects, but it becomes morally detrimental" (*Althea* 85).

Not all her anti-Wagnerism is so subjective. Like many others—even the more even-handed Wagner admirers—she resented the Wagnerites who turned him into a demigod to be uncritically worshiped and the hall in Bayreuth into a temple where his operas were performed as "religious rites." The classic composers whom she admired—Bach, Gluck, Mozart, "and the greater or greatest part of Beethoven"—never exploited the listener's emotion, but "the art of Wagner, accepting the least worthy listeners and their least worthy listening, organises into a veritable cultus the cultivation of such wholesale personal emotion as such."[7] Her best Wagner criticism was written not for publication but in letters to Maurice Baring, who had been a self-proclaimed Dionysiac in his youth. "I prefer Swinburne to Browning, Rossetti and many others . . . I seek no intellectual pleasure or very little intellectual pleasure in poetry. What I want is . . . strong emotion" (2 August 1902). By 1906, however, Baring wrote to agree heartily with her condemnation of both Wagner and D'Annunzio for "slowness and hypnotic mesmerism." Like her he enjoys *Die Meistersinger* but "abhors" *Parsifal.*

Vernon Lee's wittiest and most perceptive criticism of Wagner is in a letter she wrote Baring as she was returning by train to Florence after a visit to Dresden and Bayreuth (25 September 1906): "Although I expected little enjoyment, I have been miserably disappointed. . . . What is insufferable to me is the atrocious way in which Wagner takes himself seriously, the self-complacent (if I may coin an absurd expression) auto-religion implied in his hateful unbridled longwindedness and reiteration; the element of degenerate priesthood in it all, like English peoples' contemplation of their hat linings in church." Wagner's creation of "music drama," as opposed to the more static traditional opera with its set arias, failed to impress her. She recalls the "varying dramatic expression in a single act (Act One) of Mozart's

Don Giovanni," in which the mood swings from attempted seduction, violence, and tragedy with the murder of the Commendatore, to declarations of love and devotion and broad comedy with Leporello and the Don. Mozart conveyed innumerable moods and ideals in less time "than for that old poseur Amfortas to squirm over his grail or Kundry to break the ice with Parsifal." There is no sparkle and variety in Wagner. "Even *Tristan,* so incomparably finer than Wagner's other things . . . is indecent through its dragging out of situations, its bellowing out of confessions which the natural human being dreads to profane by showing or expressing. . . . The chief psychological explanation of Wagner (and of his hypnotizer's power over some persons) [is] namely his extreme *slowness of vital tempo.* Listening to him is like finding oneself in a planet where the time is bigger than ours; one is on the stretch, devitalised as by the contemplation of a slug."

Again it is the psychological reaction, the synergy of brisk musical tempo and sound mental health contrasted with Wagner's long and repetitious motifs and morbid melancholy, that is Vernon Lee's critical criterion. She can even find merit in a work as fraught with hysteria and Dionysiac madness as Richard Strauss's *Salome.* "How Wagner would have gloated over it all; Strauss is noisy but swift and therefore (I think) wholesome and decorous." Less perverse is her judgment of the salutary effects of *Carmen:* "The humanity of it and the modesty also are due very much to the incomparable briskness of the rhythm and phrasing; the mind is made to work quickly, the life of the hearer to brace itself to action."

In her pursuit of the Apollonian, Vernon Lee came dangerously close to undermining her musical aesthetics. That she was beginning to suspect this herself is obvious in her loss of faith in the results of the questionnaires she had used in *Music and Its Lovers.* Nothing in her analyses of the questionnaires, the long, persistent inquiries into the psychological aesthetics of music, matches her spontaneous reactions to music. She knew exactly what she liked and what she disliked. With some significant exceptions, principally Wagner, she could distinguish between the merely pretentious and the genuine masterpiece. She probably overrated eighteenth-century Italian music and underrated nineteenth-century music. But until the 1920s when deafness closed all public performances of music to her, she was that best of music lovers—the independent, intelligent listener always ready to discover the new even while she cherished the old.

13 DEMONS, GHOSTS, AND THE *GENIUS LOCI*: STORIES OF THE SUPERNATURAL

The Genius Loci, *like all worthy divinities, is of the substance of our heart and mind, a spiritual reality. And as for visible embodiment, why that is the place itself, or the country; and the features and speech are the lie of the land, pitch of the streets, sound of bells or of weirs; above all, perhaps, that strangely impressive combination, noted by Virgil, of "rivers washing round old city walls."*

Vernon Lee, introduction to *Genius Loci*

ONE DAY IN THE EARLY 1880S, A SMALL BOY VISITED THE bookstore Hatchard's in London to spend some money he had received from his governess as a reward for doing his lessons well. By his own account years later, the boy, Maurice Baring, novelist, dramatist, essayist, and longtime friend of Vernon Lee's, chose "a book called *The Prince of the Hundred Soups* because of the cover. It was by Vernon Lee, an Italian puppet show in narrative, about a Doge who had to eat a particular kind of soup every day for a hundred days." Delighted with the story and noting from the title page that it was "by the author of *Belcaro*," the boy saved up five shillings and returned to Hatchard's to buy that book too, only to discover that "it was an aesthetic treatise of the stiffest and driest and most grown-up kind" (*Puppet Show of Memory* 20). In 1927 Vernon Lee made up for Baring's early disappointment with *For Maurice: Five Unlikely Stories,* a collection that is typical of all her roughly dozen and a half stories of the supernatural. They are, she wrote, "another puppet show, framing the unlikely heroes and heroines at the ends of my wires with roughly daubed scenery of places not unfamiliar to you" (xii).

Because "scenery of places" (setting) figures every bit as prominently as the "unlikely heroes and heroines" (plot), it is instructive to read Vernon Lee's stories of the supernatural, her works of pure imagination, alongside her travel writings, based on the reality of geography. For her, both the real scenes and the often wildly fantastic stories were haunted by the ghost who accompanied her happily from her childhood adventures in the wake of Mrs. Mary Sargent to her old age when she was still exploring remote Italian towns and churches in pursuit of the *genius loci:* "a spiritual reality," a spirit that lurks in all manner of places, in "the lie of the land, the shape of buildings, history and even quality of air and soil" (*Spirit of Rome* 44).

The English ghost story enjoyed a remarkable surge of popularity in the 1890s. Though Henry James had published ghost stories from the beginning of his career, he wrote at least a dozen, including his best-known story, "The Turn of the Screw," in that decade, and Vernon Lee published most of hers between 1889 and 1902. Leon Edel speculates that these stories of the "decadent nineties," the fin de siècle, the closing of a century that had defined the limits of religion and launched the unlimited possibilities of science, "exercise a fascination upon the creative imagination: they carry with them a sense of termination, a sense of death, a sense of the turning of a corner in Time" (James, *Ghostly Tales* xiv). But the appeal of the genre to Vernon Lee was more than its popularity in the 1890s. From childhood she had been fascinated with the past. Her imagination, she wrote, fed on "the remote lumber-room full of discarded mysteries and of lurking ghosts, that wonder-world of things moth-eaten and dust-engrained" (*Studies of the Eighteenth Century* xvi). Like many other children she had absorbed folklore, fairy tales, and puppet shows into her very being, but unlike most children her experience of the past was at first hand. She had read the German märchen and the tales of the Grimm brothers with her German governesses in the very atmosphere out of which they had grown. She had played amid the ruins of the ancient civilizations that had inspired mythology. Paganism, early Christianity, the saints and their miracles, the sinister power of corrupt Renaissance men and women were familiar to her not only from books but from their relics everywhere she looked in Italy.

With the exception of "Oke of Okehurst," set in an English country house, all of her stories of the supernatural are set in Italy, Germany, or Spain in places haunted not by domestic ghosts of the recent past but by ancient gods and goddesses or by long dead spirits of the Renaissance and eighteenth century. She wrote under the direct influence of the European romantic supernatural—from Goethe's evocation of the classic past in *Faust II* and Adelbert von Chamisso and E. T. A. Hoffmann's wildly imaginative tales to the drug-induced fantasies of Baudelaire and the exoticism of Théophile Gautier—and she scorned the vogue among her contemporaries in England for "real" ghosts of the kind conjured up by hypnosis and psychical research. These, she complained in her preface to *Hauntings* in 1890, have "no point of picturesqueness and [are], generally speaking, flat, stale, and unprofitable." *Her* ghosts come from "the more or less remote past . . . things of the imagination, born there, bred there, sprung from the strange, confused heaps, half-rubbish, half-treasure, which lie in our fancy" (ix).

Like Henry James, Vernon Lee was interested in the psychological rather than the psychic, not the "vulgar apparition" but the "inner ghost . . . the haunter not of corridors and staircases, but of our fancies" (*Belcaro* 93). While James found most of his ghosts in some element of himself, notably the aging bachelor who is haunted by the sense of having missed something in life ("The Beast in the Jungle," "The Altar of the Dead," "Maud-Evelyn," "The Jolly Corner"), Vernon Lee's stories of the supernatural owe their inspiration to history, mythology, and art. Her characters are purely literary; the stories are genre pieces individualized by her fascination with myth, legend, and pseudohistory. To read them as unconscious revelations of her inner self—of her sexual frustration and repressed lesbianism, of her jealousy of her brother and her bitterness toward her mother—is unrewarding. To the extent that all works of the creative imagination reflect in some degree the psyche of their creators, they are of course self-revealing, and in one instance, her story "Amour Dure," the protagonist is, like her, a historian, obsessed with the past, whose first successful book was published when he was twenty-four, her age when she published her book on eighteenth-century Italy.[1] But to probe for significance in every reference to towers, pools of water, snakes, and so on, is to pursue the dubious and unprovable and deny the stories their genuine merits as works of the imagination.

Of all Vernon Lee's stories of the supernatural, "Prince Alberic and the Snake Lady" has invited the most attention and interpretation. Because it was first published in the *Yellow Book* in July 1896—her only appearance in that short-lived publication—it has had especially close scrutiny. The reputation of the *Yellow Book* as an outlet for shocking, even erotic, literature has been much exaggerated and was based more on its cover, which was identified with the notorious French yellowback novels, than on its contents. Its contributors ranged from as respectable a novelist as Henry James through younger and bolder though hardly less respectable writers like Max Beerbohm, George Gissing, H. G. Wells, and Arnold Bennett. Even the drawings of Aubrey Beardsley and a few stories by Baron Corvo, who later became an unabashed pornographer, evoked no widespread expression of moral outrage. In the *Yellow Book* Vernon Lee was in the company of her peers, the younger generation of late Victorianism venturing into new but hardly radical variations on familiar literary genres.

"Prince Alberic and the Snake Lady" brings together Vernon Lee's major literary interests of history—specifically the degeneration of the High Renaissance as it moved into the post-Reformation baroque—and fairy tale in the wildly fantastic spirit of German romanticism. History is relatively insignificant here after the brief opening paragraph: "In the year 1701, the Duchy of Luna became united to the Italian dominions of the Holy Roman Empire, in consequence of the extinction of its famous ducal house in the persons of Duke Balthasar Maria and of his grandson Alberic, who should have been third of the name. Under this dry historical fact lies hidden the strange story of Prince Alberic and the Snake lady." This "dry historical fact" is not a fact but part of the author's invented documentation. The "facts" that she sprinkles throughout the story are pure fabrication.[2] The Gobelin tapestries that decorate the ducal palace (allegedly designed by Monsieur Le Brun for Louis XIV) never existed. The literary sources cited for the background of Prince Alberic's ancestry are real—the poems of Boiardo and *The Chronicles of Archbishop Turpin* (a spurious history of Charlemagne and Orlando published in 1812)—but a search of these reveals no Alberic nor any remotely similar tale.

In "Prince Alberic" we are in as rich and exotic a realm of fantasy as Vernon Lee ever created. Within the story of the relationship between the lonely young prince and the enchanted snake who assumes the shape of a beautiful lady is the story of the prince's ancestor Alberic the Blond, a heroic knight of the Crusades, who rescued a lovely damsel from her enchantment as a monstrous green snake. In both cases the snake is benign, the literary descendant not of the biblical tempter and the seven-headed serpent-dragon of the Apocalypse but of the guardian serpents of Eastern legend, like the Hindu Ananta, the serpent mother of the god Vishnu, and of Greek and Roman mythology, like the healing symbol of Aesculapius's staff. "Prince Alberic," like any good story of the supernatural, is the product of the author's syncretic imagination.

Young orphaned Alberic's guardian is so absorbed in his grand self that he ignores the boy, leaving him to invent his own life. The duke, though "a prince of enlightened mind and delicate taste," decorates his Red Palace ("brilliant tomato-covered plaster which gave the palace its name") in lavish rococo style and is himself a rococo relic, trying to conceal his old age with cosmetics and elegant clothing. On a rare visit to his grandfather, the boy is terrified by the sight of what appears to be a human head with long flowing locks stuck on a pole. It proves to be merely his grandfather's wig, but it serves to foreshadow the boy's ominous future. In his loneliness Alberic fantasizes over a shabby tapestry that pictures the adventures of his ancestor Alberic the Blond returning from the Crusades. Against a faded background of a garden full of exotic plants and animals is a knight embracing a beautiful lady dressed in a gown of gold cloth. Because a heavy wardrobe stands in front of the tapestry, the boy can see her only from the waist up, but one day the furniture is moved and he discovers that below her waist is "a snake's tail, with scales of still more vivid (the tapestry not having faded there) green and gold." From a wandering storyteller he learns that, by kissing the loathsome snake three times on the lips, knight Alberic rescued the lovely Oriana and restored her to human life.

Unhappily for the young Alberic, his grandfather decides to replace the shabby tapestry with a new one representing Susannah and the Elders (an appropriate choice for the lascivious old man). The boy, enraged, cuts the new tapestry into shreds and refuses food: "It had been his whole world; and now it was gone, he discovered he had no others." It therefore matters little to him when his grandfather banishes him to the long abandoned Castle of the Sparkling Waters, a medieval ruin inhabited only by some peasants. Alberic flourishes in its quaint antiquity and its lush, overgrown, and neglected grounds. Here he feels himself in the world of his beloved tapestry and is hardly surprised to discover an abandoned well where, emerging from the weeds around it, "a long green glittering thing" approaches him:

> Then, slowly, it began to glide around the well circle towards him. "Perhaps it wants to drink," thought Alberic, and tipped the bronze pitcher in its direction. But the creature glided past, and came round and rubbed itself against Alberic's hand. The boy was not afraid, for he knew nothing about snakes; but he started, for on this hot day the creature was icy cold. But then he felt sorry. "It must be dreadful to be always so cold," he said, "come, try and get warm in my pocket." But the snake merely rubbed itself against his coat, and then disappeared back into the carved sarcophagus.

The snake is the second mysterious presence to manifest itself. The first had been a beautiful lady dressed in green who appeared just after his arrival at the castle. She introduces herself as his godmother and comes every evening to play and read with him—"and, above all, to love." She educates the boy, provides him with books, fine clothes, and horses, but he never tells her about the little snake that has now become his pet. It is clear, nevertheless, that the snake and the lady are somehow connected. In a dream one night Alberic follows the song of a nightingale into an exquisite garden. Bathed in moonlight, the wildly colorful flowers are resplendent: "The moon hung like a silver lantern over the orchard; the wood of the trellises patterned the blue luminous heaven; the vine-leaves seemed to swim, transparent, in the shining air. Over the circular well, in the high grass, the fireflies rose and fell like a thin fountain of gold. And, from the sentinel pine, the nightingale sang."

Alberic realizes that it is "the hour and place of his fate." At that moment the snake appears, transfigured:

> "Oriana!" whispered Alberic. "Oriana!" she paused and stood almost erect. The Prince put out his hand, and she twisted round his arm, extending slowly her chilly coil to his wrist and fingers.
>
> "Oriana!" whispered Prince Alberic again. And raising his hand to his face, he leaned down and pressed his lips on the little flat head of the serpent. And the nightingale sang. But a coldness seized his heart, the moon seemed suddenly extinguished, and he slipped away in unconsciousness.

When he awakens, his head is resting in the lap "of the most beautiful of ladies . . . his own dear Godmother."

Under her care Alberic grows up to be a handsome and manly youth. His grandfather now has plans for him to come to court, and Alberic dutifully appears, with his snake concealed in a wicker cage under his cloak. He performs his courtly duties correctly but displays no interest in the lavish entertainments and the beautiful women with whom his grandfather surrounds him. Worse yet, he infuriates the old man, who is now deeply in debt for his extravagant habits, by refusing to marry a wealthy bride. The duke's spies—his dwarf, his jester, and his Jesuit confessor—have long suspected that Alberic has some secret companion. They persuade the duke to make an unexpected visit to his grandson's chambers. Terrified by the sight of the pet snake sleeping peacefully in a corner, the duke screams and his lackeys rush forward to kill it. Alberic fights them furiously but is overpowered. He dies of grief two weeks later, followed in death only a few months later by his grandfather. Thus ends the house of Luna. But because this is a story of the supernatural, we are told that when the servants cleaned the prince's room they found not the mutilated snake "but the body of a woman, naked, and miserably disfigured with blows and saber cuts."

The erotic implications of "Prince Alberic and the Snake Lady" are undeniable, but they are also only matters of speculation.[3] What we can positively know about this or any other story by Vernon Lee are the literary influences that were at work on her imagination and how she filtered them into her own special versions of the supernatural. There is no mystery in her fascination with the theme of the beautiful yet terrifying, healing yet destructive enchanted serpent. At the age of fourteen she had written a story of some 250 words, "Capo Serpente: A Legend of the Roman Campagna," about a huge "serpent king" who haunts a Roman ruin and frightens a young painter. Even then it was the atmosphere of the place, the *genius loci* rather than the plot, that intrigued her: "When the sun sheds upon the broken arches of the aqueduct a rosy tint, when the Alban hills are purple, when the dome of St. Peter's rises black upon a golden sky, a huge green serpent glides from beneath the tall grass."[4]

Prince Alberic's snake, however, is terrifying only to his superstitious grandfather. In her early reading Vernon Lee had encountered numerous enchanted snake ladies, from the classical Medusa to Coleridge's Christabel and Keats's Lamia. But for the innocent and benevolent snake her closest source was probably Hoffmann. She had already retold his story of Johannes Kreisler, the half-mad musician, in an essay in *Belcaro,* and her story "A Wicked Voice" shows the influence of his "Rath [Councillor] Krespel," in which a young girl is killed by her compulsion to sing (she is the Antonia of Offenbach's *Tales of Hoffmann*). But there is a more direct connection between Vernon Lee's "green-gold" snake lady and Hoffmann's Serpentina in "Der goldene Topf" ("The Golden Flower Pot"). Serpentina is one of three enchanted daughters of a magician who saves the hero Anselmus from a life of bourgeois materialism and leads him into the spiritual world of nature and art. Like Alberic, Anselmus is a young innocent, menaced by evil forces and temptations that seek to lure him away from his idealism. When he sees the "three little snakes, glittering with green and gold, twisted around the branches and stretching out their heads to the evening sun," he falls in love with one, Serpentina, who even when she assumes a human body remains serpentine in her graceful movements, sinuous and slippery, sliding away when he attempts to embrace her. To win her he must defeat a witch who guards a golden flower pot. After many fantastic adventures Anselmus wins his bride. Her magician-father declares: "And is the blessedness of Anselmus anything else but a living in poesy? Can anything else but poesy reveal itself as the sacred harmony of all beings, as the deepest secret of nature?"

Like Hoffmann's tale, and unlike her other stories of the supernatural, "Prince Alberic and the Snake Lady" is pure fairy tale. Not even the background of the duke's corrupt court shatters the mood until the last lines of the story, where we are denied the happy ending of a fairy tale and the "dry facts" of history prevail. In her other stories of the supernatural there are no benign enchanted snakes. Instead the driving force is the malign femme fatale. Nowhere is the woman more evil than in "Amour Dure." Here she is Medea da Carpi, who proves herself altogether worthy of her given name. She is a high-born Renaissance lady whose ravishing beauty ensures the destruction of every man who loves her, including the young scholar who is writing a history of her times. First published in *Murray's Magazine* in 1887, then in *Hauntings* in 1890, "Amour Dure" like "Prince Alberic" has been reprinted in several twentieth-century collections, including Italo Calvino's *Fantastic Tales: Visionary and Everyday* (1997), where the title has unfortu-

nately been changed to "A Lasting Love," missing the irony of the French
"Amour Dure" (love lasts) and "Dure Amour" (hard or unrelenting love).

There is more Medusa than Medea in Medea da Carpi. Her guiding spirit
is not vengeance on a lover who wronged her but sheer malignancy. Her
"sisters" flourished in romantic and Decadent literature. In "The Beauty of
the Medusa," the first chapter of *The Romantic Agony,* Mario Praz traced
their history to eighteenth-century aesthetics, where beauty and pleasure often have common roots in terror: "The Horrid, from being a category of
the Beautiful, ended by becoming one of its essential elements, and the 'beautifully horrid' passed by insensible degrees into the 'horribly beautiful'"
(27). The Germans, the French, and the English poets of romanticism embraced the image of the femme fatale, and later in the century the so-called
Decadents, most notoriously Swinburne, exploited the theme. Vernon Lee
was no stranger to any of this literature. For all her moral conservatism she
saw no reason to reject it any more than she had rejected the Renaissance
because many of its leaders were morally tainted. She was well acquainted
with the femme fatale in Renaissance history; in "Amour Dure" she cites as
Medea da Carpi's peers Lucrezia Borgia and Vittoria Accoramboni, John
Webster's White Devil. Closer to home she had the inspiration of Walter
Pater's "La Gioconda," not evil herself but embodying "the animalism of
Greece, the lust of Rome, the mysticism of the Middle Age with its spiritual ambition and imaginative loves, the return of the Pagan world, the sins
of the Borgias" (Pater, *Renaissance* 103).[5]

The scholar-narrator of "Amour Dure" is haunted by the ghost of a
woman who died three hundred years earlier; the story itself is haunted by
Vernon Lee's *genius loci.* Once again she teases her reader with what might
be a real Italian town in the windswept Apennines, Urbania—small, dull,
undistinguished for architecture and art but full of what Henry James called
"the redolence of the unspeakable Italy" (*Letters,* ed. Edel, 3 : 276). Vernon
Lee often pursued her *genius loci* into remote and quite unglamorous parts
of Italy. To reach Urbania her narrator, Spiridion Trepka, must take a gig
drawn by white bullocks, "slowly winding among interminable valleys,
crawling among interminable hillsides, with the invisible droning torrent
far below, and only the bare gray and reddish peaks all around." The town
itself "is a handful of tall black houses huddled to the top of an Alp," and
its populace are rugged mountain people,

dark, bushy-bearded men, riding about like brigands, wrapped in green-
lined cloaks with their shaggy pack-mules; or loitering about, great, brawny
tow-headed youngsters, like the parti-colored bravos in Signorelli's frescoes:
the beautiful boys, like so many young Raphaels, with eyes like the eyes of

bullocks, and the huge women, Madonnas or St. Elizabeths, as the case may be, with their clogs firmly poised on their toes and their brass pitchers on their heads, as they go up and down the steep black alleys.

We are seeing all this through the eyes of the young, high-strung narrator, and Vernon Lee is careful to follow her own strictures, as outlined in *The Handling of Words,* on consistent literary point of view. Written in the form of a diary precisely dated from 20 August 1885 to a final entry on 24 December of the same year, "Amour Dure" is the record of the experiences of a twenty-four-year-old Pole who has lived most of his life in Germany. He feels displaced, deracinated as it were—"thou Pole grown into the semblance of a German pedant, doctor of philosophy." Having already published a well-received book on fifteenth-century Italian history, he is in Urbania on a traveling scholarship to write a history of the town. He has no illusions about himself or his work, which he calls "modern scientific vandalism," because what he truly seeks is to "come in spirit into the presence of the Past." Such a quest, Vernon Lee knew only too well, is frustrating. Trepka plods through dusty archives, grumbles about the dull society of the town and the unattractiveness of the young women he meets: "for all my efforts, in Rome, Florence, and Siena, I could never find a woman to go mad about." He seeks "a grand passion," a woman "for whose pleasure to die."

He finds that woman in the long-dead Medea da Carpi, whose history is in the archives: "Yes, I can understand Medea. Fancy a woman of superlative beauty, of the highest courage and calmness, a woman of many resources, of genius, brought up by a petty princelet of a father, upon Tacitus and Sallust, and the tales of the great Malatestas, of Caesar Borgia and suchlike!—a woman whose one passion is conquest and empire." Married at sixteen to an elderly nobleman, having already murdered a passionate young suitor who had abducted her, Medea contrives to have her husband murdered and flees to Urbania, where the local duke falls madly in love with her. She proceeds through a succession of lovers ("her magic faculty is to enslave all men who come across her path"), all of whom meet violent or mysterious deaths, until her cruelty (she coolly watches the ghastly torture of one lover who refuses to testify against her) sickens the duke, who has her imprisoned and strangled. Her executioners are women because the duke knows that she will bewitch any male executioners.

A convincing femme fatale usually has some embodiment in a visual image—Medusa's head on Perseus's shield, for example. Vernon Lee found her model in Bronzino's portrait of Lucrezia Panciatichi in the Uffizi Gallery. Cool and self-possessed, she looks level-eyed at the viewer. She is richly dressed in dark red satin and velvet and wears her auburn hair in a neatly braided coronet. On a string of pearls around her neck is a medallion on which is inscribed a French motto, "Amour Dure Sans Fin."[6] Trepka's fatal entrapment by Medea comes when he finds in the archives a miniature portrait of her: "an exquisite work, and with it . . . it is easy to reconstruct the beauty of this terrible being":

> The face is a perfect oval, the forehead somewhat over-round, with minute curls, like a fleece, of bright auburn hair; the nose a trifle over-aquiline, and the cheek-bones a trifle too low; the eyes gray, large, prominent, beneath exquisitely curved brows and lids just a little too tight at the corners; the mouth also brilliantly red and most delicately designed, is a little too tight, the lips strained over the teeth. . . . The mouth with a kind of childish pout looks as if it could bite or suck like a leech.

Vernon Lee has transformed Bronzino's portrait of a dignified young matron into a sensual and erotic image, and she has turned the message of Lucrezia's medallion from a pledge of fidelity to a grim warning to love Medea at one's peril: "AMOUR DURE—DURE AMOUR." Already inflamed by this miniature portrait, Trepka by accident comes upon another portrait, this one full-sized: "And such a portrait—Bronzino never painted a grander one." This is "the real Medea, a thousand times more real, individual, and powerful," seated in a high-backed chair: "The face is the same as in all the other portraits . . . she looks out of the frame with a cold, level glance . . . round the throat, white as marble, partially confined in the tight dull-red bodice, hangs a gold collar, with the device on alternate enameled medallions, AMOUR DURE—DURE AMOUR." From there it is only a small step for Trepka to hallucination. He encounters a woman in the street, a real enough presence, but when he glimpses her face, "I felt myself grow quite cold; the face of the woman outside was that of Medea da Carpi!"

Like many other writers of ghost stories, Vernon Lee is careful to honor the borders between the supernatural and the real. By representing her narrator as obsessed with his scholarship and contemptuous of the provincialism of his surroundings, by sustaining his point of view as he increasingly questions his sanity (he admits to a family history of madness), she positions her reader firmly in the world of sanity and reality. But her final thrust undermines all certainties—as a good ghost story should. She undermines history itself as Trepka comes to recognize that his passion for a dead woman is real:

> Shall life for me mean the love of a dead woman? We smile at what we choose to call the superstition of the past, forgetting that all our vaunted science of today may seem just another superstition to the men of the future;

but why should the present be right and the past wrong? . . . No, no; all is explained by the fact that the first time I read of this woman's career, the first time I saw her portrait, I loved her, though I hid my love to myself in the garb of historical interest. Historical interest indeed!

Medea da Carpi comes to life for him. He follows her elusive figure through the deserted nighttime streets of Urbania. He receives a letter from her commanding him to destroy the bronze equestrian statue in the square of the duke who had ordered her death. One night he follows her into a long-abandoned church where she stands near the altar but disappears when he approaches her. On Christmas Eve, happily resigned to dying like her other lovers and ignoring their ghostly warnings, he attacks the statue with a hatchet. His diary ends with his breathless excitement as he awaits her visit to his room: "It is she! It is she! At last, Medea, Medea! Ah! AMOUR DURE—DURE AMOUR!" But the story ends with a terse note that on Christmas morning 1885 the local authorities found the equestrian statue mutilated and the body of "Professor Spiridion Trepka of Posen, in the German Empire . . . dead of a stab in the region of the heart, given by an unknown hand."

There are genuinely artistic touches in "Amour Dure"—the snowy winter landscape of the surrounding mountains and the chill of the ruthless Medea, the abandoned church named San Giovanni Decollato in honor of another victim of a femme fatale, the self-imposed isolation of a romantic young man trapped in a dreary Italian small town. Vernon Lee delights in ironic contrasts: the scholar's obsession with the mysteries of the past and his bumptious landlord, who indulges in superstitious ceremonies that mock the mysteries of the Roman Catholic past

> and believes that if only you lay a table for two, light four candles made of dead men's fat, and perform certain rites about which he is not very precise, you can, on Christmas Eve and similar nights, summon up San Pasquale Baylon, who will write you the winning numbers of the lottery upon the smoked back of a plate, if you have previously slapped him on both cheeks and repeated three Ave Marias. The difficulty consists in obtaining the dead men's fat for the candles, and also in slapping the saint before he has time to vanish.

The femme fatale reappears in two other Vernon Lee stories, "Oke of Okehurst" and "Dionea." In "Oke of Okehurst" the *genius loci*—the essential character of a particular place—is only a plot device, useful because a story of the supernatural requires an appropriate framework for atmosphere and mood. "Oke of Okehurst" is Vernon Lee's only English ghost story, and it draws heavily on the conventions of such stories—an isolated English country house, usually of Jacobean vintage, with dark paneling, heavy carved furniture, faded tapestries, and stately halls lined with ancestral portraits.[7] She follows the formula conscientiously through a narrator who is a witness to ghostly horrors but is not an active participant in them. "Oke of Okehurst" and "Dionea" were published in *Hauntings* in 1890, but "Oke," of novella length, had been published earlier by William Blackwood as *A Phantom Lover: A Fantasy Story* in 1886. Vernon Lee had only recently begun her annual summer visits to England, discovering the peculiar charms of English scenery and English weather:

> We had meanwhile driven into a large park, or rather a long succession of grazing-grounds, dotted about with large oaks, under which the sheep were huddled together for shelter from the rain. In the distance, blurred by the sheets of rain, was a line of low hills, with a jagged fringe of bluish firs and a solitary windmill. It must be a good mile and a half since we passed a house, and there was none to be seen in the distance—nothing but the undulation of sere grass, sopped brown beneath the huge blackish oak-trees, and whence arose, from all sides, a vague disconsolate bleating. At last the road made a sudden bend, and disclosed what was evidently the home of my sitter.

The narrator is a portrait painter, recalling for a visitor in his London studio the background of one of his paintings. He is self-assured, coolly objective in the manner of Browning's Duke of Ferrara: "That sketch up there with the boy's cap?" the story begins. "Yes, that's the same woman. I wonder whether you could guess who she was. A singular being, is she not?" Her singularity is not the murderous witchery of Medea da Carpi. She is a Victorian lady, Alice Oke, wife of a landed gentleman of stereotypical Englishness —handsome, blond, with military bearing and "beautifully fitting clothes; absolutely like a hundred other young men you can see any day in the Park and absolutely uninteresting, from the crown of his head to the tip of his boots." His wife, however, fits no stereotype. When the painter meets her, he is instantly struck by her unconventional and unearthly beauty. As the story develops, he also perceives her destructive powers, though these are limited to one victim—her husband. She is in short a modern femme fatale, possessed not by some outside evil but by inner demons of psychotic delusion.

With his painterly eye the narrator also observes that Oke, in spite of his wholesome Englishness, shows signs of insecurity—hesitant speech, shyness, a nervous solicitude about his wife, and "a very odd nervous frown between his eyebrows, a perfect double gash—a thing which usually means something abnormal: a mad-doctor of my acquaintance calls it the maniac frown." The Okes are first cousins. Portraits of their ancestors hang in the halls, and the narrator notices a close resemblance between Alice Oke and a seventeenth-century ancestor. One day she tells him the story of the family curse, involving the lady in the portrait and her husband. They had allegedly murdered a neighbor, a dashing Cavalier poet. Alice Oke has discovered hidden away a manuscript of his love poems addressed to the lady. She torments her husband with constant talk about the poet, as if he were a living lover, until Oke begins to see apparitions of the poet. Yet the painter, the modern man of hard facts and reality, dismisses the business as "a very harmless psychological mania." When he finally recognizes the seriousness of the problem, he urges Oke to seek medical help, but it is too late. Imagining that he has caught his wife with her ghost lover, Oke shoots her and dies himself a few days later, raving mad.

"Oke of Okehurst" has its admirers. It meets the conventions of the English ghost story competently, but its narrator fails to engage himself, and consequently the reader, in his characters until it is too late. John Clute has argued that the tragedy "comes as a direct consequence of the narrator's creation of the story that he needs for his art" (1:332). Obtuse and smug in his judgments of others, the painter fails to realize the enormity of the problems in the Okes' marriage: their isolation in a country house, their sexual incompatibility, and their family history of madness. The weakness of the story, however, is not the unreliable narrator but its author's failure to give it the color and immediacy that distinguish most of her stories of the supernatural—the absence here of the *genius loci*. Her femme fatale and the husband-victim are psychotic case histories, and we are obliged to dismiss them with the same callousness as the painter-narrator.

Apparently Vernon Lee's *genius loci* did not flourish in the damp country houses of England. He demanded genuine antiquity and the brilliant colors of the Mediterranean, where Medusa and Medea were born. "Dionea," first published in *Hauntings,* offers us not a neurotic Englishwoman but a genuine and enchanting femme fatale and a setting as enchanting as she. Although its conclusion is even more violent and terrible than the fate of the Okes, the story is told with such disingenuous directness that it reads like a myth. And well it should, for "Dionea" is one of many stories about dispossessed pagan gods returning to the modern world with dire consequences, sometimes for themselves, more often for the mortals who encounter them. These "gods in exile," as Heinrich Heine called them, caught the imaginations of the romantics and the Victorians.[8] They were especially prominent in the art and writings of the Pre-Raphaelites and the Decadents. Even without the examples of Walter Pater's imaginary portraits "Denys

L'Auxerrois" and "Apollo in Picardy," Vernon Lee would have been attracted to the revenant gods of antiquity because, as literary motifs, they came without the baggage of modern psychology. As characters they can move freely and spontaneously; they can be wildly eccentric and arbitrary without being accountable to common sense or the moral codes of society. They are absolutely natural—personifications of natural forces, pure creatures of the *genius loci*.

Such at least is Dionea, a mysterious waif washed up on the shores of a Ligurian town in June 1873. She is apparently the sole survivor of a shipwreck, identified only by a scrap of paper bearing her name. Her clothing and the few words she speaks appear to be of eastern origin, probably some Greek dialect. We learn her story in a series of letters by an elderly Italian doctor addressed to an English lady married to an Italian nobleman. The most interesting feature of the story is not its plot. Given the framework of the return of the pagan gods, what follows is predictable: Dionea will bring disaster to those who love her. The reader's attention is on the doctor who writes the letters. He is a much traveled man who has retired to this quiet seaside village where he serves a poor superstition-riddled community. Since writing *Miss Brown* and "Lady Tal" Vernon Lee had learned the dangers of introducing characters from real life into her fiction, but she was comfortable in modeling her Dr. Alessandro on Giovanni Ruffini, the genial revolutionary turned novelist (*Doctor Antonio*) who had been so helpful to her in her early writing days. Having lived most of his life abroad as a political exile (a man "of Mazzinian times," as she describes the good doctor), Ruffini retired to a small town on the Italian Riviera much like the setting of "Dionea," where he continued to correspond with young Violet Paget until two years before his death in 1881. In "Dionea" she pays him a gracious tribute. Her Dr. Alessandro takes up the cause of the little castaway and over the next fourteen years writes to his English friend seeking her financial help and keeping her posted on the child's extraordinary development. She is adopted by the Sisters of the Stigmata, the local Franciscan convent, and confounds the nuns by growing up beautiful but hopelessly wayward, resistant to all their efforts to civilize her. She is drawn to the sea from which she came and to the countryside, a creature of the *genius loci* with whom she seems to share a natural affinity:

> Another of Dionea's amusements is playing with pigeons. The number of pigeons she collects about her is quite amazing; you would never have thought that San Massimo or the neighbouring hills contained as many. They flutter down like snowflakes, and strut and swell themselves out, and furl and unfurl their tails, and peck with little sharp movements of their

silly, sensual heads and a little throb and gurgle in their throats while Dionea lies stretched out full length in the sun, putting out her lips, which they come to kiss, and uttering strange, cooing sounds; or hopping about, flapping her arms slowly like wings, and raising her little head with much the same odd gesture as they.

Innocent as she appears to be, Dionea casts a sinister shadow: "an amazing little beauty, dark, lithe, with an odd, ferocious gleam in her eyes, and a still odder smile, tortuous, serpentine, like that of Leonardo da Vinci's women." Small wonder that rumors spread: that she has "the evil eye," that she upsets the moral order and causes married women and even some of the nuns to run off with lovers and young girls to elope with ne'er-do-wells. Even the rational Dr. Alessandro reports to his correspondent that strange things are happening. A young priest, confessor to the convent, grows feverish and commits suicide, apparently for love of Dionea; a rich old man who makes advances to her is killed by a bolt of lightning. Skeptic that he is, the doctor acknowledges the possibility "that the Pagan divinities lasted much longer than we suspect, sometimes in their own nakedness, sometimes in the stolen garb of the Madonna or the saints. Who knows whether they do not exist to this day?" Not even he, however, can anticipate Dionea's destructive powers. A famous sculptor brings his wife and children to the village, and his wife, struck by Dionea's beauty, suggests that he use her as a model for a statue of Venus. The conclusion is inevitable: the sculptor becomes infatuated with his model, his wife is murdered, and his body is found at the foot of a cliff. Dionea disappears, but a sailor reports that while at sea he saw a Greek vessel, "And against the mast, a robe of purple and gold about her, and a myrtle-wreath on her head, leaned Dionea, singing words in an unknown tongue, the white pigeons circling around her."

Italy is not the only homeland for displaced pagan gods or the only setting in which to reenact classical mythology. A coastal town in northern Europe is the scene of "Marsyas in Flanders" (in *For Maurice*) where the traveler-narrator becomes fascinated by a medieval church and hears from the antiquarian guide the story of a statue, presumably representing the Savior, that washed up on the shore in the thirteenth century. Hailing it as a miraculous gift from the sea, the parishioners decided to build a cross on which to rest the statue, but the figure, twisting and contorting itself, resisted all their efforts. When they finally forced it into position, the statue broke the cross to which it had been attached. It was then secretly stowed away with a stake driven through its heart. Years later the antiquarian, a student of ancient art, finds the statue and realizes that it had never represented the crucified Jesus but was "Marsyas awaiting punishment."

Germany, where the child Violet Paget first tasted the delights of the supernatural, provided a setting for two more stories with pagan-classical analogues. One, "The Lady and Death," first published in *Pope Jacynth and Other Fantastic Tales*, resets the Alcestis legend in sixteenth-century Germany; the other is a broadly comic story, "The Gods and Ritter Tanhûser," first published in *For Maurice*. The subtitle to "The Lady and Death" is "A Companion-Piece to Dürer's Print." There is no work in the Dürer canon that remotely resembles the story, but Vernon Lee freely invented saints and works of art and wrote her own versions of history and mythology as her stories demanded.[9] For this story she invented a town in Thuringia or Bavaria, Erlach, much like the quaint towns where she had spent so much of her childhood and where, during the Renaissance, the image of Death was ever present in both secular and religious art. Dürer dominates the scene; her narrator refers specifically to *The Knight, Death, and the Devil*. The narrator tells the story of his ancestor, the Lady of the title, who offers herself in the place of her physician husband, who, in desperation to find a cure for the plague, had pledged his soul to the Devil. In an appropriate updating she is rescued by a latter-day saint, one Theodulus, who conquers Death in a tournament.

Having no commitment to any religion, Vernon Lee did not hesitate to mix pagan and Christian myths. She took special pleasure in parodying the Tannhäuser legend, treated with religious awe in Wagner's opera and feverish eroticism in Swinburne's "Laus Veneris." Her Tanhûser ("that is the proper medieval form and less evocative of brawny *Heldentenors* than the usual one") is "a very mediocre High Dutch poet," bored with the passion of Venus (Aphrodite here) and eager to return to earth to participate in a singing contest. Two gods agree to go along to watch the contest. They appear in various disguises: Athene as a necromancer named Klingsor ("who enjoyed much vogue in the magical circles of that day"), Apollo as a Greek grammarian. In another Wagnerian dig, Aphrodite presents Tanhûser with a helmet of invisibility designed by her husband Ares. The story descends into farce and slapstick; after a dousing in a moat for an audacious reference to Aphrodite, Tanhûser goes on his pilgrimage to Rome and receives the papal staff, which flowers only because the "forsaken" Aphrodite persuades Zeus to grant her this last favor. "It is something connected with a foolish superstition about what he calls being saved (as if he hadn't been safe enough when I was there!)."

Viewed overall, Vernon Lee's stories of the supernatural display a remarkable variety of styles and moods. They gave her the opportunity not only to indulge in her love for place—to describe in her overflowing and colorful prose and to evoke the spirit of the long dead past—but also to test her versatility as a writer. Here she proved herself more than a scholarly historian and an outspoken critic of the arts. She had a healthy sense of humor, apparent to her close friends though invisible to the many who found her pedantic and heavy-handed. She could also assume a childlike simplicity and innocence, qualities that had endeared her to young Maurice Baring; and for one who claimed no religious affiliation, she could write tender little religious fables that in others' hands might have been banal. The strongest feature of her stories, however, is their setting—the *genius loci* at work, especially in the authenticity of Italy, where most of these stories take place. For example, her "Sister Benvenuta and the Christ Child" (published in the *Fortnightly Review* in December 1905), a simple miracle tale of a nun's devotion to a doll that represents the Christ child in the Christmas pageant, is enriched by her picture of eighteenth-century Venice in carnival mood and the puppet shows that delighted her in her own childhood.

In other stories she assumes a more sophisticated attitude somewhat similar to the series of boldly satiric anticlerical tales that Frederick Rolfe, the self-styled Baron Corvo, contributed to the *Yellow Book* from 1895 to 1896 and collected as *Stories Toto Told Me*.[10] Her "Pope Jacynth" and "Saint Eudaemon and His Orange Tree" (first published in *Pope Jacynth and Other Fantastic Tales* in 1904) have for their themes the rivalry among the early saints for earthly rewards, the sanctimonious piety of some of them, their human frailties in the face of worldly temptations. Pope Jacynth, another creation of Vernon Lee's private hagiography, is a priest of such piety and humility that he becomes the subject of a Job-like wager between Satan and the Lord. This time the terms of the contest are reversed. Satan endows Jacynth with beauty, strength, and wisdom and persuades the Lord to make him pope, surrounding him with lavish splendor. But the pious Jacynth remains ascetic and humble, distributing all his wealth to the poor. His fatal error, however, is "the sin of vaingloriousness," because "he gloated in his humility." Satan's triumph is brief, for though when Jacynth dies his corpse burns, the angel Gabriel retrieves his heart, from which a flowering pomegranate tree grows.

"Saint Eudaemon and His Orange Tree" is also set in "the new Christian Rome," where the ruins of paganism still dominate the landscape. Told with absolute simplicity ("Eudaemon was a saint; persons who did not molest their neighbours were mostly saints in those days; and so, of course, he could work miracles"), the story celebrates a man who has retreated to a house in the country to mourn the death of his young bride. Here he plants a garden, converts a Roman temple into a chapel, and serves the poor. He has two neighbors who are also saints—one a theologian, the other a stylite. They enjoy his hospitality but are highly critical of his generosity to others and his friendly association with the peasants. Because Eudaemon defends the pagan gods as "deserving compassion" and as fellow-creatures of God, they accuse him of consorting with devils. They are further scandalized when Eudaemon unearths a statue of Venus and rashly slips his wedding ring on her finger while he is bowling with the peasants. The ominous expectations of his neighbor-saints seem to be fulfilled when he seeks to remove the ring and the statue's finger becomes rigid. Here Vernon Lee writes her own cheerful variation on Prosper Mérimée's gruesome "Venus de l'Ille," in which a young bridegroom who slipped his ring on the finger of a pagan statue is crushed to death by her on his wedding night.[11] No such fate awaits Eudaemon. He firmly orders his Venus to return the ring and change herself into "a fair white tree with sweet-smelling blossoms and golden fruit which blooms to this day on the Aventine hill."

The mood of the *genius loci* varies with place and time. The Italy that provides the scene for these lighthearted pieces is the same Italy in which "Amour Dure" takes place. Although Vernon Lee's puritanism provoked her revulsion at the lurid and erotic in the work of others, it did not inhibit her from indulging in the lurid and erotic herself. Most of her stories, to be sure, reflect the general tastes of the reading public of her time. She wrote the stories for publication—though not all of them were easily placed or widely appreciated. But there is also an element of the subjective in some of them, revealing the darker side of her sensibility. Nowhere is this more apparent than in the only story she set in Spain, "The Virgin of the Seven Daggers," conceived during her visit there when she was recovering from the nervous breakdown she suffered after Mary Robinson's marriage. The overwrought sensuous imagery of the story reflects a mind shaken with illness and a feverish imagination.

Even in normal health Vernon Lee had little appreciation for Spanish culture, especially its art of the baroque age, which is the setting for this story. Her years in Italy had made her sympathetic to Latin culture, but it was the joyous, wholesome, open spirit of Italian life to which she responded. Describing herself to Maurice Baring as "an old agnostic adorer of true Catholicism," she scorned the Calvinism of the Counter-Reformation, "with its sour aping of Geneva." She was also repelled by the grim, morbid spirit of Spanish art with its cult of "death, damnation, tears and wounds . . . Asiatic *Fleurs du Mal* sprung of the blood of Adonis, and taking root in the Spanish mud half and half of *auto da fée* and bullfights . . . the melancholy lymphatic Hapsburgs of Velasquez, the lousy, greedy beggars of Murillo, the black and white penitents of Ribera and Zurbarán, above all the elongated ecstatics and fervent dullards of Greco" (*For Maurice* xviii).[12]

The tone of "The Virgin of the Seven Daggers," in *For Maurice,* is witty

but also bitterly ironic. The "hero" Don Juan, not the wicked but irresistible Mozartian Don nor the guileless Byronic Don, but an arrogant, ruthless seducer and murderer, is saved from the damnation he thoroughly deserves by one act of faith in a long career of faithlessness—loyalty to the
gaudy, sanguinary image of the Spanish Madonna of the Seven Daggers. In
a scene of dazzling sensuous imagery, the spirit of the long dead Infanta,
buried beneath the Alhambra, is summoned up:

> The breast of the princess heaved deeply; her lips opened with a little sigh,
> and she languidly raised her long-fringed lids; then cast down her eyes on
> the ground and resumed the rigidity of a statue. She was most marvellously
> fair. She sat on the cushions of the throne with modestly crossed legs;
> her hands, with nails tinged violet with henna, demurely folded in her lap.
> Through the thinness of her embroidered muslin shone the magnificence
> of purple and orange vests, stiff with gold and gems, and all subdued into
> a wondrous opalescent radiance. . . . Her breast was covered with rows and
> rows of the largest pearls, a perfect network reaching from her slender throat
> to her waist, among which flashed diamonds embroidered in her vest.

She offers her love, provided he swear that she is more beautiful than the
Virgin of the Seven Daggers. When he refuses to do so, he is beheaded, but
his soul flies to heaven. The story ends on an ironic note with a comment
by the playwright Calderón to the Archpriest Morales that he wishes he
might make this story the subject of a play, for it is "well calculated to spread
the glory of our holy church."

Vernon Lee's first ghost story—inspired by her visits with John Sargent
to see the portrait of Farinelli in the gallery of the Accademia Filarmonica
in Bologna and published in 1881 in *Fraser's Magazine*—was called "A Culture Ghost; or Winthrop's Adventure." She was never entirely certain herself what "culture ghost" meant, defining it in *For Maurice* as "anything
vaguely connected with Italy, art and, let us put it, the works of the late J.A.
Symonds" (xxxvi). Symonds was a distinguished cultural historian, but his
name offers no clue. Noting the variety of scenes, subjects, and moods in
her stories, we may only conclude that the culture ghost was some manifes-
tation of art—painting, sculpture, music—that gives each story its unique
flavor: a Bronzino portrait in "Amour Dure," a tapestry in "Prince Alberic,"
a Dürer print in "The Lady and Death," a memento mori by Zurbarán in
"The Virgin of the Seven Daggers," the suggestion of a Sargent painting in
"Oke of Okehurst."

The culture ghost even haunts two of her stories that have no elements
of the supernatural. These are "A Wedding Chest" and "The Doll," both, it
should be noted, set in Italy and centering on objects of art associated with

a distant past. In both, the central characters are mortal and "normal" in the eyes of society. One is a collector of art, the other a creative artist. The artist in "A Wedding Chest" (first published in 1904 in *Pope Jacynth and Other Fantastic Tales*) is a gifted sculptor who carves an elaborate *cassone* on the commission of a wealthy young nobleman, notorious for his pursuit of women. Four panels on the front of the chest depict scenes from Petrarch's "Triumph of Love," celebrating famous lovers of legend ruled over by the god of love. The sculptor is about to marry a beautiful young woman of his own class, but the nobleman has her kidnapped, rapes her, and a year later returns her mutilated corpse in the same *cassone* with a mocking note to the sculptor. Also in the coffin is "the body of an infant, recently born, dead like herself." The grieving sculptor has his beloved's body preserved in the *cassone* and buried with all due religious rites, but he throws the infant in a refuse heap. He then sets out to avenge her death, kills the nobleman, drinks his blood, disinters the chest, and flees with it to another city, where he spends the rest of his life.

A less grisly culture ghost haunts "The Doll" (originally published in *Cornhill* in 1896 as "The Image," retitled and collected in *For Maurice* in 1927). Here too the story centers on an artifact with no supernatural qualities. In contrast to "A Wedding Chest" with its darkly evil Renaissance atmosphere and its passionate characters, "The Doll" is contemporary, set in an Italian small town (Foligno in Umbria), and totally lacking in violence or melodramatic action. The culture ghost here is a life-sized cardboard effigy of a beautiful young woman ("with Ingres Madonna features") in early nineteenth-century dress. She, or it, is discovered by an Englishwoman, a collector of antiques, who narrates the story. A dealer of absolute probity takes her to a now neglected but once beautifully decorated seventeenth-century palace to look at some ancient Chinese plates. Now in the hands of a dissolute heir, the treasures are for sale, but none catches the interest of the collector until she stumbles upon the dusty effigy. She learns that it was made for the present heir's grandfather in memory of his first wife, who had died young in childbirth. Her husband so idolized her that he had the image made to keep her, as it were, alive. He worshiped it for years but finally remarried, and the doll was relegated to a storage room. Fascinated, the Englishwoman buys it, removes it to a garden, and then, without any stated reason, burns it, retrieving from the ashes only the wedding ring from the doll's finger. "Keep it, signore," the sympathetic antiques dealer tells her. "You have put an end to her sorrows."

Recent comment on "The Doll" concerns the enigmatic nature of the story. Susan J. Navarette traces its origin to Vernon Lee's early and lifelong fondness for puppet shows and effigies and considers the story "her briefest, her most complex, her most uncanny and perhaps her best" (166). She finds a certain mystique in it involving "a disintegrating society that encases women in roles that efface the reality of their lives . . . [and the burning] an encoded rite of passage, accessible only to the initiated, who could share sympathetically in its essence" (169).[13] The framework of the story, however, does not support so heavy a burden of allegory, but it does offer a sensitive sketch of a middle-aged woman finding fulfillment for something missing in her own life. That missing something, suggested by her retrieving the doll's wedding ring, involves her marriage and her husband's indifference to her wants and needs: "I was alone at the inn, for you know my husband is too busy for my *bric à brac* journies." The living model for the doll had been doted upon by her husband as an object of art but was unappreciated as a human being. Or so at least the narrator imagines: "[H]e never made an attempt to train this raw young creature into a companion, or showed any curiosity as to whether his idol might have a mind or character of her own." She further imagines that the young woman had loved her husband dearly but was too inarticulate to express her feelings, "painfully though she longed to do so." Such reflection leads her to speculate on her own marriage: "Do you suppose I could ever have told all this about the Doll to my husband? Yet I tell him everything about myself; and I know he would have been kind and respectful."

John Sargent had early recognized the affinity between Vernon Lee's culture ghosts and her *genius loci*. On reading "A Culture Ghost; or Winthrop's Adventure" in 1881 he wrote her, "I like its Italian colour very much and the delicate observation throughout, so much so indeed that the local atmosphere, so to speak, strikes me as the real raison d'être of the thing, and the ghost story a pretext, but this is prying behind the scenes" (*For Maurice* xxxvii). Some years later, she wrote another version of the story, "A Wicked Voice" (published in *Hauntings* in 1890). Both stories prove that Sargent was correct: in both versions, the ghost story is an excuse for indulging the *genius loci*. Both have long-dead singers as their centers. In the 1881 story, Winthrop is a young painter traveling in Italy to indulge "his love of the picturesque." In a small town in Lombardy he meets an eccentric collector of old musical instruments and manuscripts who shows him a portrait of a once famous tenor, Rinaldi, who had been murdered some years earlier. Fascinated by the picture, Winthrop spends the night in the deserted house that was the scene of the murder. The ghost of the tenor appears and sings a song just before the ghost of the jealous husband appears and stabs him to death. Winthrop might have dismissed all this as a nightmare, but a year later, staying in a villa in Bellosguardo, he hears his hostess singing the same song. She tells him that buried away in a lumber room she found a copy of the song dated 1780. Moreover, she has learned from a musicologist that hers is a unique copy and that Winthrop could never have heard it before in waking reality.

The early "Winthrop's Adventure" is not particularly interesting as a ghost story. Its charm is in its many digressions, long and loving descriptions of summer in Lombardy ("God's own orchard on earth"), sleepy old provincial towns, and the friendly Italian peasants whom Winthrop meets along the way. "A Wicked Voice," the later version, published in *Hauntings,* is a far more chilling story, set in Venice and narrated in the first person by Magnus, a man who is obsessed and possessed. He might have stepped out of a tale by Edgar Allan Poe—a monomaniac in the throes of composing an opera in the modern age. A disciple of "the great master of the future," Richard Wagner, Magnus professes to despise the virtuoso singers of the baroque past: "O execrable art of singing, have you not wrought mischief enough in the past, degrading so much noble genius, corrupting the purity of Mozart, reducing Handel to a writer of high-class singing exercises, and defrauding the world of the only inspiration worthy of Sophocles and Euripides, the poetry of the great poet Gluck?" His nemesis is one such singer, Zaffirino, who boasted "that no woman had ever been able to resist his singing." Magnus has studied an eighteenth-century engraving of the singer so closely that he has come alive for him, much as Medea da Carpi's portrait gave life to her: "That effeminate, fat face of his is almost beautiful, with an odd smile, brazen and cruel. I have seen faces like this, if not in real life, at least in my boyish romantic dreams, when I read Swinburne and Baudelaire, the faces of wicked, vindictive women." In short, Zaffirino is *un homme fatale.* His voice pursues the composer wherever he goes and finally drives him to madness.

The evil of the story, however, lies not in the ghost of the tenor who can literally kill with the beauty of his voice, but in the place, the scene of the story—a deadly, mephitic Venice haunted by its past: "this cursed Venice, with its languishing moonlights, its atmosphere as of some stuffy boudoir, long unused, full of old stuffs and potpourri!" Though she loved Venice, Vernon Lee claimed to be overwhelmed by its man-made, unnatural beauty: "I cannot cope with it, it submerges me . . . Wagner was right to die there." [14] Only in Venice could the Italian *genius loci* prove to be an evil genius:

> It was a breathless evening under the full moon, that implacable full moon beneath which, even more than beneath the dreamy splendor of noontide, Venice seemed to swelter in the midst of the waters, exhaling like some great lily, mysterious influences, which make the brain swim and the heart faint —a moral malaria, distilled, as I thought, from those languishing melodies,

those cooling vocalizations which I had found in the musty music-books of a century ago.

As Horace Gregory noted of what he called "the romantic inventions of Vernon Lee," her stories of the supernatural

are possessed by genii of time and place as well as by the personality of their author. It is through her eyes that a generation of readers at home or abroad may set their blue guide books aside to rediscover Europe. And if the Italy they find is unlike any other Italy in English fiction, it is because no English writer since Vernon Lee (and I am aware of the Italys of Henry James, E. M. Forster, Norman Douglas, and D. H. Lawrence, all excellent of their various kinds) has peopled Italy with such enduring ghosts and shades. (24)

14 DEMONS, GHOSTS, AND THE *GENIUS LOCI:* TRAVEL WRITING

How much I like, too, your generalizations about the Genius Loci! One may be born a worshipper of more spectacular deities—from Jehovah to D. H. Lawrence's Dark God, from Dionysius to the object of Boehme's ecstasies—one may be born, but it is useless to try to make oneself consciously a worshipper at such shrines. For most of us, I fancy, Wordsworth's Natural Pieties are the most decent and satisfactory thing. Of the theory and practice of the Natural Pieties your books are a most delicate and beautiful exposition.

Aldous Huxley, to "Miss Paget," 26 May 1925

WHETHER TRAVEL INSPIRED VERNON LEE'S STORIES OF THE supernatural or her stories were an excuse for travel writing is immaterial. The *genius loci* was equally at home in both genres. It flourished in works of pure imagination like the ghost stories and her verse drama *Ariadne in Mantua,* in her histories of Renaissance and eighteenth-century Italian culture, and in the many essays she wrote over her lifetime recording her travel impressions. Fiction and fact overlapped at her will. In her stories of the supernatural she invented historical and literary sources. In her histories she introduced legends—some traditional, some of her own creation. And in her travel writings she drew on literary sources as freely as on her actual experiences. The *genius loci* for Vernon Lee was a rich stew seasoned with everything she saw, read, and imagined.

"Ravenna and Her Ghosts" is representative of the melding of genres, a discursive essay that moves with easy informality from fact to fiction.[1] Vernon Lee is confident of her reader's patience, knowing that one reads her not for specific information but for a ramble among her cluttered impressions. Still she offers a portrait of the city, "modern and full of rough, dull, modern life; and the past which haunts it," that is remarkably true to the impressions that a visitor might have today:

Those pillared basilicas, which look like the modern village churches from the street, affect one with their almost Moorish arches, their enamelled splendour of ultramarine, russet, sea-green and gold mosaics, their lily fields and peacock's tails in mosque-like domes as great stranded hulks, come floating across Eastern seas among the marsh and rice-field. The grapes and ivy berries, the pouting pigeons, the palm trees and pecking peacocks, all this early symbolism with its assimilation of Bacchic, Eleusinian mysteries, seems, quite as much as the actual fragments of Grecian capitals, the discs and gratings of porphyry and alabaster, so much flotsam and jetsam cast up from the shipwreck of an older Antiquity than Rome's; remnants of early Hellas, of Ionia, perhaps of Tyre. (129)

The ghost motif is more appropriate to Ravenna than to Italian cities of even greater antiquity because the Byzantine mosaics with their jewel-like colors and glazed, staring faces summon up images of what Yeats, in "Byzantium," called "death-in-life and life-in-death." The ghost story that Vernon Lee introduces into this essay is not, however, associated with the city itself but is a medieval legend set in the neighboring woods of Classis. It is neither original with her nor reflective of the ancient culture of Ravenna. Her excuse for including it is simply that it is "a complete ghost-story of the most perfect type and highest antiquity which has gone round the world and become known to all people" (137). She duly acknowledges her sources: "Boccaccio wrote it in prose [*Decameron*, 8th story, 5th day]; Dryden wrote it in verse ["Theodore and Honoria," *Fables Ancient and Modern*]; Botticelli illustrated it [the "Nostagio degli Onesti" panels now in the Prado]; and Byron summed up its essence in one of his most sympathetic passages [*Don Juan* 3.105–8]" (137).[2] She adds that she has discovered another version in "the barbarous Romagnol dialect of the early fifteenth century," which she translated for this essay, but one suspects that this source is imaginary, there being no evidence to support it.

The story is a grisly one involving a lover spurned because, having spent his fortune in courting a lady, he now lacks the money to marry her. Hunting one day in the wood of Classis, he sees a knight and his company pursuing a naked woman whom he captures and then brutally murders. The lover witnesses this ghostly scene again when he returns to the spot the next week. He then arranges a party in the woods where his own lady and a large company of guests see the scene repeated. The lady is so moved that she relents and marries him. Vernon Lee is left to speculate that these ghosts still haunt the quiet little church at Classe.

Though she lived into the second quarter of the twentieth century, Vernon Lee was a creature of nineteenth-century romanticism and eighteenth-century sensibility. She described herself as "the sentimental traveller." If she has a peer among travel writers, it is not one of her contemporaries but the archetypal sentimental traveler Laurence Sterne:

> I pity the man who can travel from Dan to Beersheba, and cry, "'Tis all barren"—and so it is; and so is all the world to him who will not cultivate the fruits it offers. I declare . . . that was I in a desert, I would find out wherewith in it to call forth my affections—. If I could not do better, I would fasten them upon some sweet myrtle, or seek some melancholy cypress to connect myself to—I would court their shade and greet them kindly for their protection—I would cut my name upon them, and swear they were the loveliest trees throughout the desert: if their leaves wither'd, I would teach myself to mourn, and when they rejoiced, I would rejoice along with them. ("In the Street: Calais," *A Sentimental Journey through France and Italy*, 115–16)

Her contemporaries Ruskin, Henry James, and D. H. Lawrence shared her awareness of a *genius loci* but in different and less intense ways. That is why, probably, they are still read today, while her travel writings are out of print. They also, it must be admitted, wrote better. Virginia Woolf was excessively harsh on *The Sentimental Traveller* when she wrote to Violet Dickinson in December 1907: "I am sobbing with misery over Vernon Lee, who turns all good writing to vapour with her fluency and insipidity—the plausible woman! I put her on my black list, with Mrs. Humphry Ward." Woolf tempered her remarks somewhat in her review of the book for the *Times Literary Supplement* of 9 January 1908: "Vernon Lee, with much of the curiosity, the candour, and the sensitiveness to trifles of the true essayist, lacks the exquisite taste and penetrating clearness of sight which make some essays concentrated epitomes of precious things" (*Essays* 1:157–59). Other reviewers, however, were more charitable, some even enthusiastic. The *Spectator* (4 January 1908) judged it a collection "with unquestionable originality and charm," and the *New York Times* (4 January 1908) found its author "thoroughly alive to whatever is picturesque or quaint or amusing."[3]

The vogue for the impressionistic European travel essay died with World War I, although some writers—notably Norman Douglas and Aldous Huxley—managed to preserve something of the voice of the leisurely traveler who had no goal other than self-fulfillment. But with the shrinking market of the homebound vicarious traveler, and the introduction of cheap and rapid means of transportation and relatively safe and comfortable conditions of travel, travel writing became a service—helpful advice on sights to see, hotels, restaurants, shopping. Vernon Lee herself published only one volume of travel essays after the war, *The Golden Keys and Other Essays on the*

Genius Loci (1925), and the latest essay in that collection was written in 1917. After her death in 1935 publishers showed no interest in a 228-page typescript of her later travel essays, which is now in the Vernon Lee archive at Colby College ("A Vernon Lee Notebook, 1898–1934").

Having grown up with her mother's prejudice against "Cookites," Baedeckers, and Murrays, Vernon Lee never wrote anything remotely resembling a guidebook. Like Ruskin, who traveled but was not a travel writer, she traveled to indulge her aesthetic interests in nature, art, and human culture. Once she had overcome her early disapproval of Ruskin's religious moralism, she came to appreciate his writings on Switzerland and Italy in particular as more exalted versions of her own explorations of the *genius loci:* "Ruskin gave us one of our greatest pleasures (gave it consciously and as an artistic factor in life)—topography teaching us to feel the countries growing, forming as we move through them, teaching us to evoke the haunting presence of scenery, on dreary days or evenings, over maps; the very names of stations growing delightful, and a talk about miles and levels and surveyors' details becoming fraught with delight, a poem" (*Gospels of Anarchy* 307).

Henry James too overcame his distaste for Ruskin's "narrow theological spirit" when he read him in Venice. Among all her English contemporaries, James came closest to sharing Vernon Lee's sense of the *genius loci,* seeking the essence of places not in tourist cynosures but in the offhand, casual experiences of travel: "It is by the aimless *flânerie* which leaves you free to follow capriciously every hint of entertainment that you get to know Rome" (*Italian Hours* 149). Like Vernon Lee he appreciated the tourist off-season: "It isn't simply that you are never first or never alone at the classic and heroic spots where you have dreamt of persuading the shy *genius loci* into confidential utterance," he complained; and he looks forward to the season "when Rome becomes Rome again and you may have her all to yourself" (190). For him as for her, the *genius loci* manifests itself in unexpected places and homely details. In Venice, for example, "it is not of the great Square that I think, with its strange basilica and its high arcades, nor of the wide mouth of the Grand Canal. . . . I simply see a narrow canal in the heart of the city—a patch of green water and a surface of pink wall . . . the little bridge, which has an arch like a camel's back. . . . It is very hot and still, the canal has a queer smell, and the whole place is enchanting" (13). Like Vernon Lee, finally, he fell in love not so much with the classic Italy as simply with Italy's *genius loci,* which he found in obscure provincial hill towns like Velletri, where he stopped for coffee one afternoon: "The charm was, as always in Italy, in the tone and the air and the happy hazard of things, which made any positive pretension or claimed importance a comparatively trifling question . . . we stayed no long time and 'went to see' nothing; yet we communicated to intensity, we lay at our ease in the bosom of the past, we practiced intimacy, in short, an intimacy so much greater than the mere accidental and ostensible" (364).

T. S. Eliot, a fellow American expatriate, observed in his essay "On Henry James: In Memory" (1918), "It is the final perfection, the consummation of an American to become, not an Englishman, but a European—something which no born European, no person of any European nationality, can become." For all his love for Europe, James never achieved that condition. Vernon Lee, on the other hand, did not "become" a European; she *was* European. Although her passport was British, she was an adopted Italian with stronger roots in France, Germany, and Switzerland than she ever had in England. James remained an outsider, a visitor to the Continent. Although his travel writings are intensely subjective, they are addressed to readers much like himself, cultivated American or English travelers (not tourists) who might someday visit the places he is writing about. He is a reporter (as indeed he was in his early career) of specific sites and events—an art exhibition in London, Sarah Bernhardt's performance as Andromaque in Paris, the ices served in the Caffè Quadri in the Piazza San Marco. He guides his readers through museums and churches, taking pleasure in anticipating their pleasure and sharing his serendipitous discoveries with them. Vernon Lee wrote without such a targeted audience. She appears to be writing for the sheer joy of expressing herself. Like her conversations, her essays are solipsistic. Her erudition is formidable, but it emerges spontaneously and incidentally. Because she writes vivid descriptions, we may see places as she saw them, but we realize that it would be impossible to duplicate her experiences of them.

In a sense Vernon Lee's travel writing constitutes her autobiography, the most personal and revealing of all her published work. Yet, curiously enough, she did not regard herself as much of a traveler. Her family's gypsy existence during her childhood was, she insisted, "moving not travelling . . . my family never made excursions" (*Sentimental Traveller* 23). For her entire adult life Italy was home, which she explored not like a tourist but like a householder taking inventory of her possessions. She had a proprietary air. Maurice Baring first visited her at Maiano in 1893: "Vernon Lee showed me Florence," he wrote,

and the country round Florence, and Rome, as no other one could have done. She would take me to Michelangelo's farm house, or to a forsaken villa, or a deserted garden, or to some curious half-pagan procession in a village during Holy Week, and point out with suggestive illumination the significance of such places and of such sights. . . . For Vernon Lee nothing was

ever "done." It was there forever in the haunted, many corridored and echoing palace of her imagination, and after you had seen such things with her,
in yours as well." (*Lost Lectures* 86–87)

For her, language, not nationality, defined a country. At the Bayeaux tapestries she noted the mixture of visitors—American, British, French, German, Scandinavian, all sharing a common heritage—and she reflected on
the oddity of nationality: "The moral of which seems to be, that race is nothing and language all; for the blood carries only physical resemblance, which
is simple and very individual; while the word carries thought, custom, law
and prejudice, which are complex and universal" (*Genius Loci* 154) Having
mastered the languages of Italy, France, and Germany, she was no longer
the visiting Englishwoman but a familiar of the *genius loci* in each of those
countries. In Spain, however, though she admired Spanish literature she
confessed, "I do not know the language enough to spell through a chapter
of Cervantes" (*Sentimental Traveller* 6). As a result the Spanish *genius loci*
eluded her.

From the perspective of modern travel writing, Vernon Lee was not an
adventurous traveler. Except for brief visits to Tangier and Greece, her travels were confined to England and western Europe. The Tangier expedition
in 1888 failed in its purpose, which was to restore her mental health after the
blow of Mary Robinson's marriage. In "Sketches in Tangier," an essay she
published in the *New Review* (March 1890), she recalled a colorless countryside, "undulations of greyish-brown dried mud seem so endless," with
little gardens that "make one think of some allegorical orchard in a medieval
poem—places to which the constant lover gets at last, after much scram-
bling up stony roads, and tearing amid branches." Mainly she was shocked
by the condition of women, isolated in harems, uneducated, and in everything subservient to men. In November 1907 she had a far happier visit to
Greece. Unfortunately she fell ill with fever in early December and had to
terminate her travels, which were to have included Egypt. As a result she
wrote only a few short pieces on Greece. Although these contain some of
her best travel writing, they were not collected and exist only as six short articles in the *Westminster Gazette*.[4]

As the title of the first of these, "Greece at Last," suggests, she had long
looked forward to this trip, and she reported feeling everywhere "the sense
of fulfilled expectations. . . . Yes, the Greece I have made up is the real one;
or, the grace and loveliness of the real one is that of the Greece of my fancy."
She spent her first night in Greece in Olympia, waking the next morning
to the sound of goat bells, long familiar to her in the hills of Tuscany. "But
I knew, by that sound, that scent, that this real Greece was the one I had

loved for years, recognising, I scarce knew how, its every vestige in other places" (1 January 1910). She traveled with a copy of Pindar, seeking out, as usual, the *genius loci*. She knew that she would not find it in the popular tourist centers—the archaeological zones and the fragments of sculpture mutilated by time and war and human greed—but in remote corners of the Greek countryside, still unravaged by time's "qualities of gravity and sweetliness, of breadth and restraint, which, whether the forms be for the eye or the ear, affect us as directly expressive of the highest, fairest and, at the same time, most restrained and impersonal modes of human feeling and being" (9 April 1910). Undeterred by rough conditions of travel—crossing the Gulf of Corinth in a boat she "slept peacefully among bugs and cockroaches"—she was sometimes moved beyond words by the wild beauty of the landscape: "There are things impossible to write about: such colours are emotions, poignant like music. The blue, for instance of the further shores of the gulf, under their cloud-crown and against the blue of the water, as we saw it over the great olive woods which fill the valley" (19 February 1910).

There is an element of sadness, however, in her final response to Greece. As the ship waiting to take her back to Naples left Piraeus harbor, "a knot rose in one's throat, and tears were difficult to restrain." The sadness was for both Greece and herself:

> The sadness of understanding, what I seem never to have guessed before, that the world of Hellas has perished; is dead, buried, its very grave devastated. . . . And now I know that such a country *does not exist;* that these museums, all the world over, hold far the greater amount of the wreckage of that lost world; broken things, headless and armless, or restored; and that the temples are on archaeologists' maps, or barely more. And that beyond the sea is a little country, very poor, very new, arid and empty, with people who look, some like Turks, some like Slavs, a few like Italians, but whom it is impossible to connect with the people of marble, the people drawn in red upon black or in black upon red, whom I think of as Greeks.

The mortality of Greece leaves her with a sense of her own mortality: "It is extremely improbable at my age that I shall ever see those places again. . . . Where is it gone to? . . . Shall I ever see any of it again? I think not. And in this thought also is the sadness of time, of days gone and which will never return" (26 March 1910).

The most striking gap in Vernon Lee's travel writing is America. Her stubborn refusal of invitations to visit there is all the more remarkable because she was eager to have American outlets for her articles and books. Edith Wharton offered to arrange lectures to subsidize her travels and urged her to be a guest in her home. Other American friends invited her repeatedly. Sarah Orne Jewett stopped at Il Palmerino in 1898 while she was traveling with her devoted companion Annie Fields. Over the following years she also urged Violet to visit: "Shall you never come to New England—not for myrtle and olive . . . but for juniper and bayberry? I wish, and Mrs. Fields wishes, that you would, come, summer or winter as you like" (17 March 1907). Jewett invited her to her summer home on Mt. Desert Island in Maine and reminded her of the opportunity she would have to expand her American audience: "I hoped you would say that this is the summer when you would come—to sail over from England in June is not too long, and you should have a tin Bank when you got here and go home clinking it heavy with savings. You should be withheld from long journeys and only shown a few places. Autumn is better than midsummer; come in Autumn!" (Weber, "Jewett" 113).

Under these favorable prospects the excuse she offered Jewett was unconvincing: "I want to go to America—more and more since reading Wells and H. James—but I am what the proper call 'turned fifty'—and have little health and energy and many, too many schemes of (not much believed in!) work, and I have spent a lot of money, wisely no doubt, in buying this little place and discovering its threatened disasters, the money which one wants for a journey like that when one isn't young" (Cary, "VP to SOJ" 237). Although Violet had bouts of ill health from time to time, she was not an invalid, and she had energy enough to bicycle all over the countryside. She no longer had family responsibilities; her parents were dead, and Eugene had gone his own way. But she had her reasons, odd as they may appear, for resisting. They are summed up in an essay in *Limbo,* "In Praise of Old Houses":

> I am speaking of a peculiar sense, ineffable, indescribable, but which every one knows who has once had it, and which to many of us has grown into a cherished habit—the sense of being companioned by the past, of being in a place warmed for our living by the lives of others. To me . . . the reverse of this is almost painful; and I know few things more odious than the chilly, draughty emptiness of a place without a history. For this reason America, save what may remain of Hawthorne's New England and Irving's New York, never tempts my vagabond fancy. (30)

Also absent from Vernon Lee's published writings, but not from her actual life, are impressions of Naples, Capri, and Sicily, regions whose antiquity predates Rome and where history is packed with layers of culture— Greek, Byzantine, Norman, Arab. She did in fact tour Sicily in the spring of 1912, but the pressures of the coming war and the shrinking market for her travel writing distracted her. In 1918, still living in England in wartime exile, she discovered her notes in the bottom of a box sent to her some years earlier from Italy. They remain today in manuscript as "Pre-War Sketches 1910–1914" in the Vernon Lee archive. Brief as they are, the notes reveal an aging, increasingly critical Vernon Lee, still nervously alert to every sense impression (the approach to Sicily reveals a "diaphanous silver sea and bodiless silvery jagged mountains") but primed for instant outrage over the poverty of the peasants in southern Italy and the intrusive presence of foreign tourists.

What she admires most in Sicily are the scenes that recall the familiar countryside of her beloved Tuscany. Landing at dawn at Palermo she attends Easter Day Mass in the dazzling Byzantine Capella Palatina. She travels by motorcar, noting like the faithful horticulturist she was "the great dark-silver olives . . . carpeted with a dwarf sweet pea, orange and brown . . . marigolds flamed almost like tulips; the banks below the hedgerow of aloes and eglantine, sweet dwarf gorse . . . marked with violet and scarlet vetch and the convolvulus." She is duly impressed by the great temples of Selinunte, Agrigento, and Syracuse; and her imagination soars at the pentimento of cultures. "In Girgenti [Agrigento] Cathedral, which is being stripped of its painted 10th century gallantries, there has been laid a tile recording in Moorish characters how an Arab skipper, Ibn Somebody, landed at Girgenti about 900 A.D. In the same place once stood the beautiful Roman sarcophagus with the sick Phaedra avowing her love for Hippolytus. But what must those men of the middle ages have thought of the three male caryatids still standing at that time supporting the Temple of Zeus on their shoulders?"

Unhappily, the present impinges brutally upon the past as she notes the general misery of the South: "Greece, Sicily, southernmost Italy . . . fever-ridden, slatternly, poverty stricken as we see it now. Has our notion of Hellas as something incomparably noble and delicate, alert, clear-eyed and wholesome been nothing but delusion bred in fancy by poetry and art?" And her rage flames at the sight of tourists in Taormina, contaminating the views of Etna with their presence:

The first morning gave us an appalling impression of Taormina. The native slatternliness and grace is hung round with advertisements and specimen boxes of photographers (oh those columns of Caster and Pollux which I loved so much in their reality of Girgenti, how I have got to loathe their coffee-coloured image!). And all the footling tourist industries—pseudo-peasant crockery and false antiquities and *worse!* Real ones, all the battered time-soiled properties and derelict castles, attractive to the cosmopolitan loafer and honeymooner. I have never really resented tourists anywhere before, but in Sicily I do because they are so well off and the country so miser-

ably poor and their presence feels like a profanation of Sicily's centuries-
long tragedy.

Because for her "the lie of the land" is so intensely subjective, her experiences of travel reveal more about Vernon Lee than they do about the
places she visits. She acknowledges frankly in the opening of *The Enchanted
Woods* (1905) that with the years her "hankerings after new places" have diminished, and she consoles herself, "We need undertake no voyages of discovery to meet the *Genius Loci* . . . we enrich our life not by the making of
far-fetched plans, nor by the seeking of change and gain; but by the faithful putting to profit of what is in our grasp" (10).

Vernon Lee's object in her travel pieces is the same as her object in her
writings on aesthetics—"not to teach others, but to show them how far I
have taught myself, and how far they may teach themselves." This is the romantic self fully realized, unabashedly and unapologetically self-centered.
Appropriately, she called these journeys in quest of the *genius loci* her *amours
de voyage,* "the well-nigh passionate and certainly romantic feelings we may
have for towns wherein we are utter strangers, and for roads and paths along
which, as we know full well, we shall never pass again. *Amours de Voyage* I
have allowed myself to call them, as distinguished from the love we may
have for localities wherein our everyday lot is cast" (*Genius Loci* 203).

"Passionate" and "romantic" are words usually reserved for the intimate
emotions of human love. For Vernon Lee the *genius loci* appears to have been
the object of just such feelings. It is the quest for the ideal: "For the passion
for localities, the curious emotions connected with the lie of the land, shape
of buildings, history and quality of air and soil, are born, like all intense and
permeating feeling, less of outside things than of our own soul. . . . The
places for which we feel such love are fashioned before we see them, by our
wishes and fancy; we recognize rather than discover them in the world of
reality" (*Sentimental Traveller* 14). Her communion with the *genius loci* is a
sacramental act; the *genius* is the lover pursued and finally possessed. And
nowhere does that lover assume more reality than in Italy. Rome "is an organic city, almost a living being; its *genius loci* no allegory but its own real
self" (*Spirit of Rome* 44). Wherever she discovers the *genius loci,* that spot
becomes animated. It takes on the character of a loved one: "I have a feeling as of something like a troth plighted, or a religious rite accomplished,
binding me and this place together" (*Genius Loci* 8).

The palpable reality of Vernon Lee's Italy is a function of its climate, its
landscape, and its culture. No other country offered her a combination
more natural, more aesthetically pleasing, and more spiritually satisfying.
Returning to Italy once after a winter in London, where she had suffered

"an acuteness of aesthetic desire very near akin to starvation," she hailed the
South, "where winter is a word and the commonest objects are as lovely as
the rarest." The life of the South, she concludes, writing as a romantic only
a few generations removed from Rousseau and Wordsworth, is more natural than the North's and therefore it is morally superior:

> There is, for the healthy of soul, a moral wholesomeness, as well as that of
> sunshine and sea air, to be found in these favoured Southern places; the
> wholesome recognition of the meanness of our complicated and parasitic
> life. One gets to long for some scheme of existence which shall be open to
> the air and sun; precious in colour and flower-like in shape, like the cottages
> and belfries among these groves of oranges and olives but, even as they,
> made of homely materials, simple whitewash and sound brick for rich as
> well as poor. (*Genius Loci* 199–200)

Vernon Lee's perceptions begin with childhood and even in later life
serve always as a bridge between childhood memory and adult experience.
The links are fragile, but they hold together a whole chain of impressions.
A middle-aged woman visiting Padua, she stops for a moment in the marketplace because it reminds her of an engraving in a keepsake book of 1825
that she had once "pored over while convalescing from a childhood illness. . . . The prints were of that soft and vaporous style which made you
feel (like Turner's illustrations, for the rest) that the scenes depicted . . . were
reserved by persons of the most sensitive nerves and refined manners: Lady
Blessington and *Ennuyées* with their *Diaries*. . . . Anyhow it was a slow,
beneficent rapture, spread through the hours, days, and weeks, the timeless
time of convalescence. And something of it lasted." Years later the experience was repeated, this time in reality: "an undercurrent of delicious, faint
excitement, independent of the pleasure of the actual moment, and filling
me whenever I realized that I *was* in Verona, Bologna, or any characteristic
North Italian city" (*Sentimental Traveller* 272–73).

For Vernon Lee, as for Wordsworth, childhood had these sacramental
moments "when we possess the mystic gift of consecration, of steeping things
in our soul's essences, and making them thereby different from all others,
for ever sovereign and sacred to us." In less lofty terms she traces the roots
of her passion for the *genius loci* in sounds—birdsong or music that carries
her back to childhood—and, most especially because Italy is so rich in
them, in smells: "Not merely because smells have that unrivalled power of
evoking past states of feeling, but because smells seem to distill and volatise
so many indefinable peculiarities of season, of climate, and of civilisation."
An autumn walk to the village of Castiglione d'Olona near Milan offers "the
mingled scents of long-neglected drains, of sun-dried filth, of mint crushed

underfoot and purifying all with its sense of life and ripeness, the smell of leaves baked by a summer's heat and fresh from a frosty dew" (*Tower of the Mirrors* 150). A carriage ride to fill the hours between trains at Bologna again catches quintessential Italy: "the smell of wine-vats mingled, I fancy (though I could not say why), with the sweet faint smell of decaying plaster and wood-work . . . that same smell came to my nostrils as in a dream, and with it a whiff of bygone years, the years when first I had this impression of Italian magic" (*Limbo* 82).

These odd and not entirely pleasant mixtures are in more than a literal sense the essence of Vernon Lee's Italy. As in human love relationships, there is ambivalence in her feeling for the *genius loci*. What makes love affairs interesting—the attraction-revulsion syndrome, the tension between the taut, highly wrought emotions of the lover and the inscrutable, elusive beloved—gives Vernon Lee's pursuit of the Italian *genius loci* special intimacy and depth. Why should she, of Anglo-Saxon Protestant heritage, be drawn to an alien culture whose mingled scents are as redolent of death, decay, and corruption as they are of flowers, fine wine, and good food? Having stopped at Castiglione d'Olona to look at some undistinguished frescoes by Masolino, she asks: "Why is Italy full of such places? Why is its past not homely and warm and close to us like that of the North, but distant, forlorn, tragic with the smell of dead leaves and of charnel, with its gaunt show of splendour crumbling in base uses: a past whereof one fails to understand the reasons for greatness, and oftener still the reasons for decay?" (*Tower of the Mirrors* 151).

Her sturdy northern European sensibility was offended by the neglect, the crumbling ruins, the faded frescoes that she associated with many Italian towns and the far greater squalor and decay that she saw in cities like Rome and Venice. Nor was she blind to the miseries of the poor. In Venice she witnesses a funeral at the Frari of a young girl who had died of tuberculosis. She had been an overworked and underpaid bead threader, but she is given a lavish funeral with the mourners, dressed in their best clothes, drinking and feasting. "The poor little consumptive maker of bead garlands for cemeteries is indeed now—save perhaps for her mother—as little important as the dead kitten bobbing up and down, a sleek, grey ball, in the green water of her native canal. But that just answers to the truth. The poor (let us have the courage to say it) leave no trace behind, and are in this respect less of a fraud than the rich, who possess ancestors with names" (*Sentimental Traveller* 101). Poverty and injustice not only exist but flourish in Italy. But like the romantic lover, she creates an idealized image out of what she loves. In the drab town of Castiglione d'Olona she discovers "an exquisite, empty, forsaken little church" and some delicate carving on the facades of the medieval escutcheoned houses. Best of all, she sees a breathtaking Italian sunset. "Then the cupolas and pinnacles of Monte Rosa suddenly loomed into sight, carved out of mother-of-pearl, fabulously high above a bank of opalescent vapours, against a pure pale evening sky. Had I ever really cared for any country except Italy?" (*Tower of the Mirrors* 153).[5]

The answer to Vernon Lee's rhetorical question is that she did indeed care for other countries. She had sentimental attachments to Germany and Switzerland based on early memories. She enjoyed France for both personal and aesthetic reasons: good friends, the beautiful and fertile countryside, the charms of the provincial towns, the vitality of Paris. For England she had an affection based less on family ties than on close friendships and literary associations. Like most experienced travelers, she knew that there were no objective criteria for one's reactions and that subjective impressions are everything. "If places are hackneyed, it is only in our eyes and soul, because we see their commonplace side and the rubbish of everyday detail which we bring with us," she writes in *The Sentimental Traveller* (229). Thus she admitted to a negative view of Spain, "this unkind-looking country," because she went there to recuperate from an illness "and saw it all through my melancholy." The land was bleak: "A dreary country of rolling purple earth, ploughed by the savage-looking brown cattle, with low dusky hills at the end, with the sullen clouds resting upon them" (*Enchanted Woods* 217). Spain's history was clouded with blood and violence and its art was dark and depressing, dominated by "the black and white bony essentials of things" (*Sentimental Traveller* 7).

Nowhere is the subjective nature of her travel writing more evident than in *The Spirit of Rome* (1906), a collection of short, fragmentary pieces tracing her reactions to the city over a span of years from 1888 to the spring of 1905.[6] "I felt, with odd vividness, the various myselfs who suffered and hoped while writing them," she notes in a postscript to the book (204). Most of the entries date from spring 1895 to spring 1905, a critical decade in her life that saw the deaths of her parents, her brother's recovery, her separation from Kit Anstruther-Thomson, and her first serious doubts about the direction of her work. To all these personal changes the Eternal City stood in ironic contrast: "Only to me, in these sites, impersonal and almost eternal, on these walls which have stood two thousand years and may stand two thousand more, and these hillsides and roads full of the world's legend— there appear, visible, distinct, the shadows cast by my own life, the forms and faces of those changed, gone, dead ones; and my own" (205).

Rome evokes memories of her friends, "who have made Rome what it is to me," and throughout the book she refers to them by their initials. It also reawakens long forgotten childhood memories: "the darkish, sponge-like holes in the travertine, the reversed capital on the Trinità dei Monti steps, the caryatides of the Stanza dell'Incendio, the scowl or smirk of the Emperors and philosophers at the Capitol: a hundred details" (112). At a pontifical mass in the Sistine Chapel on 4 March 1888 her Anglo-Saxon sensibilities are offended by "the utter disconnectedness of it all, the absence of all spirit or meaning . . . [this] great rag bag of purple and crimson and gold, of superb artistic things all out of place, useless, patternless, and almost odious . . . that huge *Last Judgment,* that mass of carefully grouped hideous nudities, brutal, butcher-like, on its harsh blue ground." Gradually, though, as she watches, the scene is transformed: "the blue background of the *Last Judgment* grows into a kind of deep, hyacinthine evening sky. . . . And the huge things on the ceiling, with their prodigious thighs and toes and arms and jowls crouch and cower and scowl, and hang uneasily on arches, and strain themselves wearily on brackets, dreary, magnificent, full of inexplicable feelings all about nothing" (14–18). Similarly, at St. Praxed's her initial revulsion at the "tawdry, sluttish" church, "with the usual Roman church stifling dirty smell . . . a down-at-the-heel indifferent idolatry," turns to breathless admiration for the little side (St. Zeno) chapel: "all Byzantine splendour . . . its vaults a marvellous glory of golden—infinite tinted golden—mosaics with great white angels. A bit of Venice, of St. Mark's, in this sluttish Rome" (111).

Over the years she returned to Rome with increasing personal unhappiness. In spring 1902 she complains about the crowding, dirt, and poverty of the city: "If Rome undoubtedly gives the soul peace by its assurance that the present is as nothing in the centuries, it also depresses one, in other moods, with the feeling that all history is but a vast rubbish heap and sink; that nothing matters, nothing comes out of all the ages save rags and brutishness" (139–40). A year later she writes: "Rome is in a fashion consoling; but how empty!" The loss of Kit has become a terrible reality: "That I should feel it most on return here, find I have returned without *her,* travelled without her, that she is not there to tell; the sense of utter loneliness, of the letter one would write, the greeting one would give—and which no creature now wants" (155).

Vernon Lee was not a confessional writer. This rare open expression can be attributed only to the extraordinary power Rome held over her. It is in the very nature of her subjective reaction to the city that she comes finally to reject analysis and explanation and to accept the paradox not only of Rome but of her own ambivalent and mysterious self. The book concludes in 1905 with "Rome Again": "I feel very often that if one lived in all this picturesqueness, the horrors of the past, the vacuity of the present, would drive one I know not whither. I have had, more than ever this time, the sense of horror at the barbarism of Rome, of civilisation being encamped in all this human refuse, and doing nothing for it, and the feeling of horror at this absorbing Italy and at one's liking it!" (203).

Like Italy, the other countries about which she wrote were staging areas for self-discovery. Germany and Switzerland were the richest sources for the recovery of her childhood. Switzerland was frozen into the past for her with only happy memories. She returns to Berne a middle-aged woman to experience again her excitement at seven or eight when she fed the bears. And she makes a special visit to Säckingen in Germany to recall her reading *Der Trompeter von Säckingen* with her beloved governess Maria Schülpach twenty-nine years earlier. Continuing her sentimental journey, she visits her governess, now a matron with two grown daughters, and they reminisce about the past: "We rose and walked silently to the station. Our afternoon together was over. But we had found each other, ourselves, again" (*Sentimental Traveller* 242). A flood of memories is released: "O dear German childhood in that schoolroom panelled with a porcelain stove where we baked apples! Dear German things never seen since; books heavily embossed or girt with orange labels—Konversations, Lexikons, bound years of *Gartenlaube,* stray volumes of Schiller and Goethe with their inspired curly heads in relief on the cover, and golden lyres and laurels" (237).

Revisiting Germany, however, also brought disturbing impressions. The past, preserved so purely for her in memory, was more difficult to reconstruct in the late 1890s. "The Germany I am speaking of," she writes of a visit to Augsburg, "is not the one which colonises or makes cheap goods, or frightens the world in various ways: but the Germany which invented Christmas trees, and Grimms' Fairy Tales, and Bach and Mozart, and which seems to be vouched for in many works of classic literature" (*Genius Loci* 13). Germany, "of all countries the first to be good to me," is full of personal and literary associations. Her mind luxuriates in the German past, especially "the majesty and loveliness of life [of] the classic revival, of the eighteenth century." Seeking landmarks of *The Sorrows of Werther* she visited Charlotte's house at Wetzlar: "One realizes the utter obscurity, smallness, homeliness, out of which Goethe's romance spread its undying wings over the world" (*Tower of the Mirrors* 101). As usual she discovers the *genius loci* in the most humble surroundings. She stops for refreshments ("some beer and black bread in a terraced garden overlooking the wide, sedgy river"). Someone is playing a piano in a nearby house, "and the one-two-three-four of an old-fashioned sonata mingled pleasantly with the lap of the water and the creak of the ferry chain." The *genius loci* here is what she calls the "German Gemüt." "It is the homely love of romance, this mixing up of what we priggish Anglo-Saxons and Latins call higher and lower forms of enjoyment . . . this spirit of roast veal in ruined castles, and coffee and cinnamon cake in haunted forest glades" (*Enchanted Woods* 247–50).

The German past remains fresh and beautiful, but the present intrudes rudely. Wagner, Bismarck, and Karl Marx shatter her illusions. Even the glory of Goethe dwindles in the museum that his house in Weimar has become:

> Forbidding, but not enough, alas! for the sycophancies of Eckermann, the theatricalities of Byron, the sentimental conceit of Jane Welsh Carlyle, who sends him a copy of verses and (of all embarrassing untidy presents) a long tail of "a woman's hair" (Faugh!). There he presides, variously Olympian, over the dreary 1820 wall-papers and sofas and card-tables, key patterned or sham Gothic, but all faded and dust-engrained; among the dismal collections of ores and crystals and skulls and stuffed birds: a pantalooned and swallow-tailed *Rentier* Faust. (*Sentimental Traveller* 58–59)

The impingement of the present on the past was even more troubling for Vernon Lee when she was in England. Because the "real" England (as distinguished from the English literature she had absorbed since childhood) had played no part in her past, she never captured its *genius loci*. Her parents had been English; her maternal grandfather had been a landowner in Wales. Though she had no roots in Scotland or Ireland, she came to know and love Scotland as the home of Kit Anstruther-Thomson. She enjoyed traveling in Ireland and visiting Abbey Leix, the ancestral home of her friend Evelyn Charteris, Lady de Vesci, in 1898.[7] She admired the English countryside and the many fine English country houses where she was entertained. But she was always conscious of her position as an outsider. "I fancy all expatriated people, and perhaps all really independent ones are apt to pay this price," she wrote Mona Taylor in 1900 (Gunn 168). This lack of total engagement with her subject is apparent in the series of articles she published (but never collected) in the *Atlantic Monthly* (July 1899, October 1901) and in *Scribner's Magazine* (August, November, December 1913), under the title "An English Writer's Notes on England." Her "Notes" are precisely that— impressionistic, full of fine descriptive detail and occasionally sharp critical comments on social conditions. But in contrast to her warmly personal reactions to Germany, Switzerland, and France, these offer little more than the eye's observation—the antique charms of thatched-roofed cottages, the rugged beauty of Yorkshire and Northumberland, but also the squalor of cities ("Liverpool, Manchester, Leeds, especially London . . . strangely full of evil") and the ravaging effects on the land's natural beauty of "the ruthless barbarity of this industrialism . . . the wholesale pollution of water and ground, the killing off of trees and blackening of the sky."

Her American readers apparently were not impressed by this first series of articles. When she offered to continue her "Notes" a few years later, Sarah Orne Jewett wrote her (3 January 1908) in some embarrassment: "Mr. [Bliss] Perry, of the *Atlantic,* spoke with the most true appreciation of your work— you have had few better or more affectionate readers—but he has had some difficulties in following his personal choice. . . . But I am full of hope about these English sketches, only do not be impatient if it seems to take longer than is reasonable" (Weber, "Jewett" 107–8). It was almost six years before she was able to place her additional "Notes" in an American periodical, and their appearance in *Scribner's* probably owed something to the influence of Edith Wharton, who regularly published there. In that interval Vernon Lee's critical views were sharpened by her increasingly active socialism. The ravages of industry and modern technology that she had observed in the *Atlantic* articles are more extensively recorded in the later articles, along with her rising sense of the inequities of English society.

The first of the *Scribner's* articles, "Things of the Past" (August 1913), includes visits to Oxford, the picturesque country town of Abingdon, an unidentified cathedral town, and a castle in Devonshire. All, she concedes, are picture-book pretty but characterless: "The beauty and suggestiveness of England is a little like the voices of the college choirs: it is over-white, lacking light and shade, a trifle sugary at times, and inhumanly warbling in timbre." She complains of the English prohibition against walking about freely in cathedrals, the omnipresence of a verger or official guide: "the usual impression of being conducted over God's Mansion by the housekeeper or butler. . . . What a strange, smooth country of privilege and secure legal possession this England is! The very past becomes a pleasant ornament of gentlemanly privacy." In "Things of the Present" (November 1913) she is traveling over the Yorkshire moors in a motorcar ("the noise of the engine mingling with that of the wind") and is appalled by "the heaps of coal and cinders at the stations, the colliery shaft-machine (vaguely like gallows) on a green hillside, suggesting that the real inhabitants of this empty land are underground, like the monsters in Wells's *Time Machine.*"

In Leeds she ponders the price England has paid for its prosperity: "And is such hideous refuse of life and things the price at which certain spiritual qualities are bought?" Nowhere is that price more terrible than in London: "the foul atmosphere . . . the philistine monotony of mean, well-to-do houses and blank unpicturesque squalor of mews and slums behind." If there is a *genius loci* in London, it is "the spirit to get and hold; our English energetic appreciation of material advantages and tenacious . . . belief in private property." She sees the effects of such an evil *genius* at a lecture for workingmen and -women in Bloomsbury: "an audience of shabby people with rumpled, pathetic, eager faces, bent on a future which, alas, will never be open to them." The last of the "Notes" is entitled "The Celtic West: Cornwall, Wales, Ireland" (December 1913). The rough, wind-swept coast, haunted by ghosts of the Arthurian past, is one she should have appreciated, but the past, which she embraced so enthusiastically in Italy, Germany, and France, is here dark and threatening: "This scantily inhabited end of Europe seems given up to dead folk: Arthurian heroes at every step, and odd local saints . . . whom one suspects of having been originally giants and perhaps ogres." She finds a few redeeming features in the cathedral town of St. David's in English Wales, in the beauty of the Irish woods and the friendliness of the Irish people. But she chooses not to write about the Irish cities and Irish poverty, summing it all up simply in the phrase "this tragic squalid country."

As a self-confessed expatriate, Vernon Lee was never entirely comfortable in England. Once she had crossed the Channel, however, she reverted happily to her status as a European: "After England and after Germany, and several years of absence from France, it smote me with the familiar sense that France is already half-Southern and wholly Latin" (*Tower of the Mirrors* 43). France was also more than halfway home to Italy. In sun-warmed Touraine she has a foretaste of what awaits her: "And there is a poignant pleasure also in finding among this Northern vegetation the humble scented things of Italy, the wild thyme and balm, the fennel and peppermint, or, rather, finding these friendly herbs growing Italian fashion, on each wall and in each stone-heap" (*Sentimental Traveller* 194). She had an affinity for the land in France. A farmer herself at Il Palmerino, she noted with approval "that especially French genius for turning into a kind of poetry the peaceful sensual needs of life." Though, as some of her houseguests observed, she was indifferent to food herself, she admits to thinking about food "as a permeating essence of life" (*Genius Loci* 29). Bicycling through Touraine one day she innocently trespassed on the fields of a sternly disapproving farmer. When she told him that she had been born in France and engaged him in a conversation about vineyards and wine making, he concluded that "I must be French at heart" and invited her to inspect his wine cellar and sample his wine. Proud of his land as he was, he complained about "the decay of France, the disadvantage of sub-division of property, the growth of l'Egoïsme Bourgeois, and the depopulation of the country"—sentiments she fully shared.

The France she loved was medieval, Norman, and Gothic, but increasingly she was aware of its modernization. One day in early 1914 friends drove her to Le Mans to see Wilbur Wright demonstrate his flying machine. She understood their enthusiasm for the potential of this invention, "making the odds equal at last between the small States and the large, the rich and the poor, giving victory to skill and pluck alone, and abolishing warfare by the mere threat of destruction raining down from its wings." But she regretted spending the afternoon watching "the whirring locust flight" when she might have been revisiting a nearby church: "the elephantine Norman nave, and wonderful tartan glass, whose scarlet and green and inky purple shone wonderful in my memory. The Future! Yes. it will be agreeably free from abuses and atrocities; at least one hopes so. But will it ever build things like a great Gothic church, or know, or care, how to make such windows!" (*Tower of the Mirrors* 14–15).

Happily, the encroachments of modernization that threatened France, "the loss of tradition, of vital organisation, in this sterilizing process," had not entirely despoiled Paris. In spite of the vulgar display of replicas and relics that she saw in the Great Exhibition of 1900—"this stupid wicked carnival sacrilege towards the *Genius Loci*"—she rises to lyrical heights in describing the Paris that she still cherishes:

> O Paris of the Left Bank, the only real Paris for me, with thy stately hotels and long convent walls over-topped with discreet green; thy frowzy little Balzac pensions, tenanted once by the nymphs of the Farmers-General, and now by enthusiastic art students and warlike doctoresses, and widows from the provinces leading bowing sons in checked cravats; Paris of Faison d'Ors where we hoped in the *plat du jour* and hesitated between gratuitous blue wine and another, not gratuitous, *demi-cannette;* Paris of the crêmeries, wherein we cheated the desire for afternoon tea, and many, doubtless, thought to cheat desire for dinner or lunch; Paris of history, of romance, Dumas and Balzac, of hope and effort and day-dreams also, Socialists, and scientific struggling young girls of Rosny's novels, and ardent expatriated creatures fit for Henry James! (*Enchanted Woods* 81–82)

The Paris of the Left Bank, of the medieval abbeys and churches, and the fragrant almond trees of Provence, along with the many friends she had made over the years, endeared France to Vernon Lee. But by the early years of the new century she was forced to confront a world in which she was an uneasy stranger. Even her beloved Italy was showing the signs (for her the scars) of the Present and the menacing shadows of the Future. The "Cookites" and the developers were invading the places she held most precious. When her own city of Florence was threatened with modernization, she took action. She sent off petitions to Annie Fields and Sarah Orne Jewett in America urging them "to get *as many* (anybody's) [signatures] as possible by December! The only hope of stopping the now systematic destruction and rebuilding of Florence (a deed of jobbery in a bankrupt country!) is to convince the shop and hotel keepers etc. that foreigners, so far from being attracted by a modernised Florence, will cease to come to it." She went about the city herself posting fliers in hotels and banks, convinced that "we [must] threaten the pockets of the bourgeoisie by showing the disapprobation of foreigners" (15 October 1898).[8]

For Vernon Lee the destruction of the past was as much a moral as a cultural threat. She called herself a "sentimental traveller," but her alarm was more than mere emotional indulgence. It was based on a fundamental concern for the health of what she variously called the soul, the spirit, the mind. The Italy and the Europe that she loved were vanishing before her eyes, and her pursuit of the elusive *genius loci* was beginning to resemble the quest in Matthew Arnold's "Scholar Gypsy" for the spirit who fled "this strange disease of modern life." It was her misfortune to live until 1935, long enough to witness the fading of her romantic vision of Italy and indeed of all Europe. She continued to travel, to study, and to write as actively as her health permitted, but she was increasingly aware of her alienation from the mainstream of contemporary life.

In the winter of 1899, on the very eve of the twentieth century, she completed her only play, *Ariadne in Mantua*. A poetic drama written in prose, it tells the story of a hopeless love and is a celebration of her love for the music and art of the late Renaissance and a private lamentation for the vanishing of the *genius loci*. *Ariadne* is set in a real city, Mantua, but in imaginary time. "The action takes place," she writes in the preface, "in the Palace of Mantua through a period of a year during the reign of Prospero I of Milan; and shortly before the Venetian expedition to Cyprus under Othello." The principal Shakespearean influence, however, is neither *The Tempest* nor *Othello* but *Twelfth Night* with its cross-dressing lovesick Viola wooing another woman for an Orsino who is oblivious to her true identity.[9] Vernon Lee's Viola takes on the added role of the enchantress Ariadne, rescuing her duke from a deadly labyrinth, only to lose him to another woman. If there is any single inspiration for the play, it is a song: not, as she explains, the "Lamento d'Arianna," which is the only surviving fragment of a lost opera by Monteverdi, but a simple "air," the "Amarilli" by the more obscure composer Caccini—a snatch of song she had discovered in one of her collections of old Italian music.

In 1896 and again in 1898 she had visited Mantua, intrigued by its romantic location on three small lakes and its vast Palazzo Ducale, in the sixteenth century the seat of the powerful Gonzaga family. What impressed her most was the startling contrast between the now sadly neglected palace and the beauty of the lakes, "clear, rippled, fringed with reed, islanded with water lilies . . . the unlikely combination, the fantastic duet of the palace and the lake" (*Genius Loci* 163–65). Years earlier she had imaginatively reconstructed "the splendid and triumphant Renaissance of the Medicis, Borgias, Sforzas and Gonzagas" in *Euphorion*. Seeing its vestiges now in Mantua, the priceless art of Mantegna, Giulio Romano, and others soiled and fading, she is both depressed and exhilarated: "For of all the decaying palaces I have ever seen in Italy this palace of Mantua is the most utterly decayed. . . . But little by little, as you tramp through what seem miles of solemn emptiness, you may find that more than any similar place it has gone to your brain." Painted on the ceiling of one of the rooms is a "colossal labyrinth" of gold and blue, "the most magnificent and fantastic thing left behind by the Italy of Shakespeare . . . but one feels that it once appealed to an Ariosto-Tasso mythological romance which was perfectly genuine, and another sort of romance now comes with its being so forlorn" (*Genius Loci* 166). The word haunts her: "Forlorn, forlorn! And everywhere, from the halls with mouldering zodiacs and Loves of the Gods and Dances of the Muses, and across hanging gardens choked with weeds and fallen into a lower level, appear the blue waters of the lake, and its green distant banks, to make it all into a Fairyland." Echoing Keats, who sought relief from the burden of his mortality in the song of the nightingale, Vernon Lee is "forlorn" because the past she loves is forever lost and she is trapped in a labyrinth of the present, with no Ariadne to rescue her.

In *Ariadne in Mantua* the labyrinth of ancient legend and the frescoed labyrinth on the ceiling of the palace are metaphors for the dark depression that haunts the Duke of Mantua. Held captive by the Moors for five years, he was led out of the maze of his prison by a courtesan, Magdalen, only to collapse into a profound melancholy when he returned to Mantua. In his illness he forgets the woman who rescued him and whom he loved. To restore his health and to ensure his marriage to the Princess Hippolyta, his uncle the cardinal summons Diego, a youth famous for the beauty of his singing voice. The cardinal knows that Diego is Magdalen in disguise, but he is confident of her discretion. Like Viola in *Twelfth Night,* she never tells her love and dutifully obeys her lord when he orders her to woo Hippolyta for him; like Viola she succeeds only in arousing the princess's interest in herself. On the duke's wedding day the play of Ariadne is staged on a platform built over the lake, and Diego sings the leading role. At the triumphant finale of the masque, the grieving Ariadne, remembering that "the Past belongs to me," flings herself into the lake and drowns. The play ends with the duke at last regaining his memory and recognizing the dead Ariadne as his beloved Magdalen.

Because *Ariadne in Mantua* is Vernon Lee's most powerful work of pure imagination, it invites speculation about its sources in her own life. The theme of the ambiguous sexuality of Magdalen / Diego — her hopeless love for the duke, and Hippolyta's misdirected attraction to her as the youth Diego — strikes the reader as more than a mere spinoff of the plot of *Twelfth Night*. By 1899 when she wrote the play, unrequited love seemed to be Vernon Lee's destiny as it was her protagonist's. Although the women who enlisted in her *culte* were worshiping disciples, none of them, not even the devoted Kit Anstruther-Thomson, became a lifetime companion-partner. As both Ethel Smyth and Irene Cooper Willis, the two women who knew her best and longest, recognized, her inability to respond physically to any gesture of affection, even a friendly kiss, posed a barrier to the kind of relationship she sought. "Be merely a singer," the cardinal instructs Magdalen/Diego, "a sexless creature, having seen passion but never felt it; yet capable, by the miracle of art, of rousing and soothing it in others" (act 1). If Vernon Lee identified herself with her heroine, then the image of the athletic horsewoman Kit found its reflection in Princess Hippolyta, named by her father for the Amazon queen. As Magdalen/Diego remarks to her, the duke "has told me how your illustrious father, the late Lord of Mirandola, brought his only daughter up in such a wise as scarcely to lack a son, with manly disciplines of mind and body" (act 4). Nevertheless the princess has her assured place as a woman in society. But the woman-boy Magdalen/Diego is a pariah, forever denied physical and emotional fulfillment. "What you call *love*," she says bitterly to the duke's mother, "to me means nothing: nonsense taught to children, priest's metaphysics. What *I* mean, you do not know" (act 3).

A play as private and precious as *Ariadne in Mantua* is not a likely candidate for public production. Vernon Lee herself was quick to identify it as a literary rather than a dramatic work. In April 1903 she sent one of the first published copies of the play to Edith Wharton, who replied:

> It is exquisite, and so completely the kind of fanciful poetical thing that I long to see done, that I have only one objection to make: namely, its greater fitness for narrative than for dramatic treatment. Certainly the idea is dramatic; but even for a play read in the closet, it seems to me to lack movement and clash of emotions. In short, whatever is faulty in it seems to me faulty only from the dramatic point of view; whatever is most exquisite, would increase in value were the form narrative. (Fife 141)

Edith Wharton overrated Vernon Lee's narrative skills, but she measured her descriptive powers correctly: "I have always thought, for instance, that no one has your gift of suggesting in a few touches an Italian landscape or picture; and the little stage directions at the head of each act are so beautiful that one feels they ought to be, not the mere illuminated bottom of the page, but its central subject." Implied in her comments is that the subject itself is better fitted for poetry or verse drama, a genre that was still popular though no longer as flourishing as it had been in the mid-nineteenth century. But poetry was a medium that, self-assured as she was, Vernon Lee never attempted. Poetry, she wrote some years later in an essay *The Poet's Eye* (a slender volume published by the Woolfs' Hogarth Press in 1926), is "godlike, immortal": "In prosiest prose, and speaking as a psychologist, I think it probable that the creature thinking in verse thinks in a manner at once less trammelled and more sustained than we do; thinks thoughts differing from ours, plunging into depths, soaring to giddy heights; and very often babbles sublimities which he would be at a loss to explain" (14). Accordingly, when she introduced a song into *Ariadne* she did not write it herself but had Diego sing one of the Tuscan-inspired lyrics from Mary Robinson's *An Italian Garden,* with an acknowledgment in her preface to "my dear old friend, Mme. Emile Duclaux."

Although Vernon Lee did not write her play for the stage, she must have had some kind of performance in mind when she dedicated it to Ethel Smyth, "Thanking, and begging her for music." Smyth did not compose the music, but she lent her copy of the play to the actress-producer Lilah McCarthy (Mrs. Harley Granville-Barker), who wrote to Vernon Lee in September 1907 proposing a London production. There was no objection until the following April when McCarthy sent her a copy of the play "cut for acting purposes," which she offered to produce for two matinee performances if the author would eliminate the fourth act, rewrite the play-within-a-play of the fifth act, and waive all fees. This offer Vernon Lee politely but firmly declined. But *Ariadne* did not sink into total obscurity. It had a brief production in London in 1916 with music by Eugene Goossens and Ivor Novello, and Ethel Smyth recalled that there was talk about a production in the Boboli Gardens in Florence (*Maurice Baring* 334–35). But it was not until 1934, only a year before Vernon Lee's death, that a group of her friends mounted a faithful and beautifully decorated production in Italian at the Reale Accademia dei Fidenti in Florence. This production included music by her favorite composers—Frescobaldi, Palestrina, Caccini, and Monteverdi. She was present to receive the applause of the audience and the actors—an elegant and touching tribute—but by then ailing and deaf, she could take little pleasure in the production itself.

15 "SISTER IN UTOPIA": THE AESTHETE AS POLEMICIST

In your kind letter, I detect a certain undertone of sadness. I understand it fully. Although I have the misfortune to be, I believe, some years older than you, we belong to the same generation. We belong to a generation which has—to be blunt —passed away. I feel, as you feel, as such other friends of ours who survive might feel, the vague disappointment that Mr. Punch must feel when the crowd of gapers goes on to the next entertainment, and some fresher booth. Our tricks are precisely what they were, perhaps they are even more smoothly performed, but the crowd wants novelty. Well, it seems to me that we can only prove the reality of the faith that is in us, by going serenely on. We must do our best, even if it is to empty benches.

Edmund Gosse to Vernon Lee, "Passion Sunday, '06"

THERE IS NO EVIDENCE THAT MAX BEERBOHM, A FELLOW Italophile who lived for many years in Rapallo, no great distance from Florence, ever met Vernon Lee, but he knew her work. In his library he had a copy of her *Gospels of Anarchy,* which, as he did with many of his books, he "improved" with his comments and illustrations, some by him, others clipped from magazines or newspapers. Pasted on the title page of his copy is a sketch of a woman in black bonnet and dress, seated in profile like Whistler's mother or his Thomas Carlyle and stirring a cup of, we assume, tea. The half-face we see is severe, the expression one of distaste or stern disapproval. The face is not Vernon Lee's, but in a note on the flyleaf Beerbohm wrote: "Poor dear dreadful little lady! Always having a crow to pick, ever so coyly, with Nietzsche, or a wee lance to break with Mr. Carlyle, or a sweet but sharp little warning to whisper in the ear of Mr. H.G. Wells, or Strindberg or Darwin or D'Annunzio! What a dreadful little bore and busybody" (Gunn 3).

Vernon Lee's moral earnestness and outspokenness were her heritage from her mother, and she wore them proudly. Mrs. Paget, however, had

confined her social responsibilities to her household and to occasional outbursts against Italian peasants who mistreated their work animals. Like
Ouida, another Anglo-Florentine, both Violet and her mother were ardent
antivivisectionists. Violet had taken up that cause early, and though she later
moderated her views, she never abandoned them. One of her earliest periodical publications was "Vivisection: An Evolutionist to Evolutionists" in
the *Contemporary Review* of May 1882. Identifying herself thus with the
"new" science, as "one who believes in scientific method, in human development, and in evolutionary morality," she conceded that vivisection can be
advantageous to humanity but questioned the right of the scientist "to really estimate the moral legitimacy or illegitimacy of vivisection." She developed her arguments in greater depth in a chapter in *Baldwin* in 1886, warning against the perversion of the highest motives of science: "This deliberate
choice of advantages to mankind, brought by the unrequited and cheating
infliction of agony upon creatures who cannot participate in the gain while
they sustain all the loss, is nearly always followed by a blunting of moral
judgment, and a stultification of intellectual argument among those who
defend this retrogression in the path of moral evolution, this preference of
desire to right" (170). Even this early, her emphasis on the morally corrupting effects of killing, however justifiable the cause, was the foundation for
her pacifism in World War I.

Outrage at cruelty and sympathy for the victims, animal or human, are
not necessarily expressions of a commitment to specific social and political
issues. Vernon Lee, who declared herself dedicated to aesthetics in *Belcaro*
in 1881, had made a choice of direction for her future work—philosophical
dialogues on religion and morality in *Baldwin,* essays on Renaissance and
medieval culture in *Euphorion,* and the novel *Miss Brown.* Only in this last
did she show signs of wavering. Her portrait of aesthetic society is damn-
ing. It was intended, however, to suggest not that art is corrupting but that
its worship can become corrupting when it is not balanced with a moral and
social conscience. Unfortunately the novel missed its mark and left her embarrassed and bitterly disappointed. She retreated to Florence to rethink her
strategy. Her convictions were as strong as ever, and she had no intention
of renouncing a career in literature, but she needed a fresh start and a new
direction. To that end she turned to a woman she admired, Frances Power
Cobbe, a dedicated social reformer and fighter for women's rights.

Cobbe had read *Miss Brown* the year it was published. She wrote its author a letter of praise, comparing her to George Eliot—a tribute she modestly disclaimed: "You must not mention my name in the same breath as that
of George Eliot, dear Miss Cobbe; there is something in this that perfectly
abashes me" (13 December 1884).[1] A few months later, still wounded from

the hostile reception of her novel, Violet wrote again to ask a favor. She had
not abandoned the writing of novels but now sought a new approach:

> I am coming to London in June & want to know whether you could in-
> troduce me to any people who represent more practical interest than the
> aesthetes, with whom I have broken entirely. I feel a great desire, especially
> as a novelist, to see all kinds and conditions of men; & I especially would
> like to see something of the people who work among the poor & in similar
> matters. I know you have a great deal to do with these movements, so I ven-
> ture to ask you to help me in this matter. *Miss Brown,* you see, has thor-
> oughly brouillé [set at odds] one with such intellectual classes as I have hith-
> erto dwelt with; and I am anxious to see what other things there may be in
> the world. (26 April 1885)

Violet Paget was not quite thirty when she wrote this letter renouncing
"such intellectual classes as I have hitherto dwelt with." In fact she did no
such thing. The life of art was all the more challenging when she discovered
"psychological aesthetics" and worked out an elaborate system of analysis of
the aesthetic experience. Her curiosity about all branches of knowledge and
her determination to master them were limitless. The books that she left at
her death (now in the Harold Acton library of the British Institute of Florence), only a fraction of her lifetime of reading, are solid evidence of her appetite for knowledge. There is no "light" or imaginative literature, no poetry
or fiction, among the some 350 titles. They are without exception serious
works on science (evolution, biology, geology, psychology), history, philosophy, linguistics, aesthetics, and social science—in English, French, German, and Italian. And these books were read. Many of the texts are heavily
underlined, the margins full of scribbled questions, exclamation marks, and
lengthy commentaries, all penciled in her own hand and most written in the
languages of the books themselves. Though fragmentary, they display the
ever alert mind of the writer—questioning, argumentative, eager to challenge but also to discover and absorb new ideas.

In one thing Vernon Lee was consistent throughout her life. From her
early twenties to her death she was a liberal with socialist leanings. She carried no family heritage of political beliefs. With their wanderings over the
continent of Europe, the Pagets acquired no political roots other than a
vague sympathy for Italian independence and unification. Mrs. Paget chose
to live in the philosophical world of Voltaire and Rousseau; and Mr. Paget,
having had a taste of revolution in Poland in his youth, opted for fishing.
Though in the British diplomatic service for several years, Eugene Lee-
Hamilton was more interested in a literary career than in international rela-

tions. Young Violet's first exposure to the realities of social action was a brief and, in the adolescent's lively imagination, exciting glimpse of Paris under siege in 1870. Her mentors at this time were Giovanni Ruffini, a veteran of the Risorgimento, and his companion Cornelia Turner, who still cherished her girlhood memories of the ardent radical Shelley. With this romantic political indoctrination Violet Paget came to a London in the 1880s that was rapidly awakening to demands for widespread social change.

Her fictional Miss Brown's cousin Richard, the liberal labor reformer, and the idealistic Leigh sisters, who awaken Miss Brown to the irresponsibility of rich landowners like Walter Hamlin, represent the first stage in Vernon Lee's political development. She had no personal contact with the working classes (the occasional public lectures she delivered on writing and aesthetics were far too specialized for such an audience), but she observed conditions of poverty and injustice everywhere she traveled in England. As the contents of her library demonstrate, she read widely on social problems: Charles Booth's *Life and Labour of the People in London* (1902), Margaret L. Davies's *The Women's Co-operative Guild, 1883–1904* (1904), Henry Fawcett's *Manual of Political Economy* (1888), and Karl Marx's *Das Kapital* (1887). In the houses of her upper-class friends like Lady Dorothy Nevill and Lady Jeune she met prominent socialist and radical leaders, and she attended at least one meeting of the Fabian Society. She did not join the Fabians, however, because, like H. G. Wells, she could never subordinate her independent thinking to any body of convictions that she had not formulated herself. What in fact finally became her political agenda was not original with her but a group of issues familiar to all liberal thinkers of her time. She summed them up succinctly in the *Nation*, 10 September 1912, as "Free Trade, the remodelling of the House of Lords, the juster repartition of taxation, self-government of our dependencies and increased self-government of ourselves, better housing, better education, and less drunkenness."

Conspicuously absent from this list is women's rights. Like many other intellectual women of her time (including Beatrice Webb, who signed an antisuffrage manifesto in 1889 and did not express any sympathy for the cause until 1906),[2] Vernon Lee was reluctant to commit herself. She confessed to an initial distaste for feminism provoked by "those disconnected and disjointed personalities who are attracted by every other kind of thing in ism" (*Gospels of Anarchy* 265) and "my half-hearted acquiescence and shamefaced silence whenever I have found myself in the presence of such ardent enthusiasm for progress, that, let us say, of Suffragists, Eugenists and various brands of Socialists" (*Nation*, 2 August 1913). The suffragists who demonstrated and marched and starved themselves for the cause alienated many sympathizers. Vernon Lee's chilly distaste for Olive Chancellor in *The Bostonians* betrays her own suspicions of fanatic, neurotic women and the extremes to which feminism could drive one.[3]

Her suspicions were dispelled, however, when she read *Women and Economics* (1898) by Charlotte Perkins Stetson (later Gilman) and was, in her own word, "converted": "It opened my own [eyes] to the real importance of what is known as the Woman Question." This book, which she reviewed for the *North American Review* on 1 April 1901, offered an economic rather than an emotional argument: "that the present condition of women—their state of dependence, tutelage, and semi-idleness, their sequestration from the discipline of competition and social selection, in fact their economic parasitism—is in itself a most important factor in the wrongness of all our economic arrangements" (*Gospels of Anarchy* 267–68).[4] She shared Stetson's opposition to the rigid economic determinism of Marxism and applauded her criticism of "the inevitable pitting of one of the sexes against the other, the inevitable harping on what can or cannot or must not, be done, said or thought by women, because they are not men . . . the perpetual intrusion of the one fact of sex" (265–66).

For Vernon Lee, Stetson's strongest argument is that "women are oversexed." The phrase, she hastens to explain, "does not mean over-much addiction to sexual indulgence, very far from it. . . . What we mean by *oversexed* is that, while men are a great many things besides being males —soldiers and sailors, tinkers and tailors, and all the rest of the nursery rhyme—women are, first and foremost, females, and then again females, and then still more female" (281). Women have been conditioned for dependency in a patriarchal society. In her review she cites three books on gender questions (all in her library): Emile Durkheim's *De la division du travail social* (1893), Patrick Geddes and J. Arthur Thomson's *The Evolution of Sex* (1898), and Lester Ward's *Pure Sociology* (1903). Although she treats her subject seriously, Vernon Lee is not solemn: "For the man's virtue is to make money; the woman's virtue is to make money go a long way" (291); "We do not really know what women are. Women, so to speak, as a natural product as distinguished from women as a creation of men; for women, hitherto, have been as much a creation of men as the grafted fruit tree, the milch cow, or the gelding who spends six hours in pulling a carriage, and the rest of the twenty-four standing in a stable" (294).

Over the next fifteen years until women won the vote in England the struggle was waged fiercely, but Vernon Lee remained aloof from active engagement. She subordinated the issue to what she considered higher causes of social justice on which she produced numerous articles in newspapers and magazines and two books—*Gospels of Anarchy* (1908) and *Vital Lies*

(1912). But she did not ignore the cause of feminism. In the *Nation* of 4 September 1915 she took time from advocating pacifism to write "She for God in Him," a witty, sharply focused article on "the feminist note" in literature and society. Boldly challenging the whole notion that women exist for the purpose of being "helpmates" to men, she deflates both Milton and organized religion. She offers a "guess" that "Adam and Eve are makeshifts of that purblind and fumbling Chaos called Evolution, rather than of a fine deliberate creator who knew what he was after, namely, his own greater glory and incidental philanthropical intentions." The whole notion of women as helpmates must be reexamined, she argues. While acknowledging fundamental human instincts and needs, she sees the limitations of the idea: "And thus we may fall to wondering also whether these daughters of Milton's Eve will ever learn that, as the mother is needed only by the helpless or ailing child, so the woman who lives for love is needed by the man only in those episodes when he, too, lives only for love." But these are ephemeral needs. In the modern world, "men require not merely *helpmates* but that other and very different kind of *mate,* a fellow worker, a competitor, even a possible enemy." She foresees a time "when Eve will meet Adam not only as mother or wife, but accidentally, unintentionally, as one meets another creature interested in the same business, a possible rival, a conceivable comrade."

To judge from the image Vernon Lee projects in her writings on controversial subjects like vivisection and feminism, she was a resolute critic advocating reason and gradualism as the weapons of effective social change. We know, however, from the testimony of many who encountered her personally at private social gatherings or at public meetings that she could be dogmatic, abrasive, and, if Frank Swinnerton was correct, "overapt to attribute to any opponent either incurable stupidity or malignant dishonesty" (195). Like many inveterate talkers, she tended to talk over others' talk and to pursue her arguments stubbornly even when she had lost her audience's attention. In 1917 Aldous Huxley spent "an evening with Vernon Lee— each trying to get his or her word in edgeways" (Seymour 206–7); and Ottoline Morrell recalled a lecture by Bertrand Russell ("all the cranks who attended lectures on any subject were there") where, in the discussion period, "Vernon Lee got up and made a long speech about a cigarette-case, moving her hand about with her pince-nez dangling from it until she was finally asked to sit down" (Seymour 96).

Though undisciplined as a writer, Vernon Lee was more persuasive in her journalism than she apparently was in her public persona. From the 1890s through World War I she published articles on economics, politics, and international affairs in respected and widely circulated British and American periodicals—*Fortnightly Review, Contemporary Review, Quarterly*

Review, North American Review, Yale Review, the *Atlantic, Nation, New Statesman,* and the liberal daily *Westminster Gazette.* Collected in *Gospels of Anarchy* and *Vital Lies,* the longer pieces form an ambitious study of many of the major and most influential philosophers and social critics of the late nineteenth century. Reviewers complained about her verbosity, and the more perceptive ones identified flaws in her logic (especially in her attacks on pragmatism). Overall, however, the two collections were well received, though often patronizingly praised for "cleverness," "masculinity of thought and femininity of expression" (*New York Times Review of Books* 25 July 1908), and "feminine commonsense" (*Boston Transcript* 5 March 1913).

The essays in *Gospels of Anarchy* might have been inspired by a sentence in Beatrice Webb's *Diary* of 1884: "Social questions are the vital questions of today; they have taken the place of religion" (1:115). The concepts of secular humanism or "the Religion of Humanity" were familiar to readers of George Eliot and Matthew Arnold, among other Victorian thinkers. They came naturally to Vernon Lee, who wrote in the closing lines of *Gospels of Anarchy:* "No longer having a Personal Divinity to whom to devote our surplus moral energy, we many of us want to do something for the Future" (355). The problem, as she saw it, was not the loss of a personal divinity but the negativity and irrationality of the responses of many intellectuals to this loss: "the disorder, the passionate unruliness, the blind following of individual impulses, the derision of what other men have thought . . . the intellectual anarchy in short" (360).

In *Gospels of Anarchy* she offers no program for bringing rational order out of this intellectual anarchy except the simplistic notion that sometime in the future there will be a tempering of the intellectual passions, "the gradual coming intellectual self-restraint and good will" (372). The essays she collects here are "*marginalia,* mere puttings into shape of the notes taken, often with a pencil on the poor defaced books themselves, in the course of my readings. . . . The connecting thread throughout it all appears to be my effort to exert some kind of order from the authors under consideration" (359). Her subjects are Emerson, Max Nordau, Tolstoy, Nietzsche, William James, Ruskin, and H. G. Wells. Also included are two essays that appear to have little relationship to her thesis: her review of Stetson's *Women and Economics,* titled "The Economic Parasitism of Women," and "Rosny and the French Analytical Novel." Rosny was the pen name of the elder of two brothers (the family name was Boëx) who collaborated on a number of novels popular in France but little known in England. She met him on a visit to Paris in 1894 and wrote Eugene (12 June) that he thinks "that the borderland of science—its still unascertained fields—will furnish that natural field for personal fancy and emotion hitherto supplied by theology; one will create one's fairyland there." His novels treat human emotions analytically but not in the clinical detail of major novelists like Flaubert, Maupassant, Zola, and the Goncourts, who "[looked] at life as a subject for analysis and description instead of analysing and describing such parts of life as had been found interesting or fascinating in the process of living" (*Gospels* 247). Their work is "morally arid in its perpetual pessimism; it refuses the reader what, after all, we claim for literature, as from other art . . . the sense *that life is good*" (253–54). In contrast, Vernon Lee endorses "the school of sympathising, personal, in a way unprofessional novelists whose greatest representative is Tolstoi" (256), followed closely by Stendhal, Thackeray, and "our golden but clay-footed idol, Meredith" (258).

All the preachers of the gospels of anarchy respond in one way or another to the modern "spirit which denies," a phenomenon of an age ruled by the Will of the Ego, "the gospel of Ibsenism, which Mr. Bernard Shaw preaches with jaunty fanaticism" (19). She cites as a specific illustration what Dr. Relling in Ibsen's *The Wild Duck* calls "vital lies"—religion, spiritualism, transcendentalism, any sustaining idealism that defies rational explanation, "one of those human inventions for making life's occasional difficulties seem easier" (180). Some have resorted to mysticism. Tolstoy, much as she admired him as a novelist, was reduced to absurdity by his religious conversion. Assuming the role of prophet, he preached in *What Is Art?* a gospel of asceticism and "intellectual nihilism" that perverted normal, healthy values by rejecting much of the culture of humanism, the celebration of life. Less extreme was Emerson, another writer she had read with respect and admiration, who had "exceptional influence in maturing my thought" (44). But in his emphasis on "the transcendental Mind," Emerson "has forgotten human nature . . . [and in] his supposed union with God he has left man in the lurch" (55).[5]

Among the religious thinkers discussed in *Gospels of Anarchy* only Ruskin seems to have anything to offer the reader. More than a quarter century earlier in *Belcaro* Vernon Lee had dismissed Ruskin as dogmatic, moralistic, irrelevant in the modern world. But by the time of his death in 1900 she had revised her views radically. She discovered in him "the vital synthesis of one of the richest and noblest and really best balanced of creative personalities" (302). One wonders indeed why she included him in her company of misguided nineteenth-century thinkers. She does of course reaffirm that his religious orthodoxy warped his thinking, but she suggests that if one "will strip away the mere ecclesiastical symbolism and theological metaphysics from Ruskin's genuine and spontaneous thought," a soul "higher than Goethe's or Carlyle's, more complete than Wordsworth's or Renan's, more human than Spinoza's or Emerson's" will emerge (303). She sees him now as

the prophet of "righteous happiness," crusading against materialism and proclaiming "the art of getting the imaginative essence of things, of combining
the mysterious associations, subtle, microscopic, between loveliness of all
kinds, between all evidences of noble life" (307).

Probably the most pervasive and therefore most dangerous of all vital
lies is the presumption of belief itself. The scientific discoveries of the nineteenth century, Vernon Lee argues, have totally undermined all forms of supernatural and nonempirical belief. Yet a man as well educated in science
as William James, whom she acknowledged as the foremost psychologist of
the age, argued in *The Will to Believe* (1896) that it is necessary and therefore right to believe even where there are no rational grounds for belief. In
her essay "The Need to Believe: An Agnostic's Notes on Professor William
James," which originally appeared in *Fortnightly Review* in November 1899,
she confronted the most challenging of her gospels of anarchy. James was
not an ideologue. He argued on rational, pragmatic grounds that faith was
essential for the common good of society as well as for the individual believer. In giving primacy to the human mind to *make* truth, James seems to
be in sympathy with the humanism professed by Vernon Lee. But for the
health of the mind, always for her a major concern, James recommended
"doctrinal sources" that she distrusted—idealism, spiritualism, transcendentalism, religion. He wrote in Lecture 4 of *The Varieties of Religious Experience:* "If a creed makes a man feel happy, he almost inevitably adopts it.
Such a belief ought to be true; therefore it is."

For Vernon Lee this smacked of expediency, utility, what she would a
few years later attack in *Vital Lies* as James's pragmatism. "I disbelieve in religion's objective validity or value," she declares (*Gospels* 199), boldly affirming that there is "a type of mind which does not need to believe" and that
"all we know of good and evil is confined to man; that we are spiritually
akin only to our own kind; and that the ambiguous divinity, who has tor-
tured us with good instincts and evil examples, is but a Frankenstein Monster of our own making" (220). By including James in the company of distinguished and influential thinkers of the time and singling him out for
praise as well as censure, she was perhaps making amends for "Lady Tal,"
which had aroused his anger several years earlier. Certainly she went to great
lengths to identify herself as "one of his warmest admirers," citing "the hundred luminous suggestions with which Professor James's essays have delighted me." But there is distinct ambivalence in her feelings: "The *need* to
believe. That is the title which, in my mind, I find I give to these subtle,
brilliant, delicate, violent and altogether delightful essays of Professor William James" (193).

In contrast to these life-affirming though in her opinion self-deluding thinkers, she discusses Max Nordau, a "pathological psychologist." Nordau emphasized the imperfections of human character, the inevitable biological deterioration of all life, as he saw these phenomena reflected in the moral degeneracy of nineteenth-century culture. His book *Entartung,* published in Germany in 1893 and translated into English in 1895 as *Degeneration,* was received as a kind of epitome of fin de siècle decadence. Less destructive in their implications are the writings of Nietzsche, whom she praises for the force and originality of his thinking. But his gospel of the Ego or the "Will to Power," though brilliantly conceived, produces disorder and, in his own tragic case, madness: "the living nucleus of all his teaching is not a thought, but an emotional condition, organic and permanent" (183). For one as pre-occupied with mental health as Vernon Lee, "an emotional condition" was an alarming symptom both for the individual and for the society in which one lives.

Though most of these thinkers offered some significant ideas, Vernon Lee rejected all such diagnoses of the malaise of the age. Her gospelers had demanded too much too soon. Like her friend H. G. Wells, to whom she dedicated the book, she believed in a kingdom of heaven on earth. "The difference between us is, that while Mr. Wells would set Disinterested Thinking and Impersonal Feeling the task of actively and positively bringing about this millennium, I should be satisfied with preparing such thought and emotion for service against the coming of the new dispensation" (356). Oddly enough, the ideology that Vernon Lee endorses is Puritanism, not, it must be emphasized, as a religion or a code of moral behavior, but as a form of self-mastery, a discipline of the mind:

> Puritanism is psychologically right in its implicit recognition of the habit-ual condition of feeling over the transient impulse. If individualism is to triumph; if any good is to come (and it doubtless will) out of contemporary anarchic theories of the *ego,* it will be by an increase rather than a diminu-tion of the healthy Puritan element. It is, after all, the Puritans in temper who have done all successful rebellion against items of Puritan codes; whereas the egoist of the modern type is, nine times out of ten, the sort of person who tolerates evil for want of the self-discipline and consistency necessary to stop it. (32–33).

Of all the subjects she considers in *Gospels of Anarchy,* H. G. Wells came closest to sharing Vernon Lee's vision of a world ruled by an intellectual elite, the philosopher-kings whom Wells, in *A Modern Utopia* (1905), called the Samurai. This is an aristocracy of intelligence not birth. Samurai are men who live an abstemious life, renounce worldly possessions, and devote their energies to governing a socialist technocracy with public ownership of

land and economic security for all citizens. In his utopia women have equal
educational and economic rights with men, but since their primary mission
is to breed eugenically and care for their children, their prospects are necessarily limited.

While Wells offered another gospel of anarchy, he did not endorse the
deluding nostrums of belief in any spiritual power or the dangerous and un-
healthy indulgence of the Will or the Ego. Vernon Lee read him with sympathy and shared many of his ideas. She also respected him because he had
been educated in science and he applied Darwinian principles to social
thought. But she was suspicious of his Samurai, and she reacted to *A Modern Utopia* with "a confusion of enthusiastic assent and ill-defined suspicion": "The Samurai, therefore, may organise statistics and laboratories, but
I doubt whether they do much effective organisation of men at large" (342).
Indoctrinated with ideas from her mother's eclectic reading in eighteenth-
century rationalistic philosophy, she answered Wells's revolutionary pro-
posals with monitory references to "Panglossian theology," reminding him
of Voltaire's advice about cultivating one's garden:

> Let the Samurai educate and organise themselves and not others; if their sys-
> tem of morals and education, their new scruples and new duties, their new
> ideals and dignities and pleasures, are really good for anything, why, then,
> this better born and better bred class will gradually be imitated by their in-
> feriors; the world will rot a little less for their presence. They are the salt of
> the earth; let them not lose their savour! (342)

When in 1908 Vernon Lee included Wells among the major figures of
modern social thought in *Gospels of Anarchy* and dedicated the book to him,
she paid him a singular honor. Although he had by this time established
himself as a hugely successful novelist, popularizing theories of science otherwise inaccessible to the general public, he remained sensitive to his lower-
class provincial origins and his lack of university education and the cultural
polish of European travel. Vernon Lee's regard for him was flattering, but
their warm friendship was based on more-solid grounds than flattery. All
the more unusual was the fact that her relationships with strong-willed, intellectually aggressive men, especially one as sexually active as Wells, were
usually stormy. But in spite of some of his radical political ideas and his increasingly candid treatment of sex in his novels, they remained good friends
until the outbreak of World War I.

Vernon Lee had initiated the friendship when she wrote him, apparently
spontaneously, expressing her admiration for his novels. He replied with
humility: "I know your work very well indeed and it is a very pleasant surprise for me to find that with your nice sense of finish you can stand my

crude and floundering efforts to reason out my difficulties" (*Correspondence* 2:15–16). Thereafter they corresponded frequently and exchanged copies of each other's latest books. Vernon Lee characteristically mixed her praise with criticism, which Wells received gratefully: "Dear Miss Paget," he wrote in August 1904, "I am glad of your letter and your excellent criticisms though I'm sorry you cannot forgive the opening of *The Sea Lady* for the end. All you say of the *Time Machine* is after my heart" (*Correspondence* 2:40). She reviewed his books for the *Fortnightly Review* and the *Westminster Gazette* with respectful admiration for the vigor of his thought. In turn he looked after her interests, giving her the benefit of his experience as a journalist and polemicist. When Ford Madox Ford (then Hueffer) was slow in paying for articles they had contributed to his *English Review,* Wells informed him, "I am acting for Miss Paget as well as myself" (2:237).

Theirs was a personal as well as a professional friendship. In the summer of 1905, en route to London from Paris, she spent a night with the Wells family in Sandgate. "He and his wife are really delightful," she wrote Kit,

> living with two babies in a very plain pretty house on the cliff. He is in ap-
> pearance and a little in voice like the plumber, but told me he had begun
> as a draper's shopman; but with excellent real manners and quite the easi-
> est and most interesting—most easily [informed?] conversation I have ever
> met in an Englishman so that coming from France one seemed, in a way,
> not to have left it. We talked the whole time in the *Anticipations* line—eco-
> nomics, social arrangements, psychology, etc. Everything thank goodness
> [except] (for I am a little sick of my shop) *Art.* I believe the very word was
> never mentioned, wasn't it odd! The man is wonderfully impersonal, mod-
> est, yet with a bluff strenuousness. (dated "probably July 1905")

For all her "moralist's garb" and Puritan sensibilities, Vernon Lee was a forbearing witness to Wells's extramarital sexual activities. In 1909 he began an affair with Amber Reeves, the beautiful and brilliant young daughter of a prominent Fabian leader. They lived together openly, shocking even the presumably broad-minded Fabians. Amber did not demand marriage, which was fortunate, since Wells had no intention of leaving his wife and young sons. It troubled him that Vernon Lee, who had often visited the Wellses during her summer trips to England, stopped communicating with him. "Dear 'Sister in Utopia,'" he addressed her in September 1909: "I perceive you have been listening to scandal about me and avoiding me, instead of coming to me to find out just what the moral values were, as I think you ought to have done. I'm very sorry for I wanted to talk to you—very sorry indeed. And it wasn't kind to my wife, who likes and admires you beyond measure." She must have replied promptly and reassuringly because a few weeks later he wrote: "Your letter is just what I might have expected—warmest thanks for it" (2:259–60). Two months later he wrote her to announce: "I was and am in love with a girl half my age. . . . And she is going to bear me a child."

Vernon Lee's reply, on 22 December, was a long, thoughtful letter. Her disapproval of his behavior is evident from the cool salutation "Dear Mr. Wells," but she concedes at the outset her respect for his "unflinching frankness." In the body of the letter, however, she reveals her genuinely painful struggle of conscience:

> I have been turning the matter round and round in my thoughts, hoping, wishing to find at last a point of view from which I could find it *all right*. But I find that I always revert back to the same position which is the only one that is natural to me. The story is easy to understand, easy to sympathise with, even easy to excuse; it is familiar, the same as or related to as many which one knows or guesses. . . . It jars, moreover, in its details, with some of the notions deepest engrained in me. My experience as a woman and a friend of women persuades me that a girl, however much she may have read and thought and talked, however willing she may think herself to assume certain responsibilities, cannot know what she is about as a married or older woman would, and that the unwritten code is right when it considers that an experienced man owes her protection from himself—from herself.

Shrewdly recognizing that this was neither the first nor would it be the last of Wells's affairs, she closes her letter, "I shall always remain your *sister in Utopia*, and so long as both of you wish it," signing herself "Your and your wife's affectionate friend, Violet Paget" (*Correspondence* 2:267–68). Ten days later Wells wrote her to announce the birth of his and Amber Reeves's daughter. Her reply is a mixture of censure and forgiveness: "I cannot for the life of me like this business though I can perfectly account for what strikes me as a perfect tangle of self-contradictions on your part. But I *like* you—and I love your books. . . . And I remain, dear Mr. Wells, your sincere, affectionate, respectful (and for that very reason) decidedly distressed friend, V. Paget." That she continued to wrestle with the matter is suggested by a follow-up letter a few weeks later apologizing for the "cut and dry, crude, pedantic, self-righteous form" of her earlier letter: "But I think and feel that you are one of the greatest and dearest of living persons and that your books, even your worst, are far above the best thought and work of those who fall foul of them" (2:272–73).

Vernon Lee had greater sympathy for Wells's domestic problems than she had for his visionary utopias. But he had at least proposed goals toward

which humankind might reasonably work: an enlightened socialist technocracy that would utilize the discoveries of modern science for national
and international progress and peace. To that extent she found him less
dangerous, less the teller of vital lies, than the more highly respected intellectual obscurantists who became the subjects of another series of critical essays that she collected in 1912 under the title *Vital Lies*. Chief among these
was William James, the only subject she carried over from *Gospels of Anarchy*. Ever since she had received his angry reaction to her portrait of Henry
James in "Lady Tal," she had tried to make amends by softening or at least
trying to moderate her criticism of his philosophy. In *Gospels of Anarchy* her
ambivalence—high praise for his contributions to psychology and sharp
criticism of his "will to believe"—weakened the thrust of her essay on him.
She never gave up hope for some kind of reconciliation, and she did finally
win his respect for her writing if not her society. He appears to have read
her essay on him in *Gospels of Anarchy* without offense and even to have acknowledged that his phrase "the will to believe" was ambiguous. In 1909 he
sent her a copy of what was to be his last book, *A Pluralistic Universe*. On
29 April she wrote to thank him, confessing with her always ready contrition that she felt like "an ungrateful and ungenerous monster":

> For here you are sending me your book, after writing me (last summer) a
> letter enough to turn anyone's head with vanity, while I am spending my
> time and blackening my paper (though I hope not my conscience) in at-
> tacking your opinions with the vilest virulence. Let me correct myself: not
> *all* your opinions. For has not your *Psychology* read, re-read till it is almost
> falling to pieces, made an epoch in whatever philosophic thought I am ca-
> pable of? Indeed, I am not quite sure that my extreme hostility to your
> pragmatic or, if I may set down the word which really occurs to me—your
> *obscurantist* books and parts of books, is not envenomed by the disap-
> pointment of not receiving from you further developments of your won-
> derfully *genial* psychological theories. All this must seem merely imperti-
> nence, and, as such, I can only beg you to excuse it, in consideration of my
> horror of seeming suddenly to attack an author who has gone out of his way
> to be appreciative and encouraging towards my own work. And the only act
> of courtesy with which I can answer yours is to let you know, before almost
> anyone else, that I am attacking you in what many people will think a very
> discourteous fashion. At the same time then I remain, in many respects,
> your grateful and admiring disciple.
>
>   V. Paget[6]

James died on 26 August 1910. In the October 1910 issue of the *North
American Review* Vernon Lee published "The Two Pragmatists," an essay

she reprinted in *Vital Lies*. No longer under constraints of delicacy, she was unsparing in her attack on what she regarded as a fundamental flaw in James's philosophy: his misinterpretation and distortion of pragmatism. An advocate herself of realistic programs of social reform based upon scientific empirical principles, she had no quarrel with theoretical pragmatism and its founder Charles Sanders Peirce, James's colleague at Harvard. Unlike her obscurantists, who sought answers in various systems of *belief*, Peirce worked on a theory of *meaning*, seeking to clarify concepts with the tools of logic and language, as the title of his best-known book, *How to Make Our Ideas Clear* (1870), indicates. Where James tested truth by its capacity to work, that is, to make people happy and virtuous, Peirce—so dissatisfied with James's version that in 1905 he changed the name of his philosophy from *pragmatism* to *pragmaticism*—defined truth as "the opinion which is fated to be ultimately agreed to by all who investigate." Vernon Lee's dispute with James may have originated simply in her suspicions of faith in general, but she found sounder support for her arguments in an Italian friend, the leading proponent of Italian pragmatism, Giovanni Vailate (1863–1909), a professor of mathematical logic, to whom she dedicated *Vital Lies:* "To the memory of my friend Giovanni Vailate who, better than anyone else, explained the incompatibility between 'Willing to Believe' and 'Making One's Ideas Clear.'"

Vital Lies is a more ambitious book than *Gospels of Anarchy*. Her arguments are based on thoughtful study, not the mere jotting of random ideas on her reading. Her prose, showing occasional flashes of wit, is less idiosyncratic, and the book was received with more serious attention by reviewers than its predecessor. Its main fault is excess—of length (two volumes) and language—too many heavy guns aimed at targets that time has proved to be ephemeral. Its thesis, as summed up briefly in the preface, is "Science has undermined what used to be called *religious truths*." To support their beliefs, the thinkers she calls "obscurantists" reinvent them in symbolical and mythic terms or "apply their logic to redefining truth in such a way as to include edifying and efficacious fallacy and falsehood." In addition to William James, she discusses Father George Tyrrell, the leader of the Catholic modernist movement; the anthropologist Ernest Crawley; the syndicalist Georges Sorel; and, though not rating a chapter to himself, Henri Bergson, whose theory of creative evolution (*L'évolution créatrice*, 1907) substituted an idealistic vitalism (*élan vital*) for the empirically conceived Darwinian theory of natural selection.

In *Pragmatism* James reduced truth to utility: "On pragmatic principles," he wrote, "if the hypothesis of God works satisfactorily, in the widest sense of the word it is true" (1:25). Father Tyrrell practiced "applied pragmatism." Unwilling to abandon his Catholic faith, he attempted, in his book *Christianity at the Crossroads* (1909), to reconcile his religion with the discoveries of science, to find in the teaching of Jesus principles relevant to and compatible with modern scientific thought. For Vernon Lee this was merely the expression of the "Will Not to Disbelieve": "Nothing can be more absurd than to attribute to the Founder of Christianity a mentality in advance of his time and nation and class. . . . Jesus was not a moral innovator, since his morality was current both among the Jewish pietists and the Gentile philosophers of his day" (1:169).

Ernest Crawley and Georges Sorel, on the other hand, sowed their vital lies in the social and political sciences. In *The Tree of Life: A Study of Religion* (1905), Crawley, an anthropologist and sociologist and a nonbeliever, traced the roots of Christian belief back to pagan systems, arguing that, as Vernon Lee puts it, "religion is the direct outcome of elemental human nature" (2:17), and therefore its claim to be essential to human nature, though not necessarily true, is validated. Georges Sorel, a spokesman for the revolutionary movement syndicalism, represented to Vernon Lee the reductio ad absurdum of pragmatism. For him truth has no value either in absolute terms or in terms of utility. What follows is the denial of all authority—state, church, social institutions—and the total breakdown of society in anarchy. Vernon Lee carefully distinguishes between the socialism that she, Wells, and many of their contemporaries advocated—that is, enlightened community ownership and management of the means of production and distribution—and syndicalism, whereby workers would organize into trade unions (syndicates) and call a general strike to achieve their demands. This, Sorel predicted, would cripple the economy, create class warfare, and lead to "an indefinable Armageddon." Sorel, she writes, "has not used pragmatism as a convenience, pragmatically hesitating between *yes* and *no,* but like a thorough believer, a genuine apostle, he has carried his doctrine to its own glorious logical death" (2:61–62).

In one fashion or another, Vernon Lee's vital liars exploited the philosophy of pragmatism. Driven by the will to believe, by the hunger for a faith, a belief that will give meaning and purpose to life, they resorted to obscure, illogical, and potentially dangerous theories. In *Gospels of Anarchy* she had argued that hers is "a type of mind which does not need to believe" (194). In *Vital Lies* she concedes that under the challenges of modern times the temptation to believe is powerful: "There is a sense, forever growing in me, of the utter lack of aim in life, or rather, of the illusory nature, the perfunctoriness of the various aims with which we clap variously on to life's various pieces." However, she continues to resist the glib explanations and easy remedies of the vital liars. "But with this sense there grows, ever stron-

ger and more unfailing, the conviction that this should not make us doubt
of life's value to ourselves, or of life's greatness in itself" (2:194). After examining many of the philosophies currently in vogue, she is left with the
secular humanism with which she began. "We can know only that we, or
others like us, have arranged the thing; we know that we are contemplating
to please ourselves, and that the contemplated object has been made for
such contemplation. In the case of Religion we muddle this fact up with the
quite different fact of the existence of an independent Universe, the Universe which sensations testify to, and we persuade ourselves that we are serving someone else when we are only serving ourselves" (2:169–70). Darwin
and his fellow scientists demonstrated the absence of a divine hand or purpose in the creation of the universe. What then can we know but that "man
is the measure of all things. . . . Man is certainly not the centre of all things,
but I do not see what else is to be his centre save himself" (2:194).

Edmund Gosse's melancholy reflection to Vernon Lee in 1906 that "we
belong to a generation which has—to be blunt—passed away" was only
partly correct. Intellectually and sentimentally she was committed to the
past, the natural, preindustrial landscape and the art and music that had
been her youthful passions. But during the first decade of the twentieth century she had witnessed the irreversible course of modern European history
—expanding industrialism, militarism, and imperialism—as well as a revolution in social mores. For a woman as cosmopolitan as Vernon Lee, at
home in the society of artists, writers, men and women of culture and independent means, these changes were disturbing but not threatening. She
could not ignore them, and it was not in her nature to accept them passively.
For this reason polemics increasingly appealed to her. It was a genre in
which she had been writing since her late teens when she published scathing
criticism of modern Italian society in *La rivista europea*. With maturity she
acquired the experience and self-confidence to establish herself in the unique
position of interpreting contemporary Europe to English readers and England to Europeans. While continuing to write fiction, travel essays, and reports on her research in psychological aesthetics, she was also claiming a
place in English and American journalism, with additional ventures into
French, Italian, and German periodicals.[7]

In an age that did not demand a high degree of specialization in journalism, Vernon Lee wrote with as much assurance on political economy and
foreign affairs as she did on travel and aesthetics. Consistently liberal in politics, she was far more lucid and informative in her journalism than in the
long essays of *Gospels of Anarchy* and *Vital Lies*. From 1900 through the years
of World War I she published frequently in prominent liberal weeklies like
the *Nation* (London and occasionally the *Nation* of New York), the *New*

Statesman, and in the daily *Westminster Gazette.* She could not reach a large
public in journals like these, but she had the satisfaction of addressing an
intellectual elite who evidently respected her views. The *Westminster Gazette*
in particular was an ideal outlet for her. As she wrote to Maurice Baring: "I
am fifty and want to speak my mind on a dozen subjects; and in a way those
little Westminster articles are safe vehicles. One could preach free love
or abolition of property (neither of which I believe in) if one headed it
'Valmontone'—'Signarungen'—'Ballan'—or any name out of Bradshaw"
(3 March 1908). Founded in 1893 and edited, during the years she published
there, by J. A. Spender, the *Gazette* was directed to a small, well-informed
readership who appreciated its coverage of world and local news, as well
as book, theatre, and art reviews in short, crisply written articles. It never
had the wide circulation of the popular press, but as Stephen Koss writes:
"The *Westminster Gazette,* as its name implies, aimed at a circulation within
Parliament and its environs. Although sympathetic to the plight of the
masses, it would sooner write them off as customers than write down to
them" (2:10).[8]

It was a readership sophisticated enough to appreciate Vernon Lee's attacks on British complacency: "The growth of democracy and the spread
of intellectual 'popularisation' have for the moment put us at the mercy of
the immense, half-educated majority . . . I do not mean at the mercy of the
working classes, who have, so far, too little voice in public matters." This
was Vernon Lee writing on the need for fiscal reform ("The Superman and
the Man in the Street," *Westminster Gazette,* 22 January 1906). Still bitter
over the jingoism aroused by the Boer War, she was also troubled by the
spread of anti-Semitism. She complains of the "average citizen in his hours
of irresponsibility" who listens to the "Superman" and "as a result [forgets]
his nice house and club manners in a bout of mafficking or a little Juden-
hetze [Jew baiting]." Writing as she often did from the point of view of the
European, she felt compelled to explain to her friends on the Continent
how it is "possible that English people should be trying to make a fortune
out of institutions which the Continent is trying slowly and laboriously to
discard as mechanisms of class privilege, or national improvement, and of
political corruption."

Vernon Lee was only one among many critics of the British status quo
during the prewar years, but her special advantage was that she could examine British society from a two-edged point of view. As an outsider she
criticized the raw arrogance of colonialism in "The Ethics of Glass Houses"
(*Nation,* 13 April 1912): "[Remember] your various land grabbings—so necessary to the world's progress—and the elimination of sundry backward
races; remember the burning of the Boer farms; remember the Concentra-

tion Camps; remember the Mahdi's head." Yet in the same article she identifies herself as British: "Very properly our morality is becoming less a set of
ritual taboos presided over by some Caliban's god Setebos, than a code of
things to be sought or avoided from sheer spiritual good taste and breed-
ing." There is progress toward reform, she concedes, but the danger lies in
foreign policy, the growing rivalry between England, the most powerful
country in Europe, and the rapidly expanding Germany. On this score she
maintains strict neutrality: "Can we, conscientiously, loyally, object to others doing what we have done ourselves?"

As early as 1910 she had anticipated a conflict between these two countries. In the September 10 issue of the *Nation* she published her translation
from the German of a letter by Professor Lujo Brentano addressed to the
Antwerp Free Trade Congress ("The Lines of Anglo-German Agreement").
Brentano, a German liberal, was alarmed by reports that Germany was
preparing for a war against England, and he urged liberals of both nations
to work for peace. To this letter she added her own strong opinion that "a
peaceable attitude toward Germany is the *sine qua non* of the leisure and
economy indispensable for effecting the reforms and re-organisation which
alone signify liberty and progress." [9] The accelerating tension in Anglo-
German relations is reflected in a number of her articles and letters to the
editor in the years just preceding August 1914. Unequivocally pacifist, she
observed the ominous signs of war fever in England and on the Continent.
It was impossible for her to endorse the anti-German sentiments of many
of her friends because Germany had been the scene of her happiest childhood memories. She had close friends who were German, and though she
did not share the German enthusiasm for Wagner, she loved German music and literature and delighted in the spirit of *Gemütlichkeit* that she felt in
her travels in Germany. But the German military aggression she had witnessed in Paris in 1870 and the expansion of the German military under Bismarck and Kaiser Wilhelm II were undeniable threats.

Her response to these fears was to write warnings against nationalism on
all sides, but especially in England and France, where she had witnessed it
firsthand. In the *Nation* for 12 October 1912 ("The Sense of Nationality")
she deplored the "rhetorical self-delusion" of nationalism—citing its ramifi-
cations in the popularity of Maurice Barrès, the French writer and politician
who urged "the imperative need for a sense of nationality." [10] Even among
her closest friends—"Intellectuals, Liberals, Old Dreyfusard stalwarts"—
she detected anti-German feeling and "the barely repressed longing for war"
("Peace and the Entente Cordiale," *Nation,* 7 October 1911). In England she
ridiculed the national pride reflected in the prudery of the Lord Chamber-

lain's censorship of plays and the "elderly English men and women [who] recoil with flustered blushings from [H. G. Wells's] *Ann Veronica.*" While the French "twitch" the English for their hypocrisy, they "indulge with a smile at their own sentimental cant about *la Famille, le Foyer,* and that especially dreary personification, *la Mère.*" Even the Italians felt her ire: "Would it not be really fairer to let them know . . . that the rest of us do not agree that slackness, sluttishness, and lack of public spirit (what they themselves expressively sum up as 'fare il suo commodaccio') are not the by-products of artistic and poetic genius?"

But because Vernon Lee was writing as an Englishwoman for English readers, she directed her attention mainly to the preparations England was making for war. In "Lessons of History" (*Nation,* 18 January 1913) she warns that England, "being a colonising Empire, will duly become the prey of Japanese, Americans, especially of Germans!" In "The Educational Disadvantages of Compulsory Military Service" (*Westminster Gazette* 1 and 2 October 1913) she comments bitterly on the argument that conscription is an opportunity for educating poor boys: "instruction in the use of extremely expensive instruments of destruction by well-educated and devoted gentlemen, all whose intelligence, learning, sense of honour, and readiness for self-sacrifice are themselves specialised for the murder of similarly disciplined, moralised, instructed and specialised foreigners." She argues instead for "efficient national education for its own sake," beginning in early childhood and complemented with a public health system. To objections that such programs would be costly, she replies, "Costly, in as much as it would necessarily prohibit the wage-earners from eking out incomes left them by Dreadnoughts and war-scare economic crises, by the wages of their children in sweated industries (if German), American mines (if Italian), or such educational employments as Britain allows its errand boys and golf caddies."

Vernon Lee reserved her most fiery rhetoric for the war itself. Ironically, she directed it at her friend H. G. Wells, who from the outbreak of hostilities supported the Allied cause enthusiastically. Their debate was conducted in the pages of the *Labour Leader* and the New York *Nation,* and it reverberated internationally. Only a few weeks after Germany marched into Belgium and England declared war in August 1914, Wells wrote in the *Labour Leader:* "Our country is fighting for its existence. No one who remains sane can suppose we have any other alternative before us except victory" (*Correspondence* 2:379). This was followed by his "Appeal to the American People" in the *Daily Chronicle* (24 August) urging America to boycott German trade.

Vernon Lee responded with heavy sarcasm in a letter to the New York *Nation* (17 September) that she speaks for "thousands of English men and women who feel only shame and disgust at the proposal Mr. Wells has made in their name." Although it is the threat of famine that she finds most objectionable in his proposal—"Let America use and show her neutrality by starving Germany; by reducing, if possible, its inhabitants to the scurvy-stricken and anaemia-undermined creatures I remember still seeing in the streets and shops of Paris in the summer of 1871 [1870]"—she also reminds American readers that England is not blameless in provoking this war, that its belligerent policies and heavy naval armaments have put Germany in a defensive position. Furthermore she disputes Wells's claim that czarist Russia will be a valuable ally, citing Russian internal violence, especially its pogroms against the Jews, and she ridicules his expressed faith in France as an ally. "I know too much of France to believe that she can establish in other countries the free and orderly government which she has been unable, despite all her genius and her 'principles,' to obtain for herself." She concludes her letter with an impassioned plea to Americans to reject "Mr. Wells's invitation to starve Germany," appealing to them to act consistently with their humane open door policy, welcoming Russian Jews escaping from "the demands of that recent convert to liberalism, the peace-loving czar."

Wells replied to all this in the *Labour Leader* (*Correspondence* 2:380–81) by accusing her of naïveté. "No doubt Miss Paget thinks the Kaiser is a simple, poor man . . . [and] knows nothing whatever of Russia. She will not learn." He had the last word in a letter to the editor of the New York *Nation*, 22 October 1914, pointing out first that starvation of the German people had never been his intention: "Germany can, with a little economy, go on feeding herself without importation for an indefinite time." He calls her "abuse" of France "scarcely sane" and concludes with a patronizing thrust: "Whatever losses or gains this war brings about, it has, I fear, lost 'Vernon Lee.' But we shall do our best to reconquer her for the sake of the many precious things she gave us before she was won from us by Berlin" (2:389).

In such an emotional climate it was not possible for her to argue a rational case for pacifism. At best she could offer only a short allegory that she published in an American outlet, the *Atlantic Monthly* for November 1915. Covering less than a page and titled "The Heart of a Neutral," it tells the story of her fairy christening. The guests were the nations of Europe:

> And each brought me a gift of understanding her greatness and beauty, and enriching my life with such knowledge. England and Italy came with their poetry and humor and practical wisdom, the ripeness of modern times and the heritage of oldest civilizations; France came with her humane, laughing lucidity; and Germany with her music and philosophy and the children's tales roosting in her Christmas tree. Even Russia and Poland whose soil I

was never to tread, came as the foster-mothers (unreconciled sisters!) of my father's boyhood. And all of them said, "This child shall have the joy of loving us."

As in the classic story, one fairy whom her parents had forgotten to invite came with a cruel prophecy: "For with the knowledge of the good of each nation, this child shall know in sadness the weakness and folly also of them all." But a good fairy balanced this with a generous gift: "When all the nations shall welter in the pollution of warfare, this child's eyes shall remain clear from its fratricide fumes; she shall drink deep of sorrow, but recognize and put away from her lips the sweetened and consecrated cup of hatred."

A few years later Vernon Lee would write a long and far more powerful allegory on war and pacifism, *Satan the Waster,* but she had recognized the threat to the Europe she knew and loved much earlier. In 1903 she wrote a short preface to her play *Ariadne in Mantua* in which she described her aristocratic characters as "well-bred people, faithful to their standards and forcing others, however unwilling, into their own conformity. Of course without them the world would be a den of thieves, a wilderness of wolves: for they are—if I may call them by their less personal names—Tradition, Discipline, Civilisation." In 1914, at the outset of what she and many others foresaw would be a war that would permanently alter if not destroy their cherished values of "Tradition, Discipline, Civilisation," she found herself indeed lost in "a wilderness of wolves."

16 A WILDERNESS OF WOLVES

I take off my hat to the old guard of Victorian cosmopolitan intellectualism, and salute her as the noblest Briton of them all.

George Bernard Shaw, review of *Satan the Waster* in the *Nation*

🖎 IN HER BIOGRAPHY OF MAURICE BARING, ETHEL SMYTH PUB-lished a photo of Vernon Lee taken in early 1914 at the resort town of Sestri Levante on the Gulf of Genoa. She was traveling with her old friend Mona Taylor and Mona's sister-in-law Margery, who snapped the picture. Heavily dressed in an overcoat and grasping a walking stick, she is seated on a stone bench, posed in three-quarters profile. Her large hat does not conceal the bony face and heavy jaw nor the melancholy expression as she looks off into the distance. Smyth wrote that Vernon Lee "jestingly expressed gratification at finding herself portrayed as 'a figure of romance'; and it is true that, never good-looking, in 1914 Vernon was no longer young. But at heart she was 'a figure of romance' and that is precisely what Miss Taylor tried to convey—likewise a view you cannot see, yet felt; in fact, Vernon in her true frame, Italy" (327).

A few months later she made her annual summer trip to England, and when war broke out in August 1914, she was unable to return to Italy. For a displaced "romantic"—and Ethel Smyth had judged her correctly—exile from Italy was almost as painful as the fact of war itself. Like many others, Allies and Germans alike, she had at first assumed that the war would end swiftly with some kind of compromise between the warring powers; but as the months passed with ever increasing devastation and casualties, she realized the hopelessness of her situation. Il Palmerino was in the care of her loyal servant Carlo, and Italian friends sent her news from time to time, but even if it had been possible for her to return, she probably would have remained in England, where there was a vigorous pacifist movement and an outlet for her own strong convictions. But she could no longer reach any sizable English public. The *Westminster Gazette* and many other periodicals to which she had contributed were closed to her. Although she published a few articles on art and aesthetics in the *Contemporary Review* (November 1915, July 1916), only the *Nation,* the *New Statesman,* and the radical socialist *Labour Leader* would publish her political articles in England.[1] The only book she published during the war years was *The Ballet of Nations* (1915), a moral allegory generalizing about the horrors of war.

Failure to support the Allied cause with enthusiasm inevitably led to charges of disloyalty and pro-Germanism, as Vernon Lee only too soon discovered. Her bitter quarrel with H. G. Wells in the pages of the *Nation* and the *Labour Leader* permanently ended their friendship. The French writer Augustine Bulteau, who had been her confidante in the crisis of her relationship with Kit Anstruther-Thomson, denounced her furiously:

> I have just read your shameful letter in the *Nation* [17 September 1914]. I hope, if ever chance bring us together, you will refrain from greeting me. I know that you are a waif, a stray, that nothing very lasting, no regular family or friend, binds you to your country. I know that the English refuse to grant any importance to your adaptation of ideas picked up in Germany. I know that the "thinker," which you regard yourself, is the cause of much laughter among your countrymen. But is that, all that, enough, at such a terrible moment as this, to make you renounce the honour of being English, to make you raise your thin pretentious voice in support of the enemy of your country, your suffering country which never was so great as now? (Gunn 205)

Vernon Lee replied to this cruel letter with amazing restraint, insisting that she loved the Allied countries and their people and that her animus was directed only toward their militant leaders. She cited her long-standing pacifism, her opposition years earlier to England's role in the Boer War and in 1911 to Italy's war with Turkey that led to the Italian annexation of Tripoli. But as the war advanced, it became more difficult for her to oppose it without being charged with pro-German sympathies. Even years after the war, her good friend Ethel Smyth, who had many happy memories of her own years of music study in Germany, answered Virginia Woolf's query, "Why do you think Vernon Lees [*sic*] views on the war detestable?" with, "I hate her utter lack of patriotism . . . either innate or acquired" (*Letters* 5:146). Many old friends—English, French, Italian—were deeply involved in war service: Maurice Baring was an officer in the British army in France; Kit Anstruther-Thomson volunteered for Belgian relief work; Mary Robinson Duclaux was a volunteer nurse in France, which had become her home; even the American Edith Wharton was covering the war as a journalist and raising money for French war victims. The sympathies of all her friends were with the Allies. In 1919, looking back at the first years of the war, Vernon Lee wrote: "I seem to see how all I have written and said about the war must appear from the point of view of those puzzled or disapproving friends of mine. . . . I have been subject to occasional moments of what I call to myself 'illumination,' moments of realizing the inconceivableness, the ugliness, almost the monstrosity of my hostile aloofness, as it must have appeared to those participating in the war in hand and heart." No amount of sympathy with the suffering of those friends, however, could alter her convictions: "Never for a second have I repented or distrusted my own attitude. . . . My position about the war seems as entirely natural and inevitable given *me*, as I recognize and feel theirs to be given *them*. As *they* feel in the right, so also do I" (introduction to *Satan the Waster* xii–xiii).

To compensate she should have at least had the gratification of the support of the staunchly pacifist circles at Garsington and Bloomsbury — Ottoline Morrell (whose husband Philip went to jail along with Bertrand Russell for refusing to serve), the Ponsonbys, and French writers like Romain Rolland and Daniel Halévy. But, as so often before, she pushed too hard. According to his biographer E. M. Forster, the philosopher G. Lowes Dickinson, not a declared pacifist but a sympathizer with their cause, "exasperated" Vernon Lee when they were houseguests of the Ponsonbys in the summer of 1915. She "complained to her hostess that he was 'wrinkled with scruples,' and he for his part sat silent when she poured forth fantastic diatribes against the allies" (159). Logan Pearsall Smith wrote to Ethel Sands in February 1916: "She has made herself so unpopular by her war talk that she now, by a great effort, confines herself to strictly neutral subjects" (98). But such self-discipline was rare. Frank Swinnerton, who was taken to visit her in her lodgings in Chelsea in 1916, called her "the very pro-German Miss Paget. . . . And we spoke — or perhaps it would be more accurate to say that Vernon Lee spoke . . . of the war, of books, and of national character, as to which she was, with dignity, dogmatic" (*Autobiography* 194–95).

There is an element of romantic melancholy in Vernon Lee's isolation during the war years. Away from Italy she seems to have lost her firm resolution to work without grieving and to accept the loneliness of her life without a loving companion. Antaeus-like she drew her strength from Italian soil, and deprived of it she lost much of her creative energy. When war broke out, she was staying at the country house of her friend Emily Ford in Yorkshire, but by winter she was back in London "in grubby but not unsympathetic lodgings," she wrote an American friend, Mrs. Charles Fairchild. "Dickensian furniture with every window rattling and every knob coming off in one's hands — in an old-fashioned Bloomsbury square [Torrington Square], with big trees back and front." Recalling the recent deaths

of friends—Annie Fields, Gabrielle Delzant, and "others you may not have
known who are now doubly a thing of the past, of the peaceful, hopeful past,
full of good will and serene philosophy which has disappeared *utterly* out of
the life of us miserable Europeans since that atrocious first week of last August," she found comfort only in the past, in memories of her first visit to
London in 1881 when she stayed with the Robinsons and met Browning,
William Rossetti, Oscar Wilde, "and strange epigones of pre-Raphaelitism."
She sought escape to an even more remote past in the nearby British Museum, "although I have seen the last horsemen and canephora of the frieze
disappear behind the sacred bays and asbestos paper of Zeppelin-panic"
(23 March 1915).[2]

Books at least never failed her. Three months before the war ended in
1918 she wrote:

> In these four years which the war has filled with more deaths and weeping
> than any other four-score, I have found most relief in books such as take
> one back to civilisations distant or forgotten beyond all grief, take one also
> to the countries where droughts and earthquakes and riotous vegetation
> have long effaced scars inflicted by the angry and wasteful hand of men.
> In my spare time I have been turning over dusty atlases of pre-hellenic pot-
> tery, of Egyptian temple-reliefs and of the cavern frescoes and carving of
> men whose Europe was still covered with ice and reindeer-moss. And in the
> grim evenings of war-darkened London (sometimes indeed while air raids
> screeched around) I have kept thoughts of present and future misery at bay
> with old-fashioned books of travel in Classic Lands: *Eothen*, Curzon's *Mon-
> asteries of the Levant* and Fellowes' quite equally delightful ramples [ram-
> bles?] among Lycian tombs. ("Pre-War Sketches 1910–1914")

The most poignant expression of her homesickness for Italy was in an
obituary article she wrote for the *Nation*, 9 October 1915, on the death of
the philosopher-historian Alfred William Benn. She had been introduced
to him in 1881 by Eliza Lynn Linton and saw him often when she moved to
Il Palmerino, directly adjacent to his house. "We had been neighbors in that
little valley under Fiesole some fifteen years now, my windows looking on
to a field of vines and a reach of reeded stream which belonged to him, once
farms but raised by the Florentine tax-gatherer to the dignity of 'civil habita-
tions,' being separated by only a few hundred yards of unfrequented road."
They took long walks together, accompanied by their dogs, "who had got
to know that certain words, 'Hegel,' 'Bergson,' 'Exegesis,' 'Ancestor Worship' meant opportunity for canine truancy and misdemeanor." Though
not a close personal friend, Benn represented to her a genuine humanist, "a
student not of holy but human writ . . . meaning one who judges by human

standards and in relation to human welfare and dignity." With Italy always foremost in her thinking, she counted on renewing her friendship with him when the war ended and she ("myself so aged and impoverished in spirit, so many persons and so many beliefs gone from me") could return home. "And today a letter from my servants tells me he is dead." It was less a personal loss than the end of an idyll: "It is not only he who is gone, it is a whole side of one's thinking, wondering, questioning, will be silent like the keys of which the piano strings have broken." Like all genuine romantics Vernon Lee understood that the ego is engaged in a constant struggle with social conscience. Retreat to the palace of art—for Vernon Lee the past— was at best only temporary.

The moral imperative of action to advance the cause of her social ideals demanded a return to reality. Even as she reported her attempts to escape the present in her reading, she had closed her letter to Mrs. Fairchild with: "Also I am working the little I can with those who are trying to prepare a peace which shall not be a mere prelude to more wars." A lasting peace, "not a mere prelude to more wars," was the ideal toward which a small but dedicated and articulate group of English and European intellectuals had begun to work some years before the outbreak of World War I. Vernon Lee's association with their cause began in 1911 when she joined them in opposition to British intervention in Agadir, where the Germans and French had clashed over rival imperialist claims. The group remained dissenters against official British foreign policy, and in the crisis of 1914 they argued that England should remain neutral and press for immediate negotiations for a peace settlement. In November 1914, with British neutrality no longer an issue, they established the Union of Democratic Control: "An organisation created to secure the control over their Foreign Policy by the British people, and for the promotion of International understanding." The founders of the organization were Ramsay MacDonald, E. D. Morel, Norman Angell, and Charles Trevelyan. From the outset the group looked ahead, their slogan "the war that will end wars," their agenda "to secure real parliamentary control over foreign policy" and "to aim at securing such terms that this war will not either through the humiliation of the defeated nation or an artificial re-arrangement of frontiers merely become the starting point of new national antagonism and future wars" (Harris 54–55). She also shared their long-range goals, which included repudiation of all balance-of-power alliances, "the drastic reduction of armaments," and the promotion of a policy of free trade. Two years later these policies were incorporated in Woodrow Wilson's Fourteen Points, and by the war's end they had become the foundation of the League of Nations.

During the war years the membership of the UDC, as it came popularly to be known, included a roster of eminent liberals and socialists—Arthur Ponsonby, Bertrand Russell, H. N. Brailsford, J. A. Hobson, F. W. Pethick Lawrence, B. N. Langdon-Davies. Special efforts were made to recruit women and members of the Labour Party. Beginning in September 1914 the UDC published a series of pamphlets that were as outspoken in their criticism of Germany as they were of the Allied nations, condemning "all claims based on conquest, imperialistic ambition or strategic considerations, such as a German demand for a revision of strategic frontiers in Belgium and elsewhere" (Swanwick 81). Vernon Lee's contribution to the series, "Peace with Honour" (1915), cited the division of Alsace-Lorraine as an example of the evils of creating artificial boundaries based on political interests. Her thesis was "the futility of trying to redraw the map of Europe on the principle of nationalities," and she argued that "the territory belongs to its inhabitants and not that the inhabitants belong to a territory" (Harris 97).

Vernon Lee, like her fellow members of the UDC, looked to the future. The war was a grim reality. The only hope, therefore, was the peace that was to come. In a letter to the editor published in the *Nation,* 20 February 1915, she warned against "self-righteous vindictiveness or short-sighted self-seeking." She endorsed Bertrand Russell's argument in the same journal, 13 February 1915, that the Allies should offer Germany "honorable" peace terms, adding that such an offer is desirable "not only to take the wind out of the German war party's sails, but also to take the wind of unlawful hopes out of the sails of the war parties among our Allies." In the *New Statesman* of 20 February 1915 she published an article, "Bismarck Towers," tracing the whole course of German militarism and expansionism to Prussia, which "drew the first fraternal blood cementing German unity in 1866." Until that time—and the invasion of France in 1870—Germany had been a center of culture, of music and poetry, but it had no identity as a nation, "Germany, poor sentimental frump among nations." Under the leadership of "that odious man of genius" Bismarck, a new German pride developed, a sense of nationhood and power emerged. And here Vernon Lee releases her rhetoric full blast: "Bismarck, by howsoever ruthless means, undoubtedly delivered them [the Germans], an atrocious historical accoucheur, cutting into the tissues of our common mother humanity, to bring to quicker birth a new nation." But, she reminds her readers, the Allies have no grounds for moral superiority, having produced an Oliver Cromwell in Ireland and a Napoleon warring on the Continent ("Pre-War Sketches 1910–1914").

In the UDC Vernon Lee found a voice for ideals she had long cherished: a democratic Europe governed by an intellectual elite in which barriers to free trade would disappear and national borders would be drawn not by a single or a few powerful states but by the self-determination of the native population. Such ideals could not be realized by the belligerent powers. They could be effectuated only by neutral nations like Switzerland, Sweden, and Norway and, until 1917, the United States.

Vernon Lee could not speak authoritatively as an advocate for political neutrality, but she was uniquely qualified to survey the impact of the war on English and European intellectuals. That is precisely what the UDC invited her to do in March 1915. A long report she sent in response survives among her unpublished papers. Dated 17 April 1915, it is headed simply "Dear Sir," but the context makes it clear that she was addressing a Swede ("You mention the Nobel Committee of your country") and replying to a series of specific questions. Describing herself at the outset as isolated from the English intellectual community, one of the few who "have kept a European way of thinking in these months of natural war prejudice and artificially kept up war delusion," she disclaims authority but proceeds to write simply of her own necessarily limited experience. Of the state of literature in general she writes: "I have given up reading the Germanophobe literature of my former friend Mr. H. G. Wells and so many others, but I believe some of these Englishmen advocate an intellectual as well as a commercial boycott of Germany at the end of the war." She herself has been urged by an unnamed French publisher to sign a contract binding her "never at any future time" to have dealings with Baron Tauchnitz, whose firm had published several of her novels,[3] or with any other German or Austrian firm. She rejected the offer, she writes, "with a few words of contemnation of such particular methods."

To a question about English reaction to scientific and philosophical works by Germans, she replies: "I notice a tendency in the less accredited ones who have time for popular work, to run down German achievements and at best to publish lists showing that for every German achievement there is always a French or English parallel; parallels so vague as for instance between Freud's Theory of Dreams and that contained in the works of Bergson!" But she acknowledges that "at least in periodicals devoted to philosophy recent German books are being reviewed without any bias." She is more sanguine about the reception of German music in wartime England:

> Let me on the other hand call attention to the fact that no attempt seems to have been made to boycott German music in England. Bach's Christmas and Passion music has been performed as usual in many London churches and *Parsifal* was given as an oratorio in Passion Week. Beethoven, Haydn, Mozart, Wagner and Brahms are constantly being performed at all the great concerts. And I have recently had the pleasure of hearing one of the best-known singers give Brahms' magic love-Lieder with the *German* words. This

makes me think that the attempt to boycott or depreciate German intellectual products is merely part of an irresponsible and childish screaming of reciprocal abuse which has no more real importance than the accusations and expletives of fighting boys.

The remainder of her letter deals with her hopes for a just and honorable peace settlement. "If Europe is to regain her former moral and intellectual as well as material prosperity and progress, she will require, in order to repair this war's spiritual as well as material devastation, to unite as she never has united before in a work of scientific, philosophic, artistic and above all, *democratic* cohabitation." Primarily, a lasting peace depends upon free trade in intellectual as well as economic matters. "Any nation, or group of nations, which, after such universal destruction, shall attempt to surround itself by a spiritual or material custom-house system will merely fall a prey to its own despotic and dogmatic monopolists, and reduced to live bodily and mentally upon worse and worse and fewer and fewer commodities, will gradually drop out of its position among the actively competing and collaborating lands of progress."

She closes with an appeal to the Nobel committee to use its peace award in the cause of "intellectual pacification and cohabitation" by honoring a French writer whom she much admired—"the writer who, before the war, but when its bitterness was preparing, set the German Jean Christoph alongside of the Frenchman Olivier as his companion and complement, the writer since the war of *Au-dessus de la mêlée,* Monsieur Romain Rolland." Long an admirer of his multivolume novel *Jean-Christophe* (1910–13) for its romantic portrait of a musical genius, Vernon Lee was also deeply moved by the articles that Rolland published in the *Journal de Genève* protesting the war and affirming his staunchly pacifist convictions. Such views and the fact that he was living in Switzerland cost him dearly in France. He was widely accused of being pro-German, and, like Vernon Lee, he lost many friends. In November 1916, when the Swedish Academy named him winner of the Nobel Prize for Literature, the French threatened to boycott the award. Deeply embarrassed, Rolland offered to withdraw his name, but finally he accepted the prize "in the interests of the ideals for which he was fighting." He donated the prize money to the International Red Cross for the aid of all war victims, German and French alike. Vernon Lee, who was probably the first to propose his name, had the satisfaction of a small victory.[4]

Vernon Lee's commitment to pacifism brought her few other satisfactions. Her intransigence, her refusal to enlist in any cause that embraced religious or politically radical philosophies, isolated her even from those who shared her beliefs. She remained a loner, supporting many causes but always independent. It did, however, bring her closer to the struggle for women's rights. One month after war was declared, she wrote a strongly worded attack on the British government's participation. She addressed this as a letter to Rosika Schwimmer, the Hungarian-born feminist then living in neutral America. Schwimmer had joined with Jane Addams to establish the Women's Peace Party. Vernon Lee did not join the party but by allowing her letter to be published in the *New York Post* on 3 October 1914 she openly identified herself with their cause. But even as she joined in solidarity with many women who opposed the killing of young men of whatever nationality, she alienated herself from the English Women's Suffrage Movement, which supported the war effort, seeing in it an opportunity for women to prove themselves in the workforce.

Vernon Lee's pacifism allowed for no compromises. The cause of women was necessarily subordinated to what she saw as the cause of humanity. She agreed with her fellow members of the UDC that what must emerge from the war should be "an international system . . . founded upon the consent not merely of governments but of the peoples." These words are from the preface to *Towards a Lasting Peace* (1915), a collection of essays by UDC members and sympathizers. Her contribution, "The Democratic Principle and International Relations," was a relatively brief and (for her) straightforward statement of the importance of self-determination in any peace treaties that would emerge from the war. "To transfer a province is therefore as undemocratic as to sell a slave." She condemned equally German aggression on the Continent and British aggression in Ireland: "Self-determination will itself imply that the Democratic Principle must supersede—if you can call it a principle!—of which we see the crassest and most antiquated embodiment in the present attempt of each and every nation to establish security by violence and to vindicate liberty by brute compulsion, to obtain the economic and moral blessing of peace by means of the economic ruin and the moral devastation of war" (216).

When the war ended and the peace terms of the Treaty of Versailles were announced, Vernon Lee saw the fulfillment of her grimmest prophecies: a Europe redivided with artificial borders, a shattered German economy, an alarming rise of nationalism and militarism. Living in Italy in the 1920s, she was witness to the emergence of even more-threatening forces of militarism, colonialism, and repression of freedom. Her advanced age, her deteriorating health, and her loss of any kind of large-scale readership limited but did not altogether crush her engagement in politics and foreign affairs. In 1928 she wrote to G. Lowes Dickinson to congratulate him on his book *The International Anarchy, 1904–1914* (1926). Lowes Dickinson had been active in the League of Nations Union, but by the mid-1920s it was apparent to him and to many others that the organization was ineffectual in preventing military aggression. Irene Cooper Willis had told him that Vernon Lee was interested in promoting a series of books on "the psychological preparations for war in various countries" to which she would contribute a book on France. Visiting Florence in April 1929, he wrote her that he thought it an interesting project, but "it would be better for you, if you feel the impulse, to try as an independent book, what you have to say about France." He was plainly discouraging, even expressing a doubt that she could find a publisher for the subject (Sutherland 193–94).

One suspects that Lowes Dickinson's dismissal of Vernon Lee's idea stemmed in part from his memory of her "fantastic diatribes" of 1915. But beyond that lingering prejudice, he recognized correctly that she had nothing more to contribute to a cause—world peace—that was itself dying of attrition in 1929. Sadly enough, Vernon Lee was recognizing this herself. Nothing better exemplifies the frustration of her ideals than the total failure of her most ambitious wartime undertaking, the huge, unwieldy allegory *Satan the Waster*. In an unpublished sketch of about eight pages, *"Nosce teipsum,"* dated 6 May 1930, she wrote: "I have to recognise that the lack of recognition of *Satan* and my other philosophical books is depressing not really because (as I pretend to myself) they are wasted, but because I find myself left out in the cold. *To be useful* is only, I recognise, a mode of *being heard at the party,* feeling one's importance. Not really one's importance to others, but importance to one's self." For four years Vernon Lee had spoken out against the war as vigorously as she could, but hers was a small voice lost in the wilderness. Stronger voices than hers were drowned out in the years of actual battle. But once the Armistice was signed and the great powers had settled down to peace negotiations, she seized the opportunity to crystallize all her thinking of the past decade—her aesthetics, her studies in psychology, her knowledge of world history—in a single polemical work in the cause of a lasting world peace. The aim of this work was to demonstrate that such an ideal would never be achieved by the victors' dictating punitive peace terms to the vanquished but only by a transformation in the human psyche.

"The most common and the most abiding delusions of all are about something which we cherish (and rightly!) more than any lover, detest (also rightly!) more than any enemy: our good opinion or our bad opinion of our self" ("Notes to Prologue," *Satan* 145–46). To demonstrate this self-centeredness, Vernon Lee uses the metaphor of a ballet, a Dance of Death, choreographed by Death himself but produced and stage-managed by her spokesman Satan. The lengthy introduction, prologue, and notes that accompany the text (230 pages to only 110 pages of text) are a loosely connected

series of reflections (she calls them "little psychological essays") on the war
written at various times from 1915 to 1919—all building up to a single
"practical corollary":

> That, contrary to the views of our latter-day spiritual guides, we shall secure
> a tolerable existence (including tolerable to our moral nature) by seeking to
> understand what other things, processes and persons *are,* irrespective of our
> own desires about them. Instead of thinking quite so much about our aims,
> we should pay more attention to our *means,* which always include some-
> thing or somebody not ourself, and most often regarded as having no char-
> acteristics except those which may save or thwart our own purposes. ("Post-
> script to the Notes" 299–300)

A lasting peace, Vernon Lee argues, can be achieved only by considering the
needs and suffering of "the other." That other was the enemy during the
war, but in time of peace her belief in alterity becomes "a moral philosophy
[which] really pivots entirely upon a kind of altruism; in fact upon the importance of the *alter,* the other or otherness, to the *ego*" (300). Rather than
denying the centrality of the ego, she urges an extension of one's self into
the selves of others, an act of empathy similar to the experience of art in her
aesthetics.

Earlier on, Vernon Lee had explored the psychology of the aesthetic experience. In *Satan the Waster* she attempted to explore the psychology of
war as a basis for the cultivation of a psychology of peace. One could never
accuse her of modesty of ambition. But writing *Satan the Waster* was less an
act of hubris than simply an explosion of the emotions she had been forced
to suppress during the four long years of war. True, as she freely admits in
her introduction, she suffered no personal losses—no sons or brothers, not
even any close friend. But it was not in her character to stand *au-dessus de
la mêlée* as her much admired Romain Rolland had done. She felt herself
very close to the *mêlée,* sensitive to the suffering not only of English, French,
and Belgian women but of the Germans as well. As a self-designated psychologist, she writes of the psychology of those (on both sides) who supported the war: "the *modus operandi,* psychological far more than political,
whereby that very fact of spiritual participation in the war prevented those
who did participate from seeking the realities of the case; and in so far prevented their taking the steps toward peace which those unperceived realities
demanded" (xx).

Whether Vernon Lee could have made her case more strongly in a
straightforward study of the psychology of war is questionable. She had neither the training in psychology nor the disciplined prose that such a work
would have demanded. Her choice of the genre of allegory was, for its time,

appropriate, since it allowed for freedom of expression without the responsibility of factual documentation.

That was the rationale behind her brief (16 pages) *Ballet of the Nations: A Present-Day Morality*, published in 1915 by Chatto and Windus in a handsomely designed edition, profusely decorated with "a pictorial commentary" by Maxwell Armfield.[5] With a dedication to Romain Rolland—"fraternellement / V.L. / et in terra pax hominibus bonae voluntatis"—there was no mistaking the political and polemical intent of the essay. It is allegory because the characters are capitalized abstractions (Satan, Death, Heroism, Fear, Love, etc.); but with the introduction of such figures as Politicians, Armament Shareholders, and Trade Unionists, and the appearance of Madam Science ("a lady in the spectacles and smock most commonly seen in laboratories") and Councillor Organisation ("like a city clerk who should have joined the Red Cross"), the relevancy of the work to the ongoing war is obvious. And Vernon Lee makes that clear from the opening lines:

> For a quarter of a century, Death's celebrated Dances had gone rather out of fashion. Then, with the end of the proverbially *bourgeois* Victorian age, there set in a revival of taste, and therefore of this higher form of tragic art, combining, as it does, the truest classical tradition with the romantic attractions of the best Middle Ages. In South Africa and the Far East, and then in the Near East quite recently, the well-known Ballet Master Death had staged some of his vastest and most successful productions.

Satan, "the Lessee of the World" and "the World's immortal Impresario," oversees the production, giving the choreographer Death little to do. The Nations dance in pairs: each "repelling the aggression of its vis-à-vis, and at the same time defending its partner." As the dance becomes more rapid, the scene slowly changes from a peaceful August sunset over a fertile harvest to a devastated, burned-out "lurid chasm" with the weapons of war blazing all around. The Dancers, now bloody and mutilated, continue their savage dance while Satan exults: "I prefer the Ballet of the Nations to any of the other mystery-plays, like Earthquake and Pestilence, which Death puts on our stage from time to time. The music is not always very pretty, at once too archaic and too ultra-modern for philistine taste, and the steps are a trifle monotonous. But it gives immense scope for moral beauty, and revives religious feeling in all its genuine polytheism." Though exhausted, the Dancers continue, spurred on now by Revenge. "And thus the Ballet of the Nations is still a-dancing."

In 1915 there could be no other ending to the allegory. As Vernon Lee wrote four years later, "It was in its origin merely such an extemporized shadow-play as a throng of passionate thoughts may cast up into the lucid

spaces of one's mind" (introduction to *Satan* vii). The way was therefore
prepared for a long sequel-finale, which she supplied in *Satan the Waster* in
1919. Here *The Ballet of the Nations* is the center of a full play with a prologue that introduces as Satan's honored guest Clio, the Muse of History,
and an epilogue in which Satan purportedly interprets the whole drama for
the audience. The *Ballet* is fully staged with dialogue between Death and
Satan and commentary by the Muse of History. The cast is the same, but
the production is enhanced now with gramophone and Pianola accompa-
niment and a chorus singing the "Marseillaise" and "Wacht am Rhein" at
appropriate moments. Obviously, Vernon Lee had no expectations of ever
actually staging the ballet, but she adds "A Note for Stagemanagers (other
than Satan)" in which she orders "that no attempt be made at showing the
Dancing of the Nations, that nothing beyond the footlights, the Orchestra
and the auditorium shall be visible to the real spectators . . . [that] none of
the music must be audible, except the voice and drum of Heroism. Anything beyond this would necessarily be hideous, besides drowning or inter-
rupting the dialogue" (57).

   In the epilogue Vernon Lee virtually discards the devices of allegory and
introduces the actual issues of the war and its aftermath. Satan, more urbane
and self-assured than ever, now stages a series of debates by changing discs on
his gramophone and cinematograph, moving from the abstractions of the
ballet to the reality of the moment. "These are the real ones," he tells Clio,
"the Masters of Men's Destiny, even if not always of royal birth or Cabi-
net rank, sometimes mere humble specimens of the Investor, the Homo
Economicus, who sways the modern world" (64). They include journalists,
a German-hating Frenchman, generals and admirals intent on spending
money for armaments, diplomats blithely rearranging the borders of nations, manufacturers greedily expanding the number of colonies they ex-
ploit. More immediately, they are alarmed by the Bolshevik Revolution:
"The medicine for political assassination, and for all Socialistic and irreli-
gious unrest, your Majesty, is the ancient purge and tonic vouchsafed by
Heaven for a sickly world: War!" But Vernon Lee cannot leave her readers
with so terrible a message. The epilogue ends with a confrontation between
Satan and "his illegitimate offspring" Death, the Ballet Master. Silent until
now because he has been lying in a drunken stupor sprawled over the sleeping body of "the jolly blind boy" Heroism, Death rises to proclaim his victory: "*I* am the great reality." He calls on Heroism, who until now "never
doubted the power of your old crony Death," to help him to his feet. But
the blind youth Heroism suddenly opens his eyes and sees Death for the obscene horror that he is. And Satan has the last word, defying Death as "a preposterous, indecent anachronism" and suggesting that by chance "a brand

new set of manners" will emerge: "peaceful, fraternal, full of thought for the future" and that then "this will have been the last of our Ballets of the Nations" (110).

To the modern-day reader removed by nearly a century from the events of which Vernon Lee was writing, and toughened by decades of new revolutions, wars, and futile peacemaking, *Satan the Waster* is a pompous, bombastic exercise in futility. It displays her every fault—wordiness, shrillness, illogical thinking. Even the high-mindedness of her appeal for altruism, her idealistic vision of a democratic socialist society and world peace, is undermined by the demands she makes on her reader's patience and concentration. Yet one must admire the passion, conviction, and imagination she brought to the work.[6] Although she had behind her a variety of models of political allegory and polemical satire, she anticipated the revolutionary developments in the theatre of the 1920s like expressionism, the use of film and recorded music for dramatic effects, and the combination of dance and dialogue. And her conception of Satan, while by no means original, is witty and daring. He is part Miltonic, part Shavian, and a good deal Vernon Lee. "Why have I chosen Satan as my spokesman in a discussion of what is, or is not right?" She answers:

> Seeking in the bottom of my heart, I think the answer might be: Because I am sick of hearing this war discussed from the point of view of God, as if the writer, English, French, German, American, or what not, held a brief from on high to "justify the ways of God to man" or rather, to identify the ways of his own particular nation with the ways of God. I do not know who or what God is; but in these five years he has been called upon to back so many abominations and imbecilities, that it seems more decent not to take his name once more in vain, but rather speak of Evil in that of him who had the gentlemanly frankness to say to it, "Be thou my Good." ("Notes to Prologue" 115)

Like Shaw's Devil in the "Don Juan in Hell" episode of *Man and Superman*, Vernon Lee's Satan, though he is the waster of human virtue, is intelligent and genial. He is also an advocate of reason and common sense.

In 1919 *Satan the Waster* had its admirers as well as its detractors. Reviewers generally seemed bemused or exhausted by the overwhelming weight of her arguments. As a result, most of them avoided detailed discussion of the book and tended instead to pursue their special interests. The *Times Literary Supplement* (24 June 1920) gave the book pride of place on its first page. But the reviewer dismissed it with a few negative comments, arguing that the pacifist cause could have been stated "more naturally and easily by Vernon Lee speaking in person and without this transparent artifice of a philosophic war trilogy. . . . It is merely an expression of her opinions in a very artificial form . . . an unconvincing fable." The remainder of the article expands on the title of the review, "The Decay of Satire," arguing that—Alexander Pope, Samuel Butler, and Shaw notwithstanding—satire is not the appropriate medium for modern-day political argument. Desmond MacCarthy, writing under his pen name Affable Hawk, sprang to Vernon Lee's defense a few days later in the *New Statesman* (3 July 1920). He wrote that *Satan the Waster* "was crammed with psychological analysis of feeling and conviction" and was amply justified as good satire because "beyond delighting the mind, it destroys apathy." At least one American reviewer (*New Republic* 3 November 1920) noticed the Shavian spirit of the book but found it more serious and profound than Shaw's *Heartbreak House* with its "glib accessibility. . . . Vernon Lee has a large set of ideas, a tough adhesion to them, an agglutinative mind. Her book is a remarkable representation of them, and consequently not a parlor toy."

By far the most enthusiastic reviewer of *Satan the Waster* was Shaw himself. Writing in the *Nation* (18 September 1920), he offered a textbook example of political rhetoric with his hyperbolic praise: "This book is something more than the latest literary product of a well known author. It is a trophy of the war for England. It proves what everyone has lately been drawn to doubt, that it is possible to be born in England and yet have intellect." After the first two sentences, however, it becomes apparent that for Shaw *Satan the Waster* is a mere device, a weapon for battering the foreign policy of Lloyd George's administration. "The problem remains, how is it then possible for a nation to produce a woman like Vernon Lee, and at the same time choose Mr. Lloyd George and Sir Edward Carson as its dictators?" The remainder of the article, while no doubt gratifying to Vernon Lee, is at best secondhand praise, for Shaw's target is the conservative foreign policy of the prime minister Lloyd George, supporting the Russian monarchy and sending British troops to crush the socialist revolution that had broken out in Russia in 1917. Shaw sums up the futility of that cause as simple "British boodle and British bunkum" and uses Vernon Lee as a model of all the virtues that, in his opinion, Lloyd George lacks:

> You cannot read a page of "Satan the Waster" without feeling like that about the Prime Minister. Vernon Lee has the whole European situation in the hollow of her hand; Mr. Lloyd George cannot co-ordinate its most obviously related factors. Vernon Lee knows history philosophically; Mr. Lloyd George barely knows geography topographically. Vernon Lee is a political psychologist; Mr. Lloyd George is a claptrap expert. Vernon Lee, as her dated notes to this book prove, has never been wrong since the war began;

Mr. Lloyd George has never been right. . . . Vernon Lee, by sheer intellectual force, training, knowledge, and character, kept her head when Europe was a mere lunatic asylum; Mr. Lloyd George hustled through only because, in matters of wide scope, he has no head to lose. And remember, Vernon Lee is an English woman. Had she been Irish, like me, there would have been nothing in her dispassionateness. . . . But Vernon Lee is English of the English, and yet held her intellectual own all through. I take off my hat to the old guard of Victorian cosmopolitan intellectualism, and salute her as the noblest Briton of them all.

Although they shared pacifist sympathies, Vernon Lee and Bernard Shaw were only casual acquaintances. They had first met in 1893, introduced by a friend of the Robinsons, and in a letter to her mother (3 July) she summed up her first impression of him as "a young socialist who, despite (I think) his socialism, is one of the really most brilliant writers and thinkers we have, paradoxical, wrongheaded and perhaps a little caddish, but original. He has written a little book on Ibsen, round whom a little group of young thinkers are doing some say subversive but very useful thinking, getting rid of much cant, pharisaism, false morality, which has remained from more theological times, thinkers entirely exaggerated, but in a necessary direction." Their paths may have crossed many times, but she steered clear of the Fabians, and Shaw had little interest in her more esoteric pursuits in aesthetics and psychology. Generally she regarded him as a lightweight—"enchanting and infuriating," as she judged him in a review of his *Back to Methuselah* in the *New Statesman* (24 September 1921). Of his glib treatment of vitalism—a philosophy she had dismissed in her critique of Henri Bergson in *Vital Lies*—she wrote: "O great Arch-Priest and Prophet, enchanting Sarastro-Papageno G. B. S. . . . that Creative-Evolutionist Demiurgus, consubstantial with and formed in the image of his exasperating and delightful self."

In the realpolitik of the 1920s *Satan the Waster* was at best well meaning but old-fashioned and irrelevant. Vernon Lee had indeed become what Shaw saluted a decade earlier—one of "the old guard of Victorian cosmopolitan intellectualism." Nothing confirms this better than a glance at her publication record after 1920. Her periodical articles—book reviews, travel and personal essays—shrank from an average of six to ten a year in the 1880s and '90s to a total of ten for the decade 1920–30. Of her books, not counting reprints and foreign editions, she published thirty-four titles between 1880 and 1920 and only six from 1923 to her last, *Music and Its Lovers,* in 1932. Yet in spite of advancing age and poor health, she wrote almost continuously until shortly before her death. Her complaint to her brother in

1893 that "at thirty-seven I have no public" was simply an observation that she was not a popular writer, but at that time she did command a small and loyal readership. Many of that generation died out with World War I, however, and to the younger generation, well represented by Virginia Woolf and her Bloomsbury contemporaries, she was the garrulous old woman Max Beerbohm had caricatured in his copy of *Gospels of Anarchy*.

Partly because she did not have the urgent financial needs of most professional writers, Vernon Lee never established a close relationship with any of her publishers. From her girlhood, eager though she always was to have an audience, she assumed an independence that could not have endeared her to editors. She was proud to have the firm of William Blackwood publish *Miss Brown* but balked at their editorial suggestions and insisted upon her own terms for content and style. Unlike many of her contemporaries she did not work with literary agents but preferred to handle all business matters directly with her publishers. "I greatly object to the hawking round literature to agents, syndicates, and similar arrangements," she wrote T. Fisher Unwin (18 December 1901).[7] She often complained both to her mother and to her publishers about insufficient fees, but one has the feeling that she was motivated more by pride than by financial need. In fact, considering that she was a published writer from her early twenties, she and her two most loyal publishers, T. Fisher Unwin and John Lane, realized very little profit from her work. But they carried her on their lists because she was a prestige writer, and though she often complained and at least once threatened to terminate relations with Unwin, she had no better offers. When the publisher Grant Richards faced bankruptcy, she waived all royalties and the American rights to a reprint of *Pope Jacynth and Other Fantastic Tales* so that he might publish it at a lower price (8 June 1906). On 25 October 1902, with some of her most important work yet to come, she complained to Kit Anstruther-Thomson: "I am rather depressed about my writings. Unwin behaved disgracefully, after keeping *Ariadne* a year nearly, he sprang absurd conditions on me, which I couldn't accept as they meant I should bear the main expenses. He evidently wanted to get rid of me, and succeeded. Mr. Blackwood has refused the book, and I can't place *Penelope Brandling* [which Unwin did publish in 1903], though it is far and away my best work, bar *Ariadne*."

Four years later Vernon Lee recalled in a letter to Maurice Baring that the always candid Augustine Bulteau "used to say that I lacked one of the essentials of a writer, "l'intuition du lecteur à l'autre bout"—a judgment with which any of her readers would likely agree. And she agreed herself: "It is certain that I can never imagine what I write being read, still less by anyone in particular. (I know my writings tend more and more towards the soliloquy.) It gives, perhaps, a certain freedom and decency, but sometimes, not often, it makes one feel a bit lonely, as if one were the vox clamans, not in the desert, but inside a cupboard" (25 January 1906). Vernon Lee did not discourage easily. But what she somewhat ruefully lamented in 1906 became a painful reality in the postwar years.

*As people grow more intelligent, or more people grow intelligent at all, we shall
discover other opportunities for exercising intellectual energy and for obtaining
the thrill and uplift of intellectual prowess. There will appear other adversaries to
wrestle and circumvent:* Things, Reasons why, *the Universe's riddles. The finest
sport in the world is Hunting Proteus.*

Vernon Lee, *Proteus; or, The Future of Intelligence*

AMONG VERNON LEE'S UNPUBLISHED PAPERS AT COLBY COL-
lege is a collection of notes written between 1931 and 1934 to which she gave
the title "Lore of the Ego." They are a series of reflections on the past, on
aging, a kind of summing up of her readings in psychology and philosophy.
What is most striking about them is their quality of forward rather than
backward looking. By this period of her life she had lost many of her oldest
friends; she was witnessing the emerging of militarism and Fascism in the
country she most loved and threats to peace everywhere; her health was failing and her hearing gone. But her main regret was her inability to keep pace
with time. "Je suis venue trop tôt dans un monde trop jeune," she wrote
(8 August 1932). Unlike the aged scholar Faust, she regretted not the years
she had already spent but "the years ahead that will not be mine to spend."

Reviewers and the reading public alike had relegated her to the Victorian age, which by the 1920s and '30s carried the stigma of obsolescence and
irrelevance. The fact that she enjoyed some success in that period gave her
little satisfaction:

Not in all sincerity merely that those fifty years of coming too soon have deprived me of whatever influence or utility my special gifts might, should,
have had, although I am now convinced that this is the case and that my intellectual maturity has come too late. But also, and more perhaps, because
my mind's maturity has come when I am losing all powers of work, and owing to deafness, all possibility of personal contact with the generation of

which I ought to have belonged; Pisgah-sights into the land wherein I might have flourished.

When Roger Fry praised her last major work *Music and Its Lovers* in 1933, she wrote gratefully to him, "You are quite right that I haven't had the recognition from my equals (or betters!) which I should have liked when I was young, some forty or fifty years ago. But what your letter does make up for is the incurable disappointment (even at seventy-six!) of finding my work on aesthetics utterly wasted." Her complaint was that aesthetics has been subordinated to psychology. "For this side of psychology has escaped psychologists and, thanks to Freud, is escaping them more and more." The modern world, she recognized, belonged to the specialists. "There is a living to be made out of Berensonian connoirseurship and there are professors of archaeology. But nothing comes of aesthetics as carried on by my late friend Miss Anstruther-Thomson and myself." Her sorry conclusion was that "my books have been those of an amateur and jack of all trades" (31 January 1933).

A gloomy assessment indeed; but it was one against which Vernon Lee struggled to fortify herself. Years earlier she had resolved to resist the pressures of her childhood—the smothering presence of her eccentric family, the neurasthenia that had crippled her brother emotionally as well as physically, her hunger for the love and attention that her unattractive appearance and abrasive personality denied her. Although admirers of Vernon Lee's writing often deplored her preoccupation with psychology, her pursuit of mental health was to her an absolute necessity. With the emergence of Freudian psychoanalysis in the early twentieth century, she was all the more convinced of the necessity of exploring the roots of her own psyche. She read extensively in psychological theory, no longer as a foundation for the study of aesthetics but for an understanding of what she called her "inner categorical imperatives." Generally she found no satisfaction in her readings. Sigmund Freud she dismissed as her "bête noir" while conceding of the Freudians that "their insistence on hidden springs of our thought and action is to my mind their great gift to psychology." But Freudians failed to recognize the complex and mysterious nature of the human psyche, "these imperious, violent and subtle forces of the soul, protean, lacking all definite name and all consistent aspect, hidden by and to ourselves." These "obscure psychological phenomena," she wrote, "have their explanation in something more primordial than sex." She rejected the Freudian conception of the Ego, that part of the Id that functions in human consciousness, for her own conception of the Ego, "the feeling of Self. . . . Our Self is to each man and woman the inevitable, because the only directly felt, centre of his or her Universe" ("Notes to Prologue," *Satan* 146).

The psychologist whom she found more sympathetic to her own views was Alfred Adler, Freud's onetime associate who broke with him on the same grounds that had alienated her—the emphasis on human sexuality as the driving force of the psyche. In Adler she found confirmation of her own views on self-consciousness. "If we believe that the foundation, the ultimate basis of everything has been found in character traits, drives or reflexes, the self is likely to be overlooked," Adler wrote in *Der Sinn des Lebens* (1933). "The very first requisite for a science of psychology is missing from psychoanalysis, namely, a recognition of the coherence of the personality and of the unity of the individual in all his expression" (*Individual Psychology* 175).

With the acknowledgment of the preeminence of the self comes the recognition of the struggle for self-realization, which determines the course of mental health. The healthy mind respects itself and transcends its feelings of inferiority. Struggling against depression in the last years of her life, Vernon Lee found some comfort in the fact that Adler's scientific research supported her conception of the self. "What I, at all events, owe to Psychoanalysis and quite especially to Adler. Recognition or suspicion that a large portion of our beliefs originate in our feeling of and about ourselves, but being obscure and *not in front* (not in relation to the Eye!). This origin is not suspected and the credit [is] given to outer experience, as when we assign *reasons,* which means adjustment to such outer circumstances." Intellectuals in particular are quick to assign reasons; she cites Nietzsche, D. H. Lawrence, "even H. G. Wells," who assumes "a warrant of knowledge or a power to recreate or conquer which he has not really got except in the realm of words." They rationalize and confidently assert absurdities: she gives the example of men's claim to mastery over women because of their "monthly weakness," which relegates them to "harem submission." She has learned from Adler that this kind of rationalization in men creates an illusion of self-importance. Genuine self-esteem, however, on which mental health is based, depends on the recognition that "we have been of no service to the world. But be able to say that one has not wasted over-much (or at least tried) of whatever the world offered for one's own happiness, let alone that of one's neighbour. No easy job!" (*"Nosce teipsum"* 6 May 1930).

She speculates on how the Ego works in life as in literature. King Lear assumes, after Goneril rejects him, that Regan "*must* be ready to take his part" —an example of the human tendency to take things for granted. "Hence, naturally, its tendency to intolerance, its tendency to suppress competition whether in matters of ambition, in love, in economic relations. The Ego is monotheistic par excellence, a jealous priest, a jealous God!" ("Lore of the Ego" 1 July 1933). It is as though she is clearing away all the delusions and misconceptions of the Ego—the importance of success, fame, popularity

—in the interests of a transcendent self. On 14 October 1933 she writes: "On my 76th [77th?] birthday I may boast to myself that I feel superior to these people just because what interests me is the *thing*, not my share in it. I do not mind whether I was plagiarising Adler or whether I already wrote in his sense before reading him. I am satisfied with the thought whosoever it be" ("Lore of the Ego").

Adler can hardly be credited with illuminating Vernon Lee's later years, but he confirmed a humanism, more precisely a humanitarianism, that gave her what others find in religion—a sustaining faith in the future of humankind. "In the great and small religious movements; in the great achievements of philosophy, science, art, and political wisdom, as in the individual men and women who strive to penetrate to the truth . . . there is expressed the most exalted ideal purpose: 'Love thy neighbor.' One guiding thought embraces and unites them all, the desire to create their worth and find their sense of importance in their contributions to the welfare of others" (Adler 449).[1] Altruistic and idealistic, that faith opened her mind to the realities of modern life, converting an aesthetic-Puritan-Victorian into a freethinking modernist, ready to accept and even to embrace radical social change. She rejected her Victorian heritage happily, with hardly a trace of the nostalgia of most of her generation.

For example, she challenged Henry James, who, shortly before his death in 1915, had expressed his unease with the "new" England of the twentieth century. In his posthumously published memoir *The Middle Years,* she noted the following passage, in which he contrasted his impressions of the London of his first visit in 1869 with the London of the early twentieth century: "The mid-Victorian London was sincere—that was a vast virtue and a vast appeal; the contemporary is sceptical, and, most so when most plausible, the turn of the tide could verily be fixed to an hour—the hour at which the new plausibility began to exceed the old sincerities by so much as a single sign. They could truly have been arrayed face to face, I think, for an attentive eye" (25). By "sincere" James apparently meant that Victorian London was idiosyncratic and unique: "She sat thus imperturbable in her felicities, and if that is how, remounting the stream of time, I like most to think of her, this is because if her interest is still undeniable—as that of overgrown things goes—it has not yet lost its fineness of quality" (25). James's reflection is nostalgic. For Vernon Lee, writing in 1927, his London never existed but was "a vague amalgam of his own imaginative and sentimental reactions to visible objects as much as human peculiarities." She finds equally vague his use of "sincerity" in contrast to what he called the "sceptical" and "plausible" spirit of contemporary times, but she infers that by "sincere" James meant complacent and accepting. "In this sense," she writes, "it is, I think, correct to ascribe greater *sincerity* to the people of H. J.'s and my own youth. But this *sincerity* meant, I won't say *refusal to question,* rather an inhibition, a paralysis of all questioning before a good number of subjects about which the mind acted in an invariable and automatic way . . . absolute unquestioning acquiescence . . . such *sincerity* was concerned with morals, largely of sex, of parental relations, and of proprietorship." The Ten Commandments remained, even to religious skeptics like George Eliot, "engraved" in the mind "because of the sharp impact of the divine chisel on those tablets of stone." The sincerity of these Victorians ("and most Georgians")—a group in which she significantly includes "myself til over forty"—"was to a large extent refusal or inability to see, at least to look" ("Prophets and the War," unpublished notes, 1927).

Born too early, Vernon Lee ruefully but not despairingly looked to the future, too late for her to make any significant contribution but never too late to welcome it. That is the surprisingly optimistic tone of her short book *Proteus; or, The Future of Intelligence* in 1925. The mythic god of change, like her earlier *genius loci,* informs her imagination and becomes a metaphor for exploring not a specific place this time but the country of the mind. *Proteus* was published in the Today and Tomorrow Series by Kegan Paul in England and E. P. Dutton in the United States. Books in this series were small volumes on weighty subjects like science, technology, philosophy, sexual mores, and women's causes. Other contributors included J. B. S. Haldane, Gerald Heard, Bertrand Russell, and Rebecca West, suggesting that Vernon Lee, in spite of her own sense of neglect and obsolescence, still had a significant voice in the intellectual discourse of the 1920s.

In the course of the sixty-three pages of *Proteus* she summarizes and discusses the ontology of the past—the old "certainties" of religion and social morality. "The Future of Intelligence," her subtitle, is not the mastery of knowledge but accommodation with change: "one great change which Intelligence is already initiating, namely the recognition and avowal that what one thinks (as distinguished from what primers, manuals and other authorities have taught one to believe) is, well, *just what one does think,* and neither the consensus of human opinion nor the revelation of the Deity's irrefragable truth" (3). Intelligence is the medium by which we recognize and embrace our ever changing reality. "Proteus, in my mythology, is the mysterious whole which we know must exist, but know not how to descry: Reality. For, whatever else we may believe it to be, Reality when thus partially revealed is never twice the same" (6). Intelligence can grasp single aspects of reality (in science, for example), but reality itself is protean: "mere Intelligence, with its rule-of-thumb logic and well nigh automatic movements, may be fairly fitted, not indeed to inventory and schedule separate items of Proteus' multifold embodiments, but to keep us aware that Proteus is there at that eternal game of his: changing his aspects perpetually, whether you watch him or not, nay, changing aspect by the very fact of your watching him" (9).

These are whimsical notions perhaps, displaying Vernon Lee's characteristic ambiguities of language and her delight in paradox and wordplay (e.g., "So one might say that Intelligence is a kind of Common sense, but applied to uncommon [not common or garden!] subjects, and as yet, alas, only by rather uncommon people" [12]). As in all her writing, and much of her conversation apparently, Vernon Lee was improvising, spinning out ideas that are often more interesting for what they reveal about her idiosyncratic thinking than for whatever they purport to mean. In *Proteus* she was exorcising her Victorian past: "Modes of thought . . . seem to be (slowly!) disappearing in the wake of the anecdote-mongering and epigram-and-joke button-holing of ancient bores who may have been brilliant conversationalists at Meredithian dinner-tables" (15). It is the function of Intelligence, she argues, to come to terms with Change: "Not to praise or blame it after mature deliberation . . . but just to perceive change on its passage and in so far help us to make the best of its coming" (20). And the most profound change in the modern world is the "jettisoning" (her word) of our religious and moral dogmas.

> Whether we notice it or not, Morality is already taking a new status, independent alike of an absentee (or absent) Deity, and of an indifferent Cosmos. But its new domain, narrow and self-governing, essentially *sui-generis,* has sanctions and imperatives only the stronger for being man-made and man-regarding. And, one may add, only the more austerely binding on the present that we shall recognize them as different from those of the Past and different, no doubt, from those into which the Future will transform them. (28)

In terms of practical social action, Vernon Lee foresees a tolerant and open society with a "revaluation of sexual morals": "Indissoluble marriage, which already strikes some of us as scarcely decent, will lose its practical utility once inheritance is more or less abolished, and the subsistence and education of children no longer a charge on parents" (32). She does not foresee utopias, nor does she cite "role models" in any existing society. But she looks optimistically to "Intelligence's own natural proliferation. One intelligent mode of thought inevitably leads to another and puts out of action an unintelligent one" (52). Writing on the eve of the economic and political crises that were to plunge Europe into Fascism, Nazism, and Stalinism, Vernon

Lee appears to be self-deluding, but in fact she acknowledges the threat of "the far-too-little Intelligence already at our disposal":

> There is Peril from black, brown, yellow races; from Semites, Mongols, Latins (in "Nordic" countries), Teutons (in Latin countries), Celts all over Anglo-Saxondom, Jews throughout the globe; Bolsheviks, Fascists and Junkers, International Communism and International Finance, Militarism which was put an end to by the War, besides our old friends Jesuits and Free Masons. There is Peril from the multiplication of Idiots and the multiplication of Supermen; Peril from depopulation and Peril from overpopulation, from unsexed women and over-sexed women; Peril from over-much altruism, and Peril from insufficient altruism. (58–59)

At best she can conclude only with the hope that an open future allows always for the prospect of hope: "And Intelligence itself must prepare us to expect that every change may mean a loss, but likewise an opportunity. Perhaps it may even sometimes show us how the one can turn into the other; for does not Intelligence keep an eye on Proteus?" (63).

Deprived, by the 1920s, of an effective public voice and any prospect of effective social action, she confined her views thereafter to private musings in letters to close friends, fragmentary notes and essays that she was never able to publish, and notes in the margins of the books that she continued to read hungrily on science, politics, and world affairs. She read Proust,[2] Joyce, and D. H. Lawrence, and reread Dante, Shakespeare, and Goethe. She concentrated heavily on anthropology, biology, and psychology, reading J. B. S. Haldane, Jane Harrison, and Julian Huxley. She read Spengler's *The Decline of the West,* H. L. Brose's *The Theory of Relativity,* G. D. H. and Margaret Cole on socialism, and Julian Benda on the failure of the modern intellectual to preserve the values of the life of the mind. Although impatient with the abstractness of modern philosophy ("Perhaps my dislike for Philosophy arises partly from my having had less than other folk of such theological and ritual habits whence impatience at not being, so to speak, left fair and square with a universe which I want to understand only insofar as it concerns me" ["Lore of the Ego" 27 January 1934]), she read Santayana and Bertrand Russell.

She traveled as much as her health permitted, though now mainly to revisit familiar places. Until the early 1930s she managed annual visits to England and France, mainly to see old friends like Ethel Smyth, Bella Duffy, Emily Ford, Emily Sargent, and Mary (Robinson) Duclaux. She also traveled within Italy to visit longtime Italian friends—Baroness Elena French Cini, Countess Maria Gamba, Count and Countess Pasolini.[3] Thanks to the good offices of Mary Berenson, she was reconciled with Bernard Berenson in 1920. More unusual for a woman in her seventies, she made new friends among the younger generation of writers—Aldous Huxley, Desmond Mac-Carthy, and Mario Praz. In practical terms she helped needy German students by donating her royalties from her German publisher Tauchnitz for scholarships, and she introduced Praz to the editors of English periodicals, thereby launching his literary career. If in her old age Vernon Lee failed to achieve Apollonian serenity and perfection, she successfully practiced what she had urged the readers of *Proteus*—"to perceive change on its passage [and] . . . make the best of its coming."

The Italy to which Vernon Lee returned in 1920 no longer basked in the golden glow of its past but was in the throes of postwar economic disaster, torn by political divisions and drifting into Fascist totalitarianism. For her, the country had succumbed to the parasitism and decadence she had foreseen in the 1870s. On the eve of World War I she had written a travel essay, "The Dockyard of Viareggio," that anticipated Italy's fate. Visiting the Riviera di Levante on the west coast, she had been struck by the contrast between the quiet fishing town of Viareggio and its much touristed neighbor Portofino. Viareggio was busy with the unloading of cargoes of fish and wine much as its ancient Greek settlers and Sicilian traders had done. But Portofino was crowded with tourists, its populace hawking postcards, cheap lace, and ugly souvenirs: "The Italy of beggars and backshish and Grand Hotels and Antiquaries' shops is, for the more sensitive among us, a tawdry theatrical concern" (*Tower of the Mirrors* 171). This was an omen of the vanishing of the old Italy she loved.

Why then did she choose to live out her years in Italy? Partly it was the Protean impulse. The intelligent mind welcomed growth and accepted change as inevitable. The beggars, baksheesh, and grand hotels would in their turn change, for better or worse she could not say. But Intelligence is the power "to make the best of its coming." More realistically, however, Vernon Lee returned to live and die in Italy because it was her home. Her five years in London lodgings, she confided to Mario Praz in 1925, "with the war as the chief background, and black fog even on the brightest days . . . left me with far keener relish for the beauty and peacefulness of my present surroundings" (*House of Life* 243). She had planted her roots in Tuscany in 1906 when she bought Il Palmerino, the house in which her family had lived since 1889. It remained her home, except for the years of exile in England during the war, until her death. Mrs. Paget's estate, divided between Eugene and Violet, was not magnificent, but it was enough to enable both of them to live comfortably, independent of each other. Proudly heading a letter to Kit Anstruther-Thomson "Palmerino: This picturesque country seat, the property of the eminent writer on aesthetics. V.L." she explained:

I have bought it for fear of having to buy it at a higher price when my lease was near expiration, as the man refused to prolong it, and land round Florence is going for fancy prices. I have got enough to secure the water supply and the views back and front, the long grass walks, and enough ground to raise, competent persons tell me, all the fodder and vegetables I want for 2000 including expenses. This outlay cripples me a little for the first year, as I am letting the peasant end his time instead of trying to break his contract for the peace of mind this certainly represents, and I am fond of this corner of the world and this ramshackle old house, where so much of my eventless life is clinging. (11 February 1906)

There were several small buildings on the grounds where the farmers lived. Her household staff was usually three, a couple who cooked and did the domestic chores and a man who worked on the grounds and drove the carriage, later the motorcar. The circumstances sound more luxurious than they actually were. As the many British expatriates who settled in and around Florence could have testified, a genteel life was cheaper in Italy than almost anywhere else in Europe. Nevertheless Il Palmerino proved a financial burden from the outset, and she happily accepted an offer from Irene Forbes Morse to rent and renovate one of the peasant cottages as a holiday retreat. Mrs. Forbes Morse spent little time there, however, and returned to Germany during the war years. By 1920 Vernon Lee realized that the family house was too large for her, and after some litigation she bought up her tenant's lease, rented out the larger house, and lived in the small but comfortable cottage. There was still ample room for guests, and she entertained a steady stream of visitors. Mario Praz remembered her as "an elderly lady, in a faultless grey tailor-made dress, a gleaming white piqué cravat fixed with a cameo brooch," and the house as a little ivory tower ("una torre d'avorio") (*House of Life* 227). There was a carefully tended garden, a fine view of the surrounding hills, and she had no close neighbors to disturb the peaceful scene.

Vernon Lee may have lived in an ivory tower at Il Palmerino, but she kept herself fully informed of the ominous political developments in Europe. Other English liberals—notably H. G. Wells and George Bernard Shaw—who had shared her dreams of an enlightened socialism, enthusiastically embraced the emergence of a communist USSR. Although she had earlier expressed distinct anti-czarist sentiments in her *Westminster Gazette* articles and in 1919 opposed British and American intervention to block the Bolshevik Revolution, she was implacably opposed to Leninist communism. The grounds for her opposition were not her objection to Marxist economic theory but to authoritarianism of any kind. In her unpublished notes of

1927, to which she gave the title "Prophets and the War," she wrote five pages of denunciation of communism and totalitarianism occasioned by her reading of René Fülöp-Miller's *The Mind and Face of Bolshevism* (1927). There she read that Lenin had repudiated "all morality which proceeds from supernatural ideas or ideas which are outside of class consciousness" and advanced the thesis that "Communist morality is identical with the fight for the strengthening of the dictatorship of the proletariat." To this she added: "*V. L. Loquitor*. After all this is the ethic of all war, and I wonder whether the acceptance of Bolshevism and Fascism could have come except to a people recently disciplined by War?" She read in Fülöp-Miller that Mikhail Bakunin, the nineteenth-century Russian anarchist, had once in the course of his stormy career embraced Jesuitism. "Similarly, was not Jesuitism the growth of Spain's century-long crusade against infidels? . . . Jesuitism is *war;* it has the rule of self-preservation at no matter what cost so long as self-preservation is collective and authoritarian, self-preservation of one's aims."

Two books in her personal library (now in the British Library in Florence) have notes and marginalia that reflect her thinking on totalitarianism in the last years of her life. One is the Coles' *The Intelligent Man's Review of Europe To-day* (1933). On the half-title page she carefully dated her reading "Oxford. Sept, xxxiii / finished reading Dec. 12, xxxiii." She scribbled penciled comments on a number of pages, including simply the name "Hitler" next to a passage on the political unrest in Germany. In a blank space on the last page of the book, she summed up her reaction: "Amen! Nevertheless I should be better able to believe in Socialism if it were not displayed as a panacea, if I were told of its special crop of drawbacks, for change must bring new drawbacks as [well?] as new advantages." A year and a half later she was reading *Towards the Understanding of Karl Marx* ("finished reading June 8, 1934") by Sidney Hook, later a highly vocal critic of Marxism but at this time sympathetic. The text is heavily underscored and the margins are sprinkled with exclamation marks wherever Hook expresses praise for Marx's "incorruptible revolutionary integrity." Where Hook writes about "the revolutionary dictatorship of the proletariat" (124), she scribbled, "But it isn't the proletariat; it's the leaders who dictate." There is a large question mark in the margin where Hook refers to Marx's "heroic struggles" (268), and the initials OGPU (Soviet secret police) appear opposite several passages discussing the proletariat's need to crush all counterrevolutionary movements in the interests of self-defense. Clearly Vernon Lee's voice had been stilled, but her passions continued to run deep.

She witnessed with dismay the fall of Italy to Mussolini's Fascist dictatorship in 1922, a development that, as with Russia, she attributed to the baleful consequences of World War I. Her silence on Fascism, however, is not difficult to understand. She was old and had lost whatever reading public she might have addressed years before. Repressive as Mussolini's rule was, it was tolerated by the English and Americans who lived in Italy, most of whom simply ignored politics. Jews were not persecuted in the years before Italy's alliance with Nazi Germany. Bernard Berenson, for example, gave no serious thought to leaving until war broke out, and he managed to survive, though he left I Tatti to go into hiding. Mussolini's imperialist ambitions were hollow threats until his invasion of Ethiopia in October 1935, by which time Vernon Lee was dead. There is no doubting her unhappiness with her adopted country's policies, but like her fellow expatriates, she tolerated what she was powerless to change.[4]

Although Vernon Lee complained that she had been born too early to be the freethinking twentieth-century woman she yearned to be, she was fortunate in dying just on the eve of greater horror than she had imagined in *Satan the Waster*. She was less fortunate in her longevity, suffering physical decline and the loss of many of her close friends. Though long estranged as companions, she and Kit Anstruther-Thomson remained friends. In the war years they both supported the peace movement. Their last collaboration, Vernon Lee recalled, "perhaps the consummation of our original perfect understanding in all the fundamental matters of life, was when somewhere in 1915 or 1916 Kit took the chair at a humble UDC meeting in Chelsea, where I read the symbolical fantasia which afterwards grew into my *Satan the Waster*." Kit died on 8 July 1921. During her last illness Vernon Lee came from Italy to visit her three times. "She was still extremely beautiful and looked extraordinarily young. . . . But of the things we both had in our hearts, we neither spoke a word. It was all serene and beautiful, but with the beauty and serenity of art" (*Art and Man* 62–63). Her memoir of Kit in the introduction to *Art and Man*, written in 1924, is a tribute to her dedication to their work but also a candid estimate of her limited achievement: "And, alas! why at the end there remains nothing to show what she could do except the essay in which we collaborated twenty-five years and more ago, and now these fragments which I am publishing" (6). In the end, Kit's loss was perhaps not so keenly felt as the death of Bella Duffy, a long-time Florence resident and a friend since at least 1880, to whom she dedicated *Proteus*, "with thanks for a lifetime of intelligent talk." On learning that Bella was dying, she wrote her: "Perhaps your doctor has made a mistake. Anyhow, whether you go before or after me, your words of loving farewell made (and will make) all the difference in what remains of my life. . . . If I survive you I shall do so in almost utter intellectual solitude" (3 February 1926).

"Intellectual solitude" was not her fate, although in contrast to her busy social and intellectual life in earlier years, her last decade was melancholy.

Her long struggle for mental health had its rewards because it gave her a sustaining balance and fortitude. In 1933 she wrote to Maurice Baring complaining of her deafness and ill health: "I was staying with Miss Sargent at the end of last July, but only for a week, and I didn't even ask whether you were in the neighborhood, for the mischief is that I am now almost stone deaf and that trying to hear (through the increasing noises) is what reduces me to a rag." But in the next sentence the complaints cease or at least are balanced with good cheer:

> All this, dear Maurice, although literally true, *reads* much worse than it actually is, and you mustn't be overly compassionate. I have written far too much, sickeningly too much, and (as I recognise) to little purpose. And am quite satisfied with copying out old notes (of which inconceivably many unpublished) merely for the pleasure of re-living so many delightful days. . . . And as I have always been solitary, deafness is really (except for music) as little of a loss as conceivable, for my eyes are excellent both for reading (with excitement) and for looking about me (with rapture sometimes) so that I regard myself as quite happily shelved at 75, which I am. And my few remaining friends have the tradition of my being "stimulating" even when I am dropping with weariness. (5 April 1933) [5]

The remaining friends were understandably fewer as the years passed, but there was continuity in most of those relationships. One exception was Carlo Placci. Their friendship had begun in the early 1880s when he was a frequent visitor to the Casa Paget in Florence, a friend of Eugene's, and though only five years her junior, he looked to Vernon Lee as a mentor for his own literary ambitions. She wrote favorable reviews of his books in *Fanfulla della domenica,* but like most of his friends she regarded him as a charming dilettante, too rich and too volatile in temperament to settle down to serious writing. In 1887 she dedicated *Juvenilia* to him, addressing him as a very junior colleague. Nevertheless, in the remarkable letter of 9 August 1894 (see chap. 1, p. 2) she had confided to him her anxieties about the mental health of her family. It was at the Casa Paget that Placci first met Berenson, the beginning of a long and stormy friendship. They quarreled frequently but were reconciled just as frequently.[6]

Ironically, it was Placci's tacit support of Berenson's plagiarism charges against Kit Anstruther-Thomson that caused a long-lasting rift in his friendship with Vernon Lee. She could never forgive his failure to defend his old friends, although neither could she hold a permanent grudge against him. When Eugene died in 1907, Placci published an obituary tribute to him in *Il Marzocco* that moved her to write to him after a long silence: "It was very nice, and would have given the poor fellow so much pleasure. This is another of the great debts I owe to your kindness and friendship, to add to the collection which I cherish as something precious in my life, of all these many years ago" (Pantazzi, "Carlo Placci" 113). Placci evidently took this as an invitation to renew their old intimacy, but in a long letter she addressed him on New Year's Day 1908 she made it clear that the old wounds had not healed:

My dear Carlo

I have let a few days pass without answering your letter because I wanted to make sure of my feelings and ideas. On first reading your letter my impulse was to answer at once "Come"; and my new year's eve was quite radiant not merely with the sense of good will in the past but with a very delightful hopefulness for the future. But on re-reading your letter I understood all that your hesitation implies and thinking it over has added a graver hesitation on my side.

It is not because of the doubt, which you express of our *no longer speaking the same language*. At any age, dear Carlo, one knows that no two creatures ever do really speak the same language, but one knows also that when people suit and trust one another they get on just the same as if they did. As to opinions, you may have changed yours and I intensified mine, but we have both surely learned that other people, because they *are* other people, are not and ought not to be replicas of our particular blessed self. Our differences of opinions might, in fact, make our intercourse very stormily interesting and fruitful.

What makes me hesitate is none of all this. It is the fear of misleading you. I appear to have done so already, for in writing to thank you for your article on Eugene I thought only of my pleasure in old memories. . . . But I must not allow you to be misled into supposing that because I remember gratefully the years of your friendship, I have in the least forgotten the inexplicable manner in which you not only broke it off on a mere childish excuse, but how doggedly aloof even after the death of Nencioni which ought to have reunited us; and later during an absurd but odious attack which you, with whom I had for years discussed the very ideas I was accused of stealing, had it in your power to silence with one word.

I have put the truth pretty crudely before you, my dear Carlo. In the knowledge thereof it is for you to decide whether to pick up the threads now once more in our reach or to let them drop. There need be no spoken or written explanation, perhaps better none. If within the next fortnight you telephone to propose coming to lunch or tea, I shall understand that in one way another that bad past is to be effaced. If you remain silent, I shall take it as the agreed upon signal.

V. Paget

It appears that Placci did not explain or apologize because there are no more letters until 1913. By this time Vernon Lee had put the whole business behind her, but Kit remained sensitive on the issue. When Placci offered to renew his visits in 1913, out of loyalty to her friend Vernon Lee responded that

> Miss A. T. thinks that as you were the one person in Florence to whom we had talked about the ideas afterward published in Beauty and Ugliness you might have been expected to come forward and state that they had existed independent of Berenson, instead of which she believes you went out of your way to say that she was a plagiarist. Such is her view of the matter. However, out of friendship to me she is willing to be in future perfectly civil to you when she meets you, but if it is a question of returning her good opinion of you, it would be necessary that you write her either an explanation or an apology. (23 May 1913)

No apology was offered. When she was reconciled with the Berensons in 1920, Mary Berenson urged her to meet Placci once again, but she wrote him sadly: "Somehow or other I can cut off and keep quite unsullied the past personality of those I have cared for; I apparently lack the sense of continuity which if it keeps friendship alive, often desecrates it and degrades it. This being the case, having what I want of you safe in the Past, I am reluctant to run risks with the Present" (Pantazzi, "Placci" 122). With the passing years, however, they were brought together by mutual friends. In 1932 Placci reviewed her *Music and Its Lovers* for the *Corriere della sera,* praising her eloquence and her appeal even to a younger generation of readers (Pantazzi, "Placci" 107). And less than a year before her death he took part in the elegantly staged Italian production of *Ariadne in Mantua* that an old friend of hers, Flavia Farini Cini, arranged at the Reale Accademia dei Fidenti in Florence. Though she was by then too deaf to appreciate the applause, Vernon Lee was grateful for the tribute to the play she regarded as her best and most unfairly neglected work (Gunn 231). Placci also attended her funeral at the Allori Cemetery in Florence and wrote her obituary in *La natione.*

Vernon Lee made peace with Bernard Berenson and visited I Tatti freely in the 1920s, punctuating her conversation with flourishes of her ear trumpet. That she still harbored some sensitivity to the old quarrel is evident in a letter she wrote Mary Berenson on the publication of *Art and Man,* her collection of Kit's writings: "I feel that the first copy of this book must go to you just because a certain part of it seems to conflict with the gratitude we owe you and Mr. Berenson for so much hospitality in the last few years. It would not be seemly for you to come across that passage by accident, or pointed out by anyone excepting myself" (23 January 1924). The passage in question, in Vernon Lee's long memoir of Kit that introduces the volume, does not mention Berenson by name. It simply dismisses the whole controversy as a mere "*boutade* on the part of the rather inexperienced young writer from whom it came." By this time there can be no lingering doubts about her good will toward Berenson. It was not mutual, however. Long after her death Berenson was interviewed by Burdett Gardner. Berenson paid homage to her gifts as a writer: "Her essays have a lyrical form. I didn't read her for the fact,—it was for the vision, the inspiration she gave me." But an edge of the old bias remains: "She was an incredibly spontaneous, impulsive, reckless person and she spat out ink. I don't think there was a malicious thought in her mind except when she got into a fight. She literally oozed ink —and without the slightest malice. She spent her life in three pursuits: writing, pumping people and in her love affairs with lady friends" (Gardner 61).[7]

Vernon Lee's closest friends—Ethel Smyth, Emily Sargent, Mary Robinson, and Maurice Baring—remained loyal to the end. The irrepressible Ethel Smyth, busily writing her volumes of memoirs during the 1930s, left the most perceptive and sympathetic accounts of her. She was honest enough to report her weaknesses but also to acknowledge her warmth and generosity of character. Emily Sargent left no memoir, but her steady friendship, from their childhood days in France and Italy onward, is recorded in their exchange of letters and in the memoir that Vernon Lee appended to Evan Charteris's biography of John Singer Sargent.[8] Until his death, Emily remained part of her brother's brilliant life, content to live in his reflected glory. She traveled with him and served as his hostess at tea and dinner parties. In 1906, after their mother's death, Emily took her own lodgings in Chelsea, close to John's studio in Tite Street. A plain-looking woman, slightly handicapped by a spinal injury suffered in childhood, she seldom sat for her brother, but he did several watercolors in which she was a shadowy figure. In an oil painting, *Mosquito Nets* (1908), he represents her and a companion, Eliza Wedgwood (of the pottery family), in Majorca—two eminently genteel elderly ladies reading under huge netting hoods. In *Simplon Pass: The Lesson* (1911) she sits in front of an easel, a stolid figure flanked by two young nieces, with a paintbrush between her lips and a paint box in her lap. Vernon Lee called her "an accomplished water colorist," and John Sargent encouraged her work.

As far as John Sargent himself was concerned, "our real intimacy," Vernon Lee wrote in her memoir, "did not last beyond those years of childhood" (Charteris 246). Nevertheless she maintained cordial relations with him during the 1880s. She wrote her mother proudly about his success in French art circles, and he in turn followed her published work with interest, writing her (18 March 1880), "My compliments, most illustrious twin, for what you are achieving" (R. Ormond 163). He congratulated her on the publication of *Belcaro:* "I hope it is very much read, for your view of art is the only true one" (24 March 1882). He sketched her and painted the striking portrait that now hangs in the Tate. He also painted a rough but remarkably romantic portrait of Mary Robinson, with whom it was said he was briefly infatuated (L. Ormond 168), and two portraits of Kit Anstruther-Thomson. Vernon Lee admired his work, especially his daring use of color in *Carnation, Lily, Lily, Rose.* She noted the influence of the French Impressionists on his work, but praised his restraint in not actually imitating them. Although less than enthusiastic about his decorations for the Boston Public Library ("put-together things"), she was deeply moved by his wartime painting of the blinded soldiers in *Gassed* (1919). In later years Sargent continued to admire her short stories and travel essays but, like other friends, disapproved of her increasing attention to psychological aesthetics. "In his eyes this was preposterous and, I suspect, vaguely sacrilegious" (Charteris 250). She, however, felt that it was precisely his lack of psychological insight that made much of his most famous work superficial: "Like other painters of those ingenuous, unpsychological days, John Sargent did not know that *seeing* is the business of the mind, the memory and the heart quite as much as of the eye, and that the *valeurs* which the most stiff-necked impressionist could strive after were also *values* of association and preference" (251).

None of this affected her warm friendship with Emily Sargent. In 1905 the three were reunited in Bern, Switzerland. "The Sargents have been here for a week," she wrote Kit. "I see Emily often, but scarcely anything of John. And when one does see him he is in a quite impersonal way wonderfully self-absorbed" (9 July). As long as her health permitted, Vernon Lee saw Emily on her summer visits to England. She last stayed with her for a week in July 1932. Two years later Emily Sargent died, having survived her brother by nine years.

Continuity does not precisely describe the course of Vernon Lee's relationship with Mary Robinson. There was a dramatic break for a few years immediately following Mary's marriage to James Darmesteter. The shock of the marriage itself, the physical incongruity of the sickly Darmesteter and the beautiful Mary, and the meddling of Eugene Lee-Hamilton and Mrs. Paget exacerbated Vernon Lee's grief and sense of loss and precipitated her nervous collapse. In time, and with the solicitous care of Kit Anstruther-Thomson, she recovered and made her peace with Mary. But something irretrievable had been lost. On Mary's side it was the hero worship of her youth. Her respect for Vernon Lee's intelligence and talent had not diminished, but she had moved too far into European intellectual society to remain in awe of her learned friend. Vernon Lee in turn had awakened to

Mary's dependency on others: her need for a "master" to encourage her own intellectual activities. Sylvaine Marandon quotes a letter written by Mary shortly before her marriage in which she says that she looks up to Darmesteter as a brilliant scholar and "is at his feet, like Magdalen at the cross." She asks him to send her a copy of his translation of the *Zend-Avesta,* a Persian dictionary, and "a good French cookbook with instructions in handling servants. She will learn it by heart!" (51).

After being widowed for a second time, Mary did not remarry. She had settled in Paris with her first husband, and France remained her home until her death in 1944. She lived there not as an English expatriate but as a respected French woman of letters, maintaining a salon in Paris where she entertained literary and political friends—Renan, Taine, Bourget, Maurice Barrès, Daniel Halévy. Because these men shared her liberal social ideals, they were also congenial to Vernon Lee, who became a frequent visitor. She was never fully reconciled with Mary, but in fact they had never quarreled. From 1894 onward, when Mary wrote her to apologize for Anatole France's allusions to them in *The Red Lily* in a journal edited by Darmesteter, they maintained a polite but distant friendship.[9] Vernon Lee especially admired Emile Duclaux, Mary's second husband (see chap. 10, p. 178), and the circle around Madame Duclaux—all staunch defenders of Captain Dreyfus, freethinkers, and actively engaged writers—consisted of many people whom Vernon Lee respected.

George Robinson, Mary's father, died in 1897, and her mother and sister Mabel settled in Paris near her. After Mrs. Robinson's death in 1917, Mary and Mabel took adjoining apartments at 88 rue de Varennes, neighbors of Edith Wharton, who lived at number 58. Mary had an active literary career. For many years she reviewed French books for the *Times Literary Supplement,* and she published a number of her own books in English and in French. Like Vernon Lee, she kept up with current literature and wrote sympathetically, in *Twentieth Century French Writers* (1920), of Barrès, Romain Rolland, Gide, Claudel, Péguy, Proust, and Colette. With the possible exception of Bernard Berenson's reference to her multiple given names as "alphabet Robinson" (*Letters* 48), no one who knew her failed to write admiringly about her. Mary appears to have been oblivious to all the adulation that continued into her old age. Daniel Halévy, one of her younger admirers, paid her a glowing tribute in *Les Trois Mary* (1959); the title refers to Mary Robinson, Mary Darmesteter, and Mary Duclaux. He described her as "platonicienne," sensitive to the beauty of forms, "but the forms to which she attached herself were the invisible ones of soul" (19). An even younger admirer, Emmanuel Berl, also remembered her in his confessional memoir *Rachel et autres grâces* (1965) as "platonicienne." As a young man, rebellious against bourgeois morality and, by his account, very active sexually, he looked up to Mary as "ma marraine," a godmother who showered him with gifts and letters and advice on reading (she recommended Proust and Freud) and listened patiently to his confessions of his turbulent emotional life. In 1943 she suffered several months of blindness before she had successful cataract surgery; she died in the following year at Aurillac, where she and Mabel had settled after the German occupation of Paris. Mabel died in 1956.

The most unlikely and yet the most enduring of Vernon Lee's close friendships was with Maurice Baring. It was unlikely because he was almost twenty years her junior, of an old and aristocratic English family, a convert to Roman Catholicism, and an army officer who served on active duty in World War I. But it endured because he was a prolific writer, a cosmopolitan and world traveler (Emma Letley, his biographer, called him "a citizen of Europe"), and a witty, warm-hearted man. The son of a peer (his father became Lord Ravelstoke in 1885) and the nephew of Sir Henry Ponsonby, Queen Victoria's private secretary, he was born in 1874 into the banking family of Baring Brothers and grew up in an atmosphere that Vernon Lee described as "silver spoonery" (Letley 18). The only shadow on an otherwise idyllic childhood was a strict public school, but this was only temporary. He had happy years at Eton, where his enthusiasm for languages, music, modern fiction, and poetry were encouraged. Planning a career in diplomacy, he spent five years in Germany learning the language and enjoying himself. In 1892 he proceeded to Florence to polish his Italian. In spite of his failure to master mathematics at both Oxford and Cambridge, he managed after several tries to pass the examination for the diplomatic service, and in 1898 he began a career in foreign service that took him, over the years, to Paris, Copenhagen, Rome, and Moscow. When the Russo-Japanese War broke out in 1904, Baring was posted to Manchuria as a newspaper correspondent on the front lines. He returned to Moscow to witness the first days of the revolution of 1905 and traveled all over the country, becoming something of an expert on Russian life and literature. Subsequent assignments took him to Turkey, Serbia, and Albania. After four years of war service in the Royal Flying Corps working as a translator and liaison to the press, he resumed his writing career, producing a number of, in their time, popular novels and plays.

The real joys of Maurice Baring's life were not his career achievements but his many friends, who included all the major writers of the Edwardian and Georgian eras and some of the most glamorous women of upper-class English life. But the longest lasting of these friendships were with women in whom glamour was conspicuously absent—Ethel Smyth and Vernon

Lee. He first met Ethel through his aunt Lady Ponsonby (who later introduced Ethel to Vernon Lee) when he was only nineteen, and though tempestuous Ethel tried his patience on many occasions, they remained close friends until his death in 1944. His acquaintance with Vernon Lee goes back even further, for he was the little boy so enchanted by her *Prince of the Hundred Soups* that he spent his allowance on *Belcaro,* only to discover that it was a dry aesthetic treatise (see the beginning to chap. 13).

Their friendship began in 1893 when young Baring, on his first visit to Florence, was introduced to Vernon Lee by Countess Sophie Benckendorff at a luncheon party. In her severely tailored clothes, she struck him at once as "very like Sargent's portrait," and, he recalled years later, "it is one of his most remarkable portraits, for he is successful in giving you the piercing gleam of her intelligent eyes" (*Lost Lectures* 85). Baring soon became a frequent visitor to Il Palmerino. Always attracted to young men with literary aspirations, especially when their ambition was accompanied by a sense of humor and an insatiable love for travel, she assumed the role of his mentor and Italian guide. "Sight-seeing with Vernon Lee was sight-seeing indeed. It was the opposite of scampering through a gallery with a Baedeker and ticking off what had been 'done'" (*Lost Lectures* 86).

In her mentor role she encouraged Baring's writing career. Her critiques were severe, even sometimes wounding. But unlike Berenson, Baring received them without rancor. During one of his earlier stays at Il Palmerino, he confessed to her that he had written and then in discouragement destroyed a novel. "Every one ought to write one novel, if only to lose the desire of writing another," she told him, very likely with the unhappy memory of the fate of *Miss Brown.* By 1903 Baring was a published poet and an aspiring playwright. Vernon Lee wrote him a characteristically candid criticism of his plays. "This much I see, that you have very remarkable poetic power, and that it has undergone a process of refining, of weeding and pruning, since the *Black Prince* [poems, 1902]. . . . Moreover it seems to me in all these plays, the play part is exceedingly weak, and, as I don't care a *button* what happens to anyone, and I am never made to feel *how* it happens, I wish the play or story element were left out" (30 October 1903). She continued to read his work with increasing admiration, especially his books on Russia (*Landmarks of Russian Literature,* 1910; *The Russian People,* 1911; *The Mainsprings of Russia,* 1914). "I *hate* Russia as a power (like Germany, as ditto and most others)—but I am always fearfully attracted to Russians through their writers—they seem to me to be bringing some new element of goodness and depth left out of our Franco-Roman-Germanic tripos. I wish I knew Russia and someday I want to go there" (25 January 1906). But a year later, though she repeated her fascination with Russia, reflecting that her paternal grandfather "must have left me some Slav blood wherewith to disconnect both the Anglo-Saxon and the Latin," she wrote, "I should like to go to Russia. But I am now too poor and too old to travel" (15 December 1907).

Their correspondence flourished. In the early letters she signed herself "Affectionately, V. Paget"; in later years she was simply "Vernon." Baring first addressed her as "Miss Paget," but he headed a letter of 7 January 1906 "My dear Vernon (allow me this familiarity)" without any objection from her. In reply she wrote, "Bless you, dear Maurice, for your fine, clean tender humaneness of feeling, for your courage in being capable of sorrow and pity and yet no sentimentalist" (25 January 1907). She confided to him her ambivalent feelings about the final illness and death of Eugene Lee-Hamilton: "My brother's death . . . was a mere relief; I seemed to have lost him years ago. And I don't feel I could have done or been otherwise than I was. A dreadful unfatality of temperament, of inability to take and to give, seems to have hung over all his life, except the strange years of his illness, when he was happy and delightful" (15 December 1907).[10]

There are two gaps in their correspondence. One was during World War I, when most of Vernon Lee's friends were estranged by her pacifism. The other was earlier and followed Baring's conversion to Roman Catholicism in 1909. There are no surviving letters between 24 June 1909 and 14 December 1913. Her letter of 1909, one of her most affectionate, was to acknowledge his gift of his latest book, *Russian Essays and Stories* (1908):

> I have been turning over, with the leaves of your books, the invisible leaves of my secret living book called *Maurice,* with the headings "What! he thinks that? Oh, how we agree! . . . No! I fear he's a bit of a *codina* [ultra Tory]. . . . There of course he is *really* liberal. . . . Why, he is the only person who loves and hates alternately like me! . . . Maurice, can you mean that? . . . Maurice, you are the greatest possible dear, and the more I know of your doings and feelings and thinkings in your 3rd class Russian trains, among your fine statesmen, among your books, and among the haycocks, the more I like you! One has to read little, and to live in great spiritual solitude, as I do, to *savourer* in this way whatever appeals to one, and turn one's books into chapters of one's innermost life. Thank you dear Maurice for the feeling of perfect companionship you have, in being yourself, contrived to give me.

In 1913, acknowledging the gap in their correspondence, she wrote:

> A great many things—and time and space not unhappily the most separating—have come, as you know, between us of late years. You have taken different views of politics and religion. And I, as I grow older, become less,

instead of more, able to live with people without agreement on such matters; I am, I suppose, a fanatic. And in reading both your books, the tragic one [*Letters from the Near East,* an account of the failure of young Turkish liberals to free their country from Moslem domination] and the funny [*Lost Diaries,* a lighthearted account of his life as "a citizen of Europe"], I have felt with a rush of pleasure how very fond I am of you, dear Maurice. (14 December 1913)

The war was a far greater challenge to their friendship than was his religious conversion. Baring's social and family connections with the conservative British establishment had never inhibited their easy, fond relationship. But as a journalist with close connections to the Foreign Office and expert knowledge of Russian and eastern European politics, Baring felt obligated to serve his country. He enlisted promptly in 1914 and emerged from the war a major with an OBE and citations for gallantry and distinguished service (Letley 185). Apparently, he had little difficulty adjusting to peacetime, and he quickly resumed his literary career. He took the initiative in resuming his friendship with Vernon Lee. Writing from Il Palmerino soon after she had returned from England, she welcomed him:

Yes indeed you shall have a letter from me, and I am greatly touched by your wanting one. . . . And I feel that my fantastical susceptibilities have increased with age and with the War, to the extent . . . [her ellipsis] well! Of having for instance utterly lost touch with you. But I want you to know that, by an odd compensation, when my friends drop me or I drop them there remains in me a perfect fidelity to what they were to me in the past. . . . All this dreadful analysis (but I have turned psychological, as you perhaps know) means that, dear Maurice, I have the vividest impression of, the warmest affection for, the very dear friend you were all those years ago in Rome and elsewhere, when we played together, and when, as I then imagined, we also had the same ideas about things which weren't play. (9 December 1919)

Thereafter they corresponded and from time to time met, in Italy when Baring's travels took him there, in London when she made her summer visits. Their letters are full of details about their work. They exchanged their newly published books—sadly few by Vernon Lee but numbers of novels, plays, poems, and essays by Baring. In 1927 she wrote to acknowledge some of these with the news of her forthcoming collection *For Maurice.* "I am trying to make you a slight return by a volume of stories which is already in the publisher's hands, and which is going to be called after *you—Maurice's story book* or something like that, because it tries to make up for the fright-

ful unintended way I sold you as a small boy over *Belcaro*. The stories you
mayn't care for, but I shall try (if well enough) next summer to set them in
such 'aus meinem Leben' as you have sometimes asked me to write" (20 April
1927). Baring had not been the first to ask Vernon Lee to write a memoir or
autobiography, but she resisted all such suggestions: "Well, well, dear Maurice, and since people are pestering me for biography ('Impressions which
Remained,' in E[thel] S[myth]'s elegant words), which of course I shall never
give except as incidental *Wahrheit und Dichtung*" (12 December 1932). She
even insisted to her executor Irene Cooper Willis that her biography must
never be written: "My life is my own and I leave that to nobody" (Gunn ix).
But she left memoirs of her childhood in her long chatty introduction
to *For Maurice* and of her adventures with John Sargent in Rome and Bologna in her essay "J.S.S.: In Memoriam" appended to Evan Charteris's *John
Sargent* (1927).

Vernon Lee's letters to Baring over the last decade of her life testify to
the increasing isolation that deafness and general debility imposed on her.
Conversation, she wrote him, is "a great strain" (26 September 1930). As a
result she found herself reading more novels, a genre she had tended to dis-
parage in her younger days. "I have *Tinker's Leave* [1927, a novel drawn from
Baring's experience as a war correspondent in the Russo-Japanese War] in
my little store of novels which I put by like an aged squirrel, against solitary
evenings" (26 April 1928); "I saw your new book [*Comfortless Memory*, a no-
vella] read in the train by quite a pretty long-legged girl. I, who am neither,
will read it this winter" (9 August 1928); "I am more than ever in my solitude and deafness and general invalidism, dependent on novels [referring to
his 1933 *Friday's Business*]" (12 December 1932).

Her last letter to Baring, written only two months before she died, contains probably her warmest tribute to him. After thanking him for his latest book, which arrived "just when I am fagged and stupefied by one of my
little heart attacks, which make most things disagreeable," she reports a series of domestic problems—her two house servants have gone off for a family funeral, her "dear old maid" is ill, and her laundress and charwoman has
influenza; "and I must manage with the son of the house, an eighteen-year-
old electrician, for my dinner etc. etc." Nevertheless she offers a witty and
affectionate closing: "I can only stick a stamp (such a monumental fascist
stamp with a heroic group and illegible numerals!) on this tiresome letter
and say, dear, incomparable, unreliable Historian, thanks, thanks, thanks,
thanks, THANKS from your affect. Vernon" and an afterthought: "It was
rather funny. I had a birthday just now [actually two months earlier] and
was covered with flowers like a prima donna from people who have never
before left so much as a card. It turned out that the report had spread that

I was *80!* It was a sort of Chapelle Ardente. But I am only 78, which is surely ever so much less! Finis" (1 December 1934).

Vernon Lee entertained no illusions about the immortality of her soul or of her work. She remained consistently a secular humanist. In an unpublished fragment of 11 February 1931 headed "When I Say *Divine,*" she denied "something more or less mysterious behind phenomena. . . . Whereas what I mean when I say *divine* is just phenomena, lights, sounds, movements, even persons, which, by some happy coming together of them and our soul seem all-sufficient, transcending our wishes and imaginings. . . . For *Divine* is the word signifying what we have canonised, that we have accepted it for our highest. It is Man who invests certain things with divinity." She had no illusions either of her immortality as a writer. Sometime in the late 1920s she caught a glimpse of the Chateau St. Léonard, her birthplace, from a train window as she was traveling to Boulogne. She reflected that the site would not be recorded "and pilgrimaged to by my passionate Readers of Future Ages. For one of the few certainties that life has brought me is that the competition for immortality much exceeds nowadays the immortality available for distribution, and that literature is ceasing to be *aere perennius* and assuming its true status as journalism and perishable, and which fact, though at moments disappointing to my secret hopes, I cannot fairly complain" (20 June 1930).

The last entry in "A Vernon Lee Notebook" was written on the evening of New Year's Day 1934. It is the most beautiful and characteristically gallant prose she ever wrote:

> "Come Ho! And wake Diana with a hymn"
> Although general seediness and noises in my ears should prevent even attempting such a thing, themselves perhaps, by my "Peau de Chagrin" fatality, the result, the punishment of such proceedings, yet I want to note that I have begun the dreaded New Year (and my seventy-eighth) in this spirit and with these words running in my head.
> What happened is this: after several evenings just missing it, I watched the full moon rise from my East window. She—for it was certainly she—emerged from behind the quarry hill, throwing up little beams, almost sparks, among the jagged blackness of cypress and rock, making a white furnace along them; and then, at last, when the sky above and the clouds were all silver and blue, slipping her moorings like a boat, sailing free and rising, a perfect silver disc, with extraordinary speed into the waiting firmament.
> Patet Dea!
> I had called my little cook, who was busy next door, having once noticed that she cared for moons and such sights. And we stood together at

the window, watching this lengthy assumption of the goddess, not without exclamations.

Waking Diana with an inner hymn. That hymn went on in my mind long after she had vaulted and vanished into the stormy higher sky, found appropriate voice, became an audible hymn when I strummed part of Opus 131 and was able to hear it, with aid of recollection. I have not often, at least of late years, been filled with such religious joy of beauty and happiness of being capable thereof, "Waking Diana with a hymn" at the opening of this lowering New Year. (It was a genuine emotion, with a slight heart attack brought on afterwards.)

The "little heart attacks" grew more frequent and severe. She died on 13 February 1935 having just finished reading Jules Romains's *Le couple France-Allemagne* on the conflict over the status of the Saar. Like her father, she chose to be cremated, and her ashes were buried in Eugene Lee-Hamilton's grave in the Allori Cemetery in Florence. Her name was not inscribed on the headstone until March 1996, but the new owners of Il Palmerino had earlier remembered her with an inscription on the house:

IN
QUESTA CASA
TRASCORSE LA VITA
VIOLET PAGET (VERNON LEE)
SCRITTRICE
1856–1935
SCRISSE
IN POESIA ED IN PROSA
DI PHILOSOPHIA, DI STORIA, E D'ARTE
MODESTA, DI CUORE GRANDE
INTEGRA DI VITA E D'INTELLETO
SI DEDICO ALLA RICERCA DEL VERO E DEL BELLO
PRESCELSE A SUA DIMORA L'ITALIA
CONOSCENDOLA ED AMANDOLA
TRASMISE AI VENTURI COLLE SUE OPERE
UNA EREDITA IMPERITURA.[11]

AFTERWORD

VERNON LEE BELIEVED THAT IT WAS HER MISFORTUNE TO HAVE been born before her time, a Victorian who should have been a modern. Women poets and novelists were acceptable, within the boundaries of Victorian society. But a woman who ventured into intellectual history, aesthetics, and psychology with her bold self-assurance confronted formidable obstacles. In the twentieth century, when she might rightfully have established her claims to authority as a woman of letters, she was a relic of Victorianism. Her aestheticism was Walter Pater's; her psychology a product of what she herself called "those ingenuous, unpsychological days"; her experiments in psychological aesthetics unscientific and naive; her writings on art and music superseded by more-expert specialists; her travel writing dismissed as subjective and self-indulgent. Only a handful of her exotic supernatural stories remain in print.

No doubt this neglect is partly owing to her anomalous position in society—an Englishwoman who made her home in Italy, who made no effort to conceal her attachments to women and her rejection of many of the values of conventional society, who openly deplored nationalism, colonialism, capitalism, communism, and fascism, and defied patriotic sentiment by advocating pacifism during World War I. She alienated many who might have been her friends, and others, men in particular, disliked her simply because she was a lesbian. Yet it is remarkable that everyone who knew her work gave her grudging respect and acknowledged that, however flawed, it was worthy of attention.

Even more remarkable is the persistence of her ideas. What her few twentieth-century readers dismissed as ephemera—her psychological aesthetics, her unorthodox views on religion, her neutrality in World War I, and her opposition to the terms of the Treaty of Versailles—have curious resonance in the early twenty-first century. While she squandered valuable creative energy in measuring physiological reactions to specific works of art and music, Vernon Lee was directing her (and her reader's) attention to the subjectivity of the aesthetic experience. Her emphasis on the moral value of art was based not on traditional socially prescribed standards of morality but on her independent reading of psychology in search of a key to mental health. Threatened by fears that her family's eccentricities, her brother's neurasthenic invalidism, and her own experiences of nervous collapse were, as she wrote, "a taint communicated to the race," she sought not for mere therapy but for the transcendent experience in art. The evidence that in the end she was successful in her quest lies not only in her books but in the tranquillity of her later years. The Italian past, most especially its music, sustained her. *Studies of the Eighteenth Century in Italy, Euphorion,* the short stories of a haunted but vibrant Renaissance and eighteenth-century Italy, the travel essays that re-created a Europe that no longer exists and maybe never existed, illuminate the past for her readers today more brightly than do many more-standard histories. It was also that sense of the past that enriched her understanding of the present and her sanguine vision of the future. Her essays on contemporary European and American social philosophers, many of them all but forgotten today, tell us more about her engagement with idealists and ideologues than about their vital lies. And her essays on literary creativity that she collected in *The Handling of Words* reveal an inquiring, independent mind unfettered by the conventions of academic literary criticism.

What her Victorian and Georgian contemporaries perceived as defiance or mere perverseness in Vernon Lee we now perceive as independence of spirit. For George Bernard Shaw, she was part of "the old guard of Victorian cosmopolitan intellectualism." But we read Vernon Lee as part of no tradition. She created herself in the nineteenth century and then re-created herself in the twentieth. It was her very capacity for growth that keeps her to this day a richly rewarding writer.

NOTES

1 THE INFANT PRODIGY

1. Edward Abadam inherited Middleton Hall, "a house of great magnificence." Like his father, he served as a justice of the peace and later as high sheriff of Carmarthen. See Thomas Nicholas, *Annals and Antiquities of the County Families of Wales,* 2 vols. (London, 1872), 1:280.

2. There appears to have been no connection to the distinguished Paget family, although Violet spent two days in November 1898 as the houseguest of Lady Walburga ("Wally") Paget, a close friend of Queen Victoria, who shared with Violet and the queen an abhorrence of vivisection. See Elizabeth Longford, *Queen Victoria: Born to Succeed* (New York: Harper & Row, 1964), 338.

3. The Notebook entry is titled "Boulogne-sur-Mer and Literary Immortality," and she writes that many years later she had a glimpse of her birthplace as the train in which she was traveling to Boulogne sped past it, but she did not bother to stop off, reflecting with some irony: "For have I not pilgrimaged to similar Birth (or for that matter Death) places of other writers. Which thought led to the further one that this would have happened only if Dr. P. had assisted and congratulated somewhat earlier in the History of Literature since it was easier in earlier days to attain such immortality as is stored in guidebooks simply because, given that somebody had to be immortal, there weren't so many people to do it."

4. In 1903 Vernon Lee published an autobiographical essay, "Psychologie d'un écrivain sur l'art (observation personelle)," in the *Revue philosophique* 56:225–54.

5. Stevenson, *Memoir of Fleeming Jenkin* 25–29. There is a sketch of Henrietta Camilla Jenkin in the *DNB* which cites as her best novels *Cousin Stella* (1859), "a West Indian novel showing both power and cleverness," and *Who Breaks, Pays* (1861), "a skilful delineation of an English coquette." But the sketch adds that "without having literary taste, she began to write under pressure of poverty."

6. Assuming, characteristically, a perverse minority opinion, Mark Twain wrote "In Defense of Harriet Shelley," attacking Mary Godwin (Godwin's daughter who later became Mary Shelley), and especially Cornelia Turner as a married woman trying to lure Shelley away from his wife. Richard Holmes has a more sympathetic account of her in his biography of Shelley (216–17).

2 THE EIGHTEENTH CENTURY AND AFTER

1. From time to time Vernon Lee dismissed her first book as juvenilia, but her friend Maurice Baring knew that she always valued it. In 1902 he wrote her: "I was re-reading your book on the Eighteenth Century in Italy. I feel you would now wish to black a great part of it. I am convinced it would be a mistake to *cancel one word*. . . . I finished it with a prayer of thanks to you as a wonderful wizard, an enchanter who by subtle spells invokes the magic and mysterious past" (Smyth, *Maurice Baring* 199). In 1927 Vernon Lee herself referred to it as "a big (and very good!) book" (*For Maurice* xxiii).

2. She cited such exercises as these in her article "Musical Expression and the Composers of the Eighteenth Century," *New Quarterly Magazine,* April 1877. Here she discusses the power of music to heighten the expression of a dramatic text with an example from Dr. Burney's *History of Music,* a passage from Metastasio's *Olimpiade.* Comparing three musical versions of the same lines—Cimarosa's, Galuppi's, and Pergolesi's—Burney quotes the singer Pacchierotti as favoring Pergolesi's, not for its overall beauty but for its delicate emphasis on certain lines to heighten their emotional effect.

3. She does refer to this teacher by name in her introduction to *For Maurice* (xxxiv), speaking of "the old, old people (my master Romani, for instance) on whose words about Malibran and Velluti I used to hang." To him and to another, also unnamed but obviously Mrs. Turner ("that sweet and sunny lady, whose hand, which pressed ours, had pressed the hands of Fanny Burney"), she offered a dedication of sorts—"if dedications were not advertisements to the living rather than homage to the dead"—at the conclusion of her *Studies* (294).

4. Among the holograph notes in the Vernon Lee archive there are fifteen pieces of "Notes for a biography of Muzio Clementi . . . gathered in 1873 through inquiries in an English newspaper. Originally intended to be written in collaboration with Vernon Lee's father."

5. Vernon Lee says 1872 in *For Maurice* (xxix), but it is more likely that it was 1873.

6. Vernon Lee published this early draft, "A Culture-Ghost; or Winthrop's Adventure," in *Fraser's,* n.s., 23 (January 1881): 1–29. A revised and considerably altered version of the story with the title "A Wicked Voice" was published in her collection *Hauntings* in 1890. This second version was reprinted in *For Maurice* as "Winthrop's Adventure."

7. The *Fraser's* articles include "The Arcadian Academy" and "The Musical Life," and the long essay on Metastasio. They were substantially unchanged when published in the book, with the addition of only a few brief explanatory footnotes on the spelling of proper names, and birth and death dates of some of the lesser known musicians.

8. A contemporary observer and ardent defender of the culture of eighteenth-century Italy, Giuseppi Baretti, wrote from his adopted home in England that the influence of the academies spread through many Italian towns: "The madness of pastoral now became universal. Everybody who had the least knack for poetry was metamorphosed into a shepherd and fell directly upon composing rustic sonnets, eclogues, ydylliums, and bucolics" (1:256–67).

9. Not surprisingly for the period and the British public for whom she was writing, Vernon Lee never mentioned that Farinelli was a castrato, an omission noted as "curioso" as recently as 1979 by Maria Luisa Astaldi in her biography of Metastasio (91).

10. In the 1907 "Retrospective Chapter" Vernon Lee acknowledged that she was "a little uneasy about my treatment of Metastasio's private life. . . . When I was young, I,

like all young, unscrupulous people, believed in what is called *objective historical reality;* and thinking Metastasio a timid, sentimental egoist, asserted that he was one; whereas, nowadays, I should have said, 'This is the especial reaction which half a dozen facts concerning Metastasio have provoked in my particular mind'—or, what would perhaps be simpler, I should have held my tongue altogether" (xix).

11. Dr. Burney's account of this relationship is more charitable but not unsophisticated: "Whether Metastasio's connection with the Romanina was purely platonic, or of a less seraphic kind, I shall not pretend to determine. But the husband residing in the same house with them, both at Naples and Rome, and the friendly manner in which the Poet always mentioned him in his letters to the wife, with the open manner with which he expressed his affection in writing to him after her death, would, in England, be thought indications favourable to the conjugal fidelity. But a chaste actress and opera singer is a still more uncommon phenomenon in Italy than in Great Britain" (*Metastasio* 1:100–101).

12. Symonds was so impressed with her chapter on Metastasio that two years later, when he was invited by the editors of the *Encyclopaedia Britannica* to write an article on Metastasio, he referred them to her: "I am not unwilling to do it, but I think you are far more capable of doing it well" (30 July 1882, *Letters* 2:761–62). The editors rejected his suggestion, and he wrote her on 13 September that the editors, "in spite of my urging that you should write on Metastasio, insisted I should do the article. . . . I shall depend on your book for the work" (767).

3 *BELCARO*

1. In her "J.S.S.: In Memoriam" (1925), published in Evan Charteris's biography of Sargent, Vernon Lee recalled that, close as she was to Sargent in her childhood, he was never first in her affections: "But the possession of a *bona fide* brother sufficiently my elder to engross all my juvenile worship, left for John only a comradeship which, though largely a matter of the imagination, was never anything more" (Charteris 247).

2. As recently as 1962 the poet George MacBeth published an essay, "Eugene Lee-Hamilton and the Romantic Agony," hailing him as "one of the most important English classical poets of the later nineteenth century" and judging him "fit to stand comparison at different points with Housman, with Meredith, and even with Browning." *Critical Quarterly* 4 (1962): 141–50. William Sharp, an earlier admirer, ranked him with Thomas Hardy; see his introduction to *Dramatic Sonnets, Poems and Ballads: Selections from the Poems of Eugene Lee-Hamilton,* The Canterbury Poets (London: Walter Scott, 1903). Harvey T. Lyon compiled "A Publishing History of the Writings of Eugene Lee-Hamilton" in *Papers of the Bibliographical Society* 51 (1957): 141–59. Lyon's bibliography does not include Lee-Hamilton's novel *The Lord of the Dark Red Star* (1903).

3. Symonds had earlier expressed the same idea in a letter to Eugene, 7 January 1884: "It is borne in upon me very strongly that you should serve Apollo more in the future than you have yet done in your published work. Marsyas owns a very large share —too large, I venture to think, to be quite good for yourself & entirely too large to allow you the popularity you merit as a poet" (*Letters* 3:25).

4. Mary Robinson recalled that Eugene attributed his poetic creativity to his invalidism. "What else was there left to me save my own thoughts?" he told her. "All the many interests and aims of life withdrew, retreated, like a retiring wave, and left me

high, dry, and stark on my sandbank, the jetsam of Fate. . . . There is a sort of horrible charm and disastrous leisure in suffering. It's morbid, it's awful, but it isn't vulgar. It isolates you from the small cares and worries of life, sets you thinking, shows you things *sub specie aeternitatis.*" Though Mary admired his poetry, she had her reservations: "When Eugene put his own heart, his real experience into these literary exercises he showed himself a true, an original poet. Only too often, in natural revulsion against the monotony of his sequestered days, he gave play to a certain night-mare sense that oppressed him, which I always thought a symptom of his malady: a love of the atrocious, the appalling. In this mood there is in his talent something metallic, hard and strident which cannot charm. Imagine a Baudelaire, a Poe, without their vice—but without their beauty" ("In Casa Paget" 936).

5. No authors or editors are named on the title page of *Tuscan Fairy Tales,* and the work is attributed to Vernon Lee alone in all her bibliographies.

6. *The Life of Ernest Renan* by Madame James Darmesteter was published in London in 1897; she translated the book into French in 1898.

7. In *The Cosmopolites* Harry Brewster writes of Florence in the 1870s: "Out of a total population of 200,000, there were nearly 30,000 Anglo-American inhabitants" (1).

8. Violet did not maintain any ongoing social relationship with Ouida. In 1907, summering in England, she responded sympathetically to reports that Ouida was penniless and ailing. She wrote a friend, "an English trained nurse" (possibly Kit Anstruther-Thomson) who was staying in Bagni di Lucca, asking her to call on Ouida and offer any assistance needed. She learned that Ouida was not in real need, having finally received a Civil List pension (over the opposition of the *Spectator*). In a short article "About Ouida" in the *Westminster Gazette,* 27 July 1907, she wrote a respectful survey of her achievement. "Bred in the reign of Bulwer Lytton and Disraeli, with Byronian and Sandesque romanticism still in the air, before Flaubert was heard of, or Mr. George Moore, and when the earliest style of Mr. Henry James was still in the lap of his nurse; moreover, when Italy, barely free of Austrian garrisons and Calabrian brigands, was not yet the playground of Toynbee excursions and motor-cars . . . Ouida gave her readers of every nationality, please remember—one of the many successive, constantly renewed revelations of the Land of Lands."

9. Writing to Henry Graham Dakyns, who was in Florence at the time (27 November 1882), Symonds advised: "There is the Pitti, the Uffizi, the Bargello, the Accademia! There are the churches. There is [Pasquale] Villari to talk to, & Miss Paget to quarrel with, & Mrs. Stillman to admire" (*Letters* 2:792).

10. Quoted in Grosskurth, 223n. No date is given. Burdett Gardner quotes Irene Cooper Willis: "Vernon was homosexual but she never faced up to sexual facts. She was perfectly pure. . . . She had a whole series of passions for women, but they were all perfectly correct. Physical contact she shunned" (85).

11. One visitor to the Casa Paget, the Marchesa Medici, commented on her "somewhat out of the way and a bit strange physical appearance. . . . When young, less like a girl or woman than as a marvellous brain clothed as a woman" (Gunn 174).

12. This notebook, in the Vernon Lee archive, is labeled "Some (slightly) autobiographical notes, viz. A[nnie] M[eyer] in Memoriam 1883."

13. As early as 19 April 1874 she confided in a letter to Mrs. Jenkin that she wanted to publish on "aesthetical subjects" and comparative aesthetics: "There is no subject on

which I reflect with more pleasure or write with more zest." At Mrs. Jenkin's suggestion she had begun keeping a commonplace book—"but on looking over the five or six volumes of foolscap of which it consists, I find that nearly everything in it is relative to aesthetics, particularly those of music."

4 THE LESSON OF THE MASTER

1. George Eliot to John Blackwood, 5 November 1873, *Letters of George Eliot* 6:455. She was commenting on an unfavorable review of Pater's *Renaissance* (by Margaret Oliphant, unsigned) in *Blackwood's Edinburgh Magazine,* November 1873.

2. The phrase was William Sharp's, in "Some Personal Reminiscences of Walter Pater," *Atlantic Monthly* 74 (1884), quoted in Monsman 64.

3. "Walter Pater," in Gosse, *Critical Kit-Kats* 266–67. Victorians used the word *effeminacy* much as it was used in the eighteenth century, not with reference to homosexuality but in the sense of *effeteness*. In her essay on the Arcadian Academy in *Studies of the Eighteenth Century in Italy,* Vernon Lee writes of the excesses of the baroque: "[T]he brilliant paradoxes of Marin and the elegant effeminacy of Guardi turned into systematic nonsense and studied vapidness among their successors" (11).

4. Several of Pater's contemporaries commented on his unattractive appearance, among them Henry James, who described him as "far from being as beautiful as his own prose" (Edel 224). Vernon Lee could not forgive Mallock for his cruel portrait of Pater. In the summer of 1886 she was invited to Alfred Austin's country house in Kent. "To my annoyance," she wrote her mother (31 August), "I find they have also asked Mallock, whom I have no wish whatever to meet, and he has put shameful innuendoes against some of my friends in his books."

5. See Pater's comments in a letter to her, 22 July 1883: "I write so few letters! And this strikes me as a very stiff one, after yours. Your letters *always* interest us—me, and my sister, who hopes with me that we shall see you here later in the summer, and some time or other (it is all one can say just now) in Italy" (*Letters* 52). The sister referred to here is Hester; Clara was away from home at the time. After Pater's death, his sisters undertook to collect their brother's letters, but, as Hester observed in a letter to Violet, 10 July 1895, "Walter's letters are so rare—only a stray one here and there to be found" (*Letters* 157).

6. See Pater, *Letters* 45–46. Lawrence Evans says in a footnote that he was unable to trace the photograph or the drawing.

7. The essay was reprinted in *Juvenilia* vol. 1.

8. Her impression was confirmed by Gosse's: "With natures like his, in which the tide of physical spirits runs low, in which the vitality is luke-warm. . . . " (*Critical Kit-Kats* 266).

9. In a letter of 24 February 1883 Hester Pater thanked Violet for the flowers and continued: "Walter enjoyed his visit in Rome very much. He was very much obliged for the introductions you sent him and was very sorry he had no time to use any. A month is a short time to see much of Rome. He found he had to give all his time to the galleries and churches and was so tired in the evening he was quite unfit for social intercourse. [Evans's footnote here reads, "This may be in part a rationalization, for Pater was notoriously shy with strangers, and especially so when out of England.] We are looking forward to coming to Florence this year in the beginning of September. I am

afraid it will not be the best time to see it, and that you will not be there then, which will be a disappointment. Perhaps we may see you in England before that" (Pater, *Letters* 48–49).

10. In 1896 Raffalovich published *Uranisme et unisexualité*, which Havelock Ellis hailed as "the most comprehensive book so far written on the subject." Ellis, who preferred the phrase "sexual inversion" to "uranism," wrote that Raffalovich "regards congenital inversion as a large and inevitable factor in human life, but, taking the Catholic standpoint, he condemns all sexuality, either heterosexual or homosexual, and urges the invert to restrain the physical manifestations of his instinct and to aim at an ideal of chastity." See Ellis, *Studies in the Psychology of Sex* (New York: Random House, 1935), 2:72–73.

11. Nencioni's review of *Euphorion* for the *Nuova antologia*, 15 June 1884, was reprinted in his *Saggi critici* 77–98.

12. See Symonds's letter to Mary Robinson, 24 April 1884: "She begged me to tell her frankly what was the cause of an undercurrent of disapprobation she had always noticed in me toward her. And I did tell her frankly. Now I am afraid that I have presumed too much on her disengagement from small egotisms" (*Letters* 2:908).

13. See her letter to Carlo Placci, 9 August 1894: "What a terrible loss is not that of Pater! He had achieved that splendid evolution from the cheap aestheticism of the *Renaissance Studies* to the aestheticism, which is ethical like all the highest, of his Plato; and he should have given us so much more priceless advice and experience. Although he gave himself so little in conversation, I feel a great satisfaction in having had his friendship and witnessed his kind, and in a way (being an invalid) bravely serene life" (Pantazzi, "Carlo Placci" 118).

14. In 1910 Vernon Lee reread Pater's "Denys l'Auxerrois" on the occasion of a visit to Auxerre Cathedral, where the legend of Denys is depicted in niches in the sculpture capitals. She also found another, quite different, depiction of him in banners decorating a small church in Rovolon, near Venice. See her "Dionysus in the Euganean Hills: W. H. Pater: In Memoriam," *Contemporary Review* 120 (September 1921): 346–53.

5   THE TELLER AND THE TALES

1. The career of Helen Zimmern (1846–1934) parallels Vernon Lee's, though she was far less distinguished a writer. Both had continental backgrounds. Zimmern, born in Germany, was fluent in several European languages. Just a year before she met Vernon Lee, Zimmern and her sister Alice published a two-volume anthology *Half-Hours with Foreign Novelists* (London, 1880), which displayed their wide acquaintance with nineteenth-century European authors—Russian, Scandinavian, and eastern European as well as French, German, and Italian. She published biographies of Schopenhauer (1876) and Lessing (1878) and translated Lessing's *Laocoön* (1914), Nietzsche's *Beyond Good and Evil* (1907), and many Italian authors. In 1884, the year Vernon Lee published *The Countess of Albany*, she published a biography of Maria Edgeworth in the same Eminent Women Series. In her later years she lived in Florence, producing articles and books on Italian history and culture, among them *The Italy of the Italians* (1906) and *Italian Leaders of Today* (1915).

2. Examining the role of women as observers in the nineteenth century, Hilary Fraser cites Browning's reference to Vernon Lee in "Inapprehensiveness": "The invoca-

tion of first the eminent art critic John Ruskin and then Vernon Lee, an art historian and aesthetician also of some repute in her own day, allows us to locate the poem within the larger frame of the sexual politics of spectatorship. It is with Vernon Lee that the disgruntled male speaker aligns his female companion, not Ruskin—with the woman, that is, who asserted the significance of the 'real setting of place and moment, and individuality and digression' (Lee, *Belcaro* 7) in her aesthetic, rather than with Ruskin, whom she characterized as 'this strange knight-errant of righteousness' (*Belcaro* 203)" (78).

3. See Hillebrand's essay "About Old and New Novels," *Contemporary Review* 45 (March 1884): 388–402. Here he faults George Eliot, Zola, Howells, and Henry James for their overly subtle analysis of character.

4. ALS (autograph letter signed). Berg Collection of English and American Literature, The New York Public Library, Astor, Lenox and Tilden Foundations.

5. Throughout the novel Vernon Lee drops the names of several of her contemporaries. At one point the archaeologist accuses Lady Venetia of making "a generalisation worthy of your friend Henry James" and at another, of interpreting facts as she wants them to be: "There is a volume of William James's essays called 'The Will to Believe'— you are that William in this case." Elsewhere in the novel she refers to Joseph Conrad's friend R. B. Cunninghame-Graham, a travel writer whom she had met and whose work she admired.

6   MISS BROWN

1. Julia Wedgwood recognized the popular appeal of the novel, writing of *Miss Brown* in the *Contemporary Review* 47 (1885): "The remarkable writer Vernon Lee has shown her capacity elsewhere than on the ground of fiction, and we cannot hope that she will continue to exercise her literary activity on the same soil. Interesting as is her first regular novel, it does not seem to us interesting in proportion to its power, and we cannot but surmise that these thoughts on art and life would have had more literary effect if given in some other form, although they would of course then not have had so many readers."

2. Buchanan's article is reprinted in *The Pre-Raphaelites,* ed. Jerome H. Buckley (New York: Modern Library, 1968), 437–60, quotation on p. 438. Buchanan modified his views considerably in the next two decades and in 1889 defended Zola's English publisher Henry Vizetelly against the government's charges of circulating pornography. See Decker 82–100.

3. For Kathy Psomiades this episode supports the theory that "aesthetic experience is linked to desire between women, a desire specifically defined through and against a purity polemic that condemns and reimagines sexual activity" (22). She argues that "by insistently and graphically recounting the sexual sins of the aesthetes, by locating Anne's reactions to Sacha Elaguine in her body, the novel becomes a lesbian text in the only way open to it, namely by being a perverse aesthetical text" (27). See also Psomiades's "*Miss Brown*: An Aesthetical Novel," in her *Beauty's Body: Femininity and Representation in British Aestheticism* (Stanford: Stanford UP, 1997), 165–77.

4. George Moore, "that young Irishman with the orange lock," as Violet described him to her mother, had intended to include passages from *Miss Brown* in "Literature at Nurse, or Circulating Morals," a pamphlet he published in 1885 to protest the refusal of Mudie's Circulating Library to take his novel *A Mummer's Wife* on the grounds of its

"impropriety." Moore included the "objectionable" quotations from his novel along with passages from novels by Ouida, Florence Marryat, Mrs. Praed, W. H. Mallock, and others in "an anthology of the most improper passages of all the novels Mudie had ever taken. . . . Into this charming collection he published various fragments of *Miss Brown*." But when he showed these to Mary Robinson, she demanded that he withdraw them, "which he did quite amiably" (Violet to her mother, 23 July 1885).

5. Burdett Gardner reported that Bernard Berenson recalled reading the novel as a Harvard undergraduate "and thinking it far better than any other novel of the time" (47), but in his review of her work for the *Harvard Monthly* in 1886, he wrote that *Miss Brown* was "not quite a work of art." The book had some success in America. The novelist Gertrude Atherton recalled in her autobiography: "A novelist that made an impression on me at the time was *Miss Brown,* and it looked for a while as if this really beautiful writer were to have a vogue in America. But she was quickly forgotten" (*Adventures of a Novelist* 72). In an undated letter quoted by Gardner, Kit Anstruther-Thomson wrote Violet: "O I was so delighted when the result of the examination as to which is the most popular novel in America was that Miss B had a very large number in her favor." The novel was published by Harper and Brothers in the Franklin Square Library in 1885 and reprinted the same year in G. Munroe's Seaside Library series. There is a letter from "V. Paget" to Harper, 15 March 1885, in which she asks for a copy of the American edition and copies of American reviews and mentions that she is forwarding their check for *Miss Brown* to Blackwood. (The letter is in the Harper Papers, Rare Book and Manuscript Library, Columbia University.) She refers to the American edition of the novel in a letter to Frances Power Cobbe, 26 April 1885: "By the way, an American paper wrote that "Mesrs Harper have befouled their Franklin Square Library collection by reprinting V.L.'s Miss Brown, perhaps the most indecent and immoral novel that has ever been produced."

6. The letter to Cobbe just cited in n. 5 reflects distinct ambivalence on Violet's part. She reports that "the book has been almost universally stigmatised as a scandal production, unfit for decent readers, and showing a most corrupt mind in the writer." Looking back several months later to the initial shock of its first reception, she seems less conscience-stricken than in her New Year's journal entry: "At first these things pained me very much, for with the shock of surprise came of course the terrible doubt 'have I written a disgraceful book?' Now I am quite indifferent; and for all the scandal the book has caused and the enemies (every Pre-Raphaelite has imagined himself and his to be portrayed in my book) I have made myself, I am on the whole very glad I wrote Miss Brown. And I may tell you that your letter, and the consciousness of your opinion, has done not a little to prevent my being utterly discouraged. The most sickening part of the matter is the revelation of the frightful state of dirt of many people's fancy, for such alone can explain the extraordinary meanings that have been read into Miss Brown: inuendoes [*sic*] which I never dreamed of, about things which were so much Arabic to me." This letter is in the Department of Manuscripts of the Huntington Library.

7   THE BURIED LIFE

1. Characteristically, Violet matched her respect for Mary Ward as a woman with ridicule for her as an intellectual. "Mrs. Ward was extremely friendly; she struck me as

so complete the unfortunate woman of letters who is forced to squeeze into her work more wits than she has in her head," she wrote her mother (16 June 1882). A decade later she had not substantially changed her opinion:

I liked being at the Wards so much more than I anticipated. *He,* who is rather a blundering, bumptious snob, was luckily away; and she is really an extremely nice woman, really modest and serious at bottom. It is *he,* with his absurd swagger, talking as if she were writing the Tables of Stone at the very least, saying "of course Robert Elsmere virtually destroyed Christianity" and so forth, has made her ridiculous. And she, unluckily, has neither keen literary sense to perceive her own mediocrity, nor sense of humour—not a shadow of it—to see that the sort of prophetic-hereditary (Arnold) prophetic position—which her husband makes for her is ludicrous. (24 August 1893)

2. Irish-born, Bella Duffy was educated in European languages and wrote several scholarly books—a monograph on Madame de Staël for the Eminent Women Series (1887), *The Tuscan Republics* (1893), and in 1923, two years before her death, she translated from the German Richard Semon's *Mnemic Psychology,* to which Vernon Lee contributed a long introduction. In 1925 Vernon Lee dedicated her book *Proteus; or, The Future of Intelligence* to Bella Duffy.

3. See Hutton's essays "Mr. Cotter Morison on 'The Service of Man'" and "Ardent Agnosticism," in *Contemporary Thought and Thinkers* (London: Macmillan, 1894), 1:271–87.

4. See *Memories of Fifty Years by Lady St. Helier (Mary Jeune),* 210.

5. She had originally sent the essay to the *Contemporary Review,* but Lady Archibald Campbell insisted that she send it to the *Nineteenth Century* instead for immediate publication. When she did this, she learned that it had arrived too late for publication in the forthcoming issue.

6. Amy Levy's biographer Linda Hunt Beckman finds ample evidence in Levy's letters and poems that she was in love with Violet. Levy wrote another poem, "Neue Liebe, Neue Leben," for her—the German phrase that Violet herself used later in reference to her feelings for Kit Anstruther-Thomson. She did not reciprocate Levy's love, however, being at the time still attached to Mary Robinson. See her letter to her mother (5 September 1889) concerning her search for a secretary for Eugene: "In despair of not bringing Eugene anybody, I have asked Miss Levy. I don't love her, but she's a poor little person and clever and can talk poetry. . . . No answer yet." A victim of severe depression, Levy found some if only temporary happiness in Violet's friendship. On 26 November 1886 she wrote her: "I can't tell you what a difference it has made to me to have known you. I thought I was beyond the reach of human aid as it were (this sounds rather melodramatic, but you know what I mean and if you have not converted me to optimism, you will say, I know, that you are not an optimist yourself, you have made things look and feel a good deal better" (Beckman 256).

7. In striking contrast, John Addington Symonds wrote her, 24 April 1884, that the book was excellent and that he would send a copy to Walt Whitman: "What this means for me, I think you know. I have never sent him a volume of any verse. Up to now I have never met with one which 'tallied' (in a very different style & mood, 'tis true) [with] his own conception of the poetry of actual life" (*Letters* 2:907).

8. Preface to Mary Robinson's *The Collected Poems Lyrical and Narrative.*

9. See Symons's introduction to a selection of her poems in A. H. Miles, ed., *Poets and Poetry of the Century* (London: Routledge, 1891).

10. "The Poetry of Mary Robinson," in James Darmesteter, *English Studies,* trans. Mary Darmesteter (London: Fisher Unwin, 1896).

11. The fullest account of Darmesteter's background is in Solomon Reinach, "James Darmesteter," *Cahiers d' études juives,* no. 2 (1932): 1–32.

12. Sargent painted Kit in full length, in a mannish shirt and tie, with a floppy gardener's hat, firmly grasping the lapels of her tailored jacket, chin thrust boldly forward as if to proclaim her independence and self-confidence. The painting is called *Arbor Vitae.* He also did a small pencil profile of her and a charcoal sketch "in the costume of one of the ladies in Titian's 'Sacred and Profane Love.'" There is also a portrait in oils by Gordignani, 1896. Her expression is serious but not stern, and the effect of the stiff collar of her shirtwaist is softened by a lacy jabot. All these are reproduced in *Art and Man.*

13. The news reached Symonds in Davos a few months later. He had not been in correspondence with Mary for some time. See his letter to T. S. Perry, 9 February 1888: "You speak of going to the 'Darmesteters.' Do you mean the Professor of Oriental Languages in the Rue de Vaugerard 192? He is a bachelor, is he not, & somewhat deformed in physique. I have reason to be interested in him personally at present, which I am not at liberty to mention" (*Letters* 3:291).

14. Eugene is alluding to Paul Bourget's novel of 1885, a sensationally popular exposé of sexual and political corruption in French high society. To Henry James's embarrassment, Bourget dedicated the novel to him.

15. From her study of their correspondence, Phyllis F. Manocchi concluded that "there is no direct expression of physical attraction or of the physical aspects of the love relationship. These feelings are most often voiced in idealized form or in a kind of childishly affectionate tone. In their playful communication, the two women often create a love language of their own that includes quick pencil sketches to illustrate their points, symbols for kisses, pet names and catch-all phrases intended to evoke humorous scenes or people from their past together" (134).

8 "THIS CLEVER WOMAN WHO CALLS HERSELF VERNON LEE"

1. Pronounced as in French, *culte* was defined in a glossary in Letley's *Maurice Baring* as "someone very nice and lovable; to have a culte; to have a crush on someone."

2. Kinta Beevor, Janet Ross's niece, recalls of her childhood in the late 1920s: "An even more improbable character [than Carlo Placci, "a cosmopolitan name-dropper"] was the writer Vernon Lee, alias Violet Paget, with her cropped hair and man's clothes with stiff collars. She was particularly kind and gave me copies of all her books and, more surprisingly, a loom, as if I were a character in one of her Tuscan fairy tales. Conversation with her, however, was agonizing, for she was old and very deaf. Aunt Janet, for reasons I never entirely understood, loathed her. My father, on the other hand, liked her enormously" (105).

3. Though a caricature, France's Miss Bell is a far gentler portrait than the American novelist Robert Herrick's in *The Gospel of Freedom* (1898). Here, however, the primary

target is Bernard Berenson, who appears as an unscrupulous Jewish-American art critic, all the more cruel because Berenson had been very cordial to Herrick on his visit to Italy. Violet, whom Herrick regarded as "an intolerable ass," had also entertained him at Il Palmerino. In his novel she is "the Gorgon . . . Vivian Vivasour . . . as sour as her articles are sweetly wordy." See Samuels 267.

4. Violet met Laura Gropallo in Como in 1892. According to Gunn, it was from her that Violet "acquired later the rudiments of psychology" (148), but she had already been reading in that field for several years, especially motivated by the mystery of Eugene's illness. Most of Gropallo's writings were not on psychology but were essays on contemporary Italian writers (*Autori italiani d'oggi*, 1903), some short historical dramas, and an essay on Bernard Berenson (1904). Violet and Laura Gropallo remained friends, though they often disagreed on intellectual questions. When Kit Anstruther-Thomson broke off her relationship with Violet, Laura offered sympathy. Violet reminded Kit in a letter in 1908 that they had once stayed together at the Casa Gropallo: "You went on to England and I stayed rather heart-broken and Laura came and gave me a kiss and said, 'This is the one your friend would have given you.' Well! One oughtn't forget such dearness as that" (31 October 1908).

5. Nicky Mariano wrote that from their first meeting Placci "played a great part in the life of both Bernard Berenson and Mary" (26).

6. Wimbush's generosity proved an embarrassment. Violet wrote her mother: "Myself, while feeling in a way a snob and utterly unworthy of such a token of friendship and simple kindness feel a very great repugnance to accepting. Kit thinks it would be natural and right to accept, but I cannot help thinking her biassed [*sic*] by her wish to get me well at any cost" (12 September 1888). Violet's pride also prevented her from accepting a generous check her mother sent her. Finally and reluctantly she agreed to let Wimbush pay for the Spanish trip, but she used her own money for the visit to Tangier.

7. See, for example, her letter to her mother from Rome: "I think constantly here in Rome of all that you did for me while we lived here, and how completely you *made* me intellectually, how completely 'son la tua creatura'" (4 February 1890).

8. Berenson dropped the 'h' from his first name during World War I. The scholarly books cited in the preface are *L'eresia nel medio evo*, by Felice Tocco (1884); *L'Italie mystique: Histoire de la renaissance religieuse au moyen âge*, by Emile Gebhart (1890); and *Saint François d'Assise* by Paul Sabatier (1890).

9. See Vernon Lee's review of William James's *The Will to Believe* in *Fortnightly Review*, November 1899: "Particularly on the part of those who, like myself, *will to believe* that man's highest work is the realisation of a human ideal, and that the only Godhead which can make binding laws for man is the divinity consubstantiate with his best self and shaped in the glorified image of those he loves most" (842).

10. These identifications were made by Peter Gunn, 112.

11. Preface to *Mimma Bella*. The volume consists of twenty-nine Italian sonnets, deeply felt no doubt but painfully sentimental. The first sonnet begins: "O rosy as the lining of a shell / Were the wee hands that now are white as snow / And like pink coral, with their elfin toes / The feet that on life's brambles never fell."

12. "And it seems to us to be worthwhile to try and make out what this clever woman who calls herself 'Vernon Lee' really wishes us to regard as the ideal teacher of

the new age. For all her interlocutors, without exception, treat Christianity as an absolutely exploded superstition." From an unsigned review of *Baldwin* in the *Spectator*, 1 May 1885, 573.

9   AESTHETICS AND THE HEALTH OF THE SOUL

1. Quoted s.v. "Aestheticism," *Princeton Encyclopedia of Poetry and Poetics*, ed. Alex Preminger (Princeton, N.J.: Princeton UP, 1972).

2. Quoted in F. E. Sparshott, *The Structure of Aesthetics* (Toronto: U Toronto P, 1963), 244.

3. No admirer of Vernon Lee's thinking ("such a watery mind!"), Virginia Woolf nevertheless acknowledged that she was interesting on the subject of aesthetics. In her review of *Laurus Nobilis* for the *Times Literary Supplement*, 5 August 1909, Woolf wrote: "But if Vernon Lee lacks the temper of the great aesthetic critic, she has many of the gifts of a first-rate disciple. She has read Plato and Ruskin and Pater with enthusiasm because she cares passionately for the subjects they deal with. Moreover, although we may doubt her conclusions or admit that they bewilder us, her exposition is full of ingenuity, and has often the suggestive power of brilliant talk. One may not make things more clear by talking about them, but one can infect others with the same desire" (*Essays* 1:279).

4. In his *Sketch for a Self-Portrait* Berenson wrote: "For I was born to talk and not to write and, worse still, to converse rather than to talk and then only with stimulating interlocutors" (13).

5. Vernon Lee in turn found Berenson dogmatic. In her "Commonplace Book XIII," 10 December 1895, she writes that his sole criterion for appreciation was structure. Michelangelo is good "because he is structural," but Sargent "was bad because he was the reverse of structural and after this he would never look at Sargent save with scorn, never allow Sargent's good qualities to touch him."

6. The full texts of the letters of both Berenson and Vernon Lee are in Berenson's *Letters* 55–60.

7. In her postscript to Berenson's *Selected Letters*, Nicky Mariano writes that Vernon Lee "admitted that looking through Miss Anstruther-Thomson's annotations during Berenson's talks with them she had realized that his accusation of plagiarism was not wholly unjustified" (298).

8. Hildebrand wrote, "Our ideas of form, in so far as we derive them from a visual projection or a picture, depend in reality on our vast experience of the relations existing between visual and kinesthetic sensations" (34).

9. See also her letter to Carlo Placci, 28 May 1913: "I have myself long since felt persuaded that just because Berenson was (passez moi le mot) an ill-tempered and egotistic ass to mistake us for plagiarists, we, on the other hand, were not very intelligent in mistaking him for a slanderer and a villain. The whole incident was merely a comedy in which the usual (indeed perhaps more than usual) human incapacity for understanding other people's ideas and the naive human demand that other people should *exactly* understand *one's* own played the chief and not all missing parts" (Pantazzi, "Carlo Placci" 120). Placci was another casualty of this "comedy." Violet felt that he had failed to come to her defense though he had long been acquainted with her ideas on art. They were estranged for a number of years.

10. "But there remained in my friend's mind a long-enduring aversion for the intellectual circles where such associations could arise, and even a distaste for the interests in life where *one* might be subject to such attacks" (*Art and Man* 62–63).

11. In a footnote that Kit added to *Beauty and Ugliness* in 1911 she reported that she was practicing "a system of athletics" taught by a Mrs. Roger Watts which involved exercises in muscular tension, "a facility to resisting gravitation and a consequent appearance of homogeneous existence and of freedom from weight such as we have hitherto considered the prerogative of Greek works of art" (221). Diana Maltz argues that Kit's contribution to psychological aesthetics was shallow and self-promoting: "While she freed herself from the rigors of formal study, Anstruther-Thomson continued to claim the role of seer that psychological aesthetics had afforded her in social circles" (221). Maltz follows the suggestion of Irene Cooper Willis that Kit was only pretending to an intellectual interest in aesthetics, eroticizing her spontaneous reactions to art to appeal "to an aristocratic lesbian elite." Maltz writes: "In the spirit of the fin de siècle, Anstruther-Thomson used her decadent focus on bodily sensations to subvert Lee's social and educational agendas, in effect producing a new version of psychological aesthetics, one in which social service was subordinated to sexuality. The museum gallery was in fact a social arena where Anstruther-Thomson used her body to titillate an audience of female upper-class devotees" (213). This is a subjective and I think unfounded evaluation of Kit's work. The evidence suggests rather that she was not intellectually suited for such a study but that her later efforts in the field were earnest attempts to educate working-class women.

10 LABORA ET NOLI CONTRISTARI

1. See Vernon Lee's letter to Alice Callandar of 14 November 1903 expressing surprise at hearing from her after a long silence. She recalls their friendship fondly, "despite the painful doubt in which you left me, not merely at the breaking up of our intercourse but during the time of your subsequent intimacy with Miss Anstruther-Thomson."

2. The lecture referred to was later incorporated into *The Handling of Words.*

3. A minority report was given by the aunt and niece writing team of "Michael Field" (Katherine Harris Bradley and Edith Emma Cooper). Traveling in northern Italy in 1894 or 1895, they stopped off to visit Il Palmerino. As Edith Cooper recalled the visit, "We saw a *sibyl,* in a tailor-made black dress, vine-dresser's hat and apron, sowing seeds. We advanced—it was Vernon. She looks fifty; she is thirty-nine. She is very ugly; the face very long; the eyes with a look of greed for discussion. Yet there is much suffering in the expression, or sadness that one pities." They noted the presence of Vernon's "bosom-friend" Kit Anstruther-Thomson, "a splendid example of the thorough-bred English woman, to whom dogs and horses are as familiar as books to us." They were unimpressed by the house ("no charm . . . too crowded and awkwardly disposed") or its mistress ("very stupid in what she said about art"). See *Works and Days, from the Journal of Michael Field,* 263–65.

4. Years later Russell told Burdett Gardner that she was "incredibly ugly but always able to win the devotion of young girls who were both intelligent and beautiful. This, I suppose, was owing to the brilliancy of her intellect." He called her "a vampire . . . a very masterful, dominant person—a bloodsucker!" (59–60).

5. Augustine Bulteau (1860–1922) wrote novels under the pen name Jacques Von-

tade and essays on England and the English. The best known of these is *L'âme anglais* (1910), translated as *The English Soul* by H. T. Porter (London, 1914).

6. The widow of an English army officer, Irene Forbes Morse had a distinguished German literary heritage, being distantly related to both the Brentano and the von Arnim families. She was a writer herself, and Vernon Lee wrote a preface to a collection of her short stories, *Don Juan's Daughters* (trans. Oakley Williams [New York: Dodd, Mead, 1930]), in which she noted that "this lady [is] as cosmopolitan as any of the eighteenth century, yet as deep-down German as a Brahms' *Volkslied*." Some time after Vernon Lee bought Il Palmerino, Mrs. Forbes Morse leased a portion of the land from her and converted one of the small farm buildings into a house of her own. She quarreled with Violet over expenses involved in repairs and in fact spent very little time there, but they remained friends.

7. Ottoline took a fancy to Irene Cooper Willis and introduced her to her lover Bertrand Russell in 1914 with the extraordinary idea that she might bear him the children he wanted. The "coldly beautiful Miss Cooper Willis" politely declined but worked part-time for him as a research assistant. In 1916 she had a brief affair with the critic Desmond MacCarthy which allegedly inspired a novel she published in 1923 under the pseudonym Althea Brooke, *The Green-Eyed Monster* (Seymour 255).

8. In October 1907 Edith Wharton wrote Violet a letter of condolence on Eugene Lee-Hamilton's death—"I can't tell you how I grieve for you"—and she recalled "so many pleasant memories of our first meetings in Florence, and of the delightful days he spent with us when he was in America" (Fife 139). A month later she published an article, "The Sonnets of Eugene Lee-Hamilton," in *The Bookman*. Citing his 1894 collection *Sonnets of the Wingless Hours,* she wrote that it "confirms and even strengthens the impression received from its first perusal that it contains some twenty sonnets of exceptional beauty, and four or five which rank not far after the greatest in the language" (251). Unless otherwise noted, the letters of Edith Wharton quoted are in the library of Somerville College, Oxford, quoted here with the permission of the Principal and Fellows of Somerville College.

9. Because she hoped to interest Italian readers in her work, Wharton was especially grateful for Vernon Lee's praise of *The Valley of Decision* in a review for the journal *La cultura:* "Mrs. Wharton's novel is a wonderful account of historical truth, both in the actual facts and in the human environment—a truth which, however, is not merely objective. . . . Mrs. Wharton gives us something more: a picture, a series of pictures, viewed through an artist's personality and translated into artistic symbols: the subjective truth of the soul of an age and of a country, revealed through the eyes of a real writer." Vernon Lee wrote an introduction for an Italian translation of the novel, but the translation was never published, and her introduction, once in Edith Wharton's possession, was apparently lost. See Wharton, *A Backward Glance* 133.

11 HANDLING WORDS

1. In general she had little taste for the realism of modern fiction. Her friend Edith Wharton had similar views. In a letter of 5 October 1907 she asked "Dear Miss Paget" to send her a copy of the new printing of *Studies of the Eighteenth Century in Italy* and added: "I don't send you my 'opuses,' as they are novels nowadays, and I know

novels bore you. They do me too—I mean the new ones, and my own among them" (Fife 144).

2. "These sort of Americans," Violet wrote her mother of the Curtises and Bronsons, "who shudder at Howells look up to James as a patron saint of cosmopolitan refinement" (Honour and Fleming 75).

3. Vernon Lee shared the social snobbery of many of her contemporaries. Though not anti-Semitic, she often slipped into the habits of the upper class, who regarded Jews as parvenus. Exceptions of course were made for intellectuals like Berenson. In the bitter division in French society over the Dreyfus case, she was outspoken in her support of Dreyfus, and in her journalism she expressed sympathy for the plight of Jews in czarist Russia.

4. "Lady Tal" was reprinted in 1993 in a collection edited by Elaine Showalter and titled *Daughters of Decadence*. All quotations cited here are from that edition. The paradox of the "aesthetic Puritan" Vernon Lee writing a story that can be read as an example of the literature of decadence is explored by Jean de Palacio in "Y a-t-il une écriture feminine de la Decadence?" He finds distinctly decadent characteristics in the implied reversals of sexual/gender roles: Lady Tal, whose name is shortened from the Amazonian Atalanta with all its Swinburnean echoes, conquers the reluctant and sexually ambiguous Jervase Marion. Merete Licht, studying the references to *Princess Casamassima* in "Lady Tal," finds a connection in Paul Muniment and his invalid sister Rosy. Lady Tal, we learn, had nursed her paralyzed brother until his death, suggesting Violet's experience with her brother. And Rosy Muniment, like Eugene Lee-Hamilton, though confined to her bed, is a lively conversationalist who enjoys the company of her sibling's friends. Licht makes a far more dubious connection when she identifies the Muniments' hardworking laundress mother and their insignificant father with Mr. and Mrs. Paget.

5. This last resolution of Marion's has special relevance to James, in light of his several encounters with women writers who sought his advice and approval. Violet Paget was certainly one of these, but I can find no evidence that she ever submitted a manuscript to him before its publication. His detailed criticism of *Miss Brown* came several months after its publication. He did, however, read proofs and write a critical commentary on Mrs. Humphry Ward's *Eleanor*, and he collaborated actively with the actress-novelist Elizabeth Robins in her adaptation of a Spanish play by José Echegaray, *Marianna*, in 1895. "Evening after evening," Robins wrote, "he would sit with me with that sustained patience, discussing, mending, polishing. Usually he would dictate and I would set down" (176). However, allegations (based in part on Constance Fenimore Woolson's pathetic story "Miss Grief") that James exploited his friendships with women writers by lifting ideas from their work strike me as unwarranted. Robins perceptively observed that James simply could not resist "improving" on the words of others: "He positively could not, he said, read anything now for the sake of the story. He had 'lost his innocence.' If a book interested him he wanted to rewrite it" (172). Jervase Marion's entrapment by Lady Tal may be an instance of art imitating life.

6. In February 1885 William James wrote his brother objecting to Miss Birdseye in *The Bostonians* as too obviously modeled on their family friend Miss Peabody. Henry replied: "I had absolutely no shadow of such an intention. . . . Miss Birdseye was

evolved entirely from my moral consciousness, like every other person I have ever drawn." He did, however, acknowledge the resemblance and said that he regretted it (Weber, "Henry James" 686).

7. ALS. Yale Collection of American Literature, Beinecke Rare Book and Manuscript Library.

8. See her letter to her mother, 12 June 1894: "After the lecture several smart bonnets came up to me. Margot Tennant, the famous *Dodo* [E. F. Benson's popular 1893 novel], now married to Asquith, and a lady unknown who asked me 'how she could learn to know the strength of adjectives.' It was rather pathetic."

9. *The Handling of Words* was appreciated only some years after its publication. In 1965 Kenneth Graham observed that Vernon Lee anticipated by several years Henry James's prefaces to the New York Edition. Her work, he wrote, "deserves to rank beside any single similar piece by James for its qualities of originality, reasonableness, and devotion to the craft of novel-writing. . . . Its general concern for artistic unity and for the novelist's best use of the means peculiarly at his disposal . . . connects it with all that was most scrupulous and most alert in Victorian criticism of fiction" (138). In the same year David Lodge wrote in *The Language of Fiction* that "tribute should be paid . . . to Vernon Lee's rather neglected pioneering book . . . which, considering its date, is a remarkable achievement, full of useful insights and suggestions, and which includes what are probably the first examples in English criticism of close, methodical analysis applied to narrative prose" (xi). In 1974 John Halperin acknowledged her contribution to the development of critical theory, suggesting that she was influenced by Flaubert in emphasizing the importance of form in the novel and by Henry James in deemphasizing the function of the omniscient author (16–17). Essentially she was an eclectic. In his introduction to his edition of *The Handling of Words* David Seed wrote that everything Vernon Lee studied, from the rhetoric her mother taught her out of Cobbett's *Grammar of the English Language* to Pater, Henry and William James, and the German psychologists, was absorbed into her critical thinking.

10. See "A Note on the Text," xxiii–xxiv, in Gettmann's 1968 reprint of *The Handling of Words*. (All page references here are to this edition.) The original publication of the essays is as follows: "The Craft of Words (as part 3 of her chap. "On Style"), *New Review* 11 (December 1894): 571–80; "On Literary Construction," *Contemporary Review* 68 (September 1895): 404–19; "Studies in Literary Psychology," *ibid.* 84 (November 1903): 713–23; *ibid.* (December 1903): 856–64; *ibid.* 85 (March 1904): 386–92; "The Handling of Words," *English Review* 5 (June 1910): 427–41; *ibid.* (July): 599–607; *ibid.* 6 (September 1910): 224–35; *ibid.* 9 (September 1911): 231–41; *ibid.* (October): 441–48. The longest and most rambling chapter of the book, "The Nature of the Writer," first appeared as "The Nature of Literature," *Contemporary Review* 86 (September 1904): 377–91, and November, 645–61. She made no substantial changes in any of these between periodical and book publication. In his reprint of the book Seed includes "The Handling of Words: A Page of Walter Pater," which Vernon Lee published in *Life and Letters* 9 (September–November 1933): 287–310. This is an analysis of a passage from chapter 3 of *Marius the Epicurean*. Though she faults Pater for "slovenliness"—faulty antecedents, inconsistencies in tense, repetition, and awkward phrasing—she concludes that the passage is overall so powerful that this "does not in the least affect my sense of being in the presence of one of the most enchanting and valuable minds that I know" (331).

12 MUSIC

1. In the *New Statesman and Nation* (19 November 1932), W. G. Turner judged it "a solid book . . . admirably planned, clearly and concisely written, with a refreshing absence of vague jargon." Turner refers to her throughout the review as "Dr. Vernon Lee," because she had received a Litt.D. from Durham University in 1924. In brief reviews the (London) *Times* (7 January 1933) and the *Times Literary Supplement* (10 November 1932) noted with approval her fresh psychological approach to the aesthetics of music.

2. She was not indulging in false modesty when she identified herself as "an average semi-musical hearer. . . . My ear is good in the sense of correct reproduction of notes and intervals, but not sufficient to analyze chords, to locate single notes on a scale, or to name sequences of notes." See "Religious and Moral Status of Wagner," *Fortnightly Review,* May 1911, 869.

3. The friend quoted, from a conversation in 1886, was Amy Levy. See Beckman 293 n. 6.

4. See her essay "The Riddle of Music" in the *Quarterly Review,* January 1906: "For whether a composition affect us as a beautiful and noble experience, faintly tinged, vividly tipped, with some human emotion, or whether it affect us as an emotional experience kept within the bounds of aesthetic order, shaped in aesthetic beauty, by the presence of musical form—which ever of the two possibilities we consider, there remains an action of the aesthetic element upon the emotional, and the emotional is probably purified by the aesthetic, as the aesthetic is unquestionably brought deeper into our life by the emotional" (227).

5. According to the entry for Pacchiarotti in *The New Grove Dictionary of Music and Musicians,* he was "by all accounts the greatest of the late eighteenth-century castratos and the last in the line of the finest male sopranos." He was born in Ancona in 1740 and died in Padua in 1821. Trained in the singing schools of Venice, he sang triumphantly in the major opera houses of Europe. His great triumph was in London where he was proclaimed "superior to any singer heard in this country since Farinelli." He was a close friend of the Burney family. Fanny recalled one performance she heard in May 1790: "And, oh, how Paccerotti [*sic*] sung!—HOW!—with what exquisite feeling, what penetrating pathos! I could almost have cried the whole time, that this one short song was all that that I should be able to hear!" (*Diary and Letters* 2:356). William Beckford became his patron, engaging him to sing at Fonthill Abbey for his "Gargantuan" coming-of-age party (*Travel Diaries* 1:xxiv). Stendhal was among his many admirers and reported that in an opera performance once in 1776 even the orchestra members were so moved to tears by his voice that they had to stop playing for a few minutes. Pacchiarotti spent his last years in Padua where Goldoni, Stendhal and Rossini were among a host of celebrities who visited him.

6. The books reviewed included two Italian books on the careers of the singer Pierfrancesco Tosi and the singing master Giambattista Mancini, a study of the art of song by Enrico Panofka, and Stendhal's *Vie de Rossini.*

7. "The Religious and Moral Status of Wagner," *Fortnightly Review* (May 1911): 885.

13 STORIES OF THE SUPERNATURAL

1. See Edwin F. Block Jr.'s comment that "Amour Dure" "has transformed what were for one writer the peculiar anomalies of her own emotional and artistic life . . . the

tensions of creativity and sterility, an attraction to the past and a desire to live in the present" (88).

2. Maurice Baring, who was planning to write a novel or play set in Italy in the seventeenth or eighteenth century, wrote Vernon Lee for advice. She replied, "In your place I should boldly invent a state to suit my purpose (as I did in *Alberic,* if you remember, though I had Massa Carrara in my mind). It leaves one free to be as detailed as one wishes" (20 February 1906).

3. Burdett Gardner argues at length in *The Lesbian Imagination* that Vernon Lee's work in general and her supernatural fiction in particular was stamped by her repressed lesbianism: "Can it be that the 'enchantment' is Vernon Lee's own sexual inversion and that she is presenting a fantastic allegory of her own personal struggle to achieve 'freedom' and mental health?" (28). As a Freudian he finds "oedipal implications" in Alberic's love for his fairy godmother. The most elaborate Freudian reading of "Prince Alberic" is in a German study that I have not read, Gunnar Schmidt's *Die Literarisierung des Unbewussten: Studien zu den phantastischen Erzählungen von Oliver Onions und Vernon Lee* (Frankfort: Peter Lang, 1984). I quote here from Christa Zorn's dissertation: "Schmidt sees in Lee's stories metonymic representations of continuously suppressed desires that lead to hysteric states of mind. He analyzes her stories as complex psychological 'cases,' in which works of art function as so-called 'situational imperatives' that evoke past suppression and thus become provocateurs of fears and desires" (287).

In her study of the adolescent boy as femme fatale, Martha Vicinus cites "Prince Alberic" as an example of "the lesbian subtext of much of her work" (95–96). There is certainly an androgynous quality in Alberic's character—his graceful good looks, his gentleness of character. But under the guidance of his godmother he grows up expert in horsemanship and swordplay, "marvellously assiduous in the council chamber, and still more so in following the military exercises and learning the trade of a soldier." Indifferent to "the bevy of lovely nymphs" his grandfather offers him, he resolves independently "to lead a single life until the age of twenty-eight or thirty, and he would then require the assistance of no ambassadors or chancellors, but find for himself the future Duchess of Luna." Among other analyses of the story, in "Vernon Lee's Decadent Women" Ruth Robbins sees the dying society in the court of Luna, dated precisely 1701, as analogous to the inconsistencies and contradictions of fin de siècle society, and the killing of the snake lady as a sign of the hopelessness of the feminist cause in the male-dominated 1890s. In "(P)revising Freud: Vernon Lee's Castration Phantasy" Jane Hotchkiss reads the story as a feminist protest against male hegemony and the mutilation of the snake as a symbolic clitorectomy. In contrast, Carolyn Christensen Nelson argues that Vernon Lee's supernatural tales do not reflect feminist ideology: "Instead, her work reveals the influence of the male decadents in its representation of gender 'slippage' and its preoccupation with 'perverse women characters'" (70).

4. Gunn prints this story on p. 51. Another instance of Vernon Lee's use of the motif of the enchanted snake is in her short novel *Penelope Brandling,* where the hero recalls his childhood fascination with a water snake who, he believes, will one day be transformed into a fairy. As in "Prince Alberic," the snake is caught by his cruel older brother and savagely skinned alive.

5. In her study of "aesthetic intertextuality," Zorn writes: "'Amour Dure' can be read as an animated version of 'La Gioconda' in *The Renaissance,* and at the same time

as a trope for the entire nineteenth-century craze for the Italian Renaissance—from Goethe to Burckhardt, from Browning to Swinburne." Because the narrator of "Amour Dure" is a modern historian, Zorn continues, Vernon Lee deconstructs Pater's aestheticized image "into its historical (and sexualized) components which she then reassembles to construct woman's historical visibility—on her own terms" (4). The young historian, blinded by his passion, sees Medea as a "liberated" woman rebelling against the male hegemony of the Renaissance. Zorn's reading is reasonable, in contrast to Diane Basham's astonishing argument in *The Trial of Woman* that Medea da Carpi and Alice Oke of "Oke of Okehurst" were inspired by Matilda Paget, and that "Vernon Lee's writing [is] committed to keeping this dead mother supernaturally alive. . . . As well as practicing magic [!] (for Matilda abhorred the church), Mrs. Paget was in her daughter's eyes almost literally magical in her contradictory but 'unmistakable originality'" (174).

6. Miriam Allott was the first to note that it was Bronzino's portrait of Lucrezia Panciatichi that fascinated Milly Theale in *The Wings of the Dove* when she sees it in Lord Mark's collection at Matcham. Both Milly and others in the novel notice her resemblance to the portrait. James, a frequent visitor to the Uffizi, likely knew the portrait before he read "Amour Dure" in *Hauntings* in 1890. Adeline Tintner points out two other Bronzino portraits in the Uffizi—*Elenore of Toledo Medici* and a little girl, *Bia di Cosimo de' Medici*—in which the subjects wear chains with inscriptions, but believes that the inspiration for both James and Vernon Lee was Lucrezia (*Lust of the Eyes* 95).

7. At about the same time that she was writing "Oke," she wrote another story set in an English country house, "The Hidden Door," a pseudo-ghost story because it turns out that the central character, a silly busybody, has imagined a lurid history of a family curse. The story was published in a collection edited by Henry Norman in 1886, *The Witching Time: Tales for the Year's End,* which included stories by F. Marion Crawford, Lawrence Alma-Taddema, and Mary Robinson. Vernon Lee could not have thought much of the story because she never reprinted it.

8. James G. Nelson pointed out that for the late Victorians and Edwardians paganism offered escape, a chance "to get away from it all . . . an implied rejection of both modern society and religion" (246). He cites as examples Kenneth Graham's *Pagan Pieces,* Symonds's *In the Key of Blue,* John Davidson's *A Random Itinerary.* See also Samuel Hynes: "From *The Yellow Book* to the Pan-ridden stories of E. M. Forster, one finds the same fascination with pagan deities" (146).

9. There is an engraving attributed to Dürer, *The Young Woman Attacked by Death; or The Ravisher* (ca. 1495), in which a woman struggles to tear herself from the arms of a fierce-looking, bare-chested man. But its German title, *Das Liebeskraut Eryngium,* refers to the thistlelike plant in the background, known for its aphrodisiac qualities, and the man depicted has none of the skeletal features of Death as Dürer represented him in *The Knight, Death, and the Devil.*

10. Rolfe lived in Italy for many years and died in Venice in 1913, but there is no evidence that Vernon Lee ever met him, though she certainly knew the Toto stories. Not only because of his flaunted homosexuality but also because of his reputation as a social leech who sought hospitality but never repaid debts, one understands her reluctance to know him.

11. Henry James, who translated Merimée's story when he was studying French, wrote an interesting variation on it in "The Last of the Valerii" (1874). Here a happily

married Italian count discovers, while digging in his garden, an ancient statue of a beautiful woman and falls in love with it. His sensible American wife has the statue reburied, and they are reconciled.

12. In her dedication to *The Sentimental Traveller,* Vernon Lee comments on the paradox of Spain, with "its hyperbole, all or nothing Quixotry, its cavalier aloofness from petty realities and futile advantage, its preference, as in the paintings of Velasquez compared with that of Rubens, of the black and white bony essentials of things to their pink and juicy pulpiness" (7).

13. See Rosemary Jackson, who reads the final episode of the burning as "a ritualized ending, the exorcism of a passive female role" (xxv).

14. "Out of Venice at Last," *Westminster Gazette* 1 June 1910. Carlos Caballero emphasizes Vernon Lee's "spirited indictment of Wagner's music" as decadent and morbid. He notes that the victim of Zafferino's voice in the story of his singing powers is the Procuratessa Vendramin. Wagner died in Venice in the Palazzo Vendramin in 1883. Peter Christensen similarly reads the story as the artist's vain struggle to overthrow the influence of the past. Zaffirino's haunting voice is a punishment for Magnus's hubris.

14 TRAVEL WRITING

1. The essay was first published in *Macmillan's Magazine,* September 1894, then collected in the Tauchnitz edition of *Pope Jacynth and Other Romantic Inventions* in 1906. It was reprinted in *Pope Jacynth and More Supernatural Tales: Excursions into Fantasy* (1956), with a publisher's note: "*Ravenna and Her Ghosts* is not a story, although in this vignette is retold a mediaeval legend of the supernatural, removed from the stories which make up this book, and also because it is in her vivid evocations of mediaeval Italian life that Vernon Lee's tale is shown at its height" (125). My quotations are from this edition.

2. The story also inspired Botticelli's contemporary Davide Ghirlandaio (brother of the more famous Domenico), who painted two panels illustrating the legend—the pursuit of the naked lady (now in the Brooklyn Museum) and the relenting of the lady Nostagio is wooing (in the Philadelphia Museum of Art). Byron's lines are:
    The spectre huntsman of Onesti's line,
    His hell-dogs, and their chase, and the fair throng
    Which learn'd from this example not to fly
    From a true lover, shadow'd my mind's eye.

3. Henry James had unqualified praise for her writings on Italy. Maurice Baring admired all her travel writing: "I have never met anyone who summed up so well, so precisely and yet so original and picturesque a fashion, the exact quality and essence of a person or a place" (*Lost Lectures* 90). Bernard Berenson, no partisan of hers, admitted as late as 1948: "After many years I revisited Belcaro. Vernon Lee's book, which I read while still at Harvard, invested the name with even more magic than any other Italian place name" (Diary, 30 April 1948, qtd. in Gettman's introduction to *The Handling of Words,* x–xi). In 1987, evaluating foreign writers on Italy, William M. Johnston observed, "Around 1900 an English woman, Vernon Lee, composed travel miniatures with such delicacy that even today she has more subtle things to say about enjoying places than almost anyone else" (2).

4. Her "Greek Notes" were published in the *Westminster Gazette* in 1910: "Greece

at Last," 1 January; "The Statues at Olympia," 5 February; "Delphi and the Castalian Springs," 19 February; "Farewell to Greece," 26 March; "At the Sign of the Pythian Apollo," 9 April; "Daphne and the Little Byzantine Church," n.d.

5. Edith Wharton shared these sentiments. She recalled in her *Italian Backgrounds* being amid the beautiful scenery in Switzerland one August when she suddenly decided to go to Italy. "Was it better to be cool and look at a waterfall, or to be hot and look at St. Mark's? Was it better to walk on gentians or on mosaic, to smell fir-needles or incense? Was it, in short, ever better to be elsewhere when one might be in Italy?" (*Edith Wharton Abroad* 88).

6. Maurice Baring wrote a good-natured parody, "The Spirit of Rome (with apologies to Vernon Lee)," which she enjoyed. It begins "Facts? No. Dates? No": "May 11. We drive this afternoon to the Villa Madama. On the way we talked of Richard Strauss and the non-melodiac musicians. Strauss is a Dionysian. We compared his prophetic mood-music with the old-fashioned facile melodies of Wagner that pleased our youth. While we were talking a shepherd passed us. As he passed he took off his hat and said, 'Buon Giorno.' Very Roman that" (*Round the World in Any Number of Days* 88–89).

7. She dedicated *Genius Loci* "To the Cypresses of Vincigliata and the Oakwoods at Abbey Leix."

8. ALS. The Department of Manuscripts, Huntington Library.

9. The classical Ariadne legend is here simply a frame for another of Vernon Lee's literary pastiches: a mixture of influences and allusions ranging from Ariosto, Tasso, Shakespeare, Milton, and Fletcher to her contemporary J. H. Shorthouse's allegorical tale about an innocent young boy who is sacrificed to the whims of the aristocracy he serves, *Little Schoolmaster Mark* (1883). In his preface Shorthouse had cited her "delightful book, *Studies of the Eighteenth Century in Italy*." She repaid the compliment in her preface by calling his book "a small masterpiece."

15 "SISTER IN UTOPIA"

1. ALS. The Department of Manuscripts, Huntington Library.

2. In her *Diary* for 18 July 1894, Beatrice Webb wrote: "I do not much believe in the productive power of woman's intellect, strain herself as she may, the output is small and the ideas thin and wire-drawn from lack of matter and wide experience. The woman's plenitude consists of that wonderful combination of tenderness and judgement which is the genius of motherhood, a plenitude springing from the very sources of her nature, not acquired or attained by outward training" (2:52).

3. In *The Handling of Words* she distinguishes between characters who are rationally and analytically conceived and those who are "born . . . of some strong feeling on the part of their author. Sometimes it is a violent repulsion—the strongest kind of repulsion. . . . Our whole nature tingles with the discomfort which the creature causes in us. Such characters—I take them at random—are (for myself at least) Tolstoi's Monsieur Karénine and Henry James's Olive Chancellor" (27).

4. The review had the title "The Economic Dependence of Women." It was published in *Gospels of Anarchy* as "The Economic Parasitism of Women" and reprinted in *Critical Essays on Charlotte Perkins Gilman*, ed. Joanne B. Karpinski (New York: G. K. Hall, 1992). My quotations are from *Gospels of Anarchy*.

5. Occasionally, she complains, Emerson resorts to "a cheap transcendentalism, the

metaphysics of Germany adulterated by the shoddy science, the cheap mysticism of America" (62).

6. ALS. bMS Am 1092 (641), by permission of the Houghton Library, Harvard University.

7. Her outlets ranged from specialized journals like the *Revue philosophique* and the *Zeitschrift für Ästhetik* to more generally popular American periodicals like *Harper's* and *Scribner's*. For a full list of her articles, see *ELIT* 26 (1983): 250–60.

8. Spender described his writers as "incurably 'highbrow' . . . men who are eminent and distinguished as literary craftsmen. They did not like to be cut or edited, nor have captions and subheads attached to their contributions." He recalled on one occasion having inserted subheads "into an article by a distinguished woman writer, which, though a masterpiece of its kind, did seem to me to need just that amount of relief to the reader. This brought me the deserved and expected rebuke on a postcard from Italy: 'What unspeakable office boy has been laying his obscene paw on my writing?' " (2:142–43). It is irresistible—and not unreasonable—to speculate that the writer was Vernon Lee.

9. Vernon Lee's translation of this letter was first published 25 June 1910 in the provincial edition of the *Westminster Gazette*, but seeking a wider audience, she offered it to the *Nation*.

10. In her letter to the New York *Nation*, 17 September 1914, she cites "the other vast half of French public opinion, the Nationalists, Legitimists and neo-mediaevalists with their literary representatives from Barrès and [Charles] Maurras to [Paul] Claudel."

16 A WILDERNESS OF WOLVES

1. On 11 September 1914 Olive Schreiner wrote to Havelock Ellis: "Did you see the *Labour Leader?* It is the only paper that is standing out. The other papers all refuse to take Vernon Lee's and Bertrand Russell's articles" (*Letters* 338).

2. ALS. The Fales Library, New York University.

3. Between 1906 and 1921 Vernon Lee published seven books with Tauchnitz, some of which included two titles in a single volume. They were *Pope Jacynth (with Ariadne and Other Romantic Inventions)*, 1906; *Genius Loci and The Enchanted Woods*, 1906; *Hortus Vitae and Limbo*, 1907; *The Spirit of Rome and Laurus Nobilis*, 1910; *Vanitas*, 1911; *Louis Norbert*, 1920; and *The Sentimental Traveller*, 1921.

4. At the outbreak of the war, Romain Rolland, though overage for military service, supported the French cause and appealed to German intellectuals to repudiate Germany's militarism. But in advocating cooperation with Germans in peace talks, he alienated many French and Swiss friends. The articles he published in the *Journal de Genève* opposing the war further alienated his public. According to Ellen Key, a Swedish journalist, it was Vernon Lee who first proposed his name for the Nobel Prize (Starr 130; Francis 110).

5. Armfield was a respected Anglo-American artist who specialized in book illustration in a mannered art nouveau style with abstract margin designs and vaguely Greek-looking figures in poses of battle and mourning. He wrote of his illustrations for William Morris's *Life and Death of Jason* (London: Swarthmore P, 1922): "No attempt has been made in the drawings to convey an impression with line similar in kind to that conveyed by the words of the text." This comment certainly applies to his work for *The Ballet of the Nations*.

6. There was enough interest remaining in it for John Lane to reissue *Satan the Waster* with a new preface by the author "Ten Years after Publication, 1920–1930." Here Vernon Lee somewhat disingenuously writes that at the time of its original publication her pacifist views could not have been expressed "without impiety": "So, with the generous exception of Mr. Bernard Shaw, *Satan the Waster* was boycotted by reviewers; my own friends turned away from it in silence; and I myself felt rather ashamed of having written it." In the decade from 1920 to 1930, however, disillusion set in everywhere and was articulated by many of the young men who had fought in the war:

> What Heroism, temporarily restored to sight, thought of that performance in which he had played the star part, was expressed some years later by Mr. John Galsworthy's young poet in the *White Monkey*. And Heroism, with the voice of real young poets and novelists, from Sassoon to Remarque and Hemmingway [*sic*], Williamson, Aldington and Graves, has been repeating, bitterly or sorrowfully, the same thing ever since. And people have listened without being scandalised, except with the war itself and its former promoters. . . . Now that its heresies have turned to commonplaces, it may perhaps find a few of my usual readers. So, pending a possible relapse of Heroism's constitutional cataract, I have asked my publishers to reissue the unsold edition instead of using it to make parcels of other people's books.

7. ALS. Berg Collection of English and American Literature, The New York Public Library, Astor, Lenox and Tilden Foundations.

17 HUNTING PROTEUS

1. Vernon Lee does not cite specific quotations from Adler, but such passages as these, from her unpublished "*Nosce teipsum,*" certainly articulate her views.

2. She had read *Swann's Way* before World War I: "all the parts about the little boy, grandmère, tantes, etc. delighted me." But Swann's obsession with Odette depressed her, and she was impatient with what she considered Proust's redundancy and "a certain insufficient motility and circulation, a sticky, sea-slug, slimy slowness temperamental to the man." In contrast she cites Stendhal: "There's a man so brisk, so clean in perception and movement, so energetic, so full of breeze and sunshine, that he wrote only two—at most three—novels, and spent his time at dozens of useless things" (letter to Baring, 28 March 1926).

3. In May 1932 Nicky Mariano reported to Mary Berenson that she and Bernard Berenson, visiting Rome, saw Edith Wharton and the Pasolinis: "We walked a lot about Miss Paget to whom they are all so devoted (171).

4. A regular contributor to scholarships for needy German students, she once apologized to a correspondent for refusing "to help an individual student merely because he is a German, when I am surrounded by young Italians whom the depression of the lira and the—well! *negative favouritism* of the present regime excludes from every public opportunity unless their parents or themselves pass muster with the present patriotism" (5 June 1926, ALS, the Fales Library). See also her letter to Mario Praz complaining about the political apathy of the Italians: "Of course you aren't really a *politico*, my dear Praz; you are merely *non-partisan*. But it is exactly the lack of political interest which, as we see in Italy (and indeed elsewhere!) permits the domination of partisanship" (17 January 1925, *House of Life* 244).

5. This was not Mario Praz's impression when he last saw her on 15 April 1933: "And

360   NOTES TO CHAPTER 17

perhaps it was a pity to meet her again. For it was really no longer possible to communicate with her; embittered by deafness, she had assumed an air of positively hostile detachment which displayed itself in the acid expression of her face, now devastated, alas, by old age" (*House of Life,* 245–46).

6. Mary Berenson reported that they disagreed bitterly over Italy's invasion of Tripoli, which Placci defended. She wrote to her family in England: "Placci has come round to the quarreling period and was simply full of teasing and boring little *digs* of all sorts. Finally he said to B. B., 'Our friendship is at an end. We have nothing in common.' 'If twenty years of affection counts as nothing with you in comparison to a difference of opinions over the Balkans, then there isn't really much to go on,' B. B. replied. 'The great thing is to keep out of his way till his mood changes'" (26 April 1913, *Self-Portrait* 188). Evidently that and later disagreements were patched up. There is a photo in *Self-Portrait* of Berenson, Nicky Mariano, Placci, and Walter Lippman in the gardens of I Tatti in 1937. Placci died 14 January 1941.

7. Until his last days Berenson was ambivalent about Vernon Lee, but in spite of his expressed animus against her, he respected her work and in the late 1920s saw her quite frequently at I Tatti. One suspects, however, that much of the cordiality was on Mary Berenson's part, not his. In her letters to Vernon Lee, now at Somerville College, she reports on his high regard for her—e.g., in refusing to sit for a young artist of Vernon Lee's acquaintance, Mary says of her husband, "There is no one he thinks more highly of than yourself. But this one he feels to be quite impossible" (6 March 1929). Two years later, after Vernon Lee reiterated her discouragement about her own work, Mary wrote: "BB particularly asks me to beg you, in his name, *not* to burn any of your manuscripts! Even if they are never published, they will be a mine for students of Culturgeschichte. He thinks they ought to go to the B.M., or to the National Library here" (19 March 1931). Quoted with the permission of the Principal and Fellows of Somerville College. I am grateful to David Elliott for bringing this letter to my attention.

8. A younger Sargent sister, Violet, for whom appropriately Violet Paget stood godmother, was born in 1870. She posed for a number of her brother's sketches and paintings.

9. Harboring, perhaps, some guilt about her desertion of her devoted friend, Mary was solicitous about her health, especially after Kit Anstruther-Thomson left her. In an undated letter (probably written in or near 1900), Mary wrote her friend Lady Dorothy Nevill: "Miss Paget stayed with us on her way South. She is now back in Florence—very lonely, I fear. I wish she would take a flat in Paris for the winter" (Nevill 216).

10. Baring was more candid on Eugene in an undated letter to Edmund Gosse (probably 1899 or 1900). "[He] is indeed a trying person. He is a robust egotist with all the exigence and none of the excuse of an invalid. He, as you remember, went to bed for 24 years while nothing was the matter with him—now he looks back on that time with a wistful longing and behaves as if he was still there; that is on his back he could not bear people to talk to him and on his feet he won't let them, so much does he talk himself. He takes everything with a funereal solemnity till something occurs which makes him bubble over in nervous floods of impassioned Tuscan—and he says every sentence twice over like the thrush from the fear that someone is going to interrupt him" (Letley 49). In one of Baring's later novels, *Cat's Cradle* (1925), he introduced a highly unsympathetic character who, after twenty years of helpless invalidism, "had suddenly,

in a marvellous manner, recovered, and his first act had been to climb up Mount Vesu-
vius" (Letley 48). Baring was embarrassed because of the obvious resemblance to Eugene, but Vernon Lee wrote to assure him that "any fear of hurting my feelings was entirely mistaken" (29 March 1926).

11. "In this house passed the life of Violet Paget (Vernon Lee), writer, 1856–1935.
She wrote in poetry and in prose, of philosophy, history, and art. Unassuming, of great
heart, honest in life and intellect, she dedicated herself to the search for truth and
beauty. She chose Italy for her home, knowing and loving it. With her works she leaves
behind, to those who come after, an everlasting inheritance."

I am grateful to Robin F. Brancato for this translation.

BIBLIOGRAPHY

The most comprehensive source for bibliographical material on Vernon Lee is *English Literature in Translation 1880–1920* (*ELIT*) 26, no. 4 (1983). This is as full a bibliography of works by and about her as exists, and it includes a list of her unpublished material in the Vernon Lee archive in the Miller Library, Colby College, Waterville, Maine.

There is no uniform edition of Vernon Lee's works. I have quoted wherever possible from first editions. Where these were not available, I have indicated in the end notes the later editions used. Unless otherwise noted, all my quotations from Vernon Lee's correspondence and unpublished manuscripts are from the Vernon Lee archive at Colby. Articles describing these documents are published in the *Colby Library Quarterly* (*CLQ*) and listed here under Works Consulted.

BOOKS BY VERNON LEE

Althea: A Second Book of Dialogues on Aspirations and Duties. London: Osgood, Mc-Ilvaine, 1894.

Ariadne in Mantua: A Romance in Five Acts. Oxford: B. H. Blackwell, 1903.

Art and Man. See under Anstruther-Thomson, Clementina, in Works Consulted.

Baldwin: Being Dialogues on Views and Aspirations. London: T. Fisher Unwin, 1886.

The Ballet of the Nations: A Present-Day Morality. With a pictorial commentary by Maxwell Armfield. London: Chatto and Windus, 1915.

The Beautiful: An Introduction to Psychological Aesthetics. Cambridge Manuals of Science and Literature, 77. Cambridge: Cambridge UP, 1913.

Beauty and Ugliness and Other Studies in Psychological Aesthetics. With Clementina Anstruther-Thomson. London: John Lane, Bodley Head, 1912.

Belcaro: Being Essays on Sundry Aesthetical Questions. London: W. Satchell, 1887.

The Countess of Albany. Eminent Women Series. London: W. H. Allen, 1884.

The Enchanted Woods, and Other Essays on the Genius of Places. London: John Lane, Bodley Head, 1905.

Euphorion: Being Studies of the Antique and the Mediaeval in the Renaissance. 2 vols. London: T. Fisher Unwin, 1884.

For Maurice: Five Unlikely Stories. London: John Lane, Bodley Head, 1927.

Genius Loci: Notes on Places. London: Grant Richards, 1897.

The Golden Keys and Other Essays on the Genius Loci. London: John Lane, Bodley Head, 1925.

Gospels of Anarchy and Other Contemporary Studies. London and Leipzig: T. Fisher Unwin, 1908.

The Handling of Words and Other Studies in Literary Psychology London: John Lane, Bodley Head, 1923. Reprint, with introduction and chronology by Royal A. Gettmann, Lincoln: U Nebraska P, 1968. Reprint, with introduction by David Seed, Lampeter [U.K.]: Edwin Mellen P, 1992.

Hauntings: Fantastic Stories. London: W. Heinemann, 1890.

Hortus Vitae: Essays on the Gardening of Life. London and New York: John Lane, Bodley Head, 1903.

Juvenilia: Being a Second Series of Essays on Sundry Aesthetical Questions. 2 vols. London: T. Fisher Unwin, 1887.

Laurus Nobilis: Chapters on Art and Life. London: John Lane, Bodley Head, 1909.

Limbo and Other Essays. London: Grant Richards, 1897.

Louis Norbert: A Two-Fold Romance. London: John Lane, Bodley Head, 1914.

Miss Brown: A Novel. 3 vols. Edinburgh and London: W. Blackwood and Sons, 1884.

Music and Its Lovers: An Empirical Study of Emotional and Imaginative Responses to Music. London: G. Allen and Unwin, 1932.

Ottilie: An Eighteenth-Century Idyl. London: T. Fisher Unwin, 1883.

Penelope Brandling: A Tale of the Welsh Coast in the Eighteenth Century. Pseudonym Library. London: T. Fisher Unwin, 1903.

The Poet's Eye: Notes on Some Difference between Verse and Prose. The Hogarth Essay Series, 17. London: L. and V. Woolf, Hogarth P, 1926.

Pope Jacynth and Other Fantastic Tales. London: Grant Richards, 1904. New edition, *Pope Jacynth and More Supernatural Tales: Excursions into Fantasy.* London: Peter Owen, 1956.

The Prince of the Hundred Soups: A Puppet Show in Narrative. Edited with an introduction by Vernon Lee. London: T. Fisher Unwin, 1883.

Proteus; or, The Future of Intelligence. Today and To-morrow Series. London: Kegan Paul, 1925.

Renaissance Fancies and Studies: A Sequel to Euphorion. London: Smith, Elder, 1895.

Satan the Waster: A Philosophic War Trilogy. London: John Lane, Bodley Head, 1920. Reissued, with a new preface by the author, London: John Lane, Bodley Head, 1930.

The Sentimental Traveller: Notes on Places. London: John Lane, Bodley Head, 1908.

Sister Benvenuta and the Christ Child: An Eighteenth-Century Legend. New York: Mitchell Kennerley, 1905; London: Grant Richards, 1906.

The Spirit of Rome: Leaves from a Diary. London: John Lane, Bodley Head, 1906.

Studies of the Eighteenth Century in Italy. London: W. Satchell, 1880. "New Edition," London: T. Fisher Unwin, 1887; reprint, New York: Da Capo, 1978. 2nd edition, with a Retrospective Chapter (Preface to "New Edition"), London: T. Fisher Unwin, 1907.

The Tower of the Mirrors and Other Essays on the Spirit of Places. London: John Lane, Bodley Head, 1914.

Tuscan Fairy Tales, Taken Down from the Mouths of the People. London: W. Satchell, 1880.

Vanitas: Polite Stories. London: W. Heinemann, 1892. *Vanitas: Polite Stories Including*

the Hitherto Unpublished Entitled "A Frivolous Conversion." 2nd ed. London: John
  Lane, Bodley Head, 1911.
Vernon Lee's Letters. Ed. Irene Cooper Willis. London: Privately Printed, 1937.
Vital Lies: Studies of Some Varieties of Recent Obscurantism. 2 vols. London: John Lane,
  Bodley Head, 1912.

WORKS CONSULTED

Adler, Alfred. *The Individual Psychology of Alfred Adler: A Systematic Presentation in Selections from His Writings.* Ed. Heinze L. Ansbachen and Rowena R. Ansbachen.
  London: Allen and Unwin, 1956.
Allott, Miriam. "The Bronzino Portrait in Henry James' *The Wings of the Dove.*" *Mod-
  ern Language Notes* 68 (Jan. 1953): 23–25.
Anstruther-Thomson, Clementina. *Art and Man: Essays and Fragments.* With an intro-
  duction by Vernon Lee. London: John Lane, Bodley Head, 1924.
Anstruther-Thomson, John. *Eighty Years' Reminiscences by Colonel Anstruther-Thomson.*
  2 vols. London: Longmans, 1904.
Astaldi, Maria Luisa. *Metastasio.* Milan: Rizzoli, 1979.
Atherton, Gertrude. *Adventures of a Novelist.* New York: Liveright, 1932.
———. *The Bell in the Fog and Other Stories.* New York and London: Harper & Broth-
  ers, 1905.
Baretti, Giuseppe. *An Account of the Manners and Customs of Italy.* 2 vols. London:
  T. Davies, 1768.
Baring, Maurice. *Lost Lectures, or The Fruits of Experience.* London: Peter Davies, 1932.
———. *The Puppet Show of Memory.* London: Heinemann, 1922.
———. *Round the World in Any Number of Days.* London: Chatto and Windus, 1919.
Basham, Diana. *The Trial of Woman: Feminism and the Occult Sciences in Victorian Lit-
  erature and Society.* London: Macmillan, 1992.
Beckford, William. *The Travel-Diaries of William Beckford of Fonthill.* Ed. Guy Chap-
  man. 2 vols. Cambridge: Constable; Houghton Mifflin, 1928.
Beckman, Linda Hunt. *Amy Levy: Her Life and Letters.* Athens: Ohio UP, 2000.
Beer, Gillian. "Vernon Lee and *Satan the Waster.*" In *Women's Fiction and the Great War,*
  ed. Suzanne Raitt and Trudi Tate. Oxford: Clarendon, 1997. 107–31.
Beevor, Kinta. *A Tuscan Childhood.* New York: Pantheon, 1993.
Benkovitz, Miriam J. *Frederick Rolfe: Baron Corvo.* London: Hamish Hamilton, 1977.
Berenson, Bernard. *The Selected Letters.* Ed. A. K. McComb. Boston: Houghton Mif-
  flin, 1964.
———. *Sketch for a Self-Portrait.* London: Robin Clark, 1949.
Berenson, Mary. *Mary Berenson: A Self-Portrait from Her Letters and Diaries.* Ed. Bar-
  bara Strachey and Jayne Samuels. London: V. Gollancz, 1983.
Biron, Archille H. "Paget in Paraÿs." *Colby Library Quarterly* 25 (June 1960): 123–27.
Bledsoe, Robert Terrell. *Henry Fothergill Chorley: Victorian Journalist.* Aldershot, Hants.:
  Ashgate, 1998.
Block, Edwin F., Jr. *Rituals of Dis-Integration: Romance and Madness in the Victorian
  Psychomythic Tale.* New York: Garland, 1993.
Brewster, Harry. *The Cosmopolites: A Nineteenth-Century Family Drama.* Norwich
  [U.K.]: Michael Russell, 1994.

British Women Writers: A Critical Reference Guide. Ed. Janet Todd. New York: Continuum, 1989.

Browning, Robert. *New Letters of Robert Browning.* Ed. W. C. DeVane and K. L. Knickerbocker. New Haven: Yale UP, 1950.

Buchanan, Robert. "The Fleshly School of Poetry." In *The Pre-Raphaelites,* ed. Jerome H. Buckley. New York: Modern Library, 1968. 437–60.

Bucton, Charles Roden, ed. *Towards a Lasting Settlement.* London: Allen & Unwin, 1915.

Burney, Charles. *Dr. Charles Burney's Continental Travels, 1770–1772.* Compiled from His Journals and Other Sources by Cedric Howard Glover. London and Glasgow: Blackie, 1927.

———. *Memoirs of the Life and Writings of the Abate Metastasio.* 3 vols. London: G. G. and J. Robinson, 1796.

Burney, Fanny. *The Diary and Letters of Madame D'Arblay.* Ed. W. C. Ward. 3 vols. London and New York: Frederick Warne, 1892.

Caballero, Carlos. "'A Wicked Voice': On Vernon Lee, Wagner, and the Effects of Music." *Victorian Studies* 35 (Summer 1992): 385–408.

Cambridge Companion to Edith Wharton. Ed. Millicent Bell. New York: Cambridge UP, 1995.

Cameron, Kenneth Neill. *Shelley: The Golden Years.* Cambridge, Mass.: Harvard UP, 1974.

Cary, Richard. "Aldous Huxley, Vernon Lee, and the *Genius Loci.*" *Colby Library Quarterly* 5 (June 1960): 128–40.

———. "Vernon Lee's Vignettes of Literary Acquaintances." *Colby Library Quarterly* 9 (Sept. 1970): 179–99.

———. "Violet Paget to Sarah Orne Jewett." *Colby Library Quarterly* 9 (Dec. 1970): 235–43.

Charteris, Evan. *John Sargent.* New York: Scribner, 1927.

Christensen, Peter G. "'A Wicked Voice': Vernon Lee's Artist Parable." *Lamar Journal of the Humanities* 15 (Fall 1989): 3–15.

Clute, John. "Vernon Lee." In *Supernatural Fiction Writers.* Ed. E. F. Bleiler. New York: Scribner, 1985. 1:329–35.

Corrigan, Beatrice. "Giovanni Ruffini's Letters to Vernon Lee, 1875–1879." *English Miscellany* 13 (1962): 179–240.

———. "Vernon Lee and The Old Yellow Book." *Colby Library Quarterly* 5 (June 1960): 116–22.

De Charms, Leslie. *Elizabeth of the German Garden: A Biography.* London: Heinemann, 1958.

Decker, Clarence R. *The Victorian Conscience.* New York: Twayne, 1952.

Donoghue, Denis. *Walter Pater: Lover of Strange Souls.* New York: Knopf, 1995.

Dowling, Linda. *Hellenism and Homosexuality in Victorian Oxford.* Ithaca, N.Y.: Cornell UP, 1994.

Dürer, Albrecht. *Complete Engravings, Etchings and Drypoints.* Ed. Walter L. Strauss. New York: Dover, 1972.

Edel, Leon. *Henry James: A Life.* New York: Harper and Row, 1985.

Eliot, George. *The George Eliot Letters.* Ed. Gordon S. Haight. 7 vols. New Haven: Yale UP, 1954–55.

Faderman, Lillian. *Surpassing the Love of Man: Romantic Friendship and Love between Woman from the Renaissance to the Present.* New York: Morrow, 1981.

Field, Michael, pseud. *Works and Days, from the Journal of Michael Field.* Edited by T. and D. C. Sturge Moore. London: John Murray, 1933.

Fife, Hilda M. "Letters from Edith Wharton to Vernon Lee." *Colby Library Quarterly* 3 (Feb. 1953): 139–44.

Forster, E. M. *Goldsworthy Lowes Dickinson.* 1943. New York: Harcourt Brace, 1962.

France, Anatole. *The Red Lily.* Trans. Winifred Stephens. London: John Lane, 1927.

Francis, R. A. *Romain Rolland.* New York: Oxford UP, 1999.

Fraser, Hilary. "Women and the Ends of Art History: Vision and Corporeality in Nineteeth-Century Critical Discourse." *Victorian Studies* 12 (1998/99): 77–100.

Gardner, Burdett. *The Lesbian Imagination (Victorian Style): A Psychological and Critical Study of "Vernon Lee."* New York: Garland, 1987.

Gautier, Théophile. *Mademoiselle de Maupin.* Trans. Burton Rascoe. New York: Knopf, 1920.

Geoffroy-Menoux, Sophie. "L'enfant dans les textes de Vernon Lee." *Cahiers victoriens et édouardiens* 47 (April 1998): 251–63.

———. "La musique dans les textes de Vernon Lee." *Cahiers victoriens et édouardiens* 49 (April 1999): 57–70.

Gilbert, Katharine Everitt, and Helmut Lang. *A History of Esthetics.* Bloomington: U Indiana P, 1953.

Goethe, Wolfgang. *Italian Journey, 1786–1788.* Trans. W. H. Auden and Elizabeth Meyer. London: Penguin, 1970.

Gosse, Edmund. *Critical Kit-Kats.* New York: Dodd, Mead, 1896.

Graham, Kenneth. *English Criticism of the Novel, 1865–1900.* Oxford: Clarendon P, 1965.

Gregory, Horace. "The Romantic Inventions of Vernon Lee." Introduction to *"The Snake Lady" and Other Stories by Vernon Lee.* New York: Grove, 1954.

Grosskurth, Phyllis. *John Addington Symonds.* New York: Morrow, 1981.

Gunn, Peter. *Vernon Lee: Violet Paget, 1856–1935.* London: Oxford UP, 1964. Reprint, New York: Arno P, 1975.

Gurney, Edmund. *The Power of Sound.* London: Smith, Elder, 1880.

Halévy, Daniel. "Les trois Mary." In *Mary Duclaux and Maurice Barrès: Lettres échangées.* Paris: Grasset, 1959.

Halperin, John, ed. *The Theory of the Novel: New Essays.* New York: Oxford UP, 1974.

Hamilton, Walter. *The Aesthetic Movement in England.* London: Reeves and Turner, 1882.

Harris, Sally. *Out of Control: British Foreign Policy and the Union of Democratic Control, 1914–1918.* Hull: U Hull P, 1996.

Herrick, Robert. *The Gospel of Freedom.* New York: Macmillan, 1898.

Hewett-Thayer, Harvey W. *Hoffmann: Author of the Tales.* Princeton, N.J.: Princeton UP, 1948.

Hildebrand, Adolf von. *The Problem of Form in Painting and Sculpture.* Trans. Max Meyer and R. M. Ogden. 2nd ed. New York: Stechert, 1932.

Hoffmann, E. T. A. *The Best Tales of Hoffmann.* Ed. E. F. Bleiler. New York: Dover, 1967.

Hollinrake, Roger. *Nietzsche, Wagner and the Philosophy of Pessimism*. London: Allen and Unwin, 1982.

Holmes, Richard. *Shelley: The Pursuit*. London: Weidenfeld and Nicholson, 1974.

Holroyd, Michael. *Lytton Strachey: A Critical Biography*. 2 vols. New York: Holt, Reinhart, 1968.

Honour, Hugh, and John Fleming. *The Venetian Hours of Henry James, Whistler and Sargent*. London: Walker Books, 1991.

Hotchkiss, Janet. "(P)revising Freud: Vernon Lee's Castration Phantasy." In *Seeing Double: Revisioning Edwardian and Modernist Literature*, ed. Carla M. Kaplan and Anne B. Simpson. New York: St. Martin's, 1996.

Hynes, Samuel. *The Edwardian Turn of Mind*. Princeton, N.J.: Princeton UP, 1968.

Jackson, Rosemary. Introduction to *What Did Miss Darrington See?: An Anthology of Feminist Supernatural Fiction*. Ed. J. A. Salmonson. New York: Feminst P, 1989.

James, Henry. *The Ghostly Tales of Henry James*. Ed. Leon Edel. New Brunswick, N.J.: Rutgers UP, 1948.

———. *Italian Hours*. London: Heinemann, 1909.

———. *Letters*. Ed. Leon Edel. 4 vols. Cambridge, Mass.: Harvard UP, 1974–84.

———. *Letters of Henry James*. Ed. Percy Lubbock. 2 vols. New York: Scribner, 1920.

———. *The Middle Years*. New York: Scribner, 1917.

———. *William Wetmore Story and His Friends*. 2 vols. Edinburgh: Blackwood, 1903.

James, William. *Principles of Psychology*. 3 vols. Cambridge, Mass.: Harvard UP, 1981.

———. *Psychology: Briefer Course*. 1892. New York: Fawcett, 1963.

James, William, and Henry James. *Selected Letters*. Ed. Ignas K. Skrupskelis and Elizabeth M. Berkeley. Charlottesville: UP of Virginia, 1997.

Johnston, William M. *In Search of Italy: Foreign Writers in Northern Italy since 1800*. University Park: Pennsylvania State UP, 1987.

Killoran, Helen. "Eugene Lee-Hamilton." In *The 1890s: An Encyclopedia of British Literature, Art, and Culture*, ed. G. A. Cevasco. New York and London: Gale, 1993.

Koss, Stephen. *The Rise and Fall of the Political Press in Britain*. 2 vols. Chapel Hill: U North Carolina P, 1981.

"Lee-Hamilton, Eugene Jacob." *DNB*. 2nd supplement, vol. 2, 1912.

Leighton, Angela. "Ghosts, Aestheticism and Vernon Lee." *Victorian Literature and Culture* 28, no. 1 (2000): 1–15.

Leighton, Perly L. "'To My Friend, Karl Hillebrand': The Dedication in *Ottilie* and Its Aftermath." *Colby Library Quarterly* 3 (Nov. 1953): 185–89.

Letley, Emma. *Maurice Baring: A Citizen of Europe*. London: Constable, 1991.

Lewis, R. W. B. *Edith Wharton: A Biography*. New York: Harper & Row, 1975.

Licht, Merete. "Henry James's 'Portrait of a Lady': Vernon Lee in *The Princess Casamassima*." In *A Literary Miscellany Presented to Eric Jacobsen*, ed. Graham Caie and Holger Norgaard. Publications of the Department of English, University of Copenhagen, 16. 1988. 285–303.

Lodge, David. *The Language of Fiction: Essays in Criticism and Verbal Analysis of the English Novel*. London: Routledge, 1966.

Lonsdale, Roger. *Dr. Charles Burney: A Literary Biography*. Oxford: Clarendon, 1965.

Lubbock, Percy. *Portrait of Edith Wharton*. New York: Appleton-Century, 1947.

MacCarthy, Desmond. "Out of the Limelight: Vernon Lee." In *Humanities.* London: MacGibbon & Kee, 1953. 189–93.

Mackenzie, Norman, and Jeanne Mackenzie. *H. G. Wells: A Biography.* New York: Simon & Schuster, 1973.

Mallock, W. H. *The New Republic, or Culture, Faith and Philosophy in an English Country House.* 1877. London: Michael Joseph, [1937].

Maltz, Diana. "Emerging 'Delicate Brains': From Working-Class Enculturation to Upper-Class Lesbian Liberation in Vernon Lee's and Kit Anstruther-Thomson's Psychological Aesthetics." In *Women and British Aestheticism,* ed. Talia Schaffer and Kathy Alexis Psomiades. Charlottesville: UP of Virginia, 1999. 211–29.

Manocchi, Phyllis F. "Vernon Lee and Kit Anstruther-Thomson: A Study of Love and Collaboration between Romantic Friends." *Women's Studies* 12 (Feb. 1986): 129–48.

Marandon, Sylvaine. *L'oeuvre poétique de Mary Robinson, 1857–1944.* Bordeaux: Imprimerie Pechade, 1967.

Mariano, Nicky. *Forty Years with Berenson.* London: Hamish Hamilton, 1966.

Miles, A. H., ed. *The Poets and the Poetry of the Century.* London: Hutchinson, 1892.

Mix, Katherine Lyon. *A Study in Yellow: The Yellow Book and Its Contributors.* Lawrence: U Kansas P, 1960.

Monsman, Gerald. *Walter Pater.* Boston: G. Hall, 1977.

Morra, Umberto. *Conversations with Berenson.* Trans. Florence Hammond. Boston: Houghton Mifflin, 1965.

Morrell, Ottoline. *Ottoline at Garsington: Memoirs of Lady Ottoline Morrell, 1915–1918.* Ed. Robert Gathorne-Hardy. London: Faber, 1974.

Mount, Charles Merrill. *John Singer Sargent: A Biography.* New York: Norton, 1955.

Navarette, Susan J. *The Shape of Fear: Horror and the Fin de Siècle Culture of Decadence.* Lexington: UP of Kentucky, 1998.

Nelson, Carolyn Christensen. "Vernon Lee and the Short Story." In *British Women Fiction Writers of the 1890s.* New York: Twayne, 1996. 70–79.

Nelson, James G. *The Early Nineties: A View from the Bodley Head.* Cambridge, Mass.: Harvard UP, 1971.

Nencioni, Enrico. *Saggi critici di letteratura inglese.* Firenze: Le Monnier, 1897.

Nevill, Ralph. *Life and Letters of Lady Dorothy Nevill.* New York: E. P. Dutton, 1919.

Oliphant, Margaret. *Autobiography and Letters.* Ed. Mrs. Harry Coghill, 1899. Reprint, Leicester [U.K.]: Leicester UP, 1974.

Olson, Stanley. *John Singer Sargent: His Portrait.* New York: St. Martin's P, 1986.

Ormond, Leonée. "Vernon Lee as a Critic of Aestheticism in *Miss Brown.*" *Colby Library Quarterly* 9 (Sept. 1970): 131–54.

Ormond, Richard. "John Singer Sargent and Vernon Lee." *Colby Library Quarterly* 9 (Sept. 1970): 154–78.

Palacio, Jean de. "Y a-t-il une écriture feminine de la Decadence? (à propos d'une nouvelle de Vernon Lee)." *Romantisme: Revue du dix-neuvième siècle* 42 (1983): 177–86.

Pantazzi, Sybille. "Carlo Placci and Vernon Lee." *English Miscellany* 12 (1961): 97–122.

———. "Enrico Nencioni, William Wetmore Story, and Vernon Lee." *English Miscellany* 10 (1959): 249–60.

Pater, Walter. *Letters of Walter Pater.* Ed. Lawrence Evans. Oxford: Oxford UP, 1970.

————. *The Renaissance.* Modern Library. New York: Boni and Liveright, [1919].

————. *Studies in the History of the Renaissance.* London: Macmillan, 1873.

Pollock, John. *Time's Chariot.* London: Murray, 1950.

Ponsonby, Mary. *A Memoir: Some Letters and a Journal.* Ed. Magdalen Ponsonby. London: John Murray, 1927.

Praz, Mario. *The House of Life.* Trans. Angus Davidson. New York: Oxford UP, 1964.

————. *The Romantic Agony.* Trans. Angus Davidson. New York: Meridian Books, 1956.

————. *Voce dietro la scena: Un antologia personale.* Milan: Adelphi Edizione, 1980.

Psomiades, Kathy. "'Still Burning from This Strangling Embrace': Vernon Lee on Desire and Aesthetics." In *Victorian Sexual Dissidence,* ed. Richard Dellamora. Chicago: U Chicago P, 1999. 21–41.

Robbins, Ruth. "Vernon Lee's Decadent Women." In *Fin de Siècle, Fin du Globe: Fears and Fantasies of the Late Nineteenth Century,* ed. John Stokes. London: Macmillan, 1992.

Robins, Elizabeth. *Theatre and Friendship: Some Henry James Letters.* New York: Putnam, 1932.

Robinson, A. Mary F. (Madame Duclaux). *The Collected Poems, Lyrical and Narrative.* London: T. F. Unwin, 1902.

————. "In Casa Paget." *Country Life* 22 (28 Dec. 1907): 935–37.

St. Helier, Susan (Mary Jeune). *Memories of Fifty Years by Lady St. Helier (Mary Jeune).* London: Edward Arnold, 1909.

Samuels, Ernest. *Bernard Berenson: The Making of a Connoisseur.* Cambridge, Mass.: Bellnap P, 1979.

Schabert, Ina. "An Amazon in Venice: Vernon Lee's 'Lady Tal.'" In *Venetian Views, Venetian Blinds: English Fantasies of Venice,* ed. Manfred Pfister and Barbara Schaff. Amsterdam; Atlanta, Ga.: Rodopi, 1999. 155–67.

Schreiner, Olive. *The Letters of Olive Schreiner, 1876–1920.* Ed. S. C. Cronwright-Schreiner. Boston: Little Brown, 1924.

Semon, Richard. *Mnemic Psychology.* Trans. from the German by Bella Duffy, with an introduction by Vernon Lee. London: Allen and Unwin, 1923.

Seymour, Miranda. *Ottoline Morrell: Life on the Grand Scale.* London: Hodder & Stoughton, 1992.

Shorthouse, J. H. *The Little Schoolmaster Mark: A Spiritual Romance.* 2 vols. London: Macmillan, 1883–84.

Showalter, Elaine, ed. *Daughters of Decadence: Women Writers of the Fin de Siècle.* New Brunswick, N.J.: Rutgers UP, 1993.

Smith, Logan Pearsall. *A Portrait of Logan Pearsall Smith.* Ed. John Russell. London: Dropmore, [1950].

Smyth, Ethel. *As Time Went On . . .* London: Longmans, [1936].

————. *Impressions That Remained.* London: Longmans, 1919.

————. *Maurice Baring.* London: Heinemann, 1938.

————. *The Memoirs of Ethel Smyth.* Abridged and introduced by Ronald Crichton. New York: Viking, 1987.

————. *What Happened Next.* London: Longmans, [1940].

Snow, Florence L. *Pictures on My Wall: A Lifetime in Kansas.* Lawrence: U Kansas P, 1945.

Spender, J. A. *Life, Journalism and Politics.* 2 vols. London: Cassell, 1927.

Starr, William Thomas. *Romain Rolland and a World at War*. Evanston, Ill.: North-western UP, 1956.

Sterne, Lawrence. *A Sentimental Journey through France and Italy by Mr. Yorick*. Ed. Gardner D. Stout Jr. Berkeley and Los Angeles: U California P, 1967.

Stevenson, Robert Louis. *Memoir of Fleeming Jenkin*. New York: Scribner, 1887.

Sutherland, John H. "Letters from G. Lowes Dickinson to Vernon Lee." *Colby Library Quarterly* 3 (Nov. 1953): 189–94.

Swanwick, H. M. *Builders of Peace: Being Ten Years' History of the Union of Democratic Control*. London: Swarthmore P, 1924.

Swinnerton, Frank. *Swinnerton: An Autobiography*. Garden City, N.Y.: Doubleday, Doran, 1936.

Symonds, John Addington. *Letters*. Ed. Herbert M. Schueller and Robert L. Peters. 3 vols. Detroit: Wayne State UP, 1968.

———. *The Renaissance in Italy*. 3 vols. London: Smith Elder, 1877–97.

Tintner, Adeline R. *Henry James and the Lust of the Eyes: Thirteen Artists in His Work*. Baton Rouge: LSU P, 1993.

———. *Henry James's Legacy: The Afterlife of His Figure and Fiction*. Baton Rouge: LSU P, 1998.

———. "Vernon Lee's 'Oke of Okehurst or The Phantom Lover' and James's 'The Way It Came.'" *Studies in Short Fiction* 28 (Summer 1991): 355–62.

Twain, Mark. "In Defense of Harriet Shelley." In *Literary Essays*. New York: Harper, 1899.

Usborne, Karen. *"Elizabeth": The Author of Elizabeth and Her German Garden*. London: Bodley Head, 1986.

Vicinus, Martha. "The Adolescent Boy: Fin de Siècle Femme Fatale?" *Journal of the History of Sexuality* 5 (July 1994): 90–114.

Webb, Beatrice. *The Diary of Beatrice Webb*. Ed. Norman Mackenzie and Jeanne Mackenzie. 4 vols. London: Virago, 1982–83.

Weber, Carl J. "Henry James and His Tiger-Cat." *PMLA* 68 (Sept. 1953): 672–87.

———. "Three More Letters of Sarah Orne Jewett." *Colby Library Quarterly* 3 (August 1952): 106–14.

Weintraub, Stanley, ed. *The Yellow Book: Quintessence of the Nineties*. New York: Doubleday, 1964.

Wellek, René. "Vernon Lee, Bernard Berenson and Aesthetics." In *Friendship's Garland: Essays Presented to Mario Praz on His Seventieth Birthday*, ed. Vittorio Gabrielli. Rome: Edizione di Storia e Letteratura, 1966. 2:253–51.

Wells, H. G. *The Correspondence of H. G. Wells*. Ed. David C. Smith. 4 vols. London: Pickering and Chatto, 1998.

Wharton, Edith. *A Backward Glance*. New York: Appleton Century, 1934.

———. *Edith Wharton Abroad: Selected Travel Writings*. Ed. Sarah Bird Wright. New York: St. Martin's P, 1995.

———. *Italian Villas and Their Gardens*. New York: Century, 1904. Reprint, New York: Da Capo, 1978.

———. *The Valley of Decision*. New York: Scribner, 1902.

Wilde, Oscar. "The Decay of Lying: An Observation." In *The Prose of Oscar Wilde*. New York: Cosmopolitan Book Corporation, 1916.

Woolf, Virginia. *Essays.* Ed. Andrew McNellie. 3 vols. London: Hogarth P, 1986.
———. *Letters.* Ed. Nigel Nicolson and Jaune Trautmann. 6 vols. New York: Harcourt Brace Jovanovich, 1975–80.
Zorn, Christa. "Aesthetic Intertextuality as Cultural Critique: Vernon Lee Rewrites History through Walter Pater's 'La Gioconda.'" *Victorian News Letter* 91 (Spring 1997): 4–10.
———. "Vernon Lee: Aesthetics, History, and the Female Subject in the Nineteenth Century." Ph.D. diss., University of Florida, 1994.

INDEX

Victorian Literature and Culture Series

Christina Rossetti / *The Letters of Christina Rossetti,* vols. 1–3   EDITED BY ANTONY H. HARRISON

Barbara Leah Harman / *The Feminine Political Novel in Victorian England*

John Ruskin / *The Genius of John Ruskin: Selections from His Writings*   EDITED BY JOHN D. ROSENBERG

Antony H. Harrison / *Victorian Poets and the Politics of Culture: Discourse and Ideology*

Judith Stoddart / *Ruskin's Culture Wars:* Fors Clavigera *and the Crisis of Victorian Liberalism*

Linda K. Hughes and Michael Lund / *Victorian Publishing and Mrs. Gaskell's Work*

Linda H. Peterson / *Traditions of Victorian Women's Autobiography: The Poetics and Politics of Life Writing*

Gail Turley Houston / *Royalties: The Queen and Victorian Writers*

Laura C. Berry / *The Child, the State, and the Victorian Novel*

Barbara J. Black / *On Exhibit: Victorians and Their Museums*

Annette R. Federico / *Idol of Suburbia: Marie Corelli and Late-Victorian Literary Culture*

Talia Schaffer / *The Forgotten Female Aesthetes: Literary Culture in Late-Victorian England*

Julia F. Saville / *A Queer Chivalry: The Homoerotic Asceticism of Gerard Manley Hopkins*

Victor Shea and William Whitla, Editors / *Essays and Reviews: The 1860 Text and Its Reading*

Marlene Tromp / *The Private Rod: Marital Violence, Sensation, and the Law in Victorian Britain*

Dorice Williams Elliott / *The Angel out of the House: Philanthropy and the Redefinition of Gender, 1762–1872*

Richard Maxwell, Editor / *The Victorian Illustrated Book*

Vineta Colby / *Vernon Lee: A Literary Biography*